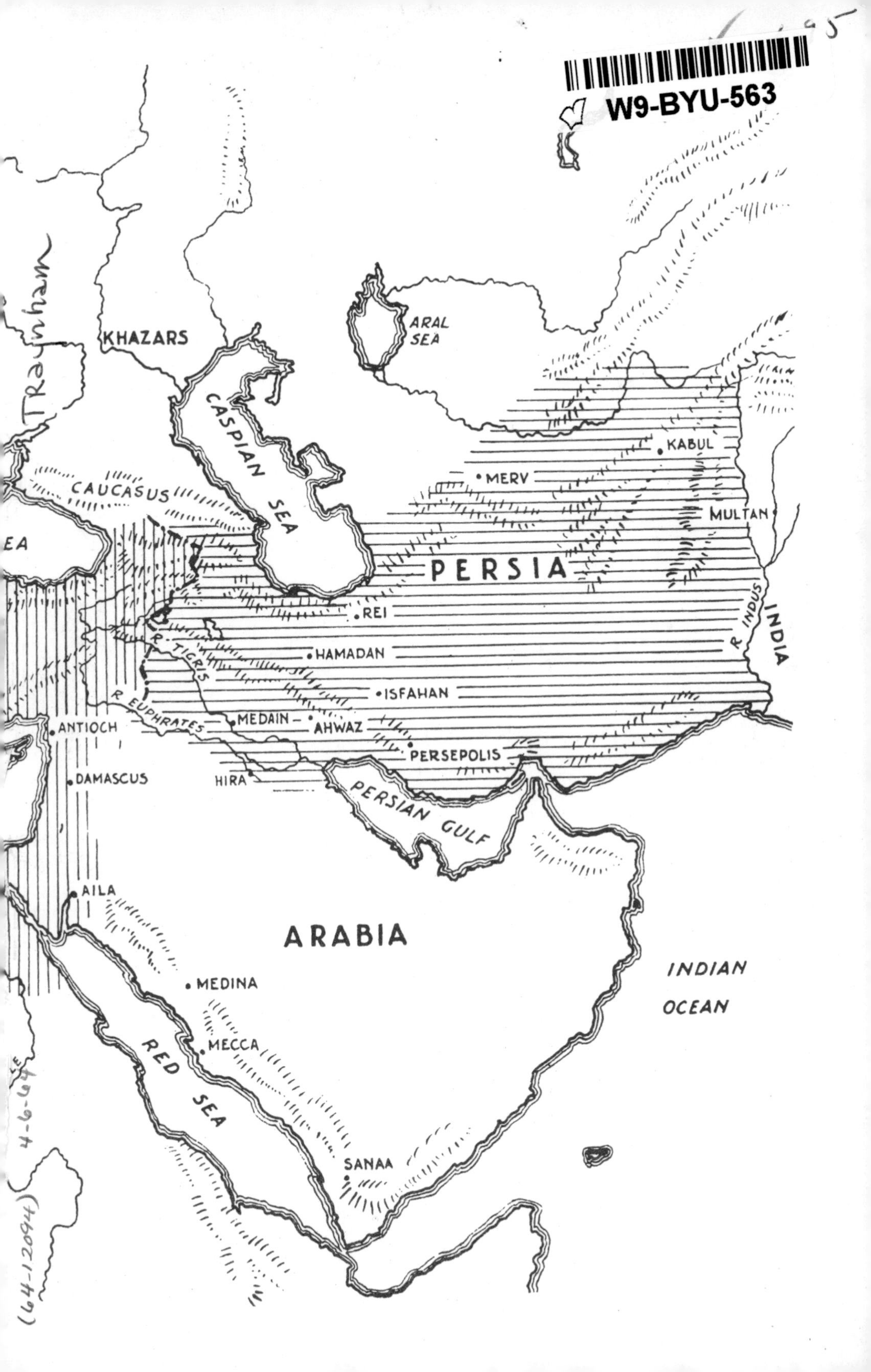
KHAZARS
ARAL SEA
CASPIAN SEA
CAUCASUS
KABUL
MERV
MULTAN
PERSIA
REI
R. INDUS
INDIA
HAMADAN
R. TIGRIS
ISFAHAN
R. EUPHRATES
MEDAIN
AHWAZ
ANTIOCH
PERSEPOLIS
DAMASCUS
HIRA
PERSIAN GULF
AILA
ARABIA
INDIAN OCEAN
MEDINA
MECCA
RED SEA
SANAA

# The Great Arab Conquests

*By the same author*

A SOLDIER WITH THE ARABS

THE STORY OF THE ARAB LEGION

BRITAIN AND THE ARABS

WAR IN THE DESERT

# THE GREAT ARAB CONQUESTS

*by*

Lieutenant-General
SIR JOHN BAGOT GLUBB
K.C.B., C.M.G., D.S.O., O.B.E., M.C.

Time should not blot out the past from mankind,
nor fame be denied to great and wonderful deeds.
HERODOTUS

PRENTICE-HALL, INC.
Englewood Cliffs, New Jersey

*First American Edition 1964*



Library of Congress Catalog Card Number:
64-12094

Printed in the United States of America

T 36350

Prentice-Hall International, Inc., *London*
Prentice-Hall of Australia, Pty., Ltd., *Sydney*
Prentice-Hall of Canada, Ltd., *Toronto*
Prentice-Hall France, S.A.R.L., *Paris*
Prentice-Hall of India Private Limited, *New Delhi*
Prentice-Hall of Japan, Inc., *Tokyo*
Prentice-Hall de Mexico, S.A., *Mexico City*

The Arabians, . . . since the time of Muhammad, rendered themselves universally remarkable, both by their arms and learning. The understanding, therefore, of their affairs seems no less if not more necessary than a knowledge of the history of any people whatsoever, who have flourished since the decline of the Roman Empire. SIMON OCKLEY, *The History of the Saracens*

We cannot understand . . . unless we are willing to bear constantly in mind two complementary truths: first the essential similarity of human nature in all ages, and secondly the dissimilarity of men's environment. . . . These will explain the remarkable self-devotion of the best characters and . . . the carelessness of the multitude, into which the theological teaching seldom penetrated beneath the surface. G. G. COULTON, *Mediaeval Panorama*

# PREFACE

I RECENTLY offered to a certain newspaper editor an article on an Arab country, in which I began by lightly sketching its history in two or three paragraphs, and then described its situation today. The editor sent the draft back, with a note to the effect that he would publish it if I could cut out the historical paragraphs. "People today," he concluded, "are not interested in history. All they want to know is your opinion on the political situation today." Judging by the many tragic errors we have made in the Middle East in recent years, this viewpoint must be widely held, both by our government and by the public.

It is curious that this should be so, in an age which talks so much about psychology and spends so much money on psychiatrists. In this field, the experts are constantly emphasizing, not only the importance of the peculiarities of our ancestors and parents, which we may have inherited, but also of the conditions under which we grew up through infancy and childhood. The circumstances of our early years, we are told, affect our mentality for the rest of our lives. If this be really so, it is surprising that we refuse to apply the same considerations to nations, and that we reject a study of their history, when we endeavour to ascertain why they behave as they do today.

History, if it is to mean anything to us, must surely be an account of the development of the human race, from its primitive beginnings to its present state. Such a process, to be intelligible, must be continuous. If we limit ourselves to turning the spotlight on one or two countries or periods in or during which events accord with our prejudices or our beliefs, and leave the remainder of our development in darkness, we can obtain no coherent picture. The whole subject remains meaningless, as indeed to school-children it often does. To learn a short period of Roman history ending with Augustus and then to jump to England in 1066 is to miss the whole idea of continuous development. Yet the great majority of people in Britain and the United States have scarcely even heard of the Byzantine Empire or the Arab Conquests. To my mind, however, the story related in this book contains one of the principal keys to the understanding of the modern world, in which Muslims are once more playing a prominent part.

* * * * *

Historians of the first Arab conquests are faced with many exasperating difficulties. When the Arabs in the seventh century burst out of Arabia to conquer an empire, they were in general rude and illiterate. Intent on action, they did not trouble to record their own deeds. The earliest and most dramatic conquests were carried out solely by Arabs from the Arabian peninsula, most of them nomadic tribesmen. The people they conquered were in the majority of cases profoundly different from themselves, most of them being the heirs of ancient civilizations. For a hundred years after the great conquests, the Central Arabians retained a considerable degree of pre-eminence in the empire which they had subdued. By the end of that period, the original Arab conquerors had been disposed of in one of two ways. Either they had settled in the conquered countries, intermarried with their varied races and become lost in the different populations concerned, or they had remained nomadic in Central Arabia and had stagnated, cut off from the centres of activity of the empire which they had created. In A.D. 750 the Abbaside dynasty seized power, a hundred and eighteen years after the death of Muhammad. Thereafter with its capital transferred to Baghdad, the empire assumed a multiracial character, the basis of which was not Arab nationalism but Islam. It was not until nearly two centuries after the Prophet, and under the auspices of this multi-national Muslim empire, that the great "Arab" historians flourished.

Thus the viewpoint of the historians was religious rather than Arab. Moreover not one of them came from Central Arabia. They originated from many different countries from Morocco and Spain to Persia, but none of them were nomads from Arabia, the people who had carried out the conquests. The historians of the Abbaside period, therefore, were not themselves familiar with the life of the early bedouin conquerors nor had they any interest in military operations. They were not even very interested in dates, numbers or "facts", aspects of history considered vital nowadays. "God put the unbelievers to flight" is often to them a sufficient description of a battle. The dates which they give are often hopelessly inaccurate. They sometimes differ from one another by as much as two years in the date of a major battle. The strengths attributed by them to the rival armies are equally vague, though they tend to give a reasonable estimate of the Muslim forces but greatly to exaggerate the numbers of the enemy.

Apart, moreover, from the lack of interest of the historians in military operations, they laboured under the handicap of possessing no maps. To us, accustomed from childhood to look at maps and to visualize the relative positions of different places, it is impossible to imagine how difficult it would be to follow a campaign without them. In fact it is obvious that the Arab historians had little idea of the campaigns which they described. Only here and there the name of some place has survived in the traditional narrative and is still in use today, thereby providing the modern historian with a clue.

One other point regarding the early Arab records may be mentioned. The historians and the traditionalists were scrupulous in mentioning the names of their informants and in tracing the sources of their information back to those who had been present when the events recorded took place. But when he had quoted his list of names, the responsibility of the historian ended. He made no further attempt to find out if the incidents which he described could really have taken place. Where alternative and even mutually contradictory reports had been handed down, the historian would record them all, each with its long chain of authorities and would leave it to the reader to sort out all the conflicting material.

These handicaps inherited from the past have been matched by equal difficulties in our own times. Firstly, Arabic was for centuries taught in England only as a dead language. European orientalists have carried out a task of immense value in translating the Arabic classics, but they have tended to concentrate on the religious, the political or the academic, rather than the military aspects of the surviving records. Professional soldiers have rarely had the time to acquire a difficult dead language.

Secondly, until the last fifty years, the Arabian peninsula has been impenetrable to any but the most daring explorers and it has thus been impossible for the Western historian to study the ground or to familiarize himself with the kind of Arabs who fought in the conquests.

Thirdly, the Muslim conquests were for many centuries regarded in Europe as terrible disasters, of which no Christian wished to be reminded. Historians are but human and are discouraged if their works find no readers. Simon Ockley, one of the earliest English historians of the Arab conquests, wrote some of his greatest works in the debtors' prison in Cambridge. The sale of his books was insufficient to enable him to support his family. How many thousands of books have been written since the Renaissance on the subject of the Roman Empire, yet the number of standard works in English on the Arab conquests can perhaps be counted on the fingers of one hand. It is no wonder that we have made so many and such profound errors in our policy towards the Arabs, when our attitude towards them is based on so frail a foundation of knowledge.

But if the historian of the Arab conquests labours under so many difficulties, he possesses one extraordinary advantage. There still exist in Central Arabia, tribesmen who are almost completely unchanged since the seventh century of our era. Such a situation is probably unique in the world. There are, of course, remote and uncivilized races which have scarcely changed for thousands of years, but these are not peoples who have played a leading rôle in the history of the civilized world as the Arabs have.

What a sensation would be caused if, on some lost island, a community of Roman republicans were discovered, living exactly as they did in the days of Marius and Sulla, or of Pompey and Caesar. Yet in Central Arabia this has actually occurred, and tribes still live there unchanged from the Hawazin and Beni Bekr of the seventh century.

* * * * *

It was religious enthusiasm which provided the impetus for the Arab conquests. Then gradually, as the first passionate devotion cooled, the nature of the new empire changed. From an idealist theocracy, it was transformed into a lay empire, which turned to power politics to defend itself and further to expand its dominions. The process of change occupied a number of years. In general, it has been my object in this book to cover the age of Religious Enthusiasm. In another work, I hope to tell the story of the Arab Empire as a Great Power, under the Umaiyid and earlier Abbasid khalifs. The reign of

Muawiya seems to represent the age of transition from a basically religious to an essentially worldly political régime. During this period, while the government may have been inspired predominantly by worldly motives, there was still much sincere religious enthusiasm among the soldiers and the people. I have therefore chosen to close this narrative with the death of Muawiya.

* * * * *

I have already said that professional soldiers have rarely had time to acquire a difficult dead language. By this confession I may seem to have condemned this book in advance. Yet a remarkable series of coincidences has emboldened me to write it. Firstly, I learned Arabic, not as a dead language, but by living with the people, until I was almost as fluent in it as in English. Secondly I actually commanded, for thirty years, soldiers recruited from those very tribesmen who carried out the great Arab conquests and who have remained unchanged for thirteen hundred years Not only so, but with these very soldiers I was engaged in military operations all over the same country across which the early Arab armies fought.

Certain features of a country—mountains, passes, rivers, deserts—are of vital importance to military operations, yet it is possible to live all one's life near to them and never to attach to them any particular significance. But as soon as one finds oneself engaged in military operations over the same countryside, all these strategically important features leap to the eye. When, after such an experience, one reads accounts of ancient campaigns fought over the same area, one immediately recognizes the intentions of former commanders. It was in this manner that the early Arab conquests suddenly came alive to my mind.

No previous author, Arab or European, has, as far as I know, ever been able to produce a lucid and reasonable narrative of the Arab conquests for the first twenty years after the death of Muhammad. Owing to the purely fortuitous circumstances which I have described, I hope that I have succeeded in doing so. Unfortunately, however, the immense advantages which, owing to a lucky chance, I have been able to enjoy may never again fall to the lot of an English language writer. Until the First World War, no British military commander had ever fought over this country. Perhaps none will ever do so again. Similarly, with the attainment of independence by these countries, British officers are no longer in command of Arab troops in these areas. And finally, with the industrialization of Arabia, the bedouin way of life, preserved for thousands of years like some buried fossil, may soon disappear from the world.

It is on these fortuitous circumstances, rather than on my own learning, that I am obliged to rely in venturing to submit to the public my reconstruction of one of the most extraordinary episodes of history—the Great Arab Conquests.

J.B.G.

West Wood St. Dunstan
Mayfield
Sussex

## AUTHOR'S NOTE

IN place names, I have in most cases used the Arabic forms. In the case of names already familiar to the English reader, I have used the best known forms. Such are, for example, Cairo, Damascus, Jerusalem, Tigris and Euphrates. I have in some places referred to Constantinople and in others to Byzantium. The two names refer to the same city, now called by the Turks Istanbul.

The Arabic personal names perhaps require a brief note. The Arabs have a confusing way of calling a man the father of his eldest son. In the seventh century, this custom seems to have been even more prevalent than now, so much so indeed that the man's original personal name seems at times to have been forgotten. The name always embodied that of the eldest son, who, as often as not, died in infancy. Thus a man might be known for the greater part of his life as Abu Qasim, although his eldest son Qasim died at the age of one month and scarcely anyone had ever seen or heard of him. This curious custom accounts for the many people in the narrative known as abu—or father of – somebody else. Incidentally also, the word abu makes abi in the genitive. The younger sons of Abu Qasim, some of whom might survive, might therefore be known as "son of the father of Qasim", which would be rendered in Arabic "ibn abi Qasim", ibn being the word for son.

In writing Arabic words and names, I have used the spelling which seemed to me most likely to enable the ordinary English reader to pronounce them correctly. Arabic is written with letters different from those of the English alphabet, so that it is not always possible to put Arabic names into English script merely by substituting the English equivalents for the Arabic letters. Some Arabic letters have no English equivalents. I have normally omitted the Arabic article al, which precedes many names of people and places in the original Arabic.

I have endeavoured, as far as possible, to obtain my narrative directly from the original Arabic sources. Of these the fullest is that of Muhammad al Tabari, who has been referred to as the Livy of the Arabs. His campaigns, however, are by no means always clear. As far as I know, there is no complete English translation of Tabari. I have, however, taken advantage of many learned translations of Arabic works by European scholars, particularly those in English and French. I have not wearied the reader by frequent footnotes or by quoting abstruse authorities for every statement. I would not venture to claim that my work is one of profound scholarship but have rather sought to apply the accepted accounts to the actual terrain and to interpret the historical texts in the light of my own practical experience.

* * * * *

I would like to express my grateful thanks to the Librarian of the School of Oriental and African Studies of the University of London, Mr. J. D. Pearson, and to the Deputy Librarian, Mr. R. J. Hoy, without whose assistance this book could scarcely have been written. I am also indebted to the Librarian of the Public Library of the Borough of Tunbridge Wells, Mr. R. G. Bird. I am most particularly grateful to Professor A. J. Arberry, Professor of Arabic at the University of Cambridge, for his generous help in clearing up a number of points in Arabic which had puzzled me.

# *Contents*

# *List of Maps*

The lower courses of the Tigris and Euphrates have changed frequently since the seventh century and it is impossible now to know how they were at the time of the Arab conquests. In general, however, it seems certain that the Euphrates at that time spread out into a great marsh, covering most of the area from the modern town of Diwaniya to that of Nasiriya.

As regards the Tigris, it seems that, prior to the seventh century, it flowed in approximately its present bed through Amara, but that, immediately before the Arab conquests, it burst its banks near the present town of Kut, and turned down the course of the present Shatt al Hai. Several centuries later, it returned to its present course. The break in the seventh century may have been due to neglect in repairing the banks, owing to the confusion in the reign of Chosroes Parwiz. Both courses of the lower Tigris are shown in the maps in this book. (See Guy Le Strange, *Lands of the Eastern Caliphate*.)

# I

# *The Ignorance*

The times of this ignorance God winked at; but now commandeth all men everywhere to repent. Because he hath appointed a day in which he will judge the world. *Acts* XVII, 30

To realize the nature and results of the changes effected by Mahomet, we must thoroughly understand the state of things which he found in existence both in his own country of Arabia, and in those adjoining empires of Rome and Persia, which were, the one wholly conquered, the other greatly diminished, by the victories of his first successors. E. A. Freeman, *History of the Saracens*

# I

## THE IGNORANCE

AT the beginning of the seventh century of our era, Arabia occupied in world politics a position not dissimilar to that which it holds today.[1] Then, as now, what we call the Middle East was torn by the rivalry between eastern and western power blocs. The West was represented by the Graeco-Roman Empire of Byzantium, the East by that of Persia. In general the upper Euphrates and Tigris formed the boundary between the two. The Arabs lay slightly to the south of, and in contact with, both parties. Then, as now, the Arabs were divided against one another. Then, as now, they sought to profit by the rivalries of the Great Powers, while themselves remaining neutral.

The struggle between Rome and Persia was centuries old. Fifty-three years before Christ, Crassus at the head of ten Roman legions had been defeated at Carrhæ, a disaster only partially retrieved thirty-three years later by the diplomacy of Augustus, who succeeeded in persuading the Parthian king to return the captured and humiliated eagles. In A.D. 115, Trajan, the soldier emperor, led the Roman legions down the length of Iraq, and, gazing over the blue waters of the Persian Gulf, wished that he were as young as Alexander had been, that he too might sweep on to India.

Here again, on the burning plains of Mesopotamia, on 26th June, A.D. 363, the Roman Emperor Julian fell mortally wounded in a desperate battle with the Persians, and Rome was obliged, in a humiliating peace, to cede five provinces of the empire to the victorious enemy. These are merely highlights of this endless struggle. For five centuries the relentless rivalry had continued, sometimes in hot war, at others in cold, the balance of victory inclining first to one side and then to the other. Then, in A.D. 475, Romulus Augustulus, the last Western Emperor of Rome, laid down the imperial dignity and Western Europe was abandoned to the barbarians. Thereafter the Eastern Roman Empire, that of Byzantium, was left alone to sustain the struggle against Persia which, for five centuries, had taxed the full resources of Rome at the height of her power.

Fifty years after the disappearance of the Western Empire, Justinian ascended the throne of Byzantium, reluctantly engaging in yet another of the unending wars with Persia, until, after five years of indecisive hostilities, he purchased in A.D. 532 a precarious truce by the payment of a heavy indemnity. On the Persian side, this treaty had been signed by Chosroes Anushirvan, who two years earlier had been proclaimed King of Persia. It was grandiloquently designated by its signatories as the Endless Peace.

Both empires, as will shortly be explained, maintained alliances with Arab

[1] See map inside front cover.

princes on their southern flanks. "Endless peace" was doubtless little to the taste of these Arab freebooters, and Khalid ibn Ghassan, the prince of Byzantium's Arab allies, hastened to shatter it by raiding Persia's Arab satellite, Al Mundhir of Hira.

Chosroes cried treachery and flew once more to arms. Invading the provinces of the Byzantine Empire, he captured and plundered Aleppo and Emessa, the modern Homs. The Byzantines were obliged to buy peace once more by the formal cession to Persia of the cities which Chosroes had already occupied. Yet the termination of active hostilities did little to reduce the rivalry of East and West, their mutual ambitions being continuously pursued by the methods (all too familiar to our own age) of intrigue, propaganda and commercial rivalry.

Chosroes Anushirvan died in A.D. 579, and was succeeded by his son Hurmizd IV, who, however, was deposed in 590, when Chosroes Parwiz ascended the throne. The Persian army revolted and the new king was obliged to flee for his life to Syria, whence he appealed for assistance to his rival, the Emperor Maurice of Byzantium. Supported by a Byzantine army, Chosroes Parwiz resumed the Persian throne, and, for a brief period, the two emperors were allies and the world had peace.

The respite was all too short. In A.D. 602, the Byzantine army mutinied in its turn and deposed Maurice. Chosroes Parwiz immediately declared himself ready to avenge his ally the emperor, who had assisted him in similar circumstances. He marched into Byzantine territory, which he was to ravage and lay waste, almost unopposed, for twenty-five years, during which the armies of Persia occupied the imperial provinces of Egypt, Palestine, Syria and Asia Minor. The Emperor Maurice had been murdered after his deposition. His successor Phocas, a drunken and brutal centurion, was for eight years, by his cruelty and debauchery, to disgrace the imperial purple.

At length, in A.D. 610, Heraclius, son of the Byzantine governor of Africa, rose in revolt and sailed to the capital in command of a fleet and an army. The vile Phocas was dragged from the throne to torture and death, and Heraclius was proclaimed emperor by a happy and grateful people.

The attacks of Chosroes Parwiz against the Byzantine Empire had ostensibly originated in his determination to avenge the murder of his benefactor Maurice, a task now accomplished by Heraclius. The fact that the Persians now redoubled their efforts against the empire revealed the falsity of the excuses under which the Great King had sought to veil his military ambition. Before Heraclius could restore order to the distracted empire, Chosroes in A.D. 613 had captured Damascus and in A.D. 614 Jerusalem, carrying off to Persia the alleged true cross of the Crucifixion. In A.D. 616 he invaded simultaneously Egypt and Asia Minor, until his armies pitched their camps within sight of the walls of Byzantium.

While these stirring events were shaking the two mightiest empires of the world, an orphan boy had been growing up in a remote desert town of Arabia. On 20th August, A.D. 570, Muhammad had been born in Mecca—the Emperor Justinian had died five years earlier while Chosroes Anushirvan was to live until A.D. 579. The Arabian prophet announced his mission in A.D. 612,

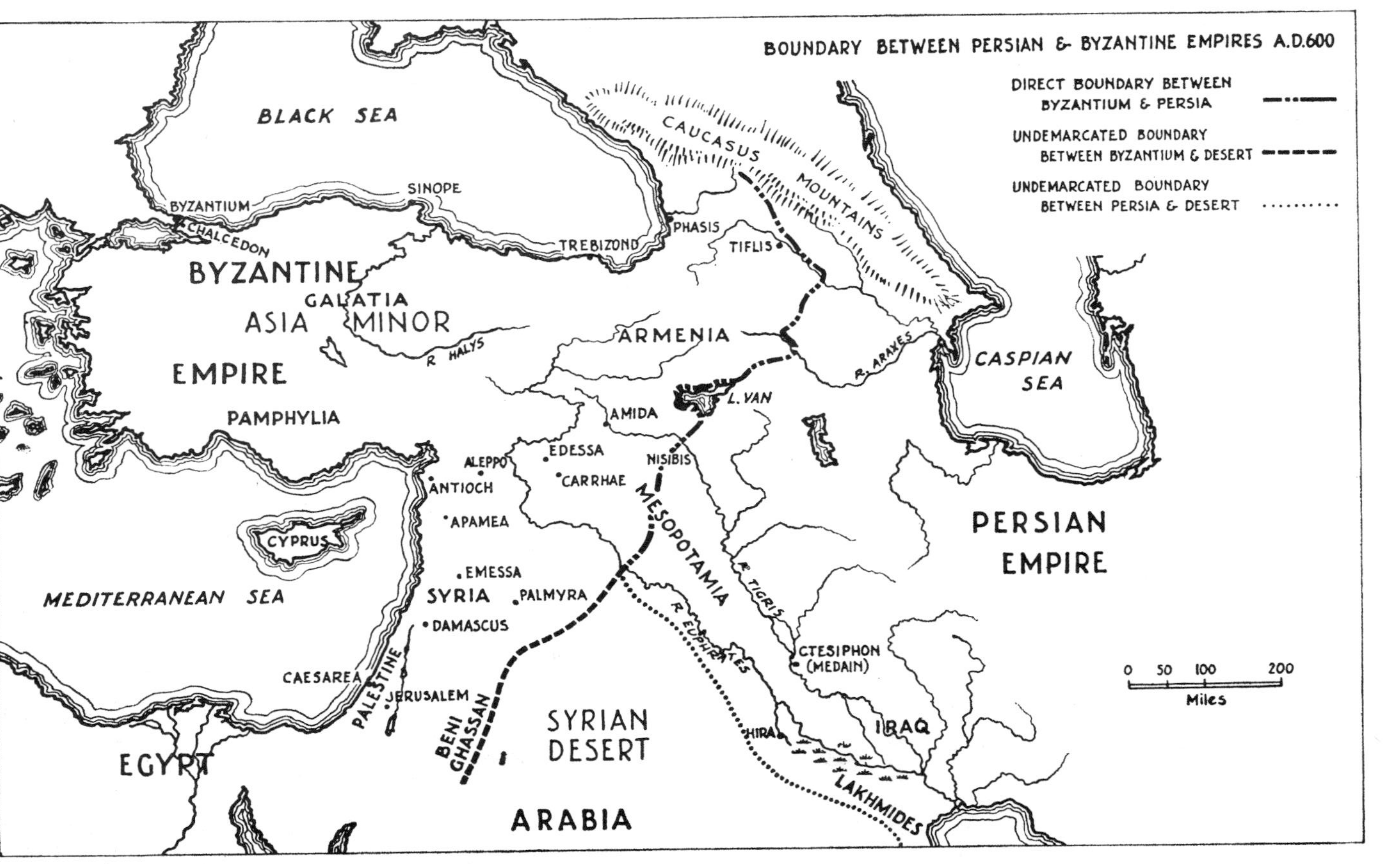
BOUNDARY BETWEEN PERSIAN & BYZANTINE EMPIRES A.D.600
DIRECT BOUNDARY BETWEEN BYZANTIUM & PERSIA
UNDEMARCATED BOUNDARY BETWEEN BYZANTIUM & DESERT
UNDEMARCATED BOUNDARY BETWEEN PERSIA & DESERT
BLACK SEA
CAUCASUS
MOUNTAINS
BYZANTIUM
SINOPE
CHALCEDON
TREBIZOND
PHASIS
TIFLIS
BYZANTINE
GALATIA
ASIA
MINOR
EMPIRE
R. HALYS
ARMENIA
R. ARAXES
CASPIAN SEA
L. VAN
AMIDA
PAMPHYLIA
EDESSA
ALEPPO
NISIBIS
ANTIOCH
CARRHAE
MESOPOTAMIA
APAMEA
CYPRUS
PERSIAN
EMPIRE
EMESSA
SYRIA
PALMYRA
R. TIGRIS
MEDITERRANEAN SEA
DAMASCUS
R. EUPHRATES
CTESIPHON (MEDAIN)
CAESAREA
PALESTINE
JERUSALEM
BENI GHASSAN
SYRIAN DESERT
HIRA
IRAQ
0 50 100 200
Miles
EGYPT
LAKHMIDES
ARABIA

Map I

when the Persian armies were already in occupation of several Byzantine provinces.

*The Cold War*

While the rivalry between Byzantium and Persia was thus carried on, by alternate periods of war and peace on their main frontiers, their unending jealousies extended cold war operations southwards to Arabia and East Africa. Their rivalry here took the form, on the one hand of commercial competition, on the other of conflicting spheres of influence, small wars and the conclusion of treaties.

Then, as now, the influence and importance of Arabia was largely due to its geographical position, separating the Indian Ocean and Southern Asia from the Mediterranean and Europe. The eastern trade was as important to the Byzantine Empire in the sixth and seventh centuries as it is to Western Europe in the twentieth, and this trade could be facilitated or impeded by whatever power exercised influence in Arabia and the Red Sea.

The secret of the monsoons had been discovered in A.D. 45 by the Greek pilot Hippalus and thereafter an active trade had been maintained between India and the Roman Empire, ships sailing directly from Bombay or even from the coasts of Southern India. Pliny, writing about A.D. 77, mentions a ship which sailed to India in the extraordinarily short period of fifteen days. But the majority of merchants avoided the navigation of the Red Sea, the waters of which were often infested with pirates, and the coasts deficient in harbours and diffcult for navigation, due to the coral reefs off-shore. The greater part of the merchandise was therefore unloaded at Aden or on the coast of the Yemen, enabling the ships to profit by the return monsoon across the Indian Ocean.

From the southern tip of Arabia, the merchandise was carried by camel caravan up the eastern or Arabian shore of the Red Sea, to the vicinity of Aila, the modern Aqaba. Thence it divided along the separate roads leading to Damascus, Gaza or Egypt, from which cities it was distributed to the Mediterranean world. From very early times, this eastern trade gave rise to thriving and civilized kingdoms in Southern Arabia, known variously as Minaeans, Sabaeans and Himyarites. The Old Testament has familiarized us with the Queen of Sheba, who paid a visit to King Solomon and "communed with him of all that was in her heart". The royal pair have been suspected of amorous dalliance. The visit may more probably be attributed to the fact that Solomon had established his control over Trans-Jordan, from Aqaba to south of Damascus, and was thus in a position to interfere with the Sabaean commercial caravans. The object of the queen's journey was doubtless to ensure that Solomon allowed her caravans to pass unmolested.

Two centuries before Christ, a northern Arab race called the Nabatæans appears to have been likewise engaged in this lucrative commerce. Perhaps the Sabaeans were already losing ground or perhaps they brought the merchandise to Al 'Ula or Teima, and handed it over there to the northern traders. The Nabatæan kingdom, with its fabulous rose-red capital of Petra in modern Jordan, reached the height of its prosperity in the first century of

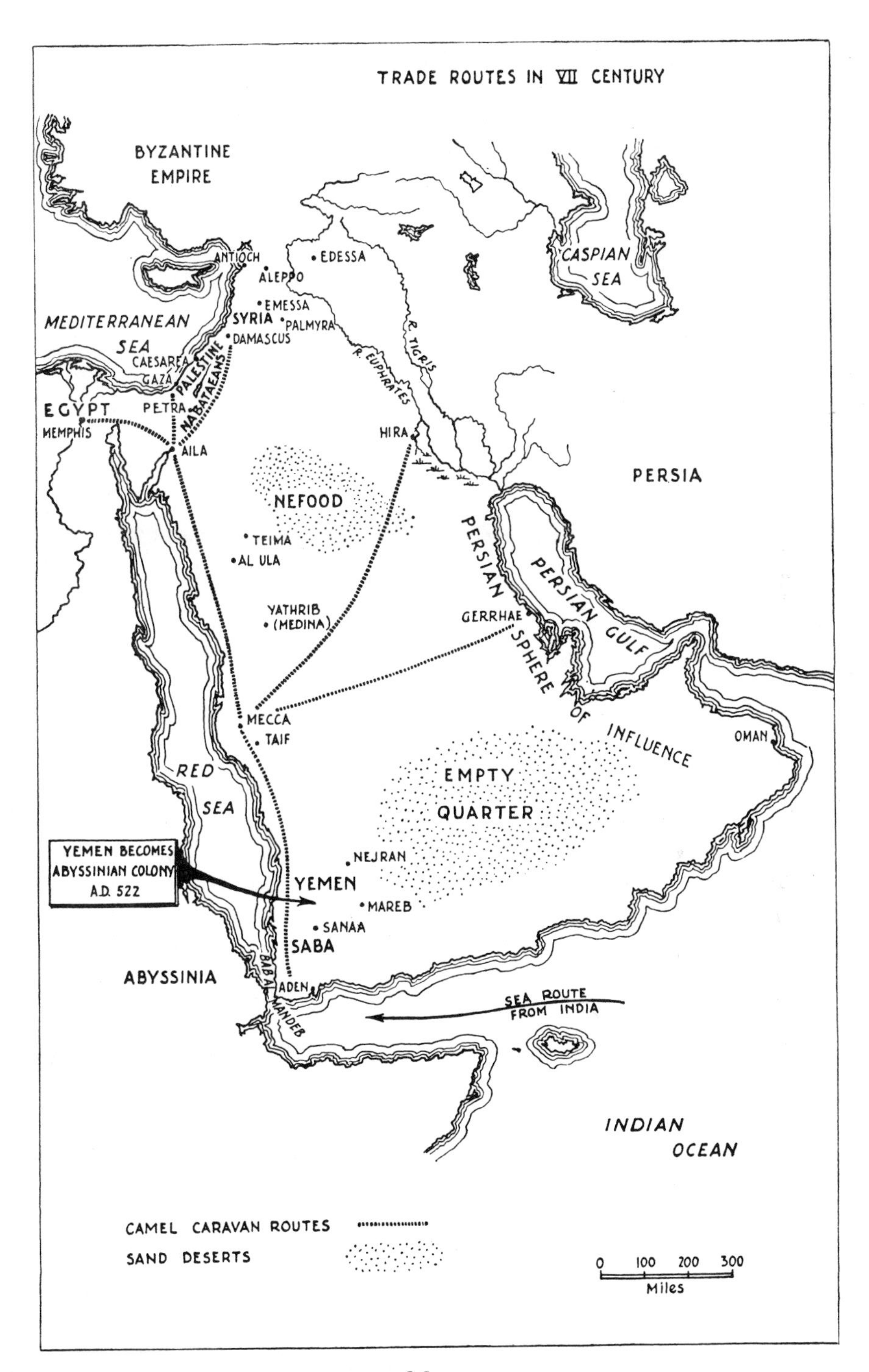
TRADE ROUTES IN VII CENTURY
BYZANTINE EMPIRE
CASPIAN SEA
ANTIOCH
EDESSA
ALEPPO
EMESSA
SYRIA
PALMYRA
MEDITERRANEAN SEA
DAMASCUS
CAESAREA
GAZA
PALESTINE
NABATAEANS
R. TIGRIS
R. EUPHRATES
EGYPT
MEMPHIS
PETRA
AILA
HIRA
PERSIA
NEFOOD
TEIMA
AL ULA
PERSIAN GULF
PERSIAN SPHERE OF INFLUENCE
YATHRIB (MEDINA)
GERRHAE
MECCA
TAIF
OMAN
RED SEA
EMPTY QUARTER
YEMEN BECOMES ABYSSINIAN COLONY A.D. 522
NEJRAN
YEMEN
MAREB
SANAA
SABA
ABYSSINIA
BAB AL MANDEB
ADEN
SEA ROUTE FROM INDIA
INDIAN OCEAN
CAMEL CARAVAN ROUTES
SAND DESERTS
0 100 200 300
Miles

Map II

our era, when its king for a time held sway as far north as Damascus. In II Corinthians XI, 32, Paul tells how "in Damascus the governor under Aretas the king kept the city of the Damascenes with a garrison, desirous to apprehend me", with the result that the apostle had to be let down from the wall in a basket. Aretas was the Greek form of Al Harith, King of the Nabatæans. Petra was captured by Trajan in A.D. 106, the Nabatæan kingdom was destroyed and their territory (the modern Trans-Jordan) became the Roman province of Arabia. As a result, Nabatæan merchants and their caravans no longer competed in the eastern trade.

In the first three centuries after Christ, the South Arabian rulers had built up a military empire. As early as A.D. 206, their king Asad abu Karib invaded Iraq with a great army and even defeated the Persians and penetrated far into that country. This was doubtless only possible because Persia was at the time torn by civil war. In any case, Asad abu Karib seems to have been undisputed ruler of the Arabian peninsula.

All the Arabs seem to have been more or less under the suzerainty of the South Arabian kingdom until as late as the Abyssinian conquest in A.D. 522, which is described below. Thus for many centuries before Muhammad, there had always been Arab states of considerable power and civilization, even if not on the same level as Rome or Persia.

In or about A.D. 450, however, the great dam of Mareb, which allegedly irrigated a large part of the South Arabian country, is believed to have collapsed. Economic troubles resulted. Many tribes migrated northwards, and the capital, which had been at Mareb, was moved to Sanaa, the capital of the Yemen today. Thereafter the name Sabaean becomes increasingly replaced by that of Himyarite.

Whatever its economic or internal political situation might be, the South Arabian kingdom was important in the cold war between Byzantium and Persia. It was a major depôt of the eastern trade and the landfall of ships from India.

Meanwhile Judaism and Christianity were spreading. Nejran in South Arabia supported a flourishing Christian population, with a cathedral and a bishop. Early in the sixth century A.D., tradition relates that the Himyar ruler, Dhu Nuwas of Sanaa, was converted to Judaism. With the fanaticism of the proselyte, he carried out a massacre of the Christians of Nejran. A fugitive victim of this persecution fled to Byzantium, carrying a charred copy of the Gospels, and appealed to the emperor to intervene to protect his fellow Christians. A military and naval expedition to South Arabia was beyond the power of the Byzantine emperor, but he gave the refugee a letter to the Christian prince of Abyssinia, urging upon the latter the duty of action to save his co-religionists.

Abyssinia had long thrown envious eyes on Arabia. As early as the fourth century A.D., we hear of her trying to extend her influence there and maintaining a fleet which attempted to control the Straits of Bab el Mandeb. Encouraged now by Byzantium, and assisted by 600 Byzantine vessels as transports, the Abyssinians invaded South Arabia in A.D. 522, dethroned Dhu Nuwas and established an Abyssinian governor in control.

The historians thus ascribe the intervention of Abyssinia in Arabia to religious motives. It is not impossible, however, that power politics were also involved, for Persia had been extending her influence down the Arab shore of the Persian Gulf to Oman. Both East and West were feeling their way towards control of the eastern trade route. Christian Abyssinia was the ally of Byzantium. With Abyssinia firmly in control of South Arabia, the trade between India and Byzantium was safe. But these political vicissitudes had perhaps impoverished the great merchants of the Himyarite kingdom, for, at about this time, we find the caravan trade passing into the hands of the merchants of Mecca, a city which had long been a posting station on the trade route.

### *The Arab Allies*

Such were the military, commercial and political struggles which were being conducted in South Arabia in the century which saw the birth of Muhammad. Meanwhile in the north, the Arabs were playing an even more active rôle in the hot and the cold wars between Byzantium and Persia.

Geographically Arabia may be said to consist of the peninsula, south of a line drawn from the head of the Persian Gulf to Aila (Aqaba), and of a triangle with this line as its base and its apex at Aleppo. The whole of this area is desert. The northern triangle consists of vast, rolling plains, the south of a great plateau extending from the summits of the Hejaz mountains, and shelving gradually to the Persian Gulf. Within this area lie two deserts of sand dunes, the smaller the Nefood in the north, the larger, the Empty Quarter, in the south. This vast peninsula was dotted here and there with oases, towns and villages, but the greater part of it consisted of immense grazing grounds over which wandered the nomadic bedouin [2] tribes.

The only means of locomotion across the desert was the camel, of which the Arabs held a monopoly. Thus neither the Byzantine nor the Persian armies could cross the desert nor make contact with one another, except north-east of Aleppo, where the desert ceased. Here they had a fixed frontier extending from the Euphrates to the Caucasus. The sea can be an obstacle to those who have no ships, but to a seafaring people it is a highway, both for trade and for war. The Arabs on their camels were the seafarers of the desert, while Persians and Byzantines were alike landsmen without ships.

The Perso-Byzantine frontier, from the Euphrates to the Caucasus, was heavily studded with frontier fortresses, but both empires exposed a soft underbelly towards Arabia—the line of the Euphrates in the case of Persia (which included what we call Iraq) and the desert border from Damascus to Aila (the modern Aqaba) in the case of Byzantium.

To protect their open southern flanks, both Byzantium and Persia maintained Arab satellite states. On the west, the princes of Beni Ghassan were allied to the emperor, while on the Euphrates, the Arab Lakhm dynasty covered the southern flank of Persia. The two Arab dynasties held high rank in their respective empires, the prince of Beni Ghassan enjoying at times

[2] Many different meanings have been given to the word bedouin. In this book it refers only to the nomadic camel-breeding tribes of the desert.

patrician status under the Byzantine government, while the Lakhmide ruler was a feudal prince under the Persian crown.

The rival Arab dynasties of Ghassan and Lakhm occupied themselves in endless desert warfare and raids against one another. We have already seen that the "endless peace" between Justinian and Chosroes Anushirvan was prematurely terminated in A.D. 532 by an attack by the Beni Ghassan on their Lakhmide rivals.

The Lakhm dynasty was at the height of its power in the middle of the sixth century under Mundhir II, and when the "endless peace" was made between Byzantium and Persia in 532, Justinian made a cash payment for reparations to Mundhir direct, in addition to that paid to Chosroes. Mundhir was eventually captured by the Byzantines and sent to die in exile in Sicily. He was succeeded by Naaman V.

We have already seen that, in A.D. 522, the Abyssinians had conquered the Himyarite Kingdom of South Arabia, at the instigation of the Byzantine Emperor. But in fifty years the south Arabs wearied of Abyssinian rule, and in or about A.D. 573 or 574, a deputation from the conquered Himyarite country visited Hira, the Lakhmide capital, to complain. Naaman took the deputation to visit the Great King. The Persians were not unwilling to gain prestige in a "war of liberation", and a Persian force was sent to South Arabia, and drove out the Abyssinians. After a period of confusion, a Persian viceroy was appointed in A.D. 597 and South Arabia (which I shall henceforward call by its modern name of the Yemen) became a Persian colony. Muhammad, the future prophet, was already twenty-seven years of age.

In A.D. 605, however, Naaman quarrelled with the Great King, who abolished the Lakhmide dynasty. Thereafter the Arabs of the Euphrates and the Persian Gulf remained in a state of semi-rebellion against Persia until the arrival of the Muslims. As a result, Persian influence, which amounted at one time virtually to colonial rule in the Persian Gulf, Oman and the Yemen, was greatly weakened. The insurgent Arab tribes of the lower Euphrates, deprived of their own Arab rulers, cut the Persian communications with their South Arabian colonies.

After the rise of Islam, the Arabs were wont to refer to the period before the ministry of Muhammad as the Ignorance. Such a term can only be justly applied in a religious sense. From the point of view of culture and of politics, some of the Arabs were already sophisticated long before the appearance of Islam, and were quite capable of playing their part in the fields of diplomacy, policy and war with the Great Powers of their time.

*Religious Factors*

In A.D. 330, Christianity had been for the first time officially tolerated in the Roman Empire. In A.D. 375, it became the state religion. The conversion of the Arabs along the desert frontiers of Syria commenced at this period. In A.D. 529, we find Harith IV of Beni Ghassan recognized by Justinian as a phylarch, with the rank of patrician, the dynasty being then probably some two hundred years old. By this time the Ghassan princes and all the Arabs of the Syrian border were Christians.

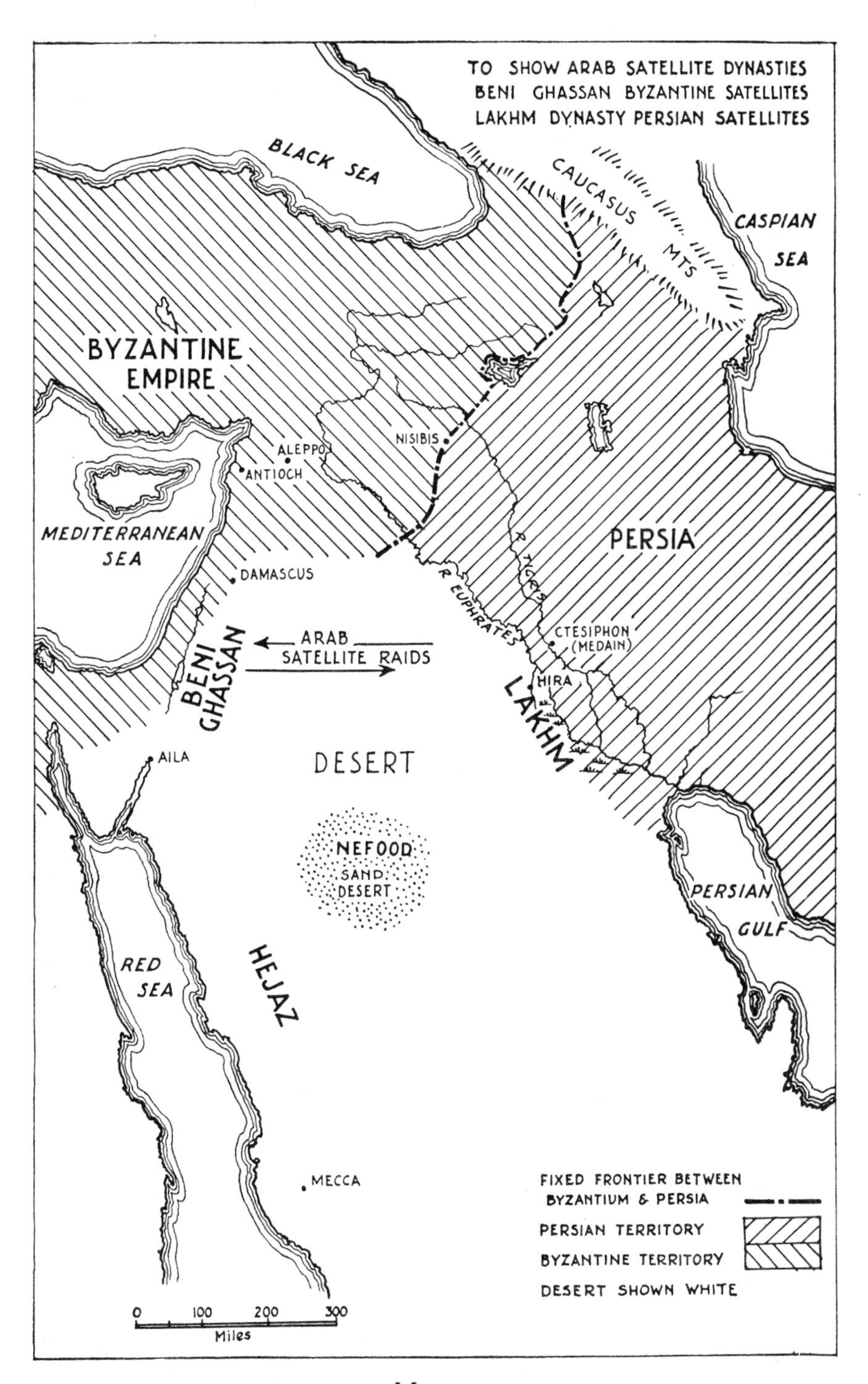

TO SHOW ARAB SATELLITE DYNASTIES
BENI GHASSAN BYZANTINE SATELLITES
LAKHM DYNASTY PERSIAN SATELLITES
BLACK SEA
CAUCASUS MTS
CASPIAN SEA
BYZANTINE EMPIRE
NISIBIS
ALEPPO
ANTIOCH
MEDITERRANEAN SEA
PERSIA
R TIGRIS
R EUPHRATES
DAMASCUS
CTESIPHON (MEDAIN)
ARAB SATELLITE RAIDS
BENI GHASSAN
HIRA
LAKHM
AILA
DESERT
NEFOOD SAND DESERT
PERSIAN GULF
RED SEA
HEJAZ
MECCA
FIXED FRONTIER BETWEEN BYZANTIUM & PERSIA
PERSIAN TERRITORY
BYZANTINE TERRITORY
DESERT SHOWN WHITE
0 100 200 300
Miles


Map III

In the fifth, sixth and succeeding centuries, schisms rent the Byzantine Greek Church. Whereas former controversies had raged over the attempt to define the nature of the Trinity, the new heresies were concerned with the analysis of the Incarnation and its expression in the technical terms employed by Greek philosophy. The furious rivalries provoked by these arguments, so dear to the subtle intellects of the Greeks, were to be one of the principal reasons for the otherwise almost inexplicable rapidity of the great Arab conquests.

In A.D. 420, Nestorius preached a new interpretation of the Incarnation, but his thesis was condemned at the Council of Ephesus in A.D. 431. Persecution followed and many of his followers took refuge in Persia, where they were welcomed at the court of the Great King. These Greek refugees were better educated than the Persians, particularly in medicine, and many of them rose to high office through the favour of the King of Kings, who professed to sympathize with them in the sufferings unjustly inflicted upon them by his enemy, the Byzantine Emperor. The Nestorians were active missionaries, and converted many of the Arabs of the Euphrates and the Persian Gulf to Christianity.

Scarcely had the Nestorians been driven from the empire than a new heresy appeared. One Eutyches, a monk of Byzantium, preached that the humanity of Christ consisted of body, mind and spirit, but that, when the Divine Spirit entered into Him, it absorbed the human spirit into Itself. In A.D. 451, the teaching of Eutyches was condemned by the Council of Chalcedon. The new heresy was termed the monophysite, a word meaning "of one nature", and signifying that Christ had only one nature—the Divine. The Orthodox Church believed that he partook of the Divine and the human. Almost all the church in Egypt became monophysite, as did the majority of the people of Palestine and Syria, especially Beni Ghassan and the Arab tribes. The civil arm of the Byzantine Empire proceeded vigorously to persecute the monophysites, who, by the year A.D. 540, were almost everywhere in semi-rebellion.

Thus, almost at the same time as the Persian king had alienated his Arab allies by the execution of their prince, Naaman, the Byzantine Emperor drove Beni Ghassan into opposition by persecuting them as monophysites. The Church of Abyssinia also adopted the monophysite creed, as probably did the Christians of Nejran, to whom reference has already been made. In A.D. 581, the ruling prince of Beni Ghassan was arrested and taken to Byzantium. His sons rose in revolt but the rebellion was suppressed, the Byzantine recognition of the Ghassan dynasty was withdrawn and their subsidy was abolished. Thereafter the Arabs of the Byzantine frontiers remained in anarchy and half-rebellion against Byzantium as were their fellow Arabs on the Euphrates against the rule of Persia. When the Arab defenders of the Byzantine Empire were thus wantonly alienated, Muhammad, the future prophet, was eleven years old.

Although at this time the Greeks and the Arabs were neighbours in Syria, an immense gulf separated their mentalities. The Greeks had always been philosophers, speculators and intellectual theorists. The Arabs, on the con-

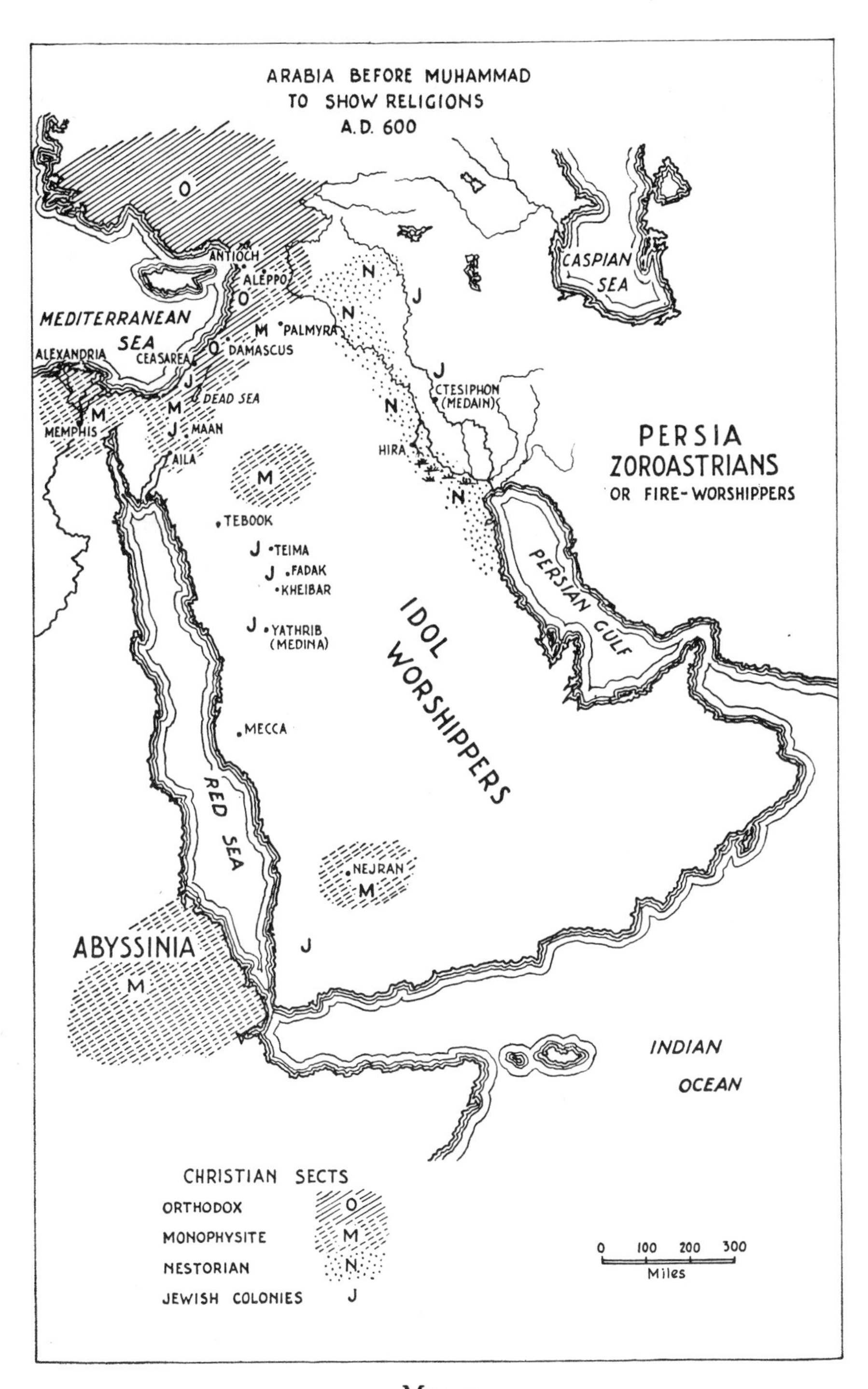
ARABIA BEFORE MUHAMMAD
TO SHOW RELIGIONS
A.D. 600
O
ANTIOCH
ALEPPO
O
MEDITERRANEAN
SEA
M
PALMYRA
N
N
J
O
DAMASCUS
ALEXANDRIA
CEASAREA
J
DEAD SEA
J
CTESIPHON
(MEDAIN)
M
M
MEMPHIS
J
MAAN
AILA
N
HIRA
CASPIAN
SEA
PERSIA
ZOROASTRIANS
OR FIRE-WORSHIPPERS
M
N
TEBOOK
J
TEIMA
J
FADAK
KHEIBAR
J
YATHRIB
(MEDINA)
IDOL
WORSHIPPERS
PERSIAN GULF
MECCA
RED SEA
NEJRAN
M
ABYSSINIA
M
J
INDIAN
OCEAN
CHRISTIAN SECTS
ORTHODOX O
MONOPHYSITE M
NESTORIAN N
JEWISH COLONIES J
0 100 200 300
Miles

Map IV

trary, were practical people, to whom purely intellectual thinking made no appeal whatever. Their genius inclined them to action rather than to thought. While the Greeks were engrossed in their attempts to define the nature of God, the Arabs were more interested in what God wanted them to do. In actual fact, both Judaism and Christianity also had at first been practical religions, concerned with how man could obey God's will, for both religions had originated among Semitic tribesmen and peasants akin to the Arabs. But Christianity did not reach the Arabs from the Jews, who had been driven from Jerusalem by Titus in A.D. 70. It reached them several centuries later, filtered through the intellectual subtlety of the Greeks. The Christianity of the Gospels would doubtless have appealed to the Arabs as it did to the poor fishermen of Galilee, but the Christianity which reached them in the fifth and sixth centuries was not the simple doctrine of the Sermon on the Mount. Islam, on the other hand, was a straightforward religion of action, entirely free from philosophic subtleties. As a result it presented to the simple Arab mind a more satisfying basis of life than did the incomprehensible hair-splitting dogmas of the Greeks. Islam has sometimes been called a Christian heresy and heresies are often over-violent reactions to genuine abuses. In this sense Islam may indeed have been an unduly vehement protest against the fact that the real message of Christianity had been submerged by the subtleties of Greek dogma.

* * * * *

In the sixth century, there were, in addition to the Christians, many Jewish colonies in Arabia. In the valley of the Tigris and Euphrates, the Jewish community, dating doubtless from the Babylonian captivity, enjoyed religious toleration under the Persian king. We have already seen an Arab Himyarite king in South Arabia converted to Judaism and persecuting the Christians of Nejran. The considerable Jewish community in the Yemen has only been reduced in number since 1948, the majority having now migrated to Israel.

In addition, however, there were, in the sixth century, many Jewish colonies in the Northern Hejaz, notably in Teima, Fadak, Khaibar and Yathrib (after Islam to be renamed Medina). No definite information is available as to where these Jews came from, or whether they were Jews by race from Judæa or Arabs converted to Judaism. When we make their acquaintance during the time of Muhammad's ministry, their language appears to be Arabic and they are organized as tribes precisely like the Arabs around them.

*The Idolaters*

Little is known of the ancient religion of Arabia, for the Muslim historians saw nothing in it worthy of record. Originally the Arabs appear to have worshipped monolithic rocks and trees, though these sacred objects were deemed holy, not in themselves, but as being the peculiar residences of certain spirits.

The adoration of carved idols may well have been a later development. In a sense, the worship of stone carved into the likeness of human beings was a retrograde tendency, transferring to material objects the veneration once directed to pure spirits. The carved idols may well, as tradition avers, have been brought from Syria, where statues of Greek and Roman gods and goddesses must have been common before the spread of Christianity.

The primitive Arabs believed that a baraka or blessing could be obtained by kissing, touching or rubbing a sacred object. To this day, tribesmen visiting the burial place of some local holy man will kiss the edge of the tomb or touch it with their hands and then draw their hands down over their faces.

It is, however, also possible that the carved idols were the remains of some age of totems, and they seem at times to have been connected with the idea of the fabulous ancestors of the tribe. More often they were associated with a sacred place, perhaps as the guardian spirit of a spring or a group of wells. As long as a certain tribe was located in the area in question, the god or spirit may have been regarded as the peculiar protector of that tribe. But when, as the result of war, famine or increase of population, that tribe was pushed on to fresh grazing areas, the new tribe which occupied their place adopted as their own the spirits of the local wells, trees or rocks.

Until the second or third decade of the present century, whenever any section of the nomadic Beni Sakhr of Trans-Jordan passed the wells of Bair, they sacrificed a camel at the supposed tomb of their ancestor Asad. Now the wells at Bair are undoubtedly thousands of years old. (They may be referred to in Numbers XXI, 16, "and from thence they went to Beer. . . . The princes digged the well, the nobles of the people digged it.") The Beni Sakhr, however, only arrived in Trans-Jordan some three centuries ago. It seems, therefore, probable that Asad, perhaps long before Islam, may have been the spirit of the wells, his sanctuary becoming rationalized long afterwards as the tomb of the Beni Sakhr ancestor when the tribe took possession of the area. We shall see later that Mecca itself passed from tribe to tribe in a not dissimilar manner.

In the midst of the worship of these spirits of stream, rock and tree, there appears at one stage to have been an intermingling of adoration of the heavenly bodies, introduced perhaps by Chaldæan influence from Iraq. The number of Arabs named Abid Shams, servant of the sun, of whom we hear before the rise of Islam, bears witness to the fact.

The outstanding accomplishment of the pre-Islamic Arabs was poetry. Deprived of spiritual influences and without belief in a future life, most of their poetry dealt with war, glory, women and wine.

"Roast meat and wine: the swinging ride
On a camel sure and tried,
Which her master speeds amain
O'er low dale and level plain:
Women marble-white and fair
Trailing gold-fringed raiment rare:

Opulence, luxurious ease,
With the lute's soft melodies—
Such delights hath our brief span;
Time is change, Time's fool is man.
Wealth or want, great store or small,
All is one since Death's are all." [3]

In the pre-Islamic period, there are alleged to have been 360 idols in the shrine of Mecca. Of these the most important were Al Uzza, Allat, and Manat, all three regarded as female deities, and Hobal, a large male image, alleged to have been brought from Syria. Tradition, in this respect, may well be correct, for his name has been found in Jordan in a Nabatæan inscription of several centuries earlier.

But although the Arabs appear thus to have worshipped, or perhaps propitiated, a great number of deities and idols before the rise of Islam, they seem also to have been familiar with the idea of Allah, as the supreme ruler of the universe. We must, I believe, beware of concluding that the Arabs, since they worshipped idols, were a race of ignorant savages. Their religion is now too remote for us to be able exactly to interpret what it meant to them. Respect for idols has, in history, been compatible with very high standards of culture and sophistication. Rome, in the golden age of Augustus or the Antonines, was still officially polytheistic, centuries after the sublime meditations of Plato and Socrates.

*Summary*

The impression that the Arabs before Islam were savage, predatory tribesmen cannot be entirely maintained. Arabia, then as now, was situated between the Indian Ocean and the Mediterranean, and the most important trade route of antiquity flowed around and across it. This strategic situation produced two results. On the one hand, Arab merchants, many of them rich and prosperous, frequented the markets of Persia, Syria and Egypt and must have formed a wealthy and cosmopolitan society. On the other hand, for many centuries before Islam, rich and highly sophisticated Arab states had grown up along the routes followed by the eastern trade. Of these were Saba (or Sheba) in South Arabia, the Nabatæans in Trans-Jordan, and the Beni Ghassan and Lakhm dynasties, the princes of which were familiar with the courts of Byzantium and Persia.

It is true that the greater part of the interior of Arabia consisted of semi-desert steppes where the inhabitants were obliged to earn a precarious living as nomadic breeders of camels, sheep and goats. The bedouin way of life in constantly moving tents renders learning, and even literacy, well nigh impossible. But it is only in our time that the culture of Western nations has made education available to all. Two hundred years ago, in France, Italy, Spain and England, the then most cultured countries in the world, the peasants and the rural population were illiterate and superstitious. In antiquity also, sophistication and savagery often lived side by side.

[3] *Hamasa*, quoted by R. A. Nicholson. *Literary History of the Arabs.*

In the field of religion, both Christianity and Judaism were well known and a great number of Arabs, including even bedouin tribes, were at least nominally Christian. The majority, it is true, still worshipped innumerable spirits dwelling in rocks, streams and trees, paid respect to some extent to the sun, moon and stars, but, at the same time, in a vague way, acknowledged the existence of a supreme divine Ruler of the world.

From this fierce, turbulent and hardy race, holding a medley of different religious beliefs and divided from one another by wide differences in their cultural levels, was soon to emerge a torrent of enthusiastic warriors, fired by a virile energy, which was to change the history of mankind. And this volcanic eruption was to coincide with a period of intense weakness and confusion in both the Persian and the Byzantine Empires. This exhaustion of the Great Powers had been brought about by their mutual destruction in their endless wars against one another, just as has occurred today to the Great Powers of Europe. In the case of Byzantium, internal weakness had been further accentuated by sedition, the result of religious controversies and persecutions.

## *NOTABLE DATES*[4]

| | A.D. |
|---|---|
| Abyssinian conquest of the Yemen | 522 |
| Birth of Muhammad | 570 |
| Expulsion of Abyssinians from the Yemen by the Persians | 574 |
| Abolition of Beni Ghassan dynasty by the Byzantine Empire | 581 |
| Chosroes Parwiz invades the Byzantine Empire to avenge the Emperor Maurice | 602 |
| Abolition of Lakhmide dynasty by Persia | 602 |
| Heraclius proclaimed Byzantine Emperor | 610 |
| Chosroes occupies Egypt and Asia Minor | 616 |

## *LIST OF RULERS*

| *Byzantine Emperors* | Date of Accession A.D. | *Kings of Persia* | Date of Accession A.D. |
|---|---|---|---|
| Justinian | 527 | Chosroes Anurshirvan | 531 |
| Justin II | 565 | Hurmizd IV | 579 |
| Tiberius | 574 | Chosroes Parwiz | 590 |
| Maurice | 582 | | |
| Phocas | 602 | | |
| Heraclius | 610 | | |

[4] A general chronology of the whole period will be found on page 372 at the end of the book.

# II

## *Quraish*

Hast Thou not seen how thy Lord dealt with the people of the elephant? Did He not cause their war to end in confusion? . . . for the protection of Quraish so let them serve the Lord of this House, who fed them against hunger and made them secure against fear. *Qoran* CV, 1, , CVI, 2, 3, 4.

## Genealogical Table of Quraish

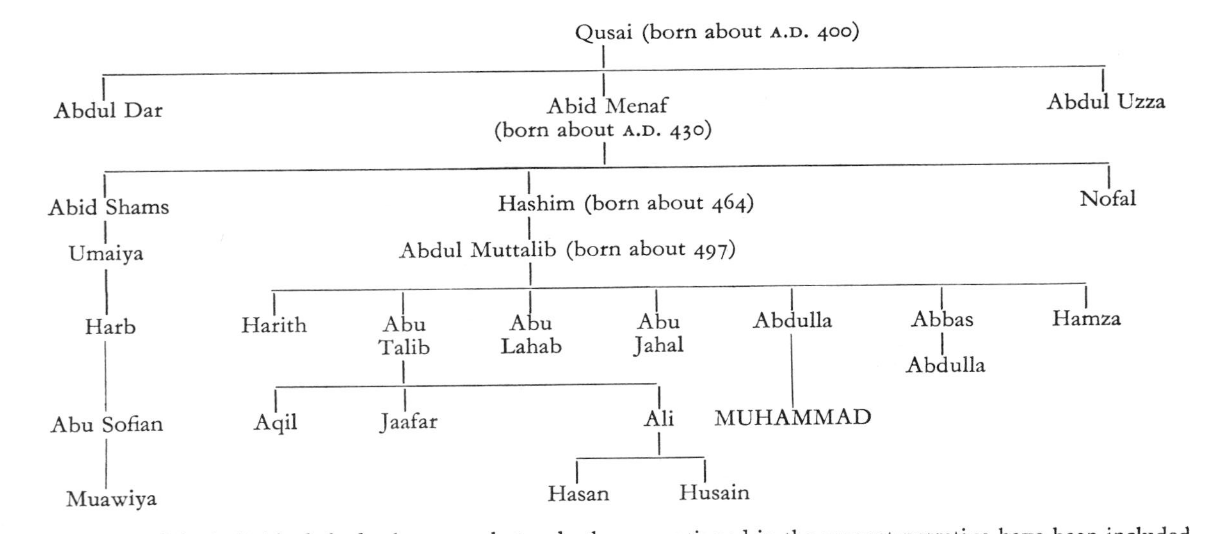


*Note.*—Some of the individuals had other sons, but only those mentioned in the present narrative have been included.

## II

## QURAISH

WE have already seen, in the previous chapter, that for the better part of a thousand years before A.D. 600, the eastern trade and the spice export trade from South Arabia itself had flowed northwards by camel caravan from the Sabaean or Himyarite kingdoms to Egypt, Syria, Rome and Byzantium. Mecca was approximately half-way between the South Arabian kingdoms and the Mediterranean distributing centres in Egypt, Gaza and Syria. From Mecca, also, caravan routes branched north-east to Gerrha (the modern Qateef) on the Persian Gulf and northwards to Hira on the Euphrates, avoiding the sand deserts of the Empty Quarter and the Nefood. Thus Mecca must have been for many centuries an important staging post.

It contained also, from very early times, a kaaba or cubical building, to which the tribes resorted from far and near on pilgrimage and which was regarded by them as sacred. From perhaps about B.C. 100, the well and the kaaba of Mecca seem to have been in the custody of a tribe known as Beni Jurham. Then, perhaps early in the third century, in the course of those northward migrations which may have resulted from the impoverishment of the Sabaean kingdom, the tribe was driven out and replaced by Khuzaa, a branch of the Azd group of tribes, migrating northwards from the Yemen.

The Northern Hejaz was already occupied by tribes of the Ishmaelite or northern group, of which one clan was known as Quraish.[1] Possibly about A.D. 235, Fihr, the then head of this family, married the daughter of the Khuzaa chief, who was the warden of the idol temple of Mecca. About A.D. 420, a descendant of this Fihr, of the name of Qusai, also married the daughter of the then Khuzaa chief of Mecca. Qusai made himself so useful to his father-in-law that he often gave him the keys of the temple and allowed him to perform the duties connected with the idolatrous rites. So much so that when the Khuzaa chief died, Qusai attempted to seize the guardianship of the kaaba for himself. The tribe of Khuzaa objected, but Qusai, who had carefully planned his *coup d'état*, called on his relatives, the neighbouring Ishmaelite tribes. The latter supported him, and in A.D. 440 Khuzaa were defeated, and Qusai was recognized as guardian of the shrine, Khuzaa being reduced to a subordinate position.

Qusai was a man of remarkable character and intelligence. No sooner was

[1] Arab historians agree in dividing the original Arab race into two stocks, the northern and the southern. The first or northern group was descended from Ishmael, the son of Abraham and thus originated from the Northern Hejaz or the south of what is now called Jordan. The southern group consisted of those tribes who migrated northwards from the Yemen to Central Arabia, where the two stocks mingled. Thus Quraish came from the Ishmaelite but Khuzaa from the southern division.

he in firm control than he set about the reorganization of the area. Hitherto there had been no buildings in Mecca except the kaaba or temple. The Arabs camped in tents in the surrounding valleys. Qusai ordered Quraish to build houses round the temple. The local Arab tribes observed the lunar year, an easy system for illiterate people, for the phases of the moon are plainly visible in the sky. But the lunar year of twelve moon months is eleven and a fraction days shorter than the solar year. Thus the pilgrimage to the kaaba, which was fixed for the twelfth month of the lunar year, moved back eleven days each year and so, in the course of about thirty-three years, moved round all the seasons. Deciding that the autumn would be the most convenient season for the pilgrimage, Qusai succeeded in persuading the Arabs to accept the insertion of a thirteenth intercalary month in every third year. This was a gallant attempt to make the lunar and solar years match, though in practice it was not quite accurate enough. (For some reason unknown to us, the Prophet Muhammad, the great-great-great grandson of Qusai, was to abolish the extra month, with the result that the Muslim year ever since has differed from the solar by eleven and a fraction days. The incident, however, illustrates the enterprise and intelligence of Qusai.)

Having thus arranged for the time of the annual pilgrimage, the chief set about organizing the internal arrangements. The duties connected with the pilgrimage were threefold: custodianship of the temple, provision of food for the pilgrims during the three days of the religious rites, and provision of water, the supply of which was always precarious. He apparently decided that, so great was the privilege of being guardians of the shrine, it was incumbent on Quraish to feed and water all the pilgrims free of charge for the three days of the pilgrimage. In order to do this, he imposed a tax on Quraish, rather than charge the pilgrims.

It may well be asked how such a heavy expenditure could be maintained. During the period of the pilgrimage, however, commercial fairs were held in Mecca and in the neighbouring valleys. When the caravans went up to Syria and Egypt with the products of the eastern trade, they returned to Mecca laden with what we should call consumer goods from the Mediterranean area. We can only assume that Quraish supported their position by the commerce of these caravans and by selling piece goods to the pilgrims at the local fairs. The free entertainment of the pilgrims, therefore, while ostensibly an act of piety, may also have stimulated the commerce of Quraish by increasing the number of their customers. Two other practices instituted by Qusai may also be mentioned. The first was the calling of a council of the tribal elders of Quraish, for which he built a council hall near the kaaba. The second was his custom, whenever the men of the tribe were to set out on a military enterprise, of presenting the leader with a lance to the end of which he in person tied a strip of white cloth, to act as a standard for rallying the tribesmen in fight. Many of the customs instituted by this extraordinary man for his half-naked clansmen in their group of mud huts round a desert well in far Arabia were to survive for centuries as revered ceremonial in some of the world's most mighty empires.

By this efficient organization, in both the religious and commercial spheres, Qusai became a man of respected influence, his fame carried to south and north by the merchant caravaners and into the deserts of the peninsula by the tribal pilgrims, who from far and wide, resorted to the shrine.

Qusai died about A.D. 450 or 460, bequeathing his position to his eldest son, Abdul Dar. (The importance attached by Qusai to his religious obligations is shown in the names of his sons—Abdul Dar, servant of the house (the kaaba), Abid Menaf, servant of Menaf, and Abdul Uzza, servant of Al Uzza.[2] Menaf and Uzza were idols.) Abid Menaf produced several sons, including Abid Shems—servant of the sun—Nofal and Hashim. Jealousies arose between the descendants of Abdul Dar and Abid Menaf, resulting in the division of the family responsibilities between them. Abdul Dar retained the custodianship of the temple and the right to carry the tribal banner in war. Meanwhile the descendants of Abid Menaf were allotted the privilege of entertaining the pilgrims.

Of the sons of Abid Menaf, the most distinguished was Hashim. The hereditary right to command the tribe of Quraish in war was acquired by his elder brother, Abid Shems, while Hashim, who had apparently grown rich in the caravan trade, gained popularity and fame by his lavish hospitality in the entertainment of the pilgrims from all parts of Arabia. In the course of his commercial journeys, Hashim married in Yathrib, a settlement some 250 miles north of Mecca, a woman of the Beni Najjar tribe settled near that town. Selma was apparently a lady of remarkable personality who gave birth in 497 [3] to a son known to history as Abdul Muttalib, who in due course assumed his father's responsibilities for the entertainment of the pilgrims in Mecca.

The fame of Abdul Muttalib soon spread far and wide, exceeding even that of his father Hashim, perhaps equalling that of his great-grandfather Qusai. The Abdul Dar branch had sunk into a subordinate position, but Harb ibn Umaiya, the grandson of Abid Shems, made bold to dispute the fame of Abdul Muttalib. His efforts were unsuccessful but the jealousies of these two remote Arab tribesmen were, more than a century later, to shake the civilized world. Meanwhile it is to be noted that Quraish were no longer controlled by one chief. Each clan had its own head and, in some cases, its peculiar duties and privileges. Particularly competition had grown up between the descendants of Umaiya and those of Hashim.

The conquest of South Arabia by the Abyssinians in 522 has already been noticed in Chapter I. In heathen times, Nejran also had possessed a kaaba, which, like that of Mecca, had been a place of pilgrimage. Since the conversion of Nejran to Christianity, it had been replaced by a cathedral. Tradition relates that Abraha, the Christian Abyssinian viceroy of the Yemen, wished to destroy the heathen kaaba of Mecca in order to divert the pilgrimage of the Arab tribes to this Christian shrine. Whether for this religious motive or through Abyssinian imperialism, Abraha marched on Mecca in 570 and reached a point a few miles from the city. Quraish were too timid or too weak to oppose the Abyssinian army and Abdul Muttalib, at the head of a

[2] See Quraish family tree, page 36.
[3] Hitherto I have marked dates as B.C. or A.D Hereafter all dates may be assumed to be A.D.

deputation, went out to negotiate with Abraha. The viceroy stated that he had no desire to damage the city, and that his only object was to demolish the heathen kaaba, a demand which the Meccans steadfastly refused to entertain.

The deputation returned to the city with heavy hearts and Abdul Muttalib advised the people to evacuate their homes and take refuge in the caves of the surrounding mountains. Before himself leaving the town, he is alleged to have leaned upon the ring of the door of the kaaba and prayed to God to defend His own house. It is impossible now to decide whether he did in reality offer up what appears to be a purely monotheistic prayer, or whether the words may have been attributed to him by later Muslim historians. The whole affair, however, would seem to establish the devotion of the Meccans to their shrine, preferring as they did to abandon their town to an enemy army rather than consent to the demolition of their idolatrous temple.

Meanwhile, it appears that smallpox had appeared in the Abyssinian army and spread rapidly. The object of the expedition was forgotten, the destruction of the kaaba abandoned, and the army commenced a disorderly retreat, Abraha himself dying on his arrival at Sanaa. The Abyssinians had brought an elephant with them, and thus the year 570 has been perpetuated until our own times and in the pages of the Qoran as the year of the elephant.

* * * * *

The year 570 saw another event, far more important than the disaster to the Abyssinian army. On 20th August[4] of that year, Muhammad, the future prophet, was born in Mecca. His father, Abdullah, a son of Abdul Muttalib, had died a few months earlier. His mother was descended from Zuhra, a brother of the famous Qusai. The child, having no father, was cared for by his grandfather Abdul Muttalib, the revered chief of the clan, now more than seventy years of age. It was the custom for the children of Quraish to be farmed out to women of the neighbouring tribes to be suckled and brought up, the free air of the desert being thought to be healthier than that of the hot, dusty town. The infant Muhammad was thus given to a woman of the Beni Saad tribe outside Mecca.

At the age of six the child returned to his mother in Mecca, but within the year she also died, leaving him an orphan of both parents. Only a slave girl, known to history as Umm Ayman, remained to care for him. The aged Abdul Muttalib took the boy into his own house, became deeply attached to him and was ever ready to play with him and fondle him. But when Muhammad was eight years of age, Abdul Muttalib also died, and the orphan was once again left in uncertainty. On his deathbed, the old chief had entrusted his little grandson to the care of another of his sons, Abu Talib, who was thus an uncle of Muhammad.

Once again the child's life was turned upside down. Tribal feeling was far too strong to allow an orphan boy to be abandoned or neglected, yet these frequent changes of household must have produced in the child a sense of

[4] Caussin de Perceval. *History of the Arabs before Islam*.

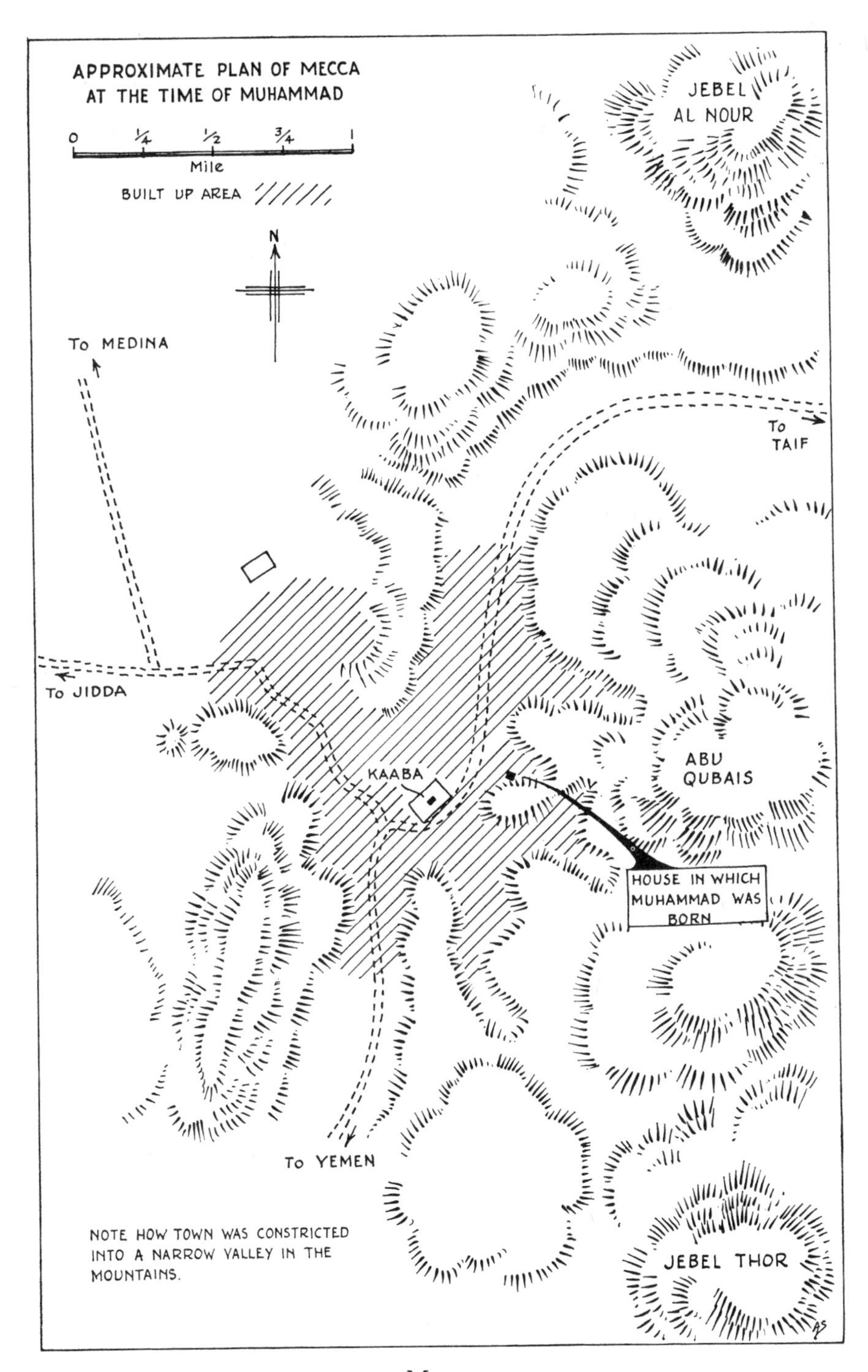
APPROXIMATE PLAN OF MECCA AT THE TIME OF MUHAMMAD
0
¼
½
¾
1
Mile
BUILT UP AREA
N
To MEDINA
JEBEL AL NOUR
To TAIF
To JIDDA
KAABA
ABU QUBAIS
HOUSE IN WHICH MUHAMMAD WAS BORN
To YEMEN
NOTE HOW TOWN WAS CONSTRICTED INTO A NARROW VALLEY IN THE MOUNTAINS.
JEBEL THOR

Map v

insecurity and perhaps of loneliness, which might result in a pensive and introspective mentality. His new protector, however, was a kindly, and indeed a noble character, who soon became fondly attached to the young Muhammad. At the age of twelve, he was taken by his uncle on one of the commercial journeys to Syria from which the Meccan merchants made their livelihood.

Except for this journey, life continued uneventful for the young Muhammad, living as a member of his uncle's family. Abu Talib, however, though kindly and generous, was by no means wealthy and his own children were increasing in number and strained all his resources. Muhammad was almost without private means, and was fain to earn what he could, sometimes in modest business transactions, at other times as a shepherd. He was a quiet and reserved youth, of a serious disposition, the result perhaps of being an orphan and of the vicissitudes of his childhood. When he was twenty-five years of age, Abu Talib suggested that he accompany a trading caravan to Syria. Khadija [5] was a wealthy widow of Quraish, who managed her own affairs, which included commercial ventures with the camel caravans. She needed a reliable agent to accompany her servants with a caravan to the north, to superintend the sale of her merchandise and with the proceeds to buy a consignment of Syrian goods for sale in Mecca. Abu Talib secured the appointment for his nephew, who already enjoyed a reputation for honesty and reliability.

This journey may have helped to stimulate the thoughts of the already pensive youth. Financially the enterprise seems to have been successful and Khadija was more than satisfied with her new agent. A few weeks after his return, she caused a proposal of marriage to be conveyed to him. She is alleged to have been at the time forty years of age, while Muhammad was only twenty-five. In other respects, however, it was a highly desirable match. Her father, Khuwailid, was a notable of Mecca, and himself a great-great-grandson of Qusai. Muhammad accepted and the wedding was celebrated.

In spite of the difference in their ages, the marriage was an unqualified success. Khadija bore him two sons, both of whom died in infancy, and four daughters, Zeinab, Rukaiya, Fatima and Umm Kulthum. The fact that she gave birth to six children may provoke doubt as to whether Khadija was in reality forty years old when she married Muhammad. Probably she was unaware of her own age as many tribal Arabs are to this day.

His wife's wealth freed Muhammad from want and improved his social standing in Mecca. She, however, continued to conduct her own commercial transactions. She thereby freed her husband from financial worries to indulge his taste for solitude and meditation, which seemed to grow upon him with age. Generally reserved and silent, he nevertheless relaxed in congenial company, and on these occasions became peculiarly pleasant and even playful and humorous.

Thus comfortably established in life, Muhammad was moved with sympathy for his uncle, who had so generously brought him up at his own expense. He accordingly offered to relieve Abu Talib of some of his expenses

[5] Pronounced Khadeeja, with the accent on the second syllable.

by taking one of his sons into his own household. Ali, then about six years old, was the one chosen and was thenceforward brought up as if he had been Muhammad's own son.

Among Khadija's servants was a slave by the name of Zeid ibn Haritha. Zeid was an Arab of the Christian tribe of Beni Odhra of Southern Syria, who had been carried off by bandits as a child and sold into slavery, eventually being acquired by Khadija. Muhammad became sincerely attached to his wife's servant, with the result that Khadija gave the youth to him as his personal slave. Soon afterwards, Zeid's father, who had been searching for him for many years, located him in Mecca and offered a large ransom to redeem him from slavery. Muhammad summoned Zeid before him and gave him the choice of returning to Syria with his father or of remaining in Mecca. The young man had already conceived an affection for Muhammad, whereas he may well not have recognized his father, whom he had not seen since infancy. He elected to remain in Muhammad's household. The latter, gratified by his devotion, hastened with him to the kaaba, where in the sacred precincts, he manumitted him from slavery and adopted him as his own son.

Although the idols of the kaaba were the objects of official worship in Mecca, there were not a few men in Arabia who had lost faith in so primitive a cult. Many Arabs, as we have seen, were Christians. Jewish colonies were numerous. Even among Quraish themselves, there were converts to Christianity. Waraqa, a cousin of Khadija, was one of these seekers after a more spiritual faith. Another, Zeid ibn Tufail of Quraish, who died about this time, is alleged to have influenced the young Muhammad in his searchings for God.

It was now the year 610, and Muhammad was forty years old, and inclined more and more to solitude and meditation. Escaping from the glaring, dusty alleyways of Mecca, he would take refuge for several days at a time in the caves of the mountains which on all sides surrounded the narrow valley in which the city lay. Amid the utterly desolate scenery of the black and grey craggy peaks, from which no spot of vegetation was visible, and divided from one another only by the deep narrow gashes of ravines and dry watercourses, his mind dwelt on the eschatology of which he had gathered fragments from the Jews and the Christians, on a single, vast, almighty, spiritual Deity, on the bliss of eternal happiness for the faithful, or on the agonies of unending tortures in hell fire. Returning home harassed by such speculations, he would confide them to Khadija, who provided for his anxious soul a continuous source of comfort and encouragement, combining the love of a wife with the comfort of a mother.

Muhammad was in the habit of retiring to the mountains for especial periods of meditation during the month of Ramadhan. One night in the year 610, when sleeping in a cave on Mount Hira, he was visited by the Archangel Gabriel. "He came to me while I was asleep, with a coverlet of brocade, on which was some writing," Muhammad subsequently related. Four times Gabriel pressed him tightly and cried, "Read!", and each time he answered, "What shall I read?" Then the Archangel replied:

"Read in the name of thy Lord who created,
Who created man of blood coagulated.
Read! Thy Lord is the most beneficent,
Who taught by the pen,
Taught what they knew not to men."

The vision was gone and Muhammad awoke in fear and turmoil of mind. "I will go to the top of the mountain and throw myself down that I may kill myself and gain rest," he thought in his alarm. "When I was midway on the mountain," he said, recalling the experience later, "I heard a voice from heaven saying, 'O Muhammad! Thou art the apostle of God and I am Gabriel.' I raised my head towards heaven to see, and lo Gabriel in the form of a man, with his feet astride the horizon."

Shattered by these visions, Muhammad returned home and poured out to Khadija an account of all that had occurred. "Rejoice, O son of my uncle, and be of good heart," she told him. "I have hope that thou wilt be the prophet of this people." [6] Khadija was the first convert to believe in Muhammad's mission. The next was his uncle's son, Ali ibn abi Talib, then ten years old, and after him his own adopted son, Zeid ibn Haritha.

Among the well-to-do merchants of Mecca was a certain Abdulla or Atiq abu Bekr, a man of a collateral branch of Quraish. Abu Bekr was a man generally popular, with a reputation for probity and a kindly genial disposition. Himself two years younger than Muhammad, he was the fourth disciple to believe in his revelation. It may be taken as evidence of the Prophet's sincerity that the first to believe in him were his wife, his two adopted sons and his best friend. These persons were in such daily intimate contact with him that any insincerity on his part would almost certainly have been apparent to them.

Scarcely a handful of converts believed in his visions. Among them may be noted Othman ibn Affan, a future khalif, Zubair ibn Awwam and Saad ibn abi Waqqas, names not many years later to resound far and wide across the civilized world. All were of Quraish. Othman was a descendant of Umaiya, whose family, it will be remembered, had competed with Hashim for pre-eminence in the tribe. Zubair was a nephew of Khadija and a cousin of Muhammad. Saad was also a cousin through Muhammad's mother.

Three years after his first vision Muhammad received the order to preach to the public in general. At the age of forty-three, his doubts and vacillations seemed to be ended and he went forth into the public square, in which stood the kaaba, to preach and to dispute with the idolaters.[7] The outlines of his teaching were simple. God, he alleged, was One, and idols must be swept away. He himself was a messenger from God. One day the dead would rise again, the righteous to paradise, the wicked and those who acknowledged many gods, to the tortures of eternal fire.

In support of these statements, Muhammad claimed direct divine revela-

[6] I have followed Professor Guillaume's translation of ibn Ishaq in this account.

[7] England at this time was still almost entirely pagan. St. Augustine had landed in 597 to effect its conversion, sixteen years before Muhammad began to preach.

tion. Sometimes, he alleged, the Archangel Gabriel appeared to him and dictated chapters of the Qoran, speaking to him as man to man. On other occasions, the messages were delivered to him by an interior voice. His intimates were soon able to detect in him the signs of an approaching revelation. He appeared to be in a state of tension, anxiety and heat. Often he lay down and was covered with a blanket until the revelation was over and a new chapter added to the Qoran. This, however, was not invariably the case, for at other times he claimed that inspiration came suddenly in the course of his normal occupations.

The basis of the new Apostle's teaching was what he himself called the religion of Abraham. The pure revelation made to Abraham, he alleged, had been subsequently distorted by the Israelites. Eventually Jesus had been sent to bring religion back from Judaistic heresies to the true faith. Muhammad believed in the Virgin Birth and stated that Jesus had been the Spirit of God, and had once again preached the pure faith of Abraham. Subsequently, however, the Christians also had adulterated the true faith, as the Jews had done before them. Now he, Muhammad, had been sent by God, in order that once more mankind be recalled to the purity of the original true religion.

The Prophet, therefore, did not claim to be the propounder of a new religion. His was identical with the faith preached by Abraham, Moses and Jesus. It was the Jews and the Christians, the self-styled disciples of Moses and of Jesus, who had deviated from the true faith preached by Muhammad and all the prophets who had preceded him. In the early stages of his ministry, he seems to have hoped that the Jews and the Christians would recognize the errors which (as he claimed) had crept into their beliefs and would rally to him to form one true, all-embracing, religious community.

In general, the Prophet seems to have had more connection with Jews than with Christians. He makes generous use of Old Testament stories, though his versions are not always the same as the originals, at least in details. As it seems probable that he himself could not read, he may have heard these stories and then repeated them from memory. In general, his preaching carried rather an Old Testament flavour. Passages in the Qoran ordering the faithful to fight against the unbelievers can be matched by many passages in the Old Testament where, for example, Jehovah is represented as ordering the extermination of the Amalekites.[8] He appears to have been less well informed on the subject of Christianity. He believed, for example, that the Holy Trinity consisted of Jesus, the Virgin Mary and God.

He insisted that the Qoran represented the actual words of God addressed to himself. All through the revelations, statements or commands are preceded by the word "Say", the divine order to Muhammad to speak. Sometimes the Prophet is warned of the arguments which will be used by his hecklers or the questions to be put to him by believers and is told how to reply.

> "They ask Thee as to what is allowed them.
> Say: The good things are allowed to you. . . ."[9]

[8] I *Samuel* XV, 3.

[9] *Qoran* Chapter V, verse 4.

"Say: Those who forge a lie against God will not succeed."[10]

"Recite to them the story of Noah, when he said to his people, 'O my people. . . .' "

The most powerful factor in promoting the great Arab conquests, however, was perhaps the promise of the immediate admission to paradise of all those who fell in battle against unbelievers. Moreover the detailed description of that paradise with its cool flowing streams, delicious fruits and above all its houris, beautiful virgins perpetually young, was precisely one to tempt the poor hardy bedouins, whose lives were one unending struggle against almost unbearable physical hardships. References to the passionate desire of the early Muslims to win immediate paradise through martyrdom are continually recurring throughout all the early narratives. Even in the 1920's the Wahhabis[11] would throw themselves on their enemies crying, "Paradise, O Muslims, paradise. O houris receive us!"

In spite of the Prophet's earnestness, however, the new faith spread but slowly. After four years of his ministry, his converts still numbered less than fifty. Nevertheless the resentment of many persons in Mecca had been aroused. Their city and the tribe of Quraish owed much of their importance to the reverence paid by the tribes all over Arabia to the idol shrine, their devotion to which has already been referred to in connection with the Abyssinian invasion in the year of the elephant. The opposition was further greatly exacerbated among the men of Quraish by Muhammad's statement that their fathers and ancestors were, at that very time, enduring the torments of hell fire. A tenderness for their ancestors had always been a characteristic of the Arabs. Even in our own days, I have often heard a bedouin, trying to conciliate a fellow tribesman, say to him soothingly, "May your father be in heaven."

While, however, many Quraish viewed Muhammad's preaching with resentment, tribal custom protected him from violence. It is necessary here to emphasize a factor which is peculiarly difficult for us to appreciate today, namely the non-existence of any government in the Hejaz in the seventh century. To us it is almost impossible to visualize a society with no controlling authority, no laws, no police and no such thing as punishment. The Persian and Byzantine Empires were, of course, highly organized states such as we know, but nothing of the kind existed in Arabia, except perhaps when the Yemen was a colony of Abyssinia or Persia.

In these circumstances, men found refuge and a sense of security in their tribes. The tribe protected all its members against the outside world. But of the tribe itself there was no exact definition. Great tribes consisting of many thousands of persons might war against one another, while similarly, on a

[10] *Qoran* Chapter X, verse 69.

[11] The Wahhabis were a fanatical Muslim revivalist sect which first appeared at the end of the eighteenth century in Central Arabia and on more than one occasion conquered the greater part of the peninsula. Their original leader was Muhammad ibn Saud, ancestor of the present King Saud of Saudi Arabia. Their last militarist outbreak was at the beginning of the present century.

lesser scale, within the great tribe, disputes and even wars might arise between clans and families. The protection accorded by the tribe or clan to its members did not depend on the morality of their actions. A murderer or a robber would be protected by his tribe as much as would a hero or a saint. In the same way today an insurance company will pay the loss caused by a traffic accident, whether or not the insured person be to blame.

Where no public authority existed, there was no question of punishment for crime. The most which could be exacted from an offender was compensation or restitution to the victim. The tribe or the clan would assist its member to secure his rights in this direction, or at least to inflict on the offender an injury equivalent to that of which he had been the cause. In Arabia, the right of retaliation was recognized, a life for a life, an eye for an eye and a tooth for a tooth. The right of the injured to retaliate was due to the absence of any public authority capable of protecting him.

Among the various clans of Quraish, Muhammad belonged to the Beni Hashim, the descendants of his great-grandfather. Whether or not they approved of his activities, Beni Hashim were bound to protect him from physical violence, as also his young converts, Ali ibn abi Talib and Zeid ibn Haritha, his adopted son. Other Quraish believers were likewise protected by their respective clans. Several of the converts, however, were slaves or servants and thus without tribal protection. On these the resentful Quraish vented their spite. A tall, lanky negro slave called Bilal was laid out by his master in the blinding midday sun with stones heaped upon his chest so that he could not rise, in the hope of obliging him to recant. Although tormented by thirst, he continued to cry "One God, one God" in defiance of his persecutors. The wealthy Abu Bekr, now devoted heart and soul to the faith of Muhammad, employed his money to buy Muslim slaves from their masters and to set them free, but many of the poorer believers recanted under persecution. Even though Muhammad himself was protected from assassination, he was exposed to manifold annoyances and humiliations. Women tipped garbage on to his head from the roofs of their houses, children called out insults in the streets and the wife of his uncle, Abu Lahab, scattered thorns outside his door to tear his feet when he went out barefoot.

In 615, five years after the first appearance of Gabriel, Muhammad, who was basically a kindly man and must have suffered to see his followers thus persecuted, advised them to emigrate. The Christian kingdom of Abyssinia was near at hand across the Red Sea. Eleven men and four women escaped from the city and sailed to Abyssinia. The party included Othman ibn Affan of Quraish and his wife Rukaiya, Muhammad's daughter.

The Prophet's prospects seemed to be at the lowest ebb. Five years of preaching had produced a mere handful of supporters, some of whom had since recanted, while several of the remainder had been forced to leave the country. Muhammad remained almost alone except for his immediate family, Khadija his wife, Ali and Zeid the two youths in his house and the kindly, ever-devoted Abu Bekr. Mecca was familiar with men seeking for a higher form of spiritual faith, but most of these men had been mere philosophers, seeking knowledge of God for themselves. Muhammad had roused opposition by his bitter denunciation of the idols in the Meccan fane and by his reiterated statements that the ancestors of Quraish were in hell fire—indeed, that his fellow-citizens who did not accept his message would soon also be in eternal torment. As a result, the angry Meccans had virtually stamped out his whole movement. Would not some compromise be possible? If he omitted his more aggressive attacks on their faith, perhaps he could lead his fellow-townsmen by more gradual methods to seek the one true God.

In the warm, dry climate of Arabia, men spend little time indoors. The courtyard of the kaaba was the place where the Meccans chiefly foregathered. Strips of carpet would be unrolled on the ground, and the elders would sit round in circles, discussing the affairs of the day. If the sun grew hot, the rugs would be moved into the shade of the kaaba itself or of the surrounding buildings. In the rare event of a rain or dust-storm, Qusai's meeting hall opened on to the square, doubtless a bare room of stone roughly laid in mud mortar, and roofed with branches, brushwood and earth.

On a certain day, the principal men of Mecca were thus seated in the open air beside the kaaba, when Muhummad approached and sat down amongst them. After a short pause, he began to recite Chapter LIII of the Qoran in their hearing. This chapter tells of Gabriel's first visit, already described, when the archangel stood less than two bowshots distance from the Prophet, and then of a second visitation "beneath the thorn tree". Verse 18 continued, "Certainly he saw of the greatest signs of his Lord. And have you seen Allat and Al Uzza and Manat, the Third, the last? These are exalted females, and verily their intercession is to be hoped for." The leaders of Quraish heard with delight this testimony to the three principal goddesses of their shrine. When, at the end of his recitation, Muhammad prostrated himself in prayer, all the assembled elders fell on their faces and worshipped with him.

This incident would appear to indicate that the Meccans themselves recognized, in a general way, the supremacy of one almighty God, but that they claimed that their local gods could be instrumental in interceding with Him. They would willingly join the Prophet in adoring God, they said, as long as he was ready to recognize the rôle played by their lesser deities. An immediate reconciliation took place and mockery and persecution ceased.

But when Muhammad returned to his house, his conscience was ill at ease. Could it be right to compromise with the truth, even to save his followers from persecution? Gabriel appeared to him once more and reproved him. He was humiliated and profoundly afraid of God's vengeance on himself. Having preached to others, he had himself become a castaway. He decided that he must withdraw the concession and face once more the resentment of his kinsmen. The offending lines were attributed to a diabolical intervention and the chapter was amended, so as to refer to the idols as "nothing but names which you and your fathers have named them, on whom God has bestowed no authority". The emendation of the passage provoked once more the fury of the Meccans and persecution was resumed.

In their indignation, the elders called upon Abu Talib to withdraw his tribal protection from Muhammad and allow them to deal with him. The old man replied to them in conciliatory terms and then sent for his nephew and confided in him his fears. Abu Talib was not himself a convert, but he could not bring himself to withdraw tribal protection from his crazy nephew, whom nevertheless he loved. Could not Muhammad do something to help him by being more conciliatory? But the Prophet had suffered too much in his mind since his previous concession. "I would not desist if they put the sun in my right hand and the moon in my left," he cried passionately, and burst into tears. His old uncle was deeply moved, and calling him to his side, assured him that he could preach as he liked, for he would never desert him.

While Muhammad's ministry seemed thus at its lowest ebb, two unexpected conversions temporarily improved his position. His uncle Hamza, a noted warrior and hunter, a man of great physical strength and widely respected, suddenly announced his adherence to the new faith. The second convert was Umar[12] ibn al Khattab, a member of a collateral branch of Quraish, a man of violent temper and hitherto bitterly hostile to the Prophet's teaching.

Umar went one day to the house of his married sister and, as he entered the front door, heard a voice reading aloud. Bursting into the room he found his brother-in-law and his sister sitting together. "What was that noise I heard?" he shouted angrily. "Nothing," they replied together, although in fact they had been reciting Chapter XX of the Qoran. Calling them renegades, Umar, beside himself, struck and kicked his brother-in-law and then hit his sister in the face. Suddenly seeing her covered with blood, his anger vanished. Humbly asking if he too could read what they had been reading, he confessed himself deeply impressed. His brother-in-law took him straight to Muhammad, who forthwith accepted his conversion. Twenty years later, Umar ibn al Khattab was to be the most powerful ruler in the world.

While, however, these conversions encouraged the Prophet, they goaded the elders of Quraish to even greater activity. Fear of starting a blood-feud with Beni Hashim made them unwilling to resort to the assassination of their fellow-tribesmen. A boycott of all Beni Hashim was decided upon. Each clan seems to have lived in its own quarter of Mecca. A narrow valley beneath the crags of Abu Qubais, the rocky hill overhanging the town, appears to have been occupied by Beni Hashim. Here they were placed under a ban by the remainder of the citizens, who drew up an undertaking in which they agreed that none should buy from Beni Hashim nor sell to them, none would take wives from them or give them women in marriage, but they would be ostracized by all. The strength of tribal feeling was such that all Beni Hashim seem to have submitted to the boycott sooner than abandon Muhammad, although many of them rejected his religion. Only one of his uncles, Abu Jahal, refused to stand by the clan and went over to the citizens. Quraish also sent two men[13] to Abyssinia to persuade the Negus to evict the Muslims who had sought sanctuary there, but the mission was unsuccessful. Thus at the end

[12] To the English reader, the nearest approximation to the pronunciation of this word is Ummer, as in "drummer".

[13] One was Amr ibn al Aasi, later to be the Muslim conqueror of Egypt.

of six years of preaching, Muhammad had everywhere been pursued by mockery and contempt. Of the tiny band of his converts, some were in exile in Abyssinia, while the remainder were besieged in their houses in Mecca.

The boycott lasted for three years, but eventually resulted in a certain revulsion of feeling towards Beni Hashim—for some of those besieged were not Muslims at all—if not towards the Prophet himself. The ban was annulled and Muhammed was free once more to move about the town. It was at about this time that the Prophet announced one morning that, during the preceding night, he had flown with the Archangel Gabriel from Mecca to Jerusalem and thence up to heaven, where he had seen Adam, Abraham, Moses and Jesus and had even reached near to the throne of God. The statement gave rise to a chorus of mockery and insult from his unbelieving fellow-citizens, though the devoted Abu Bekr stated firmly that if Muhammad said that it was so, then indeed it must be true.

With his fortunes still at this low ebb, the Prophet suffered two personal misfortunes. In December 619, the faithful Khadija died, and he was deprived of her constant sympathy and loving encouragement. About a month later, his uncle and protector, the venerable Abu Talib, also passed away. For forty years he had been a father and a protector to his nephew. Though unconvinced of his divine commission, Abu Talib had suffered threats, danger and loss in order to shield Muhammad from the bitterness of his enemies.

The Prophet's position was now more precarious and more apparently hopeless than ever. It was Abu Talib's influence which had rallied Beni Hashim. There had been no new conversions for a considerable time. At any moment violence might break out and exterminate the aggravating sectaries. The Meccans were obviously impervious to his message.

Forty miles east of Mecca, in a valley in the high rocky range of the Hejaz mountains, lay the town of Taif. It was inhabited by the tribe of Thaqeef. Accompanied only by his adopted son Zeid, Muhammad set out on foot to preach in the town. First of all, he addressed himself to the three principal men of the city but with no effect. "If God needed a messenger, could He find no one better than you?" they enquired sarcastically. Trying his fortune with the people in the streets of the town, he met only with jeering and ridicule. At last they began to pelt him with stones and he was obliged to escape on foot, bleeding from several wounds and still supported by the faithful Zeid, himself seriously injured. That day he must have drained the dregs of the cup of humiliation. "O Lord," he is said to have prayed, "I make my complaint to Thee of the feebleness of my strength and of my insignificance before men. O most Merciful! Thou art the Lord of the weak and Thou art my Lord." It was not without trepidation that he returned to his house in Mecca, from which henceforward he rarely emerged into the streets.

The season of the annual pilgrimage was at hand, when pilgrims from all over Arabia flocked to the idolatrous shrine of Mecca. Despairing of Quraish, Muhammad determined to attempt the conversion of some of the pilgrims. Chancing upon a little group of seven men from the town of Yathrib, he invited them to sit down with him in a secluded spot for a quiet talk. The people of Yathrib were in a sense his cousins, for it will be remembered that his great-grandfather, the famous Hashim, had married a woman of that town. The seven, after listening to his discourse, expressed themselves convinced of the truth of his mission. In that case, he asked, would it be possible for him to come and live in Yathrib under their protection? But on this question they were more cautious. The Arabs of Yathrib were divided into two tribes, Aus and Khazraj, which were constantly at feud with one another. Only four years earlier, a pitched battle had been fought between them. Life was still insecure, and the men hesitated to promise their protection to Muhammad.

The discussion with the men from Yathrib took place in March 620. The ensuing year passed in fear and suspense. At last the pilgrimage season came round once again, and twelve men of Yathrib met the Prophet in a narrow valley in the mountains east of Mecca. They pledged their faith in Muhammad, each swearing to worship only the one God, to obey His messenger, and to abstain from theft, adultery, infanticide and slander. If they fulfilled these simple conditions, they were promised entry to paradise. This undertaking was called the first pledge of Aqaba,[14] the name of the little valley in which the oaths had been exchanged.

Twelve converts in a town two hundred and fifty miles away was scarcely a sensational gain. The new Muslims, however, returned to Yathrib full of proselytizing zeal and the faith began to gain adherents both among Aus and Khazraj. Moreover the security situation had improved. The two rival tribes had accepted a single chief, Abdulla ibn Obay, and had thereby put an end to their mutual hostility. Musaab ibn Umair of Quraish, one of the earliest converts in Mecca, was sent by Muhammad to Yathrib to instruct the new Muslims in their faith.

Another weary year passed in Mecca. Yet Muhammad was no longer in despair; his thoughts now centred on Yathrib. In Mecca, he made little attempt to preach in public. The indignation of Quraish subsided and they turned once more to their commerce and money-making.

At last, in March 622, another pilgrimage season arrived. Musaab came in advance of the Yathrib pilgrims and reported to Muhammad all that had been achieved. On the last night of the pilgrimage, a meeting was arranged. The idolatrous ceremonies were over. At dawn, all the caravans of pilgrims would mount their camels and scatter far and wide across the deserts of Arabia. The little dry water-course of Aqaba, some three to four miles east of Mecca in the mountains, had again been chosen as the rendezvous. The time was an hour before midnight. The Prophet arrived on foot, accompanied by his uncle Abbas. Once again the strength of family feeling is illustrated by the fact that Abbas, who was the sole companion of his nephew on this precarious venture, was still an idolater. The two sat on the ground in the silence of the desert night. Then the men of Yathrib began to arrive, in twos and threes to avoid observation. Seventy-three men grouped themselves in the dark valley, lit only by the silvery radiance of the Arabian moon. "We stole along as softly as sandgrouse to our meeting with God's messenger," one of them subsequently reported.

After addressing the gathering, the Prophet invited the men to swear

[14] Not of course to be confused with the modern port of Aqaba, 600 miles away to the north.

allegiance, thereby undertaking to receive and to protect him in Yathrib. Al Baraa ibn Maroor, a chief of Yathrib, was the first to swear, and was followed by his seventy-two comrades, filing past Muhammad in the darkness, each one in turn striking his hand against his. "I am of you and you are of me," cried the Apostle at the end of the swearing. "I will war against them that war against you, and I will be at peace with those who are at peace with you." Twelve leaders were then chosen, possibly in imitation of the twelve apostles of Christ. Nine were from Khazraj and three from Aus. Then the Muslims silently dispersed, in twos and threes as they had come. This pledge was called the second Aqaba. Seventy Arab tribesmen in a dry water-course in far Arabia had changed the history of the world.

## *NOTABLE DATES*

| | A.D. |
|---|---|
| Qusai established his rule over Mecca | 440 |
| Birth of Abdul Muttalib, grandfather of Muhammad | 497 |
| Abyssinian occupation of the Yemen | 522 |
| Year of the Elephant<br>Birth of Muhammad | 570 |
| Death of Abdul Muttalib<br>Muhammad cared for by his uncle Abu Talib | 578 |
| Marriage of Muhammad to Khadija | 595 |
| Muhammad's Vision of the Archangel Gabriel | 610 |
| Emigration of Muslims to Abyssinia | 615 |
| Death of Khadija | 619 |
| Pilgrims from Yathrib agree to shelter Muslims (second pledge of Aqaba) | 622 |

## *PERSONALITIES*

Abdul Muttalib, Muhammad's grandfather.
Abu Talib, Muhammad's uncle.
Khadija, Muhammad's wife.
Ali ibn abi Talib, Muhammad's cousin, brought up in his house.
Zeid ibn Haritha, Muhammad's adopted son.
Abu Bekr, Muhammad's friend.

## *EARLY CONVERTS LATER TO BE FAMOUS*

Umar ibn al Khattab.
Othman ibn Affan, son-in-law of Muhammad, fled to Abyssinia.
Zubair ibn al Awwam, Muhammad's cousin.
Hamza, Muhammad's uncle.
Saad ibn abi Waqqas, Muhammad's cousin.

# III

## *The Well Bucket*

The Prophet who had no honour in his own country is received with homage in the city of refuge. Gradually he appears in a new character; the persecuted Apostle is transformed into the triumphant warrior; where the warnings of the Prophet have failed to convince, the strong arm of the conqueror must compel.
FREEMAN, *History of the Saracens*

When you sought the aid of your Lord, so He answered you; and I will assist you with a thousand of the angels following one another. *Qoran* VIII, 9

Indeed there was a sign for you in the two parties which met together in encounter—one party fighting in the way of Allah and the other disbelieving. . . . And Allah strengthens with his aid whom He pleases. *Qoran* III, 12

## III

## THE WELL BUCKET

A FEW days after the second pledge of Aqaba, Muhammad gave orders to his supporters to move, unostentatiously and in small groups, to Yathrib. The majority of them were poor. A few were able to procure camels, riding two and two on each animal. Many were obliged to undertake the journey of 250 miles on foot. Within seven or eight weeks, almost all the believers had emigrated from Mecca, with the exception of Muhammad himself, his cousin Ali the son of his late uncle Abu Talib, his adopted son Zeid ibn Haritha and his nearest friend Abu Bekr. A few of the Muslims recanted, or were forcibly detained by their relatives. It must be admitted that Muhammad showed considerable courage in himself remaining in Mecca, where he no longer enjoyed the protection of Abu Talib as chief of Beni Hashim.

The danger was by no means slight, for Quraish realized that the Muslims were now forming a tightly-knit community in Yathrib, far beyond their control, and were gaining converts from other tribes who might become actively hostile. A discussion was held by the elders in the council hall of Qusai, their great ancestor. Several expressed the opinion that Muhammad was the cause of all their troubles and that it would be advisable to dispose of him quickly before he joined his supporters in Yathrib. Abu Jahal, the Prophet's uncle who had disassociated himself from Beni Hashim during the boycott and was one of Muhammad's bitterest opponents, put forward a plan to kill him. To avoid a blood feud between the assassins and Beni Hashim, he suggested that the murder be carried out by one representative from every clan of Quraish, each one plunging his sword into the victim. The sons of Hashim would not be able to carry on simultaneous blood feuds with all the clans. News of the discussion reached the Prophet, who slipped out of his house and went to that of Abu Bekr. "God has given me permission to migrate," he told his devoted friend. The possibility had been foreseen by Abu Bekr and the arrangements were soon completed. The faithful Ali, now a youth of twenty, was instructed to wrap himself in Muhammad's cloak and lie on his bed, so that anyone looking into the house would imagine the Prophet to be ill. As the darkness began to fall, Muhammad and Abu Bekr climbed out of a window at the back of the latter's home and slipped away among the rocks of the mountains overlooking the town, scrambling up in the darkness until they reached a cave on Mount Thor, south of Mecca, where they had decided to lie hidden until the hue and cry had subsided. The details of their flight had already been thought out by the prudent Abu Bekr, whose daughter Asma was to bring them food every evening after dark. Meanwhile his son Abdulla was to remain in Mecca, mixing with the people, and each evening was to climb to the cave and report the events of the day. Abu Bekr's freedman was every morning to drive a flock of sheep past the cave to obliterate the tracks of the evening visitors. Meanwhile two riding camels were procured and held in readiness. Abu Bekr, careful merchant that he was, had taken with him a bag containing a large sum of money. Muhammad, to whom money was indifferent, had brought nothing. The two townsmen were too unfamiliar with the desert to be able to find their way to Medina, otherwise than along the main caravan track. A bedouin had to be hired as a guide, presumably a former associate of Abu Bekr, although a polytheist.

No sooner did the leaders of Quraish appreciate that Muhammad had disappeared than they offered a hundred camels as a reward for his apprehension. A bedouin family can live on a flock of twenty, so that the reward offered was sufficient to maintain five bedouin families. The Meccans themselves once again were not sufficiently at home in the desert to prosecute the search themselves. For three days the hue and cry continued. On the third evening, Abdulla ibn abi Bekr arrived at the cave and reported that it would now be safe for the two fugitives to escape. He was told to bring the camels the next evening.

The following night, soon after dark, three riding camels padded softly up to the mouth of the cave. Asma had brought a parcel of food, which she tied to one of the saddles with her belt. The bedouin guide rode a camel of his own. Abu Bekr took his freedman up behind him. The Prophet mounted the third camel. Silently they filed off down the rough mountain-side, the guide leading. Passing west of Mecca, they kept at first along the sea coast, then re-crossed the caravan track below Isfan and followed an unfrequented route across the spurs of the hills. At one point the little party was overtaken by a solitary horseman, who had actually ridden in pursuit of them, in the hope of winning the reward of one hundred camels. But they persuaded him not to give information of their route. By the time that news of the flight reached Mecca, the little party was already out of range of pursuit.

The group of Meccan believers who had preceded Muhammad to Yathrib had received news of his disappearance from Mecca. Unaware of the fact that he had lain hidden for four days in the cave, they had daily climbed the hills south of Yathrib at dawn, anxiously scanning the country towards Mecca for a sight of camel riders. Only at noon each day, when the scorching sun and the dancing mirage reduced visibility to a short distance, did they return to the town. It was just after midday on 28th June, 622, when the weary travellers toiled up the last defile through the wild and rocky mountains, the slopes of which were, at this point, covered with black, volcanic rocks, without tree, shrub or vegetation in sight. At last, as they topped the pass, a very different prospect suddenly opened before the eyes of the exhausted fugitives. Unlike the bare and stony ravine in which Mecca was wedged, Yathrib was blessed with ample springs and wells. The valley in which lay the town was filled with gardens of plumed date palms and with green cultivated fields, infinitely soothing to the eye after the blinding glare of the desert. Dotted over the broad valley lay the settlements of a number of different tribal groups, each living in its own self-contained village of fortified

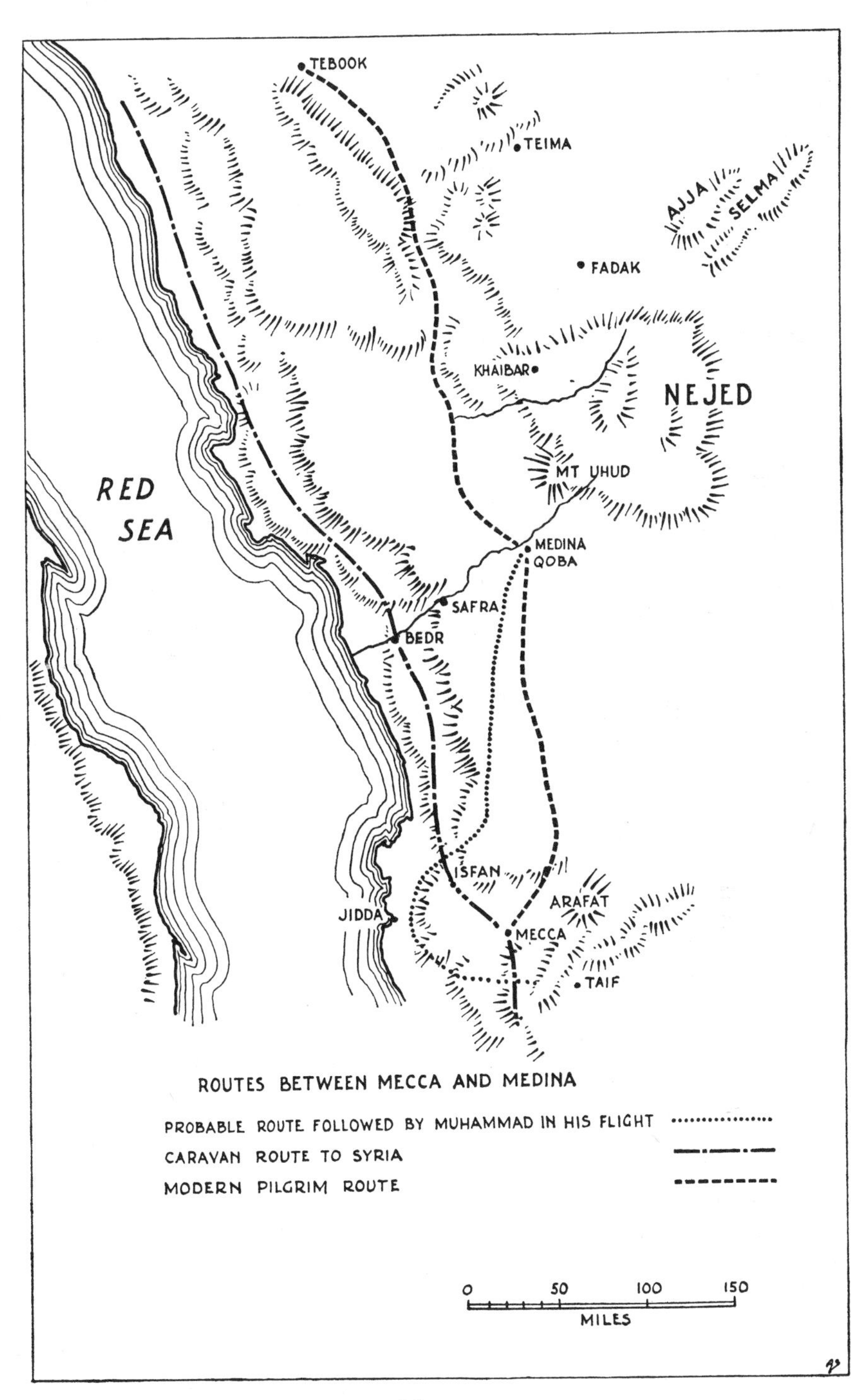
TEBOOK
TEIMA
AJJA
SELMA
FADAK
KHAIBAR
NEJED
MT UHUD
RED SEA
MEDINA
QOBA
SAFRA
BEDR
ISFAN
ARAFAT
JIDDA
MECCA
TAIF
ROUTES BETWEEN MECCA AND MEDINA
PROBABLE ROUTE FOLLOWED BY MUHAMMAD IN HIS FLIGHT
CARAVAN ROUTE TO SYRIA
MODERN PILGRIM ROUTE
0
50
100
150
MILES

Map VI

houses and towers, rudely built of stone and mud. After the burning rocks and bare pinnacles of the mountains, this fertile valley had a homely, idyllic appearance, suggesting fertility, peace, repose and contentment. The three camel-riders rode down the pass into Qoba, the first oasis settlement of Yathrib.

(The heathen town of Yathrib has, since Islam, been called the Prophet's City, Medinat al Nebi, and henceforward it is by this more famous name of Medina that I will refer to it.)

The inhabitants of Medina, when Muhammad emigrated to that city, consisted partly of Jews and partly of Arabs. (It is easiest to distinguish them in this manner, although the so-called Jews may have been emigrants from Judea or may equally well have been Arabs converted to the religion of Judaism.) The Jews were divided into three tribes of which two were agriculturalists, who cultivated palm gardens and fields. The third appears to have consisted of artisans, gold- and silver-smiths and armourers. The Arabs were divided into two tribes, Aus and Khazraj, who only three or four years previously had been at war with one another. But a reconciliation had now been effected, and a single chief, Abdulla ibn Obay, had been chosen to lead them both.

Thus at the time of the Prophet's arrival, Abdulla ibn Obay was by far the most influential Arab leader in the whole oasis. When Muhammad arrived as a helpless fugitive, ibn Obay seems to have offered no opposition. Although himself of Khazraj, he had refused to take part in the war between that tribe and the Aus, and had worked for peace and compromise. It was doubtless his reputation for neutrality and moderation which persuaded the two tribes to accept him as chief of both. Later on, when the Prophet grew in influence and power, Abdulla ibn Obay found himself relegated to a minor rôle. Perhaps he was jealous. Certainly clandestine resentment grew up between him and the Muslims. Although he was himself soon to become ostensibly a Muslim, the Apostle [1] frequently suspected him of spreading scandals or of intriguing against the believers. The many denunciations of hypocrites which appear in the chapters of the Qoran revealed during the early years in Medina probably for the greater part refer to Abdulla ibn Obay and his supporters.

The Jewish tribes were at first not openly hostile to the Prophet who, as already explained, had pronounced his doctrines to be those of the original religion of Abraham. The Muslims at this time faced the temple in Jerusalem when praying and in every way the Prophet seemed anxious to win the friendship of the Jews, with whom he concluded an agreement providing for mutual co-operation.

The Muslim Emigrants from Mecca were overjoyed at the safe arrival of their leader, a pleasure which seemed at first to be shared by the Arabs of Aus and Khazraj, most of whom of course were still idolaters. The Jews had no reason to oppose. The offer of asylum and shelter to a fugitive was, in any case, an obligation of honour amongst all the peoples of Arabia. The happy

[1] In his lifetime, Muhammad was normally called the Apostle or the Messenger of God rather than the Prophet. I have used all three designations indifferently.

news of the Prophet's safe arrival spread like wildfire among the Meccan emigrants and the Medina converts. People ran up smiling from every direction, while the cry "He is come! he is come!" passed joyfully from mouth to mouth.

In spite of this cheerful and hospitable welcome, the Apostle seems to have been aware of the precarious nature of his situation. The Meccan emigrants consisted of only some seventy men. The Medina converts were already more numerous. Most of the Meccans were destitute, having escaped by stealth, leaving all their possessions behind them. Friction between the two groups might all too easily occur. To anticipate any possible trouble, Muhammad arranged for each Medina convert to adopt a Meccan fugitive as his brother. A written charter was drawn up for the new Muslim community, which stated that the believers henceforward constituted a single group. Every Muslim would stand by every other Muslim but would not support an unbeliever against a believer. Thus the powerful hold of the tribe and the family were to be abolished, and to be replaced entirely by the solidarity of the religious community.

A few days later, a derelict palm garden near the centre of the oasis was bought with Abu Bekr's money, and work began on the construction of a mosque and of a house—no more to our minds than a hut—for the accommodation of the Prophet. Meccan emigrants and Medina converts toiled and sang together, cutting and laying mudbricks and rough stones and singing, with Muhammad at their head:

"Allahumma la aish illa aish al akhra
Allahumma irham al Ansar wa al Muhajira.
O God! There is no life but the future life.
O God! Have mercy on helpers and emigrants."

Muhammad himself, to encourage his followers, joined in the work, carrying bricks and mud with the others. Then another worker sang:

"If we sat while our Prophet worked,
It could be said that we had shirked."

Ali ibn abi Talib produced a new verse:

"There's one who labours night and day
To build us mosques of bricks and clay." [2]

Encouraging the work by singing (like sea shanties for hauling on ropes) is an immemorial custom of the Arabs. Each of the workers improvises a new verse, which the others pick up from him and chant in chorus, till someone else produces another couplet. Any who have seen gangs of Arab labourers chanting at their work will be able easily to visualize this homely scene.

Muhammad, who often showed a kindly humour and an addiction to the bestowal of nicknames, called the Medini converts the Helpers, and the Meccan exiles the Emigrants. The few hundred men who constituted these

[2] Ibn Ishaq (trans. Guillaume).

two groups were for centuries to come to form the aristocracy of Islam, their names familiar as household words in the mouths of millions of believers.

* * * * *

A short time after his arrival in Medina, the Prophet married Aisha, the daughter of Abu Bekr, his companion on his flight from Mecca. She is alleged to have been nine years old, while he was fifty-three. Before he died, Muhammad had married eleven wives, but this fact need not be attributed solely to the gross nature of his passions. For twenty-five years he had been the faithful husband of only one wife, Khadija, who was considerably older than himself. Aisha was the only young girl he chose. All the remainder were widows, and several seem to have been selected for political reasons, to conciliate their relatives. Much of his marrying was done in his late fifties, perhaps also in the hope of having a son, for he was devoted to children.

* * * * *

During the twelve years which had elapsed since the commencement of his ministry in Mecca, Muhammad had shown an extraordinary degree of patience and humility under insult and ill-treatment. Now suddenly his whole attitude was transformed. Gabriel, he claimed, had informed him that God had now commanded the Muslims to fight the unbelievers. The situation of Medina was strategically well placed for a base of operations against Mecca.

The fact that Mecca, at this time, lived almost entirely on the caravan trade between the Yemen and Syria has already been explained. The people of Medina led a completely different life. Whereas Mecca lay in a narrow sun-scorched valley between ranges of rocky hills, bare of all vegetation, Medina was in a broad well-watered depression. The people of Medina lived on the produce of their green fields and gardens, those of arid Mecca on their far-flung commercial ventures.

An incident occurred soon after the Apostle's arrival in Medina which illustrates the ignorance of agriculture among Meccans. The date palm is one of those trees which has male and female. Every year the human cultivator climbs the male tree, takes from it the seed and inserts it in his female trees. Muhammad had never heard of this process and, when he came to Medina, he forbade it. The palms of those who observed the prohibition produced no dates and the Prophet was obliged to cancel the order and to confess his ignorance.

The Western shores of Arabia consisted of a coastal plain of varying width, then a range of tangled, arid and pinnacled mountains, beyond which extended the vast plateau of Nejed, shelving down gently for six hundred miles to the Persian Gulf. The Meccan caravans travelled northwards to Syria along the coastal plain passing between Medina and the Red Sea coast, a gap only some eighty miles wide. The Muslims at Medina were thus within striking distance of Mecca's commercial lifeline to Syria.

The strategy used by Muhammad in 623–630 was the same as that used by Feisal and Lawrence in 1916–18. In the First World War, the Turks maintained large garrisons in Mecca and Medina, which depended for their maintenance not on camel caravans but on the railway from Medina to Damascus. The Amir Feisal and T. E. Lawrence placed themselves north of Medina where they were in a position to cut this lifeline to Syria.

The Prophet's military operations did not, however, begin immediately. Six months elapsed during which Muhammad and the Emigrants were settling down in Medina and, more important, during which the Prophet's extraordinary personality was gaining an ascendancy over the citizens.

Meanwhile, however, some of the Emigrants were reduced to extreme want. Many had left their families behind in Mecca and had nowhere to live except in the open courtyard of the mosque. Some worked at menial tasks for the people of Medina, although as we have seen, they knew nothing of agriculture. The Prophet shared to the full the hunger of his followers. He could doubtless have done better for himself, but was probably unwilling to live in comfort while his brethren were starving. Years afterwards Aisha was to remember that the Prophet's household often passed week after week without lighting a fire, because they had nothing to cook. Dates and water were their only diet.

To Arabs, raiding seemed a natural way to free themselves from want. The first few expeditions were carried out by small parties of Emigrants. The people of Medina took no part in these enterprises. But neither the citizens of Mecca nor of Medina were accustomed to operations of war, the pastime of bedouin nomads rather than of merchant or agricultural communities. None of the early raids achieved any success. News of intended expeditions always reached Quraish in advance, while the information received by the Muslims was inaccurate or too late. In the autumn of 623, a large caravan of a thousand camels laden with merchandise belonging to Quraish, under the command of Abu Sofian, one of the Prophet's bitterest enemies in Mecca, passed northwards on the way to Gaza. The Muslims failed to intercept it.

While, however, the men of Mecca and Medina lived in their respective towns, the open desert was scantily peopled by the nomadic, grazing tribes. The Prophet began to realize that the assistance of the bedouins was essential to these desert campaigns. Gradually he commenced to establish relations with them, particularly with Juheina, a tribe camping then as now between Medina and the sea.

In January, 624, Abu Sofian's caravan of a thousand camels was expected to pass Medina on its return journey from the north and Muhammad determined to seize it. But so little were his plans concealed that warning reached Abu Sofian while he was passing through Zerqa[3] on his way back from Syria. Immediately he despatched a fast camel rider to Mecca, calling upon Quraish to arm, to send a force to meet him near Medina and to escort him through the danger area.

On 8th January, 624, Muhammad set out with three hundred and fourteen men—eighty Emigrants and two hundred and thirty-four Medina Helpers. So poor were the Muslims that only seventy camels and two horses could be

[3] Zerqa, later to be an Arab Legion camp, is 100 miles south of Damascus.

found to mount them. In the vast distances of the desert, no man can operate on foot, and lack of animals greatly limited their mobility.

From Safra, sixty miles from Medina, the Prophet sent two scouts ahead to reconnoitre the wells of Bedr on the Syrian caravan route, through which Abu Sofian's caravan was expected to pass. The scouts heard from some women drawing water that a great caravan was indeed expected the very next day and rode back in haste to warn the Prophet in time to enable him to make the necessary dispositions.

While Muhammad, at a distance of some twenty-five miles north-east of Bedr, was awaiting the report of his scouts, Abu Sofian's great caravan was actually at about the same distance from the wells on the north-west and was slowly moving towards them with the intention of watering there. If both parties continued to move as they were then moving, the Muslims would encounter the Meccan caravan at the wells the following day. But Abu Sofian was an old and experienced caravan leader. He was anxious. No news had arrived of the escort which he had asked for from Mecca, and the next twenty-four hours, he knew, would be critical. Bedr was the nearest point to Medina on his route. He decided to ride forward himself to Bedr to reconnoitre. At the wells he found a chief of Juheina, the local bedouin tribe, and enquired of him whether he had seen any strangers in the vicinity. "None," replied the bedouin, "except two camel-riders who left here a short time ago, after watering at the well." As any desert traveller would, Abu Sofian slipped from his camel and walked carefully to the spring, gazing at the ground, until he found the tracks of the two riding camels. Before long he noticed some droppings. Picking them up and rubbing the dung between his fingers, he found some undigested date stones, which he recognised as belonging to the type of date palm peculiar to the Medina oasis. No tribal bedouin would feed his camel on dates. The two camel-riders, he correctly deduced, must have been townsmen who had come from Medina and were doubtless spies of Muhammad, who was probably lying in ambush near by. Climbing hastily on to his camel, he raced back to meet the advancing caravan, flogging his mount along at a rapid trot.

Meanwhile, unknown to either the Muslims or to Abu Sofian, the messenger sent by the latter from Syria to ask for help had reached Mecca. Alarmed for the safety of their wealth, the Meccans had seized their arms and were hastening to the rescue of their caravan. A force of seven hundred and fifty camel riders and a hundred horsemen clad in chain-mail set out up the caravan route, moving towards Bedr from the south. Thus all three parties were advancing, each unknown to the other, towards the same well.

The wily Abu Sofian met his advancing caravan some miles north of Bedr and immediately directed its course westward to the seashore. Then marching day and night without a halt and passing some twelve miles west of Bedr, he pressed on to the south and was soon out of reach of danger.

While the caravan was thus skilfully avoiding interception, Muhammad and his three hundred Muslims, riding by turn on the seventy camels, moved forward to Bedr, where they expected the weakly guarded caravan to arrive. It was escorted by only thirty men, as against three hundred Muslims. Just

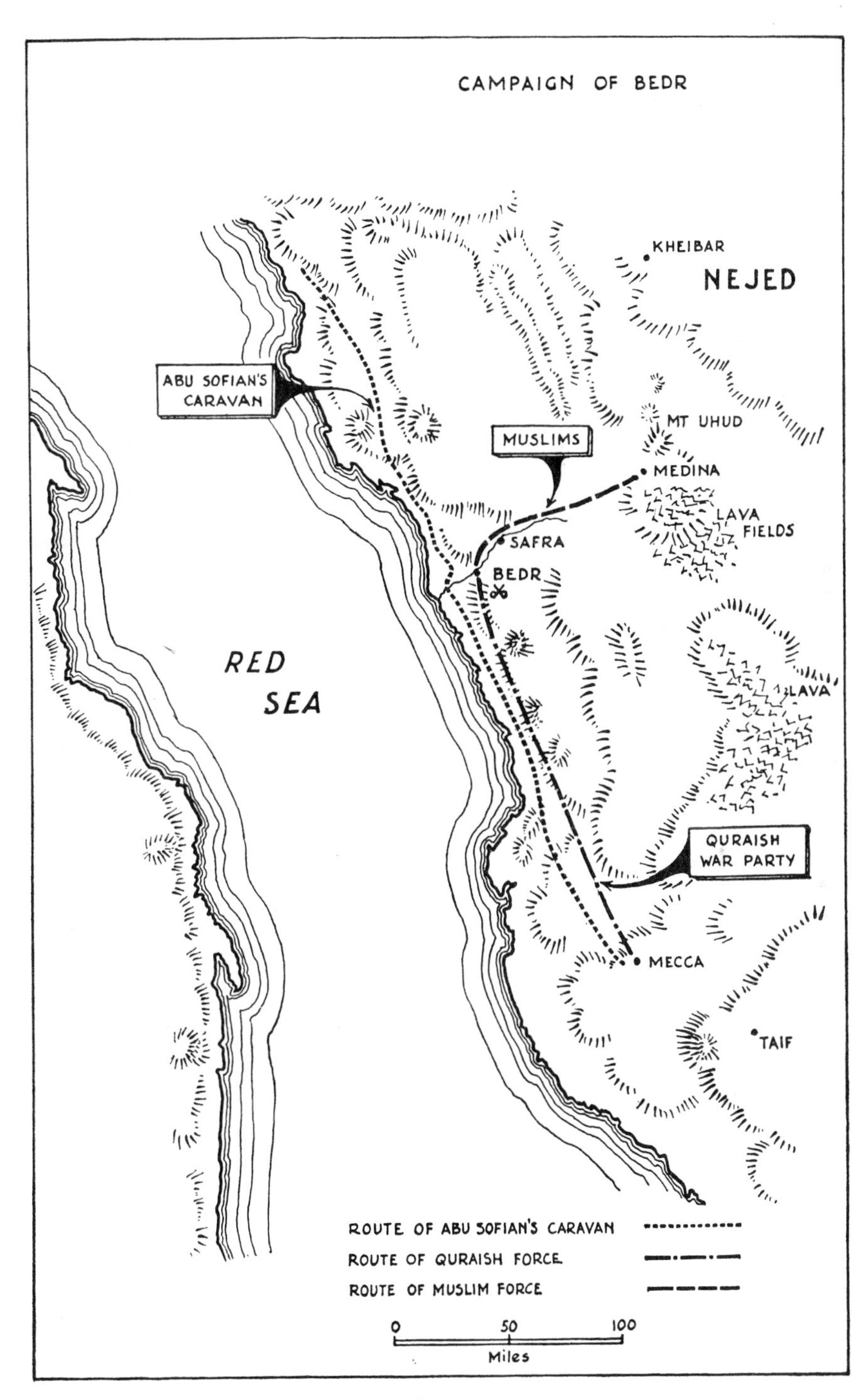
CAMPAIGN OF BEDR
KHEIBAR
NEJED
ABU SOFIAN'S CARAVAN
MT UHUD
MUSLIMS
MEDINA
LAVA FIELDS
SAFRA
BEDR
RED SEA
LAVA
QURAISH WAR PARTY
MECCA
TAIF
ROUTE OF ABU SOFIAN'S CARAVAN
ROUTE OF QURAISH FORCE
ROUTE OF MUSLIM FORCE
0
50
100
Miles

Map VII

before they reached Bedr, however, the Muslims met some travellers who informed them that a force of nearly a thousand men from Mecca was advancing to rescue the caravan. This was the first intimation which Muhammad had received of the fact that Quraish were even aware that their caravan was in danger. Alarmed at the news and uncertain of the loyalty of the men of Medina, the Prophet called a council of war. All, however, declared themselves in favour of an advance.

Approaching Bedr, Muhammad sent on Ali ibn abi Talib with a party of scouts. At the wells, they surprised some men of Quraish drawing water. These told them that their war-party lay at that very moment only a few miles away behind a line of low sandhills. Thus the Muslims, instead of the lucrative plunder of the great caravan, found themselves almost within sight of an armed force three times their own strength. They camped on the spring nearest the enemy, thus ensuring for themselves an ample supply, while denying the water to Quraish. Next morning, the little Muslim force of some three hundred men was drawn up for battle. The battle standard of the Emigrants was placed in the hands of Musaab ibn Umair, whom Muhammad two years before had sent to teach religion in Medina. The standard of Khazraj was entrusted to a certain Hubab ibn al Mundhir of that tribe, while the Aus tribal banner was committed to one of their chiefs, Saad ibn Muadh.

Meanwhile confusion reigned in the bivouac of Quraish. The strength of tribal feeling has already been shown by the fact that, when he was still in Mecca, Muhammad himself had been protected by his clan, Beni Hashim, even when most of them were still idolaters. A messenger had now reached the Meccans from Abu Sofian, telling them that the caravan was safe, and that he was going on to Mecca. A numerous party of Quraish consequently counselled a retreat, rather than the shedding of blood of their fellow tribesmen. The Meccan commercial caravans were not the sole property of the rich merchants. Everyone in the city who could raise a sum of money, however small, would take it himself or send it with a trusted member of the convoy, in the hopes of investing it in some profitable transaction. Thus the threat to the caravan involved a danger to the savings of every Meccan. But now that their wealth was safe, there was no object in fighting. The Emigrants who were following Muhammad were from every clan in Mecca. Quraish hesitated to embark on unnecessary fratricidal strife. Eventually the party in favour of fighting won the argument, largely owing to the violent language used by Abu Jahal, the Prophet's own uncle.

The Meccan force moved forward in this somewhat half-hearted manner, though the clan of Beni Zuhra, to which Muhammad's mother had belonged, deserted the army and returned to Mecca. The spirit of the Muslims was very different. The Emigrants were desperate men who had abandoned all that they possessed, and had nothing but their swords. The Muslims, moreover, had deliberately abandoned all family ties, the Prophet insisting that the only relatives of a believer were his brother Muslims. The fear of shedding the blood of a fellow tribesman, which restrained Quraish and is so deeply engrained in the bedouin mentality even today, counted for nothing with the first Muslims, several of whom are said to have killed their own unbelieving fathers or brothers. Perhaps also the act of parading five times a day for public prayer, for which they formed up in ranks and took the time from their leader, may have unconsciously introduced a sense of discipline or at least of esprit-de-corps. Helpers and Emigrants alike, moreover, were fired to reckless enthusiasm by the leadership of Muhammad in their midst.

The valley in which lay the wells of Bedr was bounded on the north and east by high hills. To the south the view was blocked by a rocky spur, but on the west, where the country sloped away to the sea, only a low line of sand dunes closed in the valley. Over these dunes the Meccan line advanced towards the Muslims, drawn up in front of the spring beneath their three tribal standards. On the side of Quraish, the war banners for the centre and the two wings were borne by members of the clan of Abdul Dar, according to their hereditary right.[4] "O God," cried Muhammad fervently, as the Meccan line appeared over the sand dunes, "O God, here are Quraish in their vanity and pride, fighting against Thee and calling Thine Apostle a liar. O God grant us help. O God destroy them."

It seems to me misleading, in describing these early Arabian battles, to speak, as some European historians have, of armies, generals and soldiers. In Arabia, every man was, in an emergency, expected to fight for his tribe. Apart from such crises there were no soldiers, nor was any training deemed necessary. The warriors fought, not in companies or battalions, but grouped by tribes and clans, each commanded by its chief. Battles normally commenced by single combats between champions, watched by the forces of both sides drawn up opposite one another. Finally the rival war parties charged and the issue was decided in a wild mêlée, consisting of a great number of confused hand-to-hand encounters. The principal weapon was the sword, though lances and spears were also carried. Bows and arrows supplied "covering fire", and there were also javelins or throwing spears which, it seems, were particularly favoured by the tribal mercenaries employed by Quraish to escort their caravans.[5] Defensive armour was highly prized, and was doubtless imported from the more technically advanced nations like the Persians or the Byzantines. It normally consisted of a pot helmet and a coat of chain-mail. Among so poor a population, however, few could afford to buy armour.

Two Meccan chiefs, Shaiba and Otba, with Waleed the son of Otba, advanced in front of the line of Quraish and defied three Muslims to meet them in single combat. Three warriors of Medina stepped forward, but Muhammad bade them stand back, and turning to the Emigrants called out, "O Beni Hashim. Stand up and fight." Three men in chain-mail stepped from the Muslim ranks. The first was Hamza, the Prophet's uncle, the second Ali ibn abi Talib, his cousin and first male convert, while the third Ubaida ibn Harith was another cousin.

The youngest pair engaged first, Ali stepping forward to meet Waleed. After a few moments of fencing, Waleed fell by the sword of his Muslim

[4] Page 39.

[5] The tribes were wont to jeer at Quraish as being people afraid to go out into the desert without an armed escort.

opponent. Then Hamza, the Prophet's uncle, engaged Shaiba and cut him down. Ubaida ibn Harith, the third Muslim champion, was already over sixty years of age. Otba, advancing upon him slashed his leg with his sword causing him to fall, himself simultaneously receiving a sword thrust. Both combatants then collapsed. Ali and Hamza hastily despatched Otba, carrying Ubaida back to die in the Muslim lines.

The Prophet had told the Muslims to stand fast and await the enemy's attack, only being careful to cover their flanks (for the Quraish line was longer) by shooting arrows. Now, preceded by a flight of arrows, Quraish advanced to the attack. Nevertheless they suffered from several tactical disadvantages. The sun had just risen and shone into the eyes of the advancing Meccans. While they lost their breath plodding through the sand dunes to attack, the Muslims stood on firm ground with the sun behind them. It was a stormy morning and rain had fallen in the night. Just as the lines were about to engage, a violent squall whipped up the sand in the faces of the Meccans. "Gabriel," cried the Prophet ecstatically, "with a thousand angels is falling upon the enemy."

A wild mêlée ensued, the air was filled with war cries and shouting and with the sound of clashing weapons. For some time neither side gave way and the issue hung in the balance. Muhammad with Abu Bekr had retired into an arbour of branches which the Muslims had made for him the night before, where he gave himself to fervent prayer. "O God," he kept crying, "fulfil Thy promises to me. If this little band of believers perishes, there will be none left on earth to worship Thee." He stretched out his hands as he cried again and again to God. His cloak fell from his shoulders unperceived, until at length Abu Bekr intervened saying, "This is enough, O Apostle. God will fulfil His promise."

Accompanied by Abu Bekr, Muhammad left the hut to watch the battle. "All who die today will go to paradise," he called. A young man was standing beside him, eating a handful of dates. "What," he cried, "is it only necessary to be killed by those people in order to enter paradise!" Throwing away his dates and drawing his sword, he rushed into the ranks of Quraish, struck several down and fell at length covered with wounds. Such was the simple faith of these early converts.

Suddenly stooping, Muhammad picked up a handful of gravel and, throwing it towards the enemy, cried out "Confusion on their faces." Quraish began to waver. The Muslims laid on with new vigour and the enemy commenced to give ground. With such undisciplined forces an orderly withdrawal was impossible. Retreat soon became a wild rout. Forty-nine Quraish were killed and a similar number taken prisoners. Abu Jahal, one of the Prophet's bitterest enemies, was among the dead. Muhammad sent his servant to seek for the corpse of Abu Jahal; when he found it he cut off his head, brought it back and threw it down at the Apostle's feet. "The head of the enemy of God," cried Muhammad jubilantly. "Praise God, for there is no god but He."

So fierce was the enthusiasm of the Muslims that some, headed by Umar ibn al Khattab, urged that all the prisoners be put to death in cold blood. At length, however, it was agreed to hold them for ransom, a more practical solution than massacre, in view of the extreme poverty of the Emigrants. The Prophet's uncle Abbas, who had accompanied him to the second oath of Aqaba, was among the prisoners, but Muhammad insisted on his paying a ransom. The Quraish dead were thrown into a common pit. Then, laden with spoils, the Muslims returned to Medina in triumph.

It is interesting to note that, while awaiting their ransoms, the prisoners were set to teach the people of Medina to read and write. Obviously the merchant community of Mecca, unlike the cultivators of Medina, found literacy necessary to their business.

* * * * *

The victory of Bedr was a milestone in the early history of Islam. Had the Muslims been defeated or had Muhammad been killed, the new sect might well have disappeared, instead of, as it did, gaining fresh converts and increased prestige. Muhammad had no hesitation in claiming the victory, against odds of three to one, as a proof of divine support. He determined to use his success further to extend his authority.

The presence of tribes of Jews at Medina has already been mentioned. At the time of his first arrival in Medina, Muhammad had adopted a conciliatory attitude towards them and had indeed made an agreement with them. Before he had been a year in Medina, however, friction arose. The Jews rejected the Prophet's mission and, in some cases, even expressed contempt and derision. After the battle of Bedr, a brawl between a Jew and a Muslim having occurred, Muhammad besieged the Jewish tribe of Beni Qainuqa in their settlement, until they surrendered. It appeared as if the Apostle were about to order their wholesale massacre. Eventually, however, Abdulla ibn Obay, the paramount chief of the Aus and Khazraj tribes, pleaded so forcibly for their lives that Muhammad relented. They were ordered to migrate from Medina to Syria, and their houses and property were divided among the Muslims. Beni Qainuqa settled at Deraa in Syria.

The defeat and exile of Beni Qainuqa alarmed all those in Medina who had been openly or secretly opposing the Apostle. Abdulla ibn Obay, the chief of the Arab community, foresaw the gradual reduction of his prestige and power in proportion as those of Muhammad increased. The remaining Jews, who had been sneering at the Prophet's claim to divine revelation, were terrorized into silence. Moreover the wealth and the houses of Beni Qainuqa were used to provide for the material needs of the Emigrants, who were thereby saved from the humiliating necessity of living on the hospitality of their Medina "brothers". In fact they were on their way to wealth.

Muhammad's authority in Medina was further reinforced by a number of assassinations. He was always extremely sensitive to any derogatory verses circulated against him and frequently denounced poets in the strongest terms. Amongst the generally illiterate Arabs, the composition of poetry and its circulation by word of mouth, whether in praise or blame, was the most generally employed form of what we should call propaganda. When two composers of such verses directed against the Muslims had been murdered, the remaining critics relapsed into silence. One of those assassinated was a woman, who was stabbed while asleep in bed with her children.

The affair, however, which created the greatest stir was the assassination of Kaab ibn al Ashraf, a man whose father had been of the Tai tribe. His mother was a Jewess of Beni Nadheer, and he lived with the Jews of Medina. Kaab had at first supported Muhammad but subsequently changed his mind. After Bedr, he paid a visit to Mecca and was thought to have encouraged the leaders of Quraish against the Muslims. It was decided that a party of five Muslims should assassinate him. They set out for Kaab's house after dark, the Apostle himself accompanying them part of the way. Then, after giving them his blessing, he returned. Kaab's foster-brother, a Muslim, was used to decoy him out of doors, whereupon the conspirators fell upon him and hacked him to pieces with their swords. Henceforward the Jews of Medina lived in continual fear.

In addition to the assassination of hostile poets, the Prophet engaged a number of men to defend him in verse. Of these the most famous was Hassan [6] ibn Thabit, a man of Medina. When informed that Muhammad desired his services, he is alleged to have put out his tongue and remarked, "There are no defences which I cannot pierce with this weapon." (Among so illiterate a people, poems circulated by word of mouth rather than by writing.) "How can you manage," enquired Muhammad, "to satirize Quraish without injuring me, seeing that I myself am of that tribe?" "I shall know how to pick you out from their midst," replied the facetious Hassan, "as a man picks a hair out of the stew."

Meanwhile Quraish in Mecca were in difficulties. Their living depended on the caravan trade and, since the battle of Bedr, they were afraid to send any more caravans to Syria. Eventually, in September 624, they determined to despatch a convoy northwards through Nejed, instead of up the Red Sea coast. But information of their intention reached Medina and Zeid ibn Haritha, Muhammad's adopted son, was sent with a raiding party to intercept it. The attempt was completely successful, the caravan was captured in its entirety, and a rich booty of silver and merchandise was divided among the Muslims.

Although at this period hostilities were basically between the two cities of Mecca and Medina, the bedouin tribes who wandered in the neighbouring deserts played an important rôle. Always coming and going, the nomads were the principal purveyors of intelligence, a military necessity in which, as we have seen, the Muslims were at first singularly lacking. Moreover the tribes occupied the great open deserts and were thus able to protect or to plunder commercial caravans. If Quraish could secure the alliance of the bedouins, their caravans might still escape from Muslim raiders, but if the Prophet were to win the allegiance of the tribes, then the Meccans would be shut into their city to starve. The Muslims had already won the friendship of Juheina on the sea coast, but the Ghatafan and Beni Suleim tribes east of Medina were allies of Quraish. As a result, a number of small Muslim raids were directed

[6] Pronounced Hassán with accent on the second syllable.

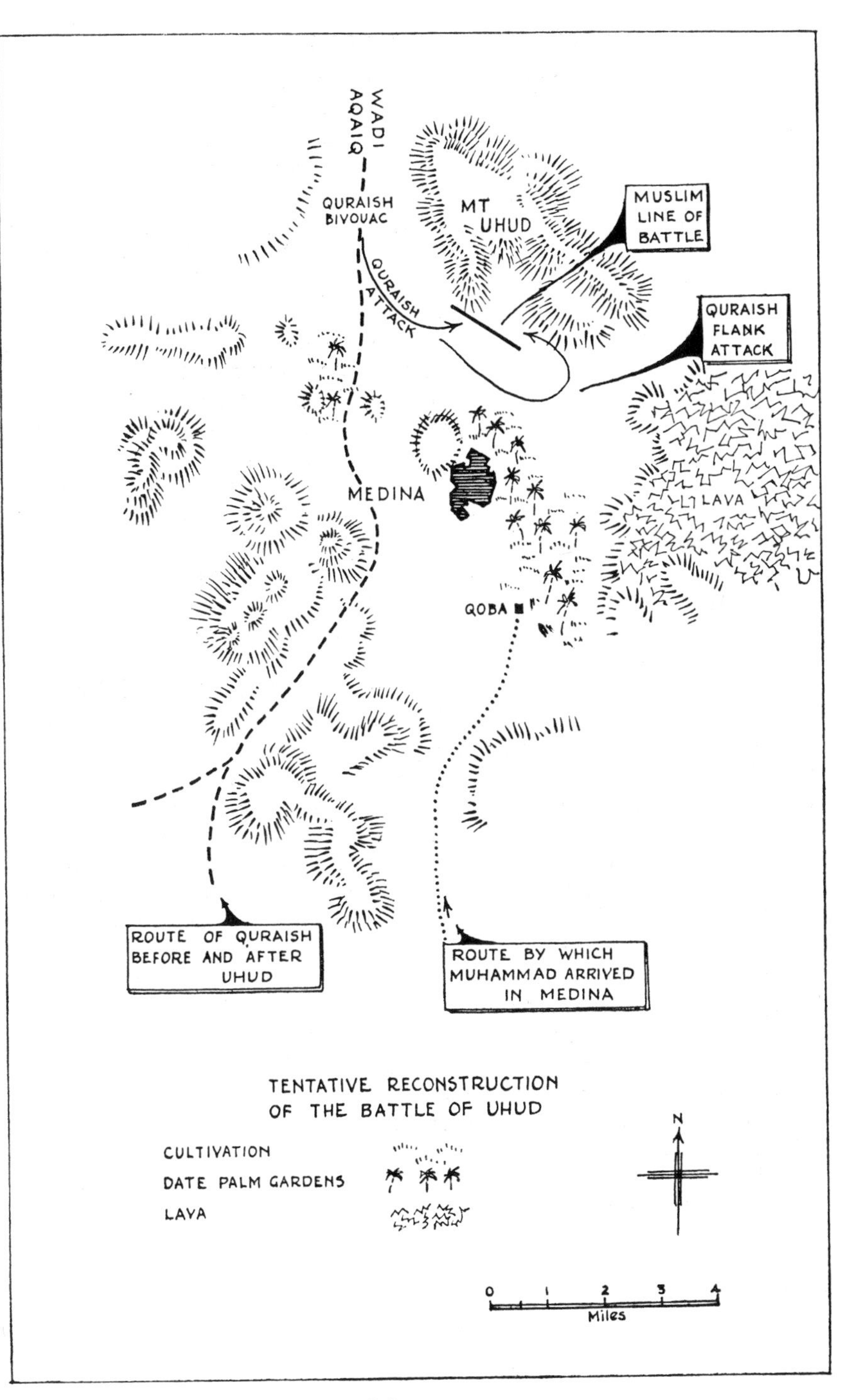
WADI AQAIQ
QURAISH BIVOUAC
MT UHUD
MUSLIM LINE OF BATTLE
QURAISH ATTACK
QURAISH FLANK ATTACK
MEDINA
LAVA
QOBA
ROUTE OF QURAISH BEFORE AND AFTER UHUD
ROUTE BY WHICH MUHAMMAD ARRIVED IN MEDINA
TENTATIVE RECONSTRUCTION OF THE BATTLE OF UHUD
CULTIVATION
DATE PALM GARDENS
LAVA
N
0 1 2 3 4
Miles

Map VIII

against these tribes, to impress them with the belief that friendship with Muhammad would be more profitable than alliance with Mecca.

The third year of Muhammad's residence in Medina opened ominously. In January 625, Quraish set out from Mecca with a force of about three thousand men, bent on obtaining revenge for their defeat at Bedr and on re-opening the caravan route to their commerce. The approaches to Medina from the south lay through rugged mountains. The Meccan force accordingly passed west of the city and then swung to the right and debouched into a wide valley north of the town at the foot of the rocky Mount Uhud. Here they bivouacked and waited for the Muslims to offer battle.

The arrival of this force, three times more numerous than the Meccan raiding party at Bedr, caused no little consternation in Medina. Muhammad, Abdulla ibn Obay and the older men were in favour of remaining in the town. Each clan, whether of Aus or Khazraj or of the Jewish tribes, lived in its own settlement, and all the houses were grouped within walls making each a small fortress, difficult to assault by men armed only with swords, bows and arrows. The Meccan force, not being an army with regular supplies, would be unable to besiege the town for long. But the younger Muslims, still elated by the memory of Bedr, clamoured to be led out to battle, and Muhammad at length gave way. After midday prayers, the Prophet rode out at the head of his followers to fight. A number of the Jewish inhabitants followed in support, but were sent back. Only Muslims could fight for God, Muhammad declared. The force bivouacked for the night and, at dawn on the following morning, advanced on the enemy. At this critical moment Abdulla ibn Obay, the jealous chief of Medina, whose advice to remain in the town had been rejected, wheeled round with three hundred followers and returned home. Thus abandoned at the moment of greatest danger, the Muslims advanced with seven hundred men against three thousand warriors from Mecca. Moreover while the Muslims could muster only one hundred men with coats of chain-mail, and no horses, Quraish and their allies included seven hundred men in armour and two hundred horsemen.

Doubtless wishing to cover their rear in view of their small numbers, the Muslims posted themselves at the foot of Mount Uhud. Their right flank and rear were covered by the mountain, but their left flank lay in open ground and was thus exposed to a charge by the enemy cavalry. To guard against this, Muhammad posted fifty archers on this flank, with orders on no account to leave their post, from which they could protect the Muslim left wing from the Quraish horse.

The Meccan force was commanded by Abu Sofian ibn Harb ibn Umaiya. It will be recollected that,[7] in the rivalries of the Quraish clans before Islam, Beni Umaiya had disputed the pre-eminence with Beni Hashim, and that, in the ensuing settlement, Beni Umaiya were awarded the hereditary leadership in war, while Beni Hashim were allotted the duty of entertaining the pilgrims. It was in the exercise of this right that Abu Sofian commanded the Meccan forces. As usual, the Quraish war banner was carried by the clan of Abdul Dar. The Apostle of God gave the banner of the Emigrants to Musaab

[7] Page 39.

ibn Umair, who had borne it at Bedr, and who was also of that clan. The Meccans now drew up their line facing the Muslims in such a way that the latter, with their backs to Uhud, were facing Medina, while the Quraish line confronted them with Medina in its rear, thereby interposing between the Muslims and the town.

The Prophet then donned two coats of mail and drawing a sword, cried out "Who will take this sword with its right?" One Abu Dujana stepped forward and asked, "What is its right, O Apostle of God?" "That you smite the enemy with it till it bends," replied Muhammad, handing it to him. Strutting up and down between the two armies, Abu Dujana recited:

"I'm the man who took the sword
When 'Use it right' was the Prophet's word.
For the sake of God, of all the Lord,
Who doth to all their food afford."

Muhammad, watching him indulgently, remarked, "This is the boastful gait which God hates except on an occasion like this."[8]

Quraish had brought a number of women with them, riding in camel-litters, a custom which survived amongst the bedouins of Nejed until the beginning of the twentieth century. These now, as the two lines drew towards one another, proceeded to rouse the enthusiasm of the Meccans, beating upon tambourines, reciting martial poetry, and letting down their long hair. Abu Sofian had taunted the clan of Abdul Dar with the charge of cowardice at Bedr. As a result, as the army was about to engage, Talha ibn Abdul Uzza of that clan, stepped out before the Meccan line carrying the Quraish banner and challenged any of the Muslims to single combat. Ali ibn abi Talib ran forward and slew him with a single blow, the Quraish banner falling to the ground, while the shout of "*Allahu akbar*," "God is most great," rose from the Muslims ranks. In an instant, Talha's brother, Othman, stepped from the ranks of Quraish, raised the fallen banner and repeated the challenge, which was accepted by Hamza, the Prophet's uncle. After a brief exchange, the Quraish banner fell once more, and Hamza strode back triumphant to the Muslim lines. Five members of the clan Abdul Dar, one after another, were struck down that day carrying the banner of Quraish.

Meanwhile, the single combats over, the Muslim line moved forward and fell with fury upon the enemy. A negro slave of Abdul Dar snatched the Quraish banner and raised it from the dust, fighting till both his hands were cut off. Falling to his knees, he still pressed the blood-soaked banner to his chest, until he fell dead, covered with sword slashes. Every believer now dashed forward convinced that death in the way of God would allow him instant admission to paradise. The Meccan line began to waver. Abu Dujana, a red kerchief tied round his helmet, swung the Prophet's sword with deadly effect. Hamza, Muhammad's uncle, towering above the battle, was killing right and left. The Meccan horse endeavoured to turn the Muslim flank but was repulsed by the fifty archers. Ali ibn abi Talib pressed on undismayed into the enemy's ranks—it was Bedr again, the Muslims were invincible.

[8] Guillaume's translation of *Ibn Ishaq*.

Led by Hind, the wife of Abu Sofian, the Quraish women were singing behind their line, accompanying themselves on their tambourines.

> "Daughters of Tariq fair are we,
> Advance—we'll give our kisses free,
> Our perfumed beds will ready be.
> But we'll desert you if you flee;
> Our love for braver men shall be."

Suddenly Abu Dujana, laying about him right and left with the Apostle's sword, burst through the Quraish line, sending the women scurrying here and there for cover.

But some of the Muslims were too soon elated. Believing the victory won, they took to looting. The very vigour of their charge had disorganized their ranks. Worst of all, the fifty archers, imagining the battle to be over, left their post on the left flank to seek for plunder. There were among Quraish that day two leaders later to win immortal fame as Muslim commanders—Khalid ibn al Waleed and Amr ibn al Aasi. These instantly saw the opportunity thus offered, and leading the horsemen round the left flank of the believers, wheeled left again and charged into the Muslim line from the rear. Muhammad, with a small escort, had been following up behind the advance of his warriors, watching the progress of the battle, when suddenly a wild torrent of horsemen poured upon the little party from behind, and past them into the ranks of the believers. Musaab ibn Umair was killed, and the banner of the Emigrants fell. The Muslims, taken completely by surprise, were everywhere swept away, struck down and scattered. The cry "Muhammad has been killed" was heard and the survivors of the believers turned their backs and fled for shelter to the rocky slopes of Uhud behind them. As his defeated followers ran past him, the Apostle cried passionately, "Where are you going? Come back, I am the Apostle of God," but all to no avail.

The banner of Quraish had lain in the dust since the death of the warriors of Abdul Dar. Now a brave girl, Amra daughter of Alqama, ran forward and raised it aloft. The Meccans rallied and, their line reformed, began to advance, raising their war-cries of Al Uzza and Hobal, and pressing hotly on the fugitives, killing them as they ran. Hearing the cry that Muhammad was dead, Anees ibn al Nadhr, a Muslim, cried to the fugitives, "Why are we still alive? Come, let us die as the Apostle of God has died." Running towards the advancing Meccans, he plunged into their midst slashing right and left until he fell. Tradition relates that, after the battle, the Muslims counted seventy wounds on his dead body.

Soon the enemy closed with the small party still surrounding the Prophet. Arrows and stones rained upon them, for slings were used as well as bows. A stone struck Muhammad in the face, breaking his front teeth. A blow on the head forced his helmet down into his forehead. "Who will sell his life for us?" cried the Prophet, and five Helpers rallied to his side. Ibn Qamia, a famous swordsman, slashed at his head, but Muhammad's cousin, Talha ibn Ubaidullah, warded off the blow with his bare hands, his fingers being broken and maimed for life. The Prophet fell to the ground, the blood running down his face, while ibn Qamia called loudly to Quraish that he had killed Muhammad. It is strange now to think how different the history of the world would have been, if, thirteen hundred years ago, ibn Qamia's sword-cut had been but a trifle better aimed.

Meanwhile some of the Muslims had gathered round the Prophet. Perhaps also ibn Qamia's claim to have killed him caused the Meccans to relax their efforts, for the quarrel was with him alone. Profiting by the opportunity, Talha ibn Ubaidullah, despite his own wounds, raised him from the ground. Abu Bekr, Ali and other intimates collected round him and half carrying, half supporting him, they hastened up the rocky side of Uhud, and dropped into a sheltered hollow. Ali fetched water and began to wash the blood from his face, while Muhammad exclaimed, "How shall a people prosper who have thus treated their Prophet who called them to their Lord!"

The battle was over. Quraish were in undisputed possession of the field. The remaining Muslims were sheltering in the crags of Mount Uhud and watching the Meccans from above. Medina lay undefended at the mercy of the idolaters. For the moment, however, the Meccans were occupied in stripping and mutilating the dead. Seventy-five of the Muslims had been killed, while Quraish had lost only twenty dead. Above all, the Prophet mourned the death of his uncle Hamza. Hind the wife of Abu Sofian had hired a famous javelin-thrower for the sole purpose of killing him in revenge for her father whom Hamza had killed at Bedr. Wahshi had stalked his victim, an incomparable swordsman, and had thrown his javelin when Hamza was engaged in a sword-fight with a Meccan. The missile pierced his groin and he fell to the ground, dying almost immediately. Hind found the body after the battle and sated her revenge by cutting off his ears and his nose. Then she slit open his body and began to chew his liver.[9]

When Quraish had finished stripping and mutilating the dead, Abu Sofian advanced alone and called out to the fugitive Muslims crouching above him among the rocks of Uhud, "Today is in exchange for Bedr. War is like a well-bucket, sometimes up and sometimes down. Thy strength O Hubal! Al Uzza and Hubal are ours. We will meet again next year at Bedr." The Meccans then climbed on to their camels and rode slowly away. Muhammad was still apprehensive lest the enemy ride into Medina and occupy the city, as they could easily have done. He sent Ali ibn abi Talib to follow them at a distance to observe and report their movements. Soon he returned, shouting that Quraish were moving southwards towards the track to Mecca and had bypassed Medina. Then the believers scrambled down the rocky hillside, and buried and prayed over their dead. Muhammad, infuriated at the sight of the mangled and mutilated corpses, especially that of his uncle Hamza, swore that he would mutilate the bodies of thirty Quraish in revenge. But later on he relented and mutilation of the dead was thenceforward forbidden.

Accustomed as we are to the idea of ruthless, total war, the casual and

[9] This habit of eating an enemy's liver is doubtless thousands of years old. A case has been reported even in the twentieth century. It probably was originally thought that the eater thereby absorbed the courage of the dead, but even in the seventh century it had become merely an act of vengeance.

desultory methods of Arab warfare seem to us almost incomprehensible. The savagery with which Quraish had mutilated the bodies of the dead Muslims would seem to us to indicate an inextinguishable hatred. Yet, when final victory seemed in their hands if they had occupied Medina, they turned home after issuing a challenge to fight again at Bedr a year later. This challenge to an annual battle seems to have been something of a tradition among the Arabs of the time. A few years earlier, when Muhammad was a young man, war had been declared between Quraish and the tribe of Hawazin. Five annual battles occurred, arranged by appointment, before peace was again concluded.

To a great extent, these methods of warfare continued between the nomadic tribes of Central Arabia well into the twentieth century. Certain tribes were almost perpetually at war with one another, without either side having the least desire for final victory. The condition of unending war provided the romantic background against which the young, the gallant and the enterprising could perform the deeds of prowess which lent poetry, colour and glory to their otherwise monotonous lives. Quraish, it is true, were not bedouins and their principal interests, as we have seen, were commercial. Nevertheless, when they did become involved in war, they tended to observe the martial custom of their age, even though these traditions had originated in a nomadic state.

The blood feud, however, cut illogically across these casual and picturesque hostilities and led to intense hatreds and to savage reprisals. Thus the paradoxical situation was reached that war was carried on in a casual and even chivalrous manner, battles being arranged by appointment and preceded by single combats. But as soon as one warrior was known to have been killed by another (in a pitched battle it was often impossible to trace who had killed whom), a savage feud was inaugurated, not between the two tribes at war, but between the two families involved in the incident in question. The mutilation of Hamza was not due to religious fanaticism but to the fact that the dead warrior had killed the father of Hind at Bedr.

The customs of Arab tribal warfare continued, as has been indicated, up to the present century. But it is interesting to notice that, throughout the intervening thirteen centuries, religious outbreaks recurred from time to time, the last being the Wahhabi revival from 1912 to 1930. These periodical outbursts of religious enthusiasm each lasted, on an average, some thirty years, during which the old tribal traditions were partly or wholly abandoned, and the revivalists fought to win. Ruthless methods, which would not have been justified in the interests of a tribe, were even commendable when their object was the service of God. We shall see in the following pages that whereas Quraish and the tribes followed the old casual methods, Muhammad was fighting to win.

* * * * *

It was not in Arabia alone that the fortune of war went up and down like the bucket in a well. The two great empires of the day were experiencing similar vicissitudes. We have already seen that Heraclius had mounted the throne of Constantinople in 610. The first news which greeted him from the

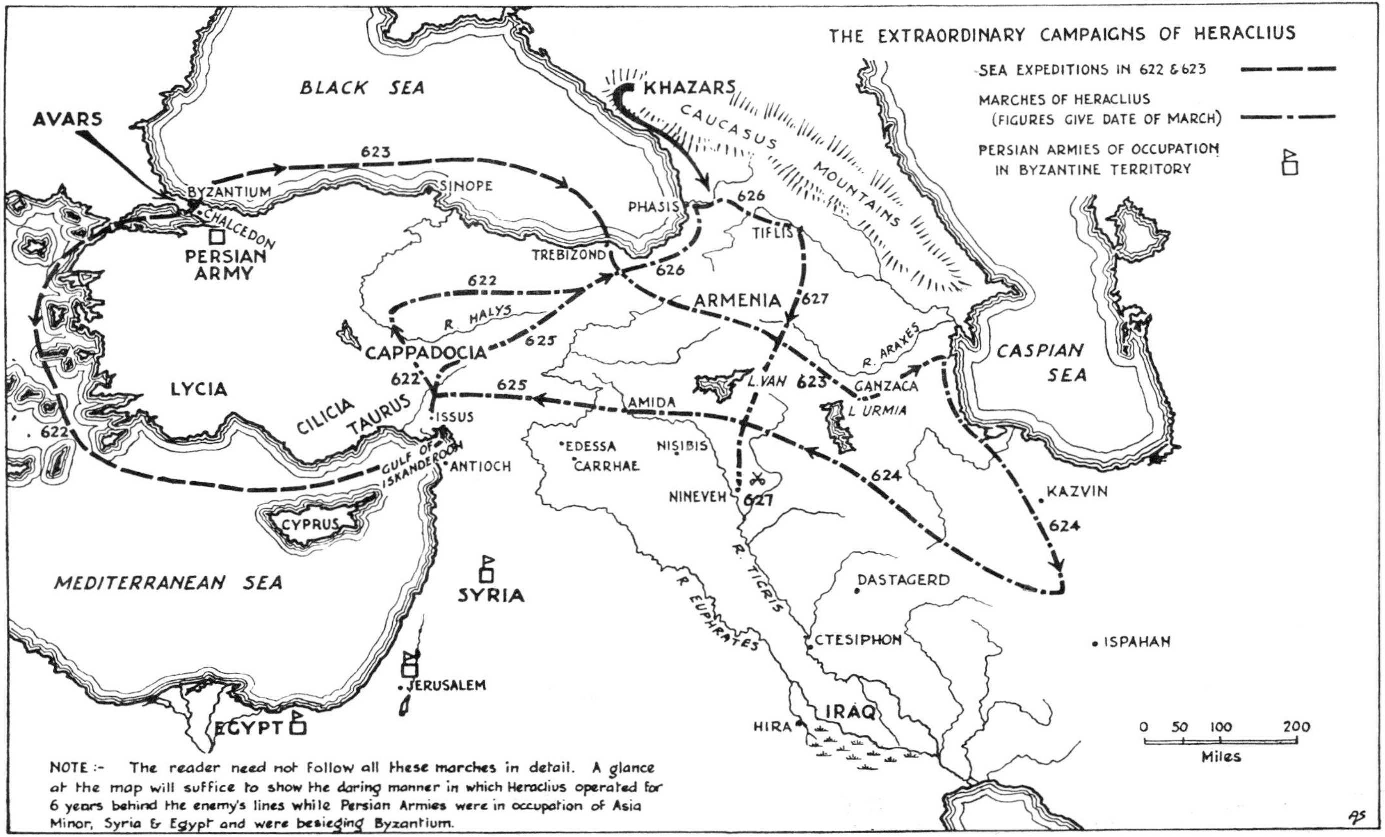
THE EXTRAORDINARY CAMPAIGNS OF HERACLIUS
SEA EXPEDITIONS IN 622 & 623
MARCHES OF HERACLIUS
(FIGURES GIVE DATE OF MARCH)
PERSIAN ARMIES OF OCCUPATION
IN BYZANTINE TERRITORY
BLACK SEA
AVARS
KHAZARS
CAUCASUS
MOUNTAINS
623
BYZANTIUM
SINOPE
CHALCEDON
PERSIAN
ARMY
PHASIS
626
TIFLIS
TREBIZOND
626
622
R. HALYS
ARMENIA
627
625
CAPPADOCIA
R. ARAXES
CASPIAN
SEA
LYCIA
622
625
L.VAN
623
GANZACA
L URMIA
CILICIA
TAURUS
AMIDA
ISSUS
622
EDESSA
CARRHAE
NISIBIS
GULF OF
ISKANDEROON
ANTIOCH
624
NINEVEH
627
KAZVIN
624
CYPRUS
R. TIGRIS
R EUPHRATES
DASTAGERD
MEDITERRANEAN SEA
SYRIA
CTESIPHON
ISPAHAN
JERUSALEM
EGYPT
HIRA
IRAQ
0 50 100 200
Miles
NOTE :- The reader need not follow all these marches in detail. A glance at the map will suffice to show the daring manner in which Heraclius operated for 6 years behind the enemy's lines while Persian Armies were in occupation of Asia Minor, Syria & Egypt and were besieging Byzantium.

Map IX

Persian front was that of the fall of Antioch. In 614 the armies of Chosroes captured Jerusalem, in 616 they occupied Egypt. Other Persian armies swept across Asia Minor and occupied Chalcedon, surveying the walls and towers of Byzantium across the narrow waters of the Bosphorus. At the same time the Avars, a nation of barbarians from southern Russia, ravaged the Balkan Peninsula up to the very walls of the capital. Thus surrounded on all sides by relentless enemies, Heraclius contemplated the transfer of the government to Carthage, but was persuaded by the patriarch to remain. He sent embassies to Chosroes, imploring peace, while he narrowly escaped assassination himself when he sought an interview with the chief of the Avars. The Great King at first rejected with contempt the supplications of the emperor but at length consented to a truce, in return for an annual payment of 1,000 talents of gold, 1,000 talents of silver, 1,000 silk robes, 1,000 horses and 1,000 virgins. Historians have blamed Heraclius for his failure, during the first twelve years of his reign, to drive out the invaders. Some, however, have opined that a struggle for power between the Senate and Heraclius made a bold national policy impossible. Our information is insufficient to enable us to reach a reliable conclusion on the subject.

Two days after Easter 622, the emperor handed over control of Constantinople to the patriarch and the senate. Although the city was hard pressed on the east and the west by the Persians and the Avars, the Byzantines still held command of the sea. Embarking his army, Heraclius sailed through the Dardanelles, and landed on the northern shore of the Gulf of Alexandretta, where he seized the narrow pass through the Taurus mountains known as the Cilician Gates. He pitched his camp near Issus, where, nearly 1,000 years earlier Alexander the Great had overthrown Darius the Persian. Defeating an army sent against him, he overran Cappadocia, cutting the communications of the Persian army camped at Chalcedon. Leaving his troops to winter on the River Halys, he returned at the end of 622 to Constantinople. (It was in June of this same year, while Heraclius was landing at Issus, that Muhammad left Mecca to seek refuge in Medina.)

In the spring of 623, Heraclius sailed from Byzantium into the Black Sea, with a corps d'élite of 5,000 men. He landed at Trebizond, and joined forces with his army which had wintered in Cappadocia. Crossing Armenia, he reached the River Araxes and wintered far inside the Persian Empire on the southern shores of the Caspian. (Meanwhile the battle of Bedr was fought in January 624.) During the summer of 624, the emperor is alleged to have reached Kazvin, a hundred miles north-west of modern Teheran, but the geography of these campaigns is vague in the extreme. Heraclius appears to have wintered the following year in the town of Amida (the modern Diyarbekr). In 625, he was back defeating the Persians again in Cilicia and in the autumn of that year, after three years of campaigning deep in Persian territory, he emerged once more on the shores of the Black Sea.

Meanwhile, Chosroes had agreed with the Avars on the necessity of capturing Constantinople. Heraclius was obliged to detach 12,000 men to reinforce the city. For ten days, in the summer of 626, wave upon wave of barbarians hurled themselves against the walls of Byzantium. The Avars had acquired some skill in war. Wooden towers were dragged up to the walls, saps and trenches were pushed forward, the enemy advanced with their shields locked to protect them from the Byzantine missiles. But after ten days of desperate battle, the Avars withdrew exhausted. Meanwhile the alliance of Chosroes with the Avars had been countered by Heraclius, who had gained the assistance of the Turkish race of the Khazars of the Lower Volga. Their chief met Heraclius at Tiflis and contributed to his army a reinforcement of 40,000 cavalry.

In the summer of 627, Heraclius moved southwards once more through Armenia and on 1st December won a decisive victory over the Persians at Nineveh. Not only Chalcedon but Egypt and Syria were evacuated and the Persian kingdom began to disintegrate. In February 628, Chosroes Parwiz was assassinated by his son Siroes and the whole structure of the state dissolved in anarchy. At length, peace was concluded, and after twenty-six years of futile war and destruction, a treaty was signed restoring the frontier of 602. Both empires had been utterly ruined, their respective treasuries were empty, their provinces laid waste, their commerce and industries destroyed.

It has been necessary to introduce this digression for two reasons. The first, and the more important, is the fact that the exhaustion produced by these twenty-six years of war was to open the door to the great Arab conquests a few years later. The second reason lies in the peculiar strategy of Heraclius, which he was to attempt to reproduce, but this time with disastrous results, against the Arab invasion of his empire.

The Muslims can scarcely be blamed if they traced the finger of God in this insane mutual butchery of Byzantium and Persia, precisely during the years in which the believers were building up their strength and unity, before breaking out of the borders of Arabia to conquer the great empires and ancient civilizations around them.

## *NOTABLE DATES*

| | |
|---|---|
| Heraclius sails from Byzantium | Easter 622 |
| Muhammad's arrival in Medina | 28th June 622 |
| Battle of Bedr | January 624 |
| Battle of Uhud | January 625 |
| Avars attack Byzantium | Summer 626 |
| Battle of Nineveh | 1st December 627 |
| Assassination of Chosroes and conclusion of peace between Byzantium and Persia | February 628 |

## *PERSONALITIES*

Ali ibn abi Talib, Muhammad's cousin, brought up as his son.
Zeid ibn Haritha, Muhammad's adopted son.
Abu Bekr, Muhammad's best friend.
Abdulla ibn Obay, jealous chief of Medina.
Abu Sofian, leader of Quraish against Muslims.

Heraclius, Byzantine Emperor.
Chosroes, King of Persia.

# IV

## *Triumph and Death*

Fight in the way of Allah against those who fight against you . . . kill them wherever you find them and drive them out from where they drove you out. *Qoran* II, 110

Surely we have won for thee an evident victory . . . that Allah might make thee victorious with a glorious victory. And He will torment the hypocrites and the polytheists both men and women. *Qoran* XLVIII, 1, 3, 6

Call him Prophet, Reformer or impostor, as we will, the camel-driver of Mecca, the conqueror of Medina, soars above every other man recorded in the history of the East. Nowhere in the history of the world can we directly trace such mighty effects to the personal agency of a single mortal.

E. A. Freeman, *Conquests of the Saracens*

They that dwell in the wilderness shall kneel before him . . . the kings of Arabia and Saba shall bring gifts. *Psalm* LXXII

# IV

## TRIUMPH AND DEATH

THE defeat of Uhud seemed to leave the Muslim cause at a low ebb. The fact that the victory of Bedr had been attributed to God's support of the believers made it all the more difficult to explain why divine help had been withheld at Uhud. A long revelation came to the Prophet's assistance in maintaining morale. In Chapter III of the Qoran, Abdulla ibn Obay and his followers are reproved for their desertion, the Muslims are promised ultimate victory and are informed that God permitted them to be defeated that He might try their faith.

No sooner were the believers rested from their exertions than Muhammad proceeded once more actively to extend his influence. Beni Asad, a powerful tribe in Nejed friendly to Quraish, were raided and their camels plundered. The chief of the tribe of Beni Lahyan, who had shown hostility to the Muslims, was assassinated, his head being cut off and brought to Muhammad in Medina. A party of six Muslims, however, were kidnapped in retaliation, four of them being killed by Beni Lahyan. The two others were sold to Quraish, to be killed by the relatives of men slain at Bedr. Zeid and Khubaib are remembered by the Muslims as martyrs. Khubaib, as the Meccans lashed him to an upright post, cried aloud, "O Lord, number these men one by one and destroy them utterly. Let not one escape."[1] When the two victims were securely bound, the children of the men killed at Bedr were given spears and were assisted in stabbing the two victims to death. The retreat of Quraish after Uhud without exploiting their victory and the ferocious stabbing of Zeid and Khubaib tied up to stakes, show on the one hand the casual methods of Arab warfare and, on the other, their savage ferocity in avenging their blood feuds.

The most striking contrast between the two sides during these years of hostilities is provided by the ceaseless activity of the Muslims as opposed to the passivity of Quraish. A constant stream of small raids emanated from Medina and its allied bedouins against those tribes which were in agreement with Quraish. Individuals who showed outstanding hostility to the Muslims or to the Apostle were, in many cases, assassinated by what we should call terrorist methods. (At about this time, the Prophet sent a man to Mecca to assassinate Abu Sofian, but the project miscarried.) The preaching, the assassinations and the propaganda proceeded simultaneously, in the attempt to win over men's minds. The fact that Muhammad was simultaneously prophet, ruler and military commander produced a perfect combination of the use of force, the persuasive methods of politics and the emotional appeal of religion. In older communities, as was indeed the case with Quraish who

[1] Compare *Acts* VII, 60.

had no single leader, these activities are often exercised by different departments, with the result that the perfect and intimate co-operation of political propaganda and the threat of armed force cannot be achieved. Thus Mohammad enjoyed, in relation to the Meccans, the same advantages as the modern dictator possesses in his dealings with the older democracies.

The comparison may even be carried further, for the Muslims, like the communists, were able to command the enthusiasm often invoked by a new idea, especially in its appeal to the young. Quraish, with their long-established way of life, were forced back on the defensive. Instead of, like Muhammad, being constantly engaged in restless aggressive action, they remained inactive except during periodic crises.

The most important event of the year after the battle of Uhud was the expulsion of Beni Nadheer. This was the second of the Jewish tribes of Medina. They lived in a separate settlement, surrounded by date palm gardens, south of the town. In September 625, after a siege of fifteen days, they consented to abandon their homes and migrate to Syria, where they settled in Jericho and in Deraa. Whereas Beni Qainuqa, the first Jewish tribe to be exiled, had been goldsmiths and armourers by profession, Beni Nadheer were cultivators. Their houses, fields and gardens were divided among the Muslims.

Thus, in spite of the defeat at Uhud, the Prophet throughout the year continued to extend his influence. By raiding the bedouins, he hoped to convince the latter that it was safer to take his side than that of Quraish, a mercantile community who did not raid. By exiling Beni Nadheer, he both weakened the potentially disloyal community in Medina and also provided a more generous means of livelihood for the Emigrants, who had left their property behind in Mecca.

At last, a year after Uhud, in January 626, the time came for the acceptance of the challenge, which Abu Sofian had delivered, for a further trial by battle at Bedr. The year had been one of scanty rainfall, an event which to this day renders movement difficult in Arabia, where horses and camels are not fed, but depend on natural grazing. Quraish sent a man to Medina to spread reports of vast preparations in Mecca, in the hope that the Muslims would be terrified into absenting themselves from the rendezvous. The ruse was nearly successful but Muhammad's determination eventually resulted in the collection of fifteen hundred men, twice the strength which he had led forth to Uhud. It was the Meccans who ultimately failed to appear. The Muslims camped for eight days at Bedr unopposed, a bloodless victory highly beneficial to their morale.

During the ensuing year, the fifth since the Prophet's flight from Mecca, the policy of ever-widening tribal raids was continued, one such extending northwards almost to the Byzantine frontiers. On one of these occasions—a raid on a small tribe called Beni Mustaliq—an unfortunate incident occurred. The Apostle often took one or other of his wives with him on these expeditions, and his companion on this occasion was Aisha, the daughter of Abu Bekr. The last night of the expedition, when the raiders bivouacked, Aisha had occasion to walk away a little distance from her tent. On returning, she discovered that she had lost her beads and retraced her steps to seek them in

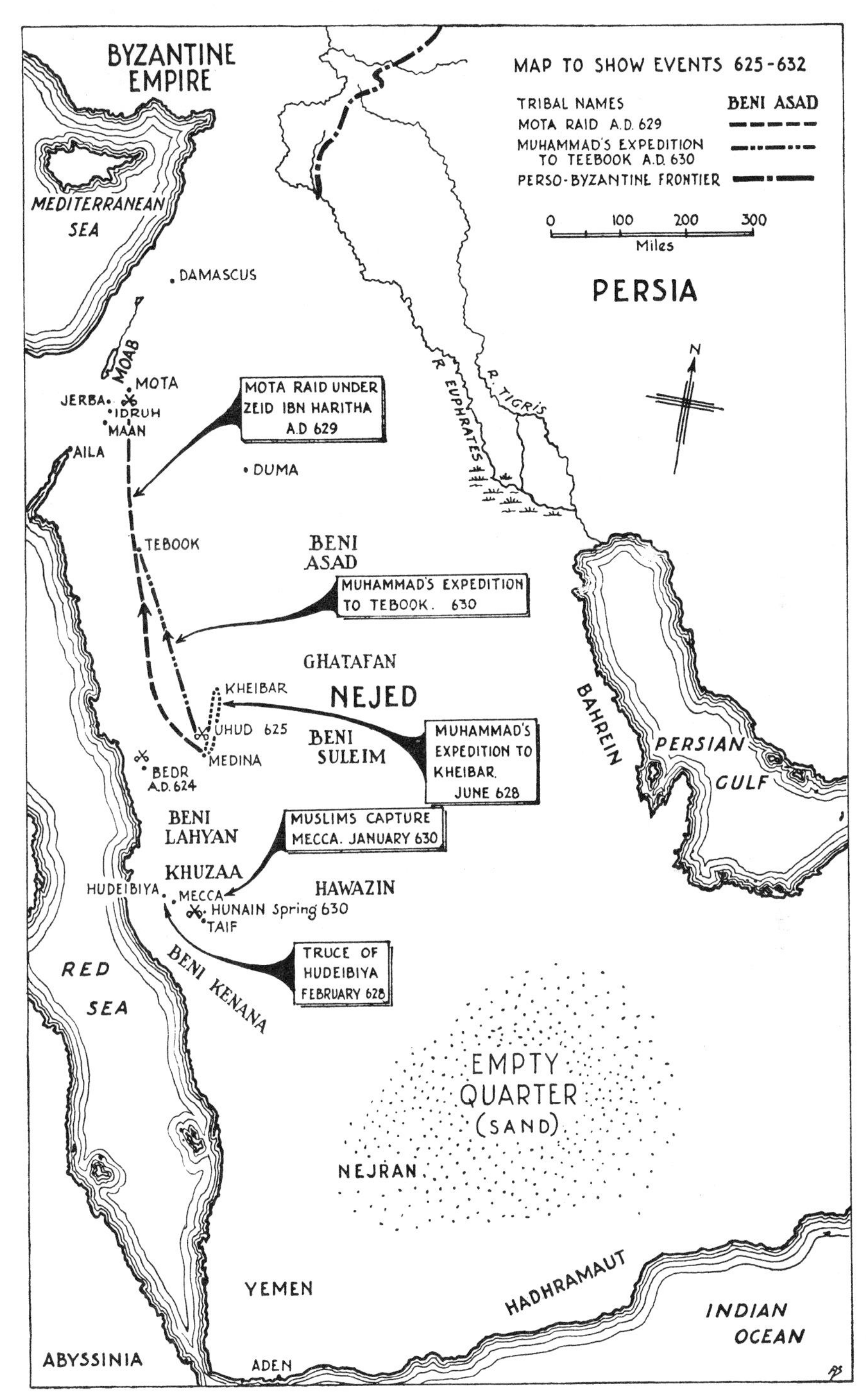
BYZANTINE EMPIRE
MAP TO SHOW EVENTS 625-632
TRIBAL NAMES
BENI ASAD
MOTA RAID A.D. 629
MUHAMMAD'S EXPEDITION TO TEEBOOK A.D. 630
PERSO-BYZANTINE FRONTIER
0
100
200
300
Miles
MEDITERRANEAN SEA
DAMASCUS
PERSIA
N
MOAB
MOTA
JERBA
IDRUH
MAAN
AILA
MOTA RAID UNDER ZEID IBN HARITHA A.D 629
DUMA
R. EUPHRATES
R. TIGRIS
TEBOOK
BENI ASAD
MUHAMMAD'S EXPEDITION TO TEBOOK. 630
GHATAFAN
KHEIBAR
NEJED
BAHREIN
UHUD 625
BENI SULEIM
MUHAMMAD'S EXPEDITION TO KHEIBAR. JUNE 628
MEDINA
PERSIAN GULF
BEDR A.D. 624
BENI LAHYAN
MUSLIMS CAPTURE MECCA. JANUARY 630
KHUZAA
HUDEIBIYA
MECCA
HAWAZIN
HUNAIN Spring 630
TAIF
RED SEA
BENI KENANA
TRUCE OF HUDEIBIYA FEBRUARY 628
EMPTY QUARTER (SAND)
NEJRAN
YEMEN
HADHRAMAUT
INDIAN OCEAN
ABYSSINIA
ADEN

Map x

the dark. While she was searching for them, the party moved on, leaving her behind. The camel carrying her litter accompanied the raiders and, as it was closely curtained, everybody assumed her to be inside. When she returned to find the bivouac deserted, she lay down and went to sleep, imagining that her absence would be discovered and that someone would return to fetch her.

Instead, however, she was woken by a young man by the name of Safwan, who was riding on his camel to Medina. Seeing her predicament, he mounted her on the camel and walked to the town, leading it by its halter. The arrival of one of the Apostle's wives in the company of a young man produced a considerable scandal. Ill-wishers were not slow to defame her character and even the Prophet himself was disturbed by doubts of her morality. It appears that Ali, most unfortunately, suggested to Muhammad that there was no lack of women, and that Aisha could easily be replaced.

After a month of anxiety, the Apostle received a heavenly revelation testifying to Aisha's innocence and harmony was restored. The coldness between Aisha and Ali was, however, to produce disastrous consequences after the death of the Apostle. Another result of this affair was the revelation of Chapter XXIV of the Qoran, laying down the necessity of four eye-witnesses for the establishment of the crime of adultery. Any who slandered married women without producing four eye-witnesses were to be flogged with eighty stripes.

* * * * *

Exasperated by the fact that they seemed to be always losing ground in face of new political methods which they did not understand, Quraish now decided to make an end of the community in Medina, once and for all. In February 627, they took the field with no less than ten thousand men, three times their strength at Uhud. Of these, some four thousand were of Quraish, while the remainder consisted of contingents from allied bedouin tribes, Ghatafan, Beni Suleim and Beni Kinana. The news of so formidable an invasion spread consternation in Medina.

It happened that there was in the town a Persian convert to Islam by the name of Sulman, who had apparently gained experience of the more technical methods of warfare in use in the Persian Empire. He suggested fortifying the town with a ditch and breastwork. It would appear that the greater part of the circumference was defended by walls and houses but that the northern side of the town was exposed. All hands were immediately turned on to dig, the Prophet himself, covered with dust, plying pick and shovel and singing with the workmen to keep up their spirits. In six days the trench was dug, just in time to prevent the enemy from taking the town by assault.

The remarkable conservatism of old Arab warfare is shown by the fact that Quraish were completely disconcerted by this unexpected development, which they contemptuously described as un-Arab and dishonourable. Camping outside the perimeter, they made little attempt to mount a general assault, although they outnumbered the defenders by three to one. With the typical Arab preference for personal bravery rather than organized tactics, a group of four horsemen charged the ditch, which the horses cleared, landing them in the midst of the defenders, whom they thereupon challenged to single combats. As usual, Ali ibn abi Talib stepped forward and killed their leader, whereupon the other three withdrew across the ditch.

Static warfare was little to the taste of the bedouin allies of Quraish. Rations soon began to fail and friction arose, fomented by a secret emissary from Muhammad. The camels and horses of the besiegers began to die for lack of grazing. Although Abu Sofian was nominally in command, a curious system was followed according to which a different leader commanded every day. While possibly necessary to calm the jealousies of the various chiefs, such an arrangement obviously made any regular siege operations impossible.

Meanwhile anxiety was spreading in Medina. The Apostle himself, doubtless alarmed at the discouragement of some of his followers, opened secret negotiations with the chief of the Ghatafan tribe, offering him one-third of the date crop of the Medina oasis if he would desert the cause of Quraish and lead his tribesmen home. The terms were accepted, but before concluding the agreement, Muhammad sent for the respective chiefs of Aus and Khazraj and explained to them the plan. Had he, they enquired, entered upon these negotiations as a result of a divine revelation? The Prophet replied in the negative. It was his own idea, he said. "In that case, O Messenger of God," replied the two chiefs, "we would like you to know that in the days of ignorance, those bedouins have never once been able to plunder our dates. Now that God has given us his grace and made us believers and is fighting on our side, are we to allow them to despoil us? Let us rely on our swords and lances and let God decide." This was one of a number of occasions on which Muslim converts seemed more determined than was the Prophet himself.

When the siege had lasted some twenty days, a violent storm one night swept across the oasis. A howling gale blew down the tents of the beseigers, extinguished their fires and sent their cooking pots bowling over and over across the ground, while rain fell in sheets. No sooner had the storm passed than Abu Sofian summoned Quraish to a meeting, and informed them curtly that he was going home. As soon as the Meccans moved away, their tribal allies dispersed into the desert. The siege was at an end.

As the enemy disappeared down the track towards Mecca, Muhammad returned wearily towards his house and the Muslims began to divest themselves of their armour. Suddenly the Archangel Gabriel, mounted upon a mule, appeared before the Prophet and enquired, "Have you already laid down your arms, O Apostle of God? The Angels have not yet laid aside their arms, for God orders you to attack Beni Quraidha and I am going on ahead of you." Muhammad thereupon called upon the Muslims to resume their weapons. Ali led the march with the Apostle's war banner unfurled, and all advanced on the settlement of Beni Quraidha, the last Jewish tribe in the Medina oasis. It is perhaps scarcely surprising that the tribe was hostile to the Muslims, who had already driven their fellow Jews into exile. The arrival of so large a force from Mecca had encouraged Beni Quraidha with the hope of revenge and they had placed themselves in communication with

Quraish. The sudden withdrawal of the Meccans had left the Jews to face the indignant Muslims unsupported.

The siege of their settlement lasted for twenty-five days. Eventually they surrendered unconditionally. The Jews had long been resident in Medina, the friends and allies of the local Arabs. Muhammad agreed to refer the decision regarding their fate to Saad ibn Muadh of the Aus tribe, formerly their ally. Saad had been one of the earliest Medina converts to Islam and had carried the banner of his tribe at Bedr. He was now dying from an arrow wound, received during the siege. A former friend of the Jews, he had perhaps become embittered by his wound. He announced his decision that every man of Beni Quraidha should be put to death, the women and children sold as slaves and their possessions taken as plunder. The Apostle welcomed the verdict as just and ordered its execution. Trenches were dug during the night and on the following day the Jews were led out in small parties, their hands tied, and made to sit down beside the trench. They were then beheaded, their bodies pushed into the trench and another batch called up. Some seven hundred men were despatched in this manner. Before execution they were offered the alternative of Islam. By the repetition of a simple sentence, they could have been transformed from condemned criminals to the equals of their conquerors, but few took advantage of the offer.

* * * * *

Quraish, by a supreme effort, had raised ten thousand men for the siege of Medina. When the grand design ended in fiasco, the prestige of Muhammad soared. The extermination of Beni Quraidha was a sufficient warning to traitors or intriguers.

Early in 628, the Apostle dreamed that he had entered Mecca unopposed and performed the pilgrimage. He immediately announced his intention of doing so. The greater pilgrimage could only be carried out on a certain day of the Muslim calendar, but Omra, or the lesser pilgrimage, was permissible at any time. It was this ceremony that Muhammad proposed to perform. Before the propagation of Islam, the idolatrous Arabs recognized in the year four sacred months, during which raiding or fighting was forbidden. It happened to be during one of these months of truce that the Apostle of God decided to visit Mecca. Thus, in theory, Quraish had no right to oppose him by force.

In February 628, therefore, a year after the siege of Medina, the Prophet set out for Mecca as a pilgrim, at the head of fifteen hundred followers. Quraish, however, were far from convinced of his peaceable intentions. They hastily armed themselves and took up a defensive position astride the track from Medina. The would-be pilgrims carried only swords and were by no means in a position to fight a battle. Indeed in thus moving half-unarmed towards the enemy, Muhammad appears to have accepted an extraordinary risk.[2] Finding the direct track closed to them, the Muslims swung to the right and, passing to the west of the enemy's position, approached the city of Mecca

[2] Margolionth suggests that Muhammad had originally intended to attack Mecca.

along the track leading up to it from the Red Sea. Here they halted at Hudeibiya, a short day's march west of the town.

When the Meccans learned that Muhammad had turned the flank of their defensive position, they fell back on the city and sent negotiators to meet him. The first was Budeil, a shaikh of the tribe of Khuzaa, who, it will be remembered, were residents of Mecca with Quraish.[3] To him, the Prophet indicated the animals which the would-be pilgrims had brought with them for sacrifice according to the rites of pilgrimage, and which thus proved his peaceful intentions. One of the Meccan emissaries, reporting back to the leaders of Quraish, has left us a vivid sketch of the prestige of the Apostle among his followers.

"I have been to Chosroes in his kingdom," he said, "and I have seen Caesar and the Prince of Abyssinia among their subjects, but never have I seen a king among his people treated with such respect as is Muhammad among his companions." When we are perplexed to account for the sudden rise of Islam, we do well to remember these few lines. We can only assess the material factors which favoured the victory of the Meccans or the Muslims. The aura of the Prophet's personality cannot be recaptured by us. Yet there was doubtless something about him which inspired this utter devotion and which constituted one of the principal causes of the success of Islam. Indeed the whole spirit of the movement was to change as soon as the last of Muhammad's companions was dead.

The Meccan envoys having returned to the city to report what they had seen and heard, the Apostle sent Othman ibn Affan to meet the leaders of Quraish. Othman had been one of the earliest converts to Islam and one of the first emigrants to Abyssinia. He had been married to the Prophet's daughter Rukaiya, and, when she died, he had married her sister, being thus twice over the Apostle's son-in-law. But he was by origin of Beni Umaiya, of the clan of which Abu Sofian was chief. Thus Othman was related to the most powerful and wealthy notables of Quraish.

The distance to Mecca was short and Othman's return was expected in a few hours. But time dragged on and he did not appear. Then, whence we do not know, a report reached Muhammad that he had been killed. If in fact Quraish, regardless of tribal ties, had killed a prominent man of Beni Umaiya, they must indeed have decided on extreme measures. Probably they were mustering a large force to attack and exterminate the Muslims once and for all. Armed only with swords, the believers were in a precarious situation. All those present realized what was at stake as the slow hours dragged by without news.

Muhammad himself seems to have thought a clash imminent. Standing beneath one of those thorny trees which are to be found here and there among the sand and rocks of these arid mountains, he called on all those present to take a renewed pledge to fight to the death. The fact that he did so proves that he himself was deeply aware of the danger in which they stood. In an atmosphere of extreme tension, they filed past him giving him their hands in turn, as the Medina pilgrims had done seven years before, on the night of

[3] Page 37.

the second Aqaba. All now were keyed to the highest pitch of devotion. Many years afterwards, when Muslim arms had built up a great empire, when former comrades spoke of the old days (as soldiers will) the deepest respect was always shown to those who had fought at Bedr and to those who had taken the oath at Hudeibiya. These long enduring memories show what suspense must have been felt during that anxious wait.

Suddenly a camel rider was seen approaching from Mecca. All eyes were strained to recognize him. It was Suhail ibn Amr, a new emissary from Quraish. No sooner did the Prophet recognize him than he exclaimed—with what relief can be imagined—"the people want peace seeing they have sent this man." Suhail was a noted speaker and diplomat with a persuasive manner. The negotiations were long drawn out before an agreement was drafted. Suhail refused to admit the phrase "Muhammad the Apostle of God" in the preamble and the agreement was concluded between Muhammad the son of Abdulla and Suhail the son of Amr. A ten years' truce was to be observed. The Muslims were to return to Medina without making the pilgrimage but were to be permitted to do so after the expiry of one year. Both sides were free to conclude alliances with the tribes, but any Meccans who left the city to join Muhammad were to be sent back by him.

As the final agreement was drafted, the son of Suhail, the Quraish negotiator, arrived as a fugitive from Mecca, declaring that he wished to accept Islam. His father invoked the agreement just concluded and Muhammad reluctantly informed the would-be convert that he must return to Mecca. As the young man was led away, the fiery Umar ibn al Khattab walked beside him for a few paces, holding out his sword. "I had hoped that he would seize the sword and kill his father," he used to say when subsequently recounting the incident.

The clause in the agreement making it incumbent on Muhammad to reject new converts from Mecca who might come to him, combined with the incident of the son of Suhail, may partly explain the reason for the weakening of Quraish, in spite of their apparent material superiority. They doubtless sensed disloyalty in their own ranks, particularly among the younger men. Throughout all the years of exile in Medina, there are frequent references to the presence with the Muslims of young men whose fathers were fighting for Quraish. At about this time, the son of Abdulla ibn Obay, the shaikh of Medina, asked the Prophet's permission to murder his own father. Perhaps the Arabs were ripe for a more advanced religion, which the young were quick to welcome, while their elders still clung to the traditions of the old days.

Many of the Muslims were disappointed at the outcome of Hudeibiya, having anticipated a triumphal entry into Mecca. Umar ibn al Khattab, as usual, voiced his indignation. "Is he not God's apostle and are we not Muslims and are they not polytheists?" he demanded angrily from the quiet and faithful Abu Bekr. "Why not fight them? Why compromise thus?" "You do what he says," answered Abu Bekr mildly, "for I bear witness that he is the Messenger of God." At the end of the first march on the homeward road to Medina, a new revelation assured the Prophet that the agreement was a manifest victory. For us it is difficult not to suspect that the advance to Hudeibiya by a small force, armed only with swords, was a dangerous military mistake. If Quraish had been more enterprising or had had a single, ruthless leader, they might have inflicted a serious defeat on the Muslims or even annihilated Islam, for these men were virtually all the Muslims then in existence. In fact, Muhammad himself was not a warrior and had few military gifts. In battle, he invariably followed behind the front line and never, if avoidable, himself engaged in hand-to-hand fighting. This was the more remarkable at a time when, as we have seen, it was the custom for the commander of a force to lead the charge in person with the war-banner in his hand.

It is true that he used, or connived at, massacre and assassination but on the whole he more often exercised a modifying influence on his more bloodthirsty followers. He lived in a savage and ruthless society and was, as we all are, to some extent the product of his age and surroundings. Yet by nature he leant rather to meditation and mildness than to ferocity. It is ironic to think that this naturally unmilitary personality gave birth to Islam, the religion of soldiers.

Just as disappointment over the defeat at Uhud was atoned for by the plunder of the Beni Nadheer Jews, so, six weeks after the affair at Hudeibiya, Muhammad restored the morale of his followers by leading them in June 628 to the attack of Kheibar, a Jewish settlement eighty miles north of Medina.[4] There was some resistance and the various settlements in the oasis were attacked one by one and taken by storm. This time the Jewish cultivators were not exiled, for the Apostle wished to keep his followers round him at Medina in readiness for action. He therefore did not wish them to acquire land and houses at Kheibar. As a result, the land was left to the Jews to cultivate on the condition of their agreeing to pay half the annual produce as tribute to the Muslims. The movable property, money and jewels, camels and sheep and stores of dates, oil and grain, were carried off as plunder.

* * * * *

The Apostle had married his daughter Fatima to Ali ibn abi Talib, his cousin who had been brought up almost as his son. Fatima had given birth to two sons, Hasan and Husain, whose tragic careers were deeply to influence the history of Islam. In these early days, however, there was as yet no foreshadowing of the disasters to come. Devoted as he was to children, Muhammad never tired of playing with his little grandsons. Even during the ritual prostrations at public prayers, they would climb on to his back and he would gently put them aside without impatience and continue his devotions.

* * * * *

According to tradition, it was at this period, the year 628, that the Prophet despatched messages to the King of Persia, the Byzantine Emperor, the Governor of Egypt and the Prince of Abyssinia, summoning them to accept the Muslim religion. The King of Persia is alleged to have torn up the missive with contempt. The Emperor Heraclius accepted his letter with less re-

[4] See Map VII, page 63.

sentment, merely enquiring who the author might be. The Governor of Egypt, however, received his epistle courteously, and while excusing himself from changing his religion, he sent in return a handsome horse, a mule, a riding ass and two Egyptian girls. Mary, one of the two, became the Prophet's concubine and was to bear him a son, who, however, died in infancy.

In so far as Heraclius is concerned, there is a tradition that, after the truce of Hudeibiya, Abu Sofian took a commercial caravan to Syria. He was picked up in Damascus by the Byzantine police. Heraclius had given orders that he wished to interview some traveller from the Hejaz and Abu Sofian was accordingly brought before the emperor in Jerusalem. Heraclius enquired of him details of the disturbances in the Hejaz and of the alleged new prophet. Abu Sofian replied that the followers of Muhammad consisted of the poorer classes or of adolescent youths. All the men of substance were opposed to him. Even if this tradition were true, it does not necessarily prove that the emperor had received a letter from Muhammad. Heraclius would naturally have been informed through government intelligence sources of the new movement in the Hejaz, and might quite reasonably have wished to cross-question a traveller from Mecca, in order to obtain further details.

Modern historians, however, have thrown some doubt on the matter of the despatch of the letters. There is little else in the records of the Prophet's life to show that he foresaw, much less himself contemplated, the conquest of Syria and Persia. The fantastic victories to be achieved by the Arabs after the death of Muhammad surprised the Muslims themselves, which would not have occurred if the Apostle had foretold them. On the other hand, Mary, the Egyptian concubine, was undoubtedly a historical personage. The picture of a simple, barefooted bedouin throwing down a challenge to the King of Kings in his Persian palace makes a dramatic scene.

* * * * *

A year after Hudeibiya, in February 629, the seventh year since the migration to Medina, the Muslims claimed the right to visit Mecca, as had been agreed in the treaty signed on that occasion. Some two thousand believers availed themselves of the opportunity to perform the lesser pilgrimage. Quraish, anxious to avoid armed clashes or perhaps fearing that the Prophet's persuasive tongue would win over more converts, evacuated Mecca en masse, and bivouacked on the mountain slopes overlooking the city, curious to watch what the Muslims would do. At length the head of the convoy appeared in the narrow dusty valley through which ran the track from Medina. Muhammad on his camel was in the lead, surrounded by Ali ibn abi Talib, Abu Bekr, Umar ibn al Khattab and a group of his close companions. Behind him, in a cloud of dust, followed his two thousand supporters, some on camels and some on foot. The Prophet went straight to the kaaba, touched the black stone,[5] and then performed the prescribed seven circuits of the house of God. This was in accordance with the pagan ritual used by Quraish themselves and now adopted by Islam.

[5] The black stone is a meteorite, embedded in the wall of the kaaba. It is still kissed by Muslims who visit Mecca on pilgrimage.

The Prophet's uncle, Abbas ibn Abdul Muttalib, had remained in Mecca and had not as yet proclaimed his conversion to Islam. Nevertheless, before Uhud, Abbas had warned Muhammad of the intentions of Quraish by sending him a secret message. Now he greeted him on his entry to Mecca and informed him that he had prepared for him a bride, to whom he could immediately be married, an apparently astute move to gain favour with his nephew, who now appeared to be worth conciliating. The conduct of Abbas has been variously interpreted by historians. Some have claimed that he was an early and sincere convert to Islam, who remained in Mecca solely to serve the interests of his nephew. Some have seen in him merely a predecessor of the Vicar of Bray, staying on overtly with Quraish but simultaneously communicating secretly with the Apostle. This prudent, if not crafty, citizen of a remote desert town was to be the ancestor of one of the world's greatest imperial dynasties. It is for this reason that his character is now so difficult to assess. A century later, when his descendants became rulers of the mighty Arab empire, historians were well advised to depict the character of Abbas in the most favourable light.

One of the most important results of Muhammad's increasing prestige at this time was the conversion of Khalid ibn al Waleed, Amr ibn al Aasi and Othman ibn Talha. It was Khalid and Amr who had been responsible for the victory of Quraish at Uhud, by leading the mounted charge round the Muslim left flank. They were to become the greatest military commanders of the Muslims. Othman ibn Talha was a man of no great distinction but he was the custodian of the keys of the kaaba, a privilege hereditary in the senior clan of Quraish, that of Abdul Dar.[6] Thus the guardian of the idol shrine had become converted to Islam. The arrival of such distinguished converts in Medina and perhaps also the good behaviour of the Muslims during their three days in Mecca on the lesser pilgrimage, had strongly impressed public opinion in the city.

While the previous year's affair at Hudeibiya had been premature, it now became clear that the Prophet's idea of performing the pilgrimage had been a masterly one. Much of the opposition to his preaching in Mecca had been due to the belief that its acceptance would discredit the kaaba and put an end to Mecca's venerated position as a holy city. By showing that he himself venerated the shrine and that it was still incumbent on Muslims to perform the ancient rites of pilgrimage, he satisfied the Meccans that Islam would not in any way injure the prestige of their city. This process was effected by the statement that the kaaba had been built by Abraham, whose religion the Apostle claimed to be reviving. The Jews and the Christians had strayed from the original purity of the religion of the patriarch, and the Meccans had done the same by filling the kaaba with idols. This heresy did not, however, in any way detract from the holiness of the kaaba, the house of God. All that was necessary was to purify it of idols. By this means, the Meccans were convinced that Islam would involve no loss to their shrine or to themselves.

At the same time, though Muhammad was still officially a public enemy in Mecca, he was becoming increasingly powerful and respected all over the

[6] Page 39.

rest of Arabia. Were they wise, Quraish began to ask themselves, to ostracize the greatest man whom their tribe had ever produced? They must have viewed with increasing jealousy the deputations from all over the peninsula flocking to pay their respects in Medina. This swing of public opinion in Mecca was soon to become a landslide.

A number of minor raids and expeditions were sent out in the year 629, some meeting with defeat, while others returned with booty. It is not without interest to compare these methods with those adopted by the Wahhabis in the eighteenth, nineteenth and twentieth centuries. The Wahhabis consciously and intentionally modelled their career of conquest on that of the first Muslims. Muhammad had never led a considerable force against the bedouin tribes, his serious operations being confined to hostilities with Quraish. Raids against the tribes were carried on casually and by small parties and as a result were sometimes successful and at other times defeated, though their frequency possessed a certain nuisance value, persuading the tribes that it might be easier to submit.

The Wahhabi tactics appear to have been more efficient. While permitting their tribes to raid non-Wahhabis if they desired, ibn Saud would periodically collect his full strength and carry out a devastating attack on some tribe which had not submitted to his rule, thereby inspiring such terror that instant submission resulted. It will be seen later that, after the Prophet's death, his successors resorted to this method. The fact that Muhammad did not use it must be primarily attributed to the fact that he was not interested in military operations and devoted little thought to them. Moreover the personality of the Apostle was so persuasive or commanding that he was able to win adherents without a really efficient military system. After his death a more rationalized use of force was necessary to keep the Muslim state in order.

In September 629, however, a more important expedition was organized, destined definitely to invade territory under Byzantine control. Tradition relates that the campaign was intended as a reprisal for the murder of certain Muslim emissaries sent to the area. Revenge, rather than campaigns of territorial conquest, were in the spirit of Arab warfare. The Prophet, now a man of sixty-one, with slightly greying hair, did not accompany any of the raids this year, the eighth after the emigration from Mecca.

A camp was formed a few miles north of Medina, where volunteers were instructed to assemble. Zeid ibn Haritha, the Prophet's freedman and adopted son, was given the command, and set out at the head of three thousand men. This was the first Muslim raid of such proportions to embark on a distant expedition. Time, however, was required for so large a force to assemble and before the expedition set out warning had already reached what is now southern Jordan.

The Muslims, who still relied for victory on divine assistance and their own spirit rather than on their skill, had apparently neglected to send spies in advance. It was not until they reached Maan that they obtained information that a large force had been mobilized in Moab—near the modern town of Kerak—to meet them. A halt was called, and the leaders spent two days in discussion, undecided whether to advance or retreat. The scales were turned by Abdulla ibn Rawaha, one of the earliest converts and most fervid believers. "Do we rely on our numbers or on the help of God?" he cried indignantly. "Victory or martyrdom and paradise—we must surely win the one or the other." The order was given for an immediate advance.

As the raiders moved northwards, the long line of the rocky hills of Moab lay on their left, its spurs running down eastwards into the vast expanses of the desert.[7] Crossing the lower foothills of the mountains, some fifty miles north of Maan, the Muslims suddenly found themselves in the presence of a force several times more numerous than themselves, consisting principally of the local Arab tribesmen but reinforced, according to tradition, by "Roman" soldiers, perhaps a local garrison of Byzantine troops. Near the village of Mota, a small plain opens between the spurs of the foothills of the Moab mountains. It was decided to give battle here. Zeid ibn Haritha, the Prophet's adopted son, seizing the white banner which Muhammad himself had entrusted to his hands, led the wild charge of the Muslims, plunging into the midst of the enemy's ranks until he fell transfixed by their spears. Jafar ibn abi Talib, the brother of Ali, seized the banner from the dying Zeid, and crying "Paradise! Paradise!" raised it aloft once more. For the commander himself to carry the banner seems to have been a system more suited to Arab warfare than to a regular battle. The enemy closed in on the heroic Jafar, who was soon covered with wounds. Tradition relates that, when both his hands were cut off gripping the banner, he still stood firm, holding the staff between his two stumps, until a Byzantine soldier struck him a mortal blow. Immediately the banner was caught up by Abdulla ibn Rawaha, he who, at Maan, had given his vote for battle. Looking around him, he saw that the Muslim ranks were already in confusion. "Are you still living?" he is alleged to have asked himself and, rushing sword in hand into the enemy's ranks, he fell seeking the Paradise he so ardently desired.

Khalid ibn al Waleed, newly converted to Islam, was fighting in the ranks. Perhaps less anxious for Paradise, he was nevertheless a more experienced commander than Zeid or Jafar. Assuming control at this moment of defeat, he succeeded in impressing his personality on the remnant of the raiders. A citizen of Medina planted the white banner in the ground and the Muslims gathered round. Then, by retiring methodically, the survivors, under Khalid's firm leadership, withdrew from the field. The enemy, perhaps severely mauled, neglected to pursue.

The field of Mota today is dominated by a Mosque with two tall minarets, marking the grave of Jafar ibn abi Talib. In the 1920's, the tomb was neglected and in ruins, and it is to me a source of pride that it was repaired and the minarets built with the assistance of the Arab Legion. The villagers of Mota still believe that, at dawn on Fridays, a ghostly Muslim army sweeps over the low ridge which bounds the plain on the east, and, with its white banner proudly displayed, pours down in a wild charge upon the place where the "Roman" army once stood arrayed in arms.

When the defeated Muslims approached Medina, the Prophet and the people of the town went out to meet them. The citizens began to throw dirt

[7] Map X, page 83.

at the crestfallen warriors, crying, "You runaways, you fled in the way of God!" But Muhammad, with that kind paternalism which he knew well how to use, interposed, "No, they are not runaways but come-agains, if God wills." Going to Jafar's house, he asked to see his children, and fondled and kissed them, his eyes full of tears. Then he hurried to the house of Zeid, whose little daughter rushed into his arms, crying passionately. Muhammad, embracing the child, himself burst into tears. Next morning in the mosque, the Prophet announced that he had, in a vision, seen the martyrs of Mota in Paradise, reclining upon couches, but Jafar was there in the guise of an angel with two wings, stained on their feathers with the blood of martyrdom. It was as a result of this vision that the martyr has since been known as Jafar the flyer, Jafar al Tayyar.

In spite of the disaster of Mota, many bedouin tribes sent deputations throughout the remainder of 629, seeking friendship and alliance with the Apostle of God.

* * * * *

Meanwhile public opinion in Mecca had swung so strongly to the side of the Muslims that Muhammad realized that the time had come for the coup de grâce. The tribes soon provided a *casus belli*. Khuzaa and Beni Bekr, two tribes long at feud, customarily camped the first on one side and the second on the other of the city of Mecca. Khuzaa had concluded an agreement with the Prophet, Beni Bekr with Quraish. It so chanced at this period that Khuzaa were watering at a well outside Mecca when they were attacked by Beni Bekr and some of their men killed. Budeil ibn Warqa, a shaikh of Khuzaa (the same who had acted as an emissary at Hudeibiya), rode to Medina and complained to Muhammad that the Beni Bekr attack was a breach of the ten years' truce.

The pretext was perhaps not unwelcome, and in January 630, the Apostle of God called the Muslims to arms. The leaders of Quraish, doubtless aware of the growing popularity of Muhammad, were profoundly alarmed. Abu Sofian, the victor of Uhud and once Muhammad's contemptuous and bitter detractor, hastened to Medina, but the proud war chief of Quraish was unable to obtain an interview. Obliged to solicit the intervention first of Abu Bekr, then of Umar ibn al Khattab and finally of Ali, he found himself everywhere repulsed and was obliged to return humiliated to Mecca.

Muhammad set out in January 630 with ten thousand followers for Mecca. The Emigrants and the Helpers followed him as one man, but the majority of the force must have consisted of contingents from the tribes. Beni Suleim, hitherto hostile, joined him on the march to Mecca. Moving rapidly, he camped at Marr al Dhahran outside Mecca, before Quraish were prepared. His uncle Abbas, realizing that the outcome was now inevitable, finally deserted Mecca and joined the advancing Muslims.

The same night Abu Sofian himself was brought in to surrender to Muhammad. The fiery Umar ibn al Khattab clamoured for leave to strike off his head, but the Prophet, in milder tones, invited him to accept Islam. The stout old warrior, even in his isolation amid ten thousand believers, admitted that there was no god but God, but confessed to a doubt whether Muhammad was His messenger. His doubts were quickly dispelled. "Testify that Muhammad is the Messenger of God before you lose your head," insisted Abbas, with the zeal of a last moment convert. The argument was unanswerable and Abu Sofian hastily complied.

The Prophet dictated his terms. Abu Sofian was to hasten back to Mecca and proclaim that all the citizens who remained in their houses and closed the doors, or who sought sanctuary in Abu Sofian's own house or in the square of the kaaba, would be safe.

Ten thousand Muslims then marched through the mountain valleys upon Mecca. Muhammad divided his force into four columns. Abu Ubaida ibn al Jarrah, of whom more will be heard later, led the Refugees, and advanced directly on the town accompanied by the Apostle himself. On the left, Zubair ibn al Awwam, moved in a parallel column. The western entrance to the city was committed to Saad ibn Ubada, shaikh of the Khazraj tribe of Medina, while Khalid ibn al Waleed with the bedouin contingents was to circle the whole city on the west and enter it from the south. Muhammad gave strict orders that no violence was to be used. His own tent was pitched on high ground immediately overlooking the town. Eight years before he had fled from Mecca under cover of darkness, and lain hidden three days in a cave on Mount Thor, which from his tent he could now see rising beyond the city. Now ten thousand warriors were ready to obey his least command and his native town lay helpless at his feet.

After a brief rest, he remounted his camel and entered the town, reverently touched the black stone and performed the seven ritual circuits of the kaaba. Then, standing before the temple, he commanded the idols to be cast down, broken and thrown away. Bilal, the gaunt negro,[8] gave the call to prayer and the Muslims lined up behind their Prophet for the ritual prostrations. This duty performed, a crier was sent through the streets, ordering the destruction of all family idols or images in private houses.

Muhammad the Conqueror was not vindictive. A general amnesty was proclaimed, from which less than a dozen persons were excluded, only four being actually executed. Ikrima, the son of Abu Jahal, escaped to the Yemen, but his wife appealed to the Apostle, who agreed to forgive him. This courageous woman then followed him to the Yemen and brought him back to be a few years later a distinguished Muslim commander. Hind, the savage wife of Abu Sofian, who had so brutally mutilated the dead body of Hamza after Uhud, was also among the proscribed.

The next step was to summon all the people of Mecca to the kaaba to swear loyalty. The men filed past first, each striking his hand against that of Muhammad and swearing fealty, as the seventy men of Medina had done at the second pledge of Aqaba eight years before. When the men were finished, all the women of the town were summoned to the square. Hind, instead of taking to flight, veiled her face and joined the crowd of women. The Apostle commenced by delivering a short address, in which he informed his audience that they would be asked to swear loyalty and also asked to swear that

[8] Page 47.

they would be loyal to him and would not associate anything with God. The men had only been asked to swear loyalty, so the irrepressible Hind called out, "You are asking us to swear something you did not require of the men." In the ensuing altercation, the Prophet recognized his heckler. "Are you Hind?" he asked. "Yes, I am Hind," she answered boldly. "This is a day on which the past is forgotten," said Muhammad quietly. "God has forgiven you."

Resuming his address, the Apostle exhorted the women to abstain from adultery and from infanticide, for the primitive Arabs had an unenviable reputation for killing unwanted girl babies. "We brought up our children when they were small," called out the argumentative Hind, "but when they were grown up you killed them at Bedr." (What a formidable woman she must have been. It is difficult not to feel sympathy for old Abu Sofian.

The Apostle then ordered Umar ibn al Khattab to accept the oaths of the women, for, we are told, he never touched the hand of a woman, except in the case of his wives. Such prudery seems remarkable to us in a man who had eleven wives and a concubine. Yet it embodies an aspect of Islam rarely appreciated in the West. The Muslims may each marry four wives, but extra-marital familiarities must be punished with the utmost severity. The West prides itself on its monogamy, but winks at, or is amused by, innumerable minor forms of dalliance. These incidents seem also to indicate that the wives of the early Muslims were far from being the languid denizens of secluded harems.[9] Although Hind was pardoned, a mere singing girl was executed for having recited verses obnoxious to the Prophet.

The Muslim occupation of Mecca was thus virtually bloodless. The fiery Khalid ibn al Waleed killed a few people at the southern gate and was sharply reprimanded by Muhammad for doing so. Although the Apostle had himself been persecuted in the city and although many of his bitterest opponents were still living there, he won all hearts by his clemency on his day of triumph. Such generosity, or statesmanship, was particularly remarkable among Arabs, a race to whom revenge has always been dear. His success had been won by policy and diplomacy rather than by military action. In an age of violence and bloodshed, he had realized that ideas are more powerful than force.

* * * * *

It will be remembered that, at the height of his persecution in Mecca, the Apostle of God had paid a visit to Taif, a town some forty miles to the east, but that he had been received with contempt and pelted with dirt and stones. The fall of Mecca filled the men of Taif with alarm and they decided to seize the initiative. They themselves were of the tribe of Thaqeef, but they were allies of the Hawazin, a large tribal confederation in the surrounding desert, which claimed with Thaqeef descent from a common ancestor. Summoning all their warriors, the two tribes prepared to move on Mecca.

Muhammad, who had now learned the importance of military intelligence,

[5] See also page 72, regarding the girl Amra who carried the war banner in the Quraish counter-attack at Uhud.

had sent a spy to the area, and received a report of these preparations. He marched to meet the enemy, at the head of his ten thousand followers. The clemency of his conquest of Mecca was rewarded by the addition to his force of two thousand Meccan volunteers.

The numerical strength of their forces perhaps rendered the Muslims careless, for they seem to have advanced without military precautions. At dawn, when they were moving down a narrow ravine debouching into the valley of Hunain, they were suddenly assailed from all sides by the enemy, who had been lying in ambush. The surprise was complete, the leading contingents panicked and fled back upon those behind them. Soon the whole force was jostling and struggling back through the narrow valley in utter confusion.

The Apostle himself was at first caught up in the rout. Then, clinging to the foot of the mountain slope bounding the narrow valley and supported by a handful of stalwarts, Abu Bekr, Umar ibn al Khattab, Ali, his uncle Abbas and Usama—the young son of Zeid who had been killed at Mota—he called aloud, "Where are you going, men? Rally to me. I am the Apostle of God. O citizens of Medina! O Helpers! O men of the pledge of the tree." [10] Old Abu Sofian, who was in personal attendance on the Prophet, whispered to a fellow Meccan slyly, "Nothing can stop them now but the sea!"

In the lead of the Hawazin, now in wild pursuit of the fleeing Muslims, rode a man on a red camel, bearing a black banner and carrying a long spear. As he overtook man after man of the fugitives, he thrust them through the back with his spear. Ali galloped after this lone rider and coming up behind him unperceived, hamstrung his camel so that he and it fell headlong. A man of the Helpers ran up and killed him.

Meanwhile the companions of the Prophet had begun to rally to his cries, especially the Helpers. Soon a hundred men surrounded him and moved forward to check the enemy's pursuit. "To me Helpers!" "To me Khazraj!" was the cry. The Hawazin were halted and the fleeing Muslims, finding that they were no longer pursued, returned to the battle. Once the believers rallied their overwhelming numbers were not to be resisted. The Beni Suleim bedouins, recently converted, also put in a spirited charge. Hawazin began to give ground, and fled for refuge to the surrounding mountains. The people of Taif retired to their town and closed the gates. To an Arab force armed only with swords, spears and bows, any masonry building was an obstacle. After besieging Taif in vain for fifteen days, the Prophet abandoned the attempt.

So complete had been the ultimate victory at Hunain that the Muslims had captured vast numbers of camels and sheep and had taken prisoners the greater part of the women and children of Hawazin. Returning foiled from Taif, Muhammad set himself to the division of the spoils. A deputation arrived from the defeated enemy, begging the release of the captive women and children, a request with which Muhammad immediately and graciously complied. Once more, in these days of victory, he sought to gain adherents rather than to exact retribution. It happened that Beni Saad, the tribe in which Muhammad had been suckled, were among the defeated at Hunain.

[10] Referring to the oath taken at Hudeibiya, see page 88.

An old woman was led up to him, claiming to be Shima, the little foster sister who had carried him about as an infant sixty years before. To prove her identity, she pulled down the shirt off her skinny shoulder and showed a faint white scar. "That was where you bit me one day when I was carrying you back to the tent," she said, looking indulgently at her former unruly charge. With that ready and democratic charm which he used so successfully to win hearts, the Apostle spread his own cloak on the ground and invited her to sit beside him to talk of old times. Later he dismissed her to her tribe with gifts.

While the Prophet had been releasing the families of Hawazin, his followers had been impatiently awaiting the division of the plundered flocks. Seeing him rise to go to his tent, the crowd closed around him crying, "O Apostle, divide the camels and flocks among us." So rudely did they push him that he lost his cloak. At length, getting his back against a tree, he called—doubtless in laughter—"Give me back my cloak, men, and I will distribute the flocks among you." To anyone familiar with the bedouin tribes of Arabia today, this little scene is pure joy. In a few lines, it epitomizes the tribesmen's greedy clamour for loot, combined with their free, humorous, familiar and yet respectful attitude to a leader whom they love and admire. Nothing has changed in these people in thirteen centuries.

Dividing the spoils, one-fifth was set apart for the Prophet himself as prescribed in the Qoran. He retained nothing of his share, but used it to win over by handsome gifts the recently converted Meccans and the chiefs of the bedouin tribes. Although he undoubtedly considered himself to be a religious reformer first and foremost, he always made use of worldly rewards to win converts and establish his authority. Believers were entitled to the best of both worlds, if God willed. His was not to urge the rich young men to sell all they had and come and follow him. Abu Sofian and his two sons, Yezeed and Muawiya, received especially generous gifts.

Few tasks are more exhausting than the division of plunder between clamorous bedouins (for I have done it in a small way myself). Muhammad showed infinite tact, patience and good humour until all had received their share. To Malik ibn Auf, the shaikh of Hawazin who had led his tribe against the Muslims, he restored his family and his flocks, in return for his conversion to Islam. Thereupon, with the peculiar bedouin facility for changing sides, Malik ibn Auf undertook to fight against his former allies, the people of Taif, cutting off their flocks and harassing all who left the city. Leaving a governor in charge of Mecca, the Prophet returned to Medina.

The manner in which he distributed the booty after Hunain nevertheless exposed the Apostle to some criticism. Admittedly he used the attraction of worldly wealth and gifts to win over his enemies or to convert unbelievers. He was always satisfied by the repetition of the Muslim profession of faith, without enquiring into the sincerity of the convert. But the principal criticism directed against his division of the plunder was that he made no effort to reward his devoted friends, but employed most of the loot in attempts to conciliate his enemies. The men of Medina in particular, who were the first to rally after the initial panic at Hunain, received scarcely any share of the plunder. When they protested, Muhammad collected the Helpers and addressed them. He pointed out that it was his complete reliance on the sincerity of their faith which had caused him to act as he had. "Others," he exclaimed, "may go home with camels and sheep, but you go home with God's Apostle. If all the world were to take one road and the Helpers another, I would go with the Helpers." Then looking up to Heaven, he cried: "Oh God! Show Thy mercy on the Helpers, and on the sons of the Helpers!" Such was the magnetism of his personality that his hearers burst into sobs "and wept," says the Arab historian, "until their beards were wet."

Muhammad was now universally recognized as the greatest power in Arabia, and deputations poured in from tribes all over the peninsula, anxious to declare their loyalty or at least to avert the hostility of the Muslims.

In September 630, the Apostle himself led a force of many thousands northwards towards the frontiers of the Byzantine Empire.[11] The weather in September in the Hejaz was intensely hot, the breath of the desert like a furnace. Many believers evinced a disinclination to take the field until the cooler weather came. But the Prophet quickly received a divine message. "They say it is too hot to go to war. Say: the fire of hell is hotter, if only they knew."

Halting at Tebook, Muhammad summoned to his presence John, the Christian prince of Aila, and concluded with him a treaty, under which he agreed to pay tribute. Deputations from the settlements at Jerba and Udhroh —the latter had once been the camp of a Roman legion—were received and arrangements concluded for them to pay an annual tax, although all the places concerned were under Byzantine protection. Meanwhile Khalid ibn al Waleed had been sent to bring the Christian ruler of Duma, the modern Jauf. With him also an agreement was made, including an annual tribute. After remaining for ten days in Tebook, the Muslim force returned to Medina without fighting.

This bloodless expedition was doubtless intended to show the flag on the Byzantine frontier. The Prophet had not forgotten Mota, but was preparing to avenge the defeat. In December 630, a deputation arrived with the submission of Taif.

In March 631, the greater pilgrimage was for the first time performed under Muslim control. Abu Bekr was sent to conduct the ceremonies. An announcement was made, forbidding non-Muslims thereafter to perform the pilgrimage. It will be remembered that the annual pilgrim rites at the kaaba had hitherto been carried out by idol-worshippers. Now, however, that the house of God had been cleansed of idols, only monotheists were to worship there. At the same time, an ultimatum was proclaimed, allowing all the tribes of Arabia four months' grace to accept Islam or to prepare for war.

Throughout 631, deputations continued to arrive from as far afield as Bahrain, Oman, Hadhramaut and the Yemen. Among the visitors was Wail ibn Hejr, prince of Hadhramaut, whom Muhammad received with honour. Muawiya, the son of old Abu Sofian, had been appointed one of the Prophet's secretaries, doubtless further to conciliate his father. Muhammad now desired Muawiya to take Wail ibn Hejr to his house in another part of the oasis and

[11] See Map X, page 83.

to entertain him. It was midday, the sun was blazing, the prince mounted his camel, leaving his host on foot. When Muawiya asked to be allowed to ride pillion behind his guest, the latter refused. "Then at least," said Muawiya, "let me borrow your sandals, for I came out barefoot." "What would my subjects say," replied Wail haughtily, "if they heard that a common man had worn the sandals of their prince"—a remark described later by the Prophet as "a remnant of heathenism". Little did Wail ibn Hejr imagine that the man running beside his camel was one day to be the most powerful emperor in the world of his time.

Muhammad had now, in the last two years, become a ruler of great power. He was occupied all day long and far into the night receiving deputations, dictating letters, settling disputes and despatching public business, with no trained staff, no facilities and being himself probably unable to read and write. Outside critics have often charged Muhammad with hypocrisy, by contrasting the poor and patient contemplative of the early Meccan ministry with the active and worldly politician of his later years. The difference is indeed striking, but the insinuation that it involved a conscious abandonment of spiritual values in favour of the fleshpots of the world may possibly be unjust. That he was fond of women cannot be denied. He himself had once said, "I love most in the world women and perfume but the apple of my eye is prayer." He was never interested in money, even when he was in a position to acquire immense riches. He died practically penniless, in so far as private wealth was concerned. The frugal simplicity of his diet never changed and to the last he lived in what we should consider a rude hut unfit for a stable.

Perhaps his transformation from a contemplative to an extremely active politician was unforeseen by him. It happened almost unawares when he migrated with his followers to Medina, where he found himself the chief of a community many of whom were destitute. A large proportion of the people of Medina resented the presence of these Meccan refugees and intrigued against them. The Emigrants took to raiding to support themselves and to vent their resentment on Quraish, who had driven them out. Before long the Prophet found himself deeply involved in war and intrigue and his religious meditations undoubtedly suffered. The Qoran itself reveals the change. The early Meccan revelations breathe an atmosphere of deep emotion. The later chapters revealed in Medina deal increasingly with politics, war and legislation.

The fact that Muhammad's career transformed him from something resembling an Old Testament prophet into a politician, a ruler and a lawgiver, has profoundly affected the development of Islam to this day. All the Apostle's successors automatically followed his example and combined religious and political rule. Islam never witnessed the rivalry between pope and emperor which so often disturbed mediaeval Europe. The Islamic lay state, in which the government is independent of the religious hierarchy, is a novelty of the last forty years, in imitation of Europe.

Morever it is well always to remember that Muhammad absorbed much more Jewish than Christian influence. In Medina there may have been as many Jews as Arabs. There was no Christian community in either Mecca or Medina, though individual Christians were to be met with occasionally. Moreover the general stage of development reached by the Arabs of the peninsula in the seventh century was not very unlike that of the Old Testament Hebrews. The Prophet's most militant pronouncements can be matched by many passages in the Old Testament, particularly in the first five books. It has been said that, if Muhammad had lived after Moses but before Christ, he might justly be recognized as one of the world's greatest reformers.

* * * * *

In February 632, Muhammad himself led a vast concourse of Muslims to perform the greater pilgrimage. Every action of the ageing Prophet on that occasion was watched and has ever since become enshrined in the ritual of the pilgrimage. Muhammad himself preached the sermon to the assembled crowds, at the conclusion of which he is said to have looked up to heaven and cried: "O Lord, I have delivered my message and fulfilled my mission." Dismissing the vast concourse of pilgrims, he returned to Medina.

During the last few months of the Apostle's life, rival prophets had set themselves up in different parts of Arabia, but their activities did not as yet appear to be formidable enough to cause any anxiety in Medina. They were only to assume importance after Muhammad's death. For the moment, all military opposition inside Arabia seemed to have ceased. Early in 632, however, Muhammad gave orders for an expedition to the Byzantine frontier. The more to emphasize that it was intended as revenge for Mota, he appointed Usama, the son of Zeid ibn Haritha killed at Mota, to command the raid, though he was only twenty years old, a selection which aroused some resentment from more experienced commanders. (This theme of private or family revenge is constantly recurring in the wars of the ancient Arabs.)

A few days later, in June 632, Muhammad complained of headache and fever, but next morning was well enough to present Usama with the banner for his raid. Nevertheless the fever and headache returned, though for two or three days he struggled to continue his usual routine. Then he gave way, and lay groaning and panting in the room of Aisha, his youngest and favourite wife, the daughter of his dearest friend Abu Bekr. An Arab woman is alleged to have told him that he was suffering from a disease of his lungs but he denied it, claiming his illness to be the result of an attempt to poison him four years earlier by the Jews of Kheibar. Perhaps by this means he hoped to achieve the crown of martyrdom, as having been killed by unbelievers. (In fact the symptoms reported by tradition seem to indicate that he was suffering from pneumonia.)

The fever, however, continued to increase. When he had been ill for a week and perceived that he was growing worse, he decided to address the people. Calling for a cold bath to allay his burning fever, he was able to stagger out of his room and say a few words to the crowd, defending his appointment of Usama ibn Zeid. The cold bath and the effort of making a speech aggravated his condition and next day he was unable to rise. In a weak voice he directed that Abu Bekr lead the public prayers in his place. Shortly afterwards, Abu Bekr happening to be absent, Umar ibn al Khattab began on one occasion to act as prayer leader, but Muhammad, recognizing his voice (for Aisha's room opened on the mosque) called loudly from his bed, "No. No. Only Abu Bekr."

On the tenth day of his illness the Prophet's symptoms became greatly aggravated. He was often unconscious, his body was wracked with pain, his fever burned like fire, he seemed at times to be delirious. Then the following morning, when Abu Bekr was leading the dawn prayer, the Prophet suddenly appeared at the door of Aisha's room, his face wreathed in smiles. He moved slowly forward, supported by two men, until he stood beside Abu Bekr. Too weak to perform the prostrations, Muhammad sat down on the ground and prayed. The congregation dispersed joyfully, imagining the Prophet to be convalescent, and Muhammad returned slowly to Aisha's room.

But this effort must have been a last rally of his strength rather than an alleviation of his illness. Exhausted by the effort, he lay down on his bed, probably a mere mattress on the earth floor. He lay half conscious, too weak to move. Suddenly he rallied again, called for water and wet his face, and cried, "O Lord, I beseech Thee assist me in the agonies of death." Aisha gently supported his head. He prayed in a whisper, "Lord grant me pardon. Eternity in paradise. Pardon."

Suddenly Aisha noticed that his head had grown heavy. Looking down she saw that his eyes were fixed. The Prophet of Arabia had passed into the presence of his Lord.

## *NOTABLE DATES*

| | |
|---|---|
| Siege of Medina | February 627 |
| Pilgrimage of Hudeibiya | February 628 |
| (Conclusion of peace between Byzantium and Persia was in | Summer 628) |
| Muslim Pilgrimage to Mecca | February 629 |
| Battle of Mota | September 629 |
| Muslim occupation of Mecca | January 630 |
| Battle of Hunain | Spring 630 |
| Expedition to Tebook | September 630 |
| Death of Muhammad | June 632 |

## *PERSONALITIES*

Othman ibn Affan, son-in-law of Muhammad.

Umar ibn al Khattab, Muhammad's principal supporter after Abu Bekr.

Hasan and Husain, infant sons of Ali and Fatima and grandsons of Muhammad.

Khalid ibn al Waleed, Amr ibn al Aasi } Quraish military leaders converted to Islam.

Muawiya, son of Abu Sofian, appointed Muhammad's secretary after the capture of Mecca.

Abbas ibn Abdul Muttalib, Muhammad's uncle.

# V

# *The Apostasy*

O you who believe, if any of you apostasize from his religion, Allah will bring a people whom He loves and who love Him, victorious over the unbelievers, battling in the path of Allah. *Qoran* V, 54

Whoever of you apostasizes from his religion, will die a heathen. . . . Their actions will be defeated in this world and the next. These are the people who will remain eternally in hell fire. *Qoran* II, 217

## V

## THE APOSTASY

WHEN Muhammad appeared smiling at the morning prayers on the day of his death, Abu Bekr, believing him now to be convalescent, had obtained leave to spend the day in an outlying oasis. As a result, Umar ibn al Khattab was the first prominent leader who came to the apostle's bedside, and raising the sheet which covered his face, gazed on the peaceful features of his master. For many years, Umar's life had been dominated by his devotion to his leader, and his mind was at first incapable of realizing that Muhammad could have died. Hastening from Aisha's room into the courtyard of the mosque, where the people were already assembling, he cried excitedly that the Apostle was not dead. Had not Moses in the wilderness spent forty days with God in the mountain, while the Children of Israel thought he was dead? In the same manner Muhammad would return, and then he would cut off the hands and the feet of any who had dared to say he was dead. Umar, almost delirious from shock, continued his excited ranting to the rapidly increasing crowd.

While this frenzied scene was in progress, Abu Bekr arrived and, walking across the courtyard where Umar was still wildly haranguing the crowd, passed into Aisha's room. Kneeling beside the dead man, he raised the sheet and kissed him on the face. Then, having assured himself that Muhammad had really passed away, he replaced the coverlet and went out into the crowded courtyard. As Umar refused to stop speaking, Abu Bekr moved to one side and began also to address the crowd. "O men," he called out, "if anyone worships Muhammad, let him know that Muhammad is dead. But if anyone worships God, God lives and does not die," and he quoted two verses from the Qoran specifically stating that Muhammad was mortal. Abu Bekr's words seemed suddenly to restore Umar to his senses, and as the dreadful truth for the first time penetrated to his understanding, he relapsed into silence.

This wild scene was scarcely over when a man hastened up to Abu Bekr to inform him that the people of Medina were gathering in the guest hall of the Beni Saeeda clan, proposing to elect Saad ibn Ubada, shaikh of the Khazraj tribe, as their successor to the Prophet. Muhammad was not dead an hour before the struggle for power threatened to rend Islam into rival factions. The mild and quiet Abu Bekr and the fiery Umar ibn al Khattab set off in haste to meet this new challenge. They were accompanied by the wise and gentle Abu Ubaida, one of the earliest converts, of whom we shall hear more later.

Ten years before, the Helpers had welcomed the persecuted Prophet into their homes and had given him their protection, but Muhammad had gradually become famous and powerful, and had been surrounded by his own Quraish relatives. The men of Medina, instead of being the protectors of the Muslims, found themselves in a subordinate position in their own town. Criticism was silenced during the Prophet's lifetime, but he was scarcely dead when the tribes of Aus and Khazraj decided to throw off the yoke of Quraish "Let them have their own chief," the men of Medina cried. "As for us, we will have a leader from ourselves." Once more Abu Bekr, a frail little man of sixty with a slight stoop, was faced with a scene of excited anarchy. He confronted it with apparent composure. "O men of Medina," he said, "all the good which you have said of yourselves is deserved. But the Arabs will not accept a leader except from Quraish."

"No! No! That is not true! A chief from us and another chief from you!" The hall was filled with shouting, the issue hung in doubt, the anarchy only increased.

"Not so," replied Abu Bekr firmly, "we are the noblest of the Arabs. Here I offer you the choice of these two, choose to which you will swear allegiance," and he pointed to his two companions, Umar ibn al Khattab and Abu Ubaida, both Qurashis.

"No, indeed," cried the excited Umar, "did not the Apostle of God appoint you to lead the prayers when he was ill? We swear allegiance to you," and seizing Abu Bekr's hand he pledged his loyalty to him.

While this noisy meeting had been in progress, a number of other Muslims had gathered round, some of them Meccans, others of different origins. These hastened to follow the example of Umar. Doubtless Abu Bekr, so loyal and simple in character, was universally trusted. The feeling of the meeting swung to his side and the men of Medina themselves rose and filed past him, giving him their hands in token of fealty. The crisis was past, but it had been a dangerous moment indeed. Ali ibn abi Talib, the Prophet's other close intimate, his cousin and son-in-law, had not been present. He was in Aisha's room, preparing the Apostle's body for burial. Some Arab historians allege that Ali was displeased with Abu Bekr's election, having himself coveted the khalifate.[1] He did not take the oath of loyalty until six months later, many of Beni Hashim following his example. Abu Bekr was of neither the rival clans—Beni Umaiya or Beni Hashim—but of a smaller branch of Quraish called Beni Taim.

Further disputes threatened on the subject of the place of interment, until Abu Bekr ordered that the Prophet be buried where he died, in Aisha's room.

* * * * *

During the last two or three years of his life, Muhammad had become the most famous man in Arabia, but he was far from being a ruler in the modern sense. The allegiance of the individual Arab was to his clan and his tribe. In Central Arabia and the Hejaz, there was no tradition of super-tribal government. For a year or two, the tribes might pay lip-service to a powerful neighbour, but few of them were ready to surrender their sovereignty to this new system. It will be recollected that the Muslims had constantly raided the

[1] The title of khalif adopted by Abu Bekr merely meant "successor".

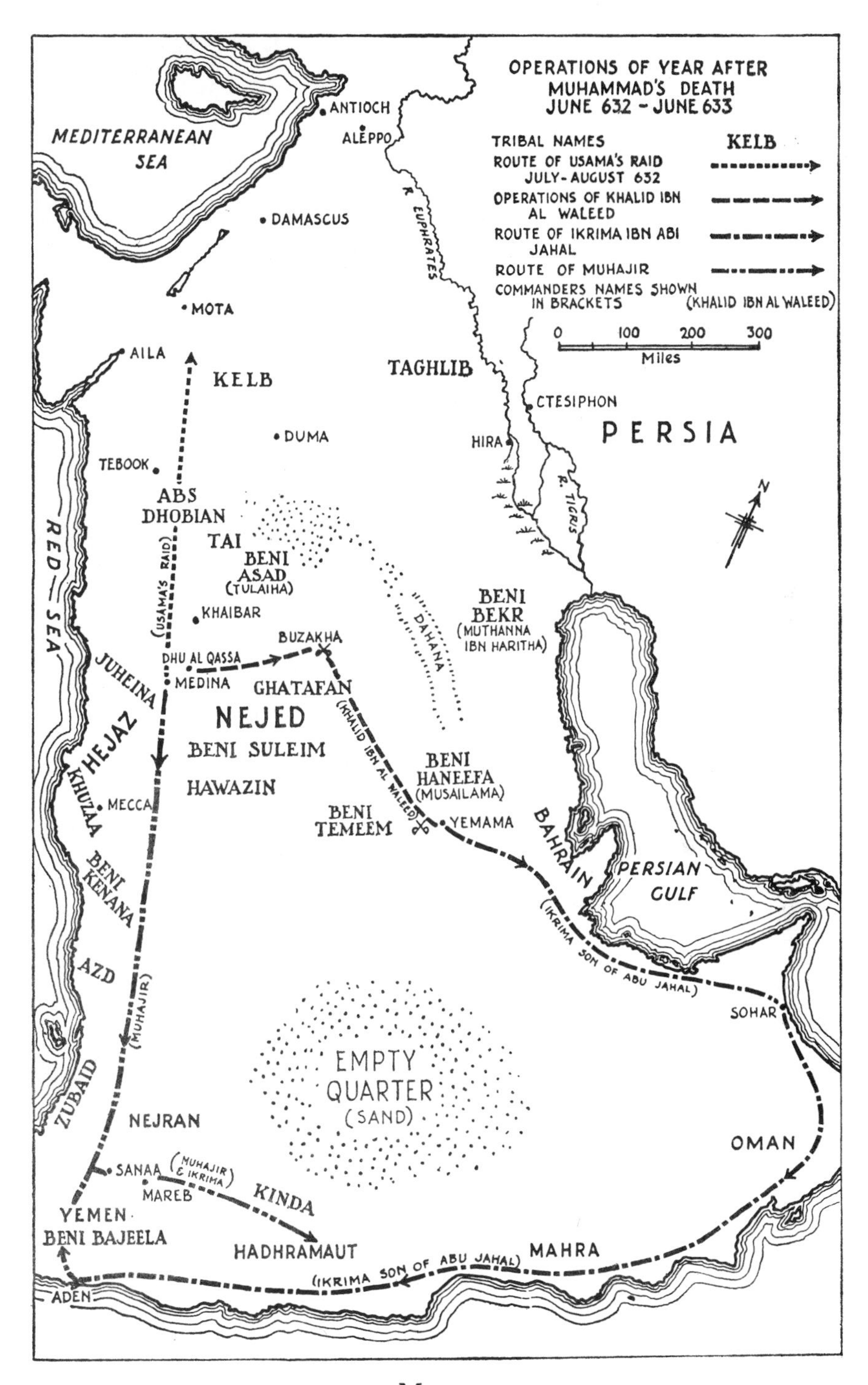

OPERATIONS OF YEAR AFTER MUHAMMAD'S DEATH JUNE 632 - JUNE 633
TRIBAL NAMES
KELB
ROUTE OF USAMA'S RAID JULY-AUGUST 632
OPERATIONS OF KHALID IBN AL WALEED
ROUTE OF IKRIMA IBN ABI JAHAL
ROUTE OF MUHAJIR
COMMANDERS NAMES SHOWN IN BRACKETS
(KHALID IBN AL WALEED)
0
100
200
300
Miles
MEDITERRANEAN SEA
ANTIOCH
ALEPPO
R. EUPHRATES
DAMASCUS
MOTA
AILA
KELB
TAGHLIB
CTESIPHON
PERSIA
HIRA
DUMA
TEBOOK
ABS
DHOBIAN
TAI
BENI ASAD
(TULAIHA)
R. TIGRIS
N
RED SEA
(USAMA'S RAID)
KHAIBAR
DAHANA
BENI BEKR
(MUTHANNA IBN HARITHA)
BUZAKHA
DHU AL QASSA
MEDINA
GHATAFAN
JUHEINA
NEJED
(KHALID IBN AL WALEED)
HEJAZ
BENI SULEIM
BENI HANEEFA
(MUSAILAMA)
KHUZAA
MECCA
HAWAZIN
BENI TEMEEM
YEMAMA
BAHRAIN
PERSIAN GULF
BENI KENANA
(IKRIMA SON OF ABU JAHAL)
AZD
(MUHAJIR)
SOHAR
EMPTY QUARTER
(SAND)
ZUBAID
NEJRAN
OMAN
SANAA
(MUHAJIR & IKRIMA)
MAREB
KINDA
YEMEN
BENI BAJEELA
HADHRAMAUT
MAHRA
(IKRIMA SON OF ABU JAHAL)
ADEN


Map XI

tribes, while the Prophet was living in Medina. Latterly, in the raid to Tebook, he had led a force several thousand strong. No nomadic tribe, scattered with its flocks in search of grazing, could easily concentrate such numbers of warriors for a battle. The bedouin is a practical diplomat, and knows what can and what cannot be done. In such circumstances, it was easier to ride with a deputation to Medina and make terms. Muhammad's conditions were not onerous. It was necessary to repeat the formula "There is no god but God and Muhammad is the Messenger of God". The majority of the tribes were heathen but a few were nominal Christians. Their Christianity sat lightly on them, for it does not appear to have changed any of their immemorial customs of raiding, plunder, poetry or blood revenge. To such, the repetition of a formula presented no great difficulty. More unwelcome was the fact that Muhammad expected them to pay a tax. The tribes were intensely wedded to their independence. A tax not only meant financial loss but signified subjection and this, to the bedouin, was a bitter pill. The tribesman's objective in life was glory, arising from bold deeds of war and plunder, and fantastic acts of generosity and hospitality, the whole celebrated in sonorous verse by innumerable poets. It was a Homeric age of poetry and bravado. Abu Bekr might claim that Quraish were the noblest of the Arabs, but to the bedouin they were mere town-dwellers—indeed a nation of shopkeepers.

Apart from the insistence on the pronouncement of the Muslim formula and the payment of a small tribute, Muhammad was in no position to rule Arabia. He had no government, no officials, no police, no army, no records. If he wished to carry out a raid, the Muslims were summoned to arms. They were paid by the division of the plunder. Thus the tribal chiefs returned from their visits to Medina very nearly as independent as they were before they left home. Nevertheless, in the Hejaz and Nejed, the tribes were more or less under the influence of the Muslims. But in the more remote areas of Oman, Hadhramaut and the Yemen, the Prophet had exercised little or no actual authority.

No sooner did the news spread that Muhammad was dead than the majority of the tribes decided to cease paying the tax. This movement is known in Islamic history as the apostasy. In reality, however, it is extremely doubtful whether more than a small proportion of the inhabitants of Arabia had seriously adopted Islam. The personality of Muhammad had inspired admiration, respect, in some cases fear. But now that Muhammad was dead, the tribes assumed that the incident was closed and that the old life could be resumed.

It will be remembered that the young Usama, the son of Zeid ibn Haritha, the Prophet's adopted son, had been ready to start for the Byzantine frontier in a raid of revenge for Mota. So threatening, however, was the situation after Muhammad's death, that even the fiery Umar advised Abu Bekr to cancel the expedition and keep the warriors of Islam concentrated in Medina to face all emergencies. But this hitherto quiet and gentle old man suddenly gave proof of unexpected determination. "Never," he exclaimed, "shall I consent to alter the smallest detail of an order given by the Apostle of God."

Usama set out, leaving Medina denuded of fighting men, and surrounded by doubtful or openly hostile tribes. Abu Bekr himself went out to a place a few miles north of Medina where the force was bivouacked and walked beside Usama a little way to bid him farewell. "Mount and ride," said the twenty-year-old commander, "or else I will dismount and walk beside you." "I will not ride," said the old man firmly. "I will walk and soil my feet for a little space in the way of God." Then after giving his blessing and parting injunctions, Abu Bekr turned back to Medina.

Meanwhile a new threat was rapidly developing. Muhammad's rise to power, resulting from his claim to a prophetic mission, had provoked imitators. Talha was a chief of the large nomadic tribe of Beni Asad, who camped in the area now known as Jebel Shammar in Northern Nejed. Talha has passed into history as Tulaiha, a scornful diminutive bestowed upon him by the Muslims—little Talha. Tulaiha now himself claimed the gift of prophecy in imitation of Muhammad. Further east, a certain Maslama put forward similar pretensions—and was also reduced by the believers to the contemptuous diminutive Musailama.[2] Meanwhile, from far and wide, the tax-collectors sent out by the Prophet were either put to death or with difficulty escaped with their lives to return to Medina.

The more remote tribes were satisfied with driving out the tax collectors, but those nearer to Medina presumably feared that the Muslims would attack them if they did not seize the initiative first. Abs and Dhobian, tribes from north of Medina, appear to have been the first to act. Camping at Dhu al Qassa, thirty miles east of Medina, they sent messengers to Abu Bekr, offering to adhere to the Muslim religion if the tax were abolished. A more subtle politician might well have temporized, hoping to gain time until Usama returned from his northern raid. But the new khalif was a simple, dedicated enthusiast. Without mincing words, he sent back the messengers with the reply that not one piece of old rope would be reduced from the tax.

Three days later, marauding bedouins appeared on the outskirts of the oasis, but the few men remaining in the town hastily sallied forth and drove them away. The gentle little khalif had suddenly become inspired with a new spirit. Collecting every available man who could bear arms, he set out by night from Medina and, at first dawn, surprised the camp at Dhu al Qassa. Bedouins, though they spent their lives in a state of desultory warfare, were ever too lazy or too undisciplined to post sentries or pickets outside the camp. The attack was a complete surprise, the tribesmen were thrown into confusion and, abandoning Dhu al Qassa, disappeared into the desert. A new energy, a ruthless aggressiveness, seemed to have been injected into Arab warfare.

In September 632, after two months' absence, Usama returned to Medina with plundered sheep and camels, though few details of his operations have been handed down to us. It appears that he raided bedouin tribes rather than Byzantine troops. No sooner was the oasis thus made safe than the indefatigable sexagenarian khalif set out once more, and, passing Dhu al Qassa, again

[2] The Arabic diminutive is formed by inserting the syllable -ai in the middle of a word. This -ai is pronounced as in the English word hay, not as in high.

fell upon Abs and Dhobian, who were camping some thirty miles further east, routing them once more. Unexpectedly, the gentle Abu Bekr had proved himself a far more aggressive commander than his master. Many of the faithful expostulated with Abu Bekr for leading these raids in person, but the old man replied, "I will go out with you and be your comrade and one of yourselves."

The Arab historians seem to suggest that, after the return of Usama, Abu Bekr organized eleven independent columns to operate simultaneously in the same number of different directions. If such a dispersal of forces was in reality contemplated, it does not appear to have been put into effect. In fact the only reasonable course was adopted and the rebellious tribes were chastised one after the other.

Meanwhile Abs and Dhobian had fallen back eastwards and joined the false prophet Tulaiha, at the head of his tribe, Beni Asad. Abu Bekr summoned all the force which the Muslims could raise and ordered a concentration at Dhu al Qassa. The khalif at the same time addressed a letter to the insurgent tribes. After quoting passages from the Qoran, he informed the rebels that he had sent an army of Emigrants and Helpers, the commander of which had been instructed first to appeal to them to repent and return to God. In the event of their refusal, however, he would fight against them, burn them with fire and kill them and carry away their women and children into captivity. He would accept nothing but Islam, he concluded.

The supreme command he entrusted to Khalid ibn al Waleed, the most experienced warrior available, who had been responsible for the Quraish victory at Uhud, and for the withdrawal from the defeat at Mota. Again the contrast with the Prophet's own military operations is striking. As we have seen, Muhammad, shortly before his death, had put the northern force under the command of the twenty-year-old Usama, because he was the son of Zeid ibn Haritha and had been brought up in the Prophet's family, and because he desired to avenge the death of his father at Mota. Thus it will be seen that the Apostle had chosen the commander for this important military operation on purely emotional grounds—the desire for revenge and love for the memory of Zeid—rather than for reasons of practical efficiency. It may well have been the warm, emotional side of the Prophet's character which enabled him to command the devotion of his followers, but war is a stern practical occupation. Khalid ibn al Waleed, the veteran fighter, had accompanied Usama's force as a volunteer in the ranks. As soon, however, as Abu Bekr was free to take his own decisions, he placed his most experienced commander in charge of his principal force.

From Dhu al Qassa, Khalid ibn al Waleed set off into Nejed with some 4,000 men, Abu Bekr at last consenting to return to Medina. Advancing against Tulaiha and his Beni Asad, who were concentrated at Buzakha, Khalid received on the way the submission of a great part of the tribe of Tai, for ever famous in Arab story for the fabulous generosity of its former chieftain Hatim. It is impossible for us today to discover wherein lay the prophetic gift of Tulaiha, for the Muslim historians have merely loaded his name with ridicule. Uyaina, the chief of the neighbouring tribe of Ghatafan, who joined

Tulaiha before the battle, perhaps gives us the most plausible explanation. "A prophet of our own," he is alleged to have argued, "is better than a prophet of Quraish. Moreover, Tulaiha is alive, whereas Muhammad is dead."

No details of the battle of Buzakha have been handed down to us by the Muslim historians. Suffice it to say that, when Beni Asad began to waver, Uyaina is alleged to have withdrawn with the Ghatafan, whereupon Beni Asad also broke and fled. Tulaiha escaped with his family to Syria, was subsequently pardoned, became a Muslim and fought bravely in the wars against Persia. He appears to have had (like all bedouins) a ready sense of humour. Some years later, when passing through Medina on his way to the pilgrimage, he paid his respects to Umar ibn al Khattab, then become khalif. Umar reproved him for the murder of a certain famous Muslim at the time of Khalid's operations. "Why," replied the imperturbable Tulaiha, "was it not better that by my hand Ukkasha should become a martyr in heaven, rather than that I by his should descend into hell-fire?" When Umar enquired what had since become of his prophetic gift, Tulaiha answered, doubtless with a twinkle, "It was but a puff or two, as if with a bellows."

Tulaiha, having made good his escape, Beni Asad now made submission, and so great was the moral effect of this victory, that Beni Suleim and Hawazin hastened to follow their example and to pay the tax. All were freely pardoned except such individuals as were known to have killed Muslims during the revolt. All these were killed by the same methods as each had used in killing a Muslim. Some were burned alive, some stoned, some thrown over precipices, some shot through with arrows.

South-east of Beni Asad and Ghatafan lay the tribal areas of Beni Temeem and Beni Haneefa (Beni Temeem indeed still live in considerable numbers in this area, mostly as oasis-dwellers. Part of the tribe migrated to Iraq and now occupies lands west of Baghdad.) Beni Haneefa were the supporters of Musailama, the other rival prophet. Many clans of Beni Temeem hastened to visit Khalid ibn al Waleed, but the Beni Yerboa branch of the tribe, under its chief, Malik ibn Nuweira, hung back. Malik was a chief of some distinction, a warrior, noted for his generosity and a famous poet. Bravery, generosity and poetry were the three qualities most admired among the Arabs. Unwilling perhaps to demean himself by bowing to Khalid, he ordered his followers to scatter and himself apparently moved away across the desert alone with his family. Abu Bekr had given orders that the test to be applied to suspected rebels was that they be asked to repeat the Muslim formula and that they answer the Adhan or call to prayer. There seemed, therefore, to be no great danger in not submitting to Khalid in person, for, if overtaken by the Muslims, Malik could always repeat the profession of faith and answer the call to prayer. Khalid, however, preferred more aggressive methods and sent out parties of horsemen to round up the fugitives and plunder their property. One such party seized Malik ibn Nuweira and his family and brought them in to Khalid, although they claimed to be Muslims. The men of Medina who were with the army protested vigorously against Khalid's ruthlessness, but without avail. The prisoners were placed under guard but, during the night, Malik ibn Nuweira and his supporters were killed in cold blood. Within twenty-four hours, Khalid had married the widow of his victim.

There was nothing wrong in marrying the widow of an enemy on the battlefield. Muhammad himself had done the same at Kheibar, when Kinana, the Jewish leader, was killed. The Prophet married his widow, the lovely Safiya, the same night. But Kinana had not been a Muslim, whereas Malik ibn Nuweira had been executed while professing to be a believer. Indeed, Khalid's immediate marriage to the beautiful Leila gave rise to the suspicion that Malik had been killed with the object of making her available to the conqueror.

The men of Medina, who had already opposed Khalid's ruthless actions, were outraged by the death of Malik. A certain Abu Qatada, an erstwhile friend and companion of the Prophet, hastened to Medina to complain to Abu Bekr, who summoned Khalid to answer the accusation. Umar ibn al Khattab, who, though fierce and impetuous, was as simple and dedicated a Muslim as Abu Bekr himself, pressed the khalif to deprive Khalid of his command. The latter, returning to Medina, claimed that he had not ordered the execution of Malik but that his instructions to the guards had been misunderstood. The wise Abu Bekr, whatever he may have thought of the morals of his lieutenant, was aware of his prowess. "I will not sheathe a sword which God has drawn for His service," he exclaimed. Khalid's excuses were accepted, but, before he left Medina, he exchanged hot words with Umar ibn al Khattab—which were to produce serious consequences in the years ahead.

Meanwhile the khalif had authorized Khalid to advance against Musailama and Beni Haneefa, who were still in arms. This tribe formed part of the greater tribal group of Beni Bekr ibn Wail,[3] who led a pastoral life in the deserts extending from the Dahana sand-dunes to the lower Euphrates. Beni Bekr were partly Christian—at least in name—and partly heathen. Now, however, the Beni Haneefa division of Beni Bekr stood stoutly in support of their prophet Musailama, a man who had laid claim to the gift of prophecy even in Muhammad's life-time, and who apparently alleged, at least after the death of the Apostle, that the latter had recognized in him the signs of a fellow-prophet.

Tradition alleges that Musailama had even communicated with Muhammad, offering to share the world with him. "From Musailama the Apostle of God to Muhammad the Apostle of God," he is said to have written. "Let us divide the earth between us, half to you and half to me."

"From Muhammad the Apostle of God to Musailama the liar," the Prophet is alleged to have replied. "The earth is the Lord's. He causes such of His servants to inherit it as He pleases."

Meanwhile Abu Bekr had sent reinforcements from Mecca and Medina to join Khalid, who now moved forward to engage the enemy. The two forces met in the sandy plain of Aqraba in Yemama, in south-eastern Nejed. It was Beni Haneefa who opened the battle with a wild charge of such impetuosity that the Muslims were at first swept from their feet and the excited bedouins even entered and plundered the tent of Khalid himself. But the Muslims

[3] No connection with Beni Bekr of Mecca, mentioned on page 94.

rallied. Zeid ibn al Khattab, the brother of Umar, bearing the banner of the Emigrants, led forward the Meccans until he himself was cut down. Thabit ibn Qais, with the standard of the Helpers, advanced at the head of the men of Medina, meeting death in the enemy's ranks. A furious sword-slashing mêlée swayed to and fro, made even more exhausting by a hot south wind blowing up the sand in the faces of the Muslims. At length, after several hours of battle, Beni Haneefa began to waver. The battle must presumably have been fought by one of the many small oases in this area, for the retreating enemy took refuge in a walled garden of date palms, barricading the door behind them. At last Beraa, the first of the twelve leaders from Medina who had pledged loyalty to the Prophet at the second Aqaba, and Abu Dujana, who had fought with the Prophet's sword at Uhud, were hoisted on to the wall near the door by their companions. Jumping down into the midst of the enemy, Abu Dujana was slashed to death in a few seconds. Beraa, however, was able to reach the door and open it. The Muslims poured in like a torrent and a desperate sword battle ensued round the trunks of the palm trees in the cramped garden. Beni Haneefa, penned in and unable to withdraw further, were fighting literally with their backs to the wall. At last they were overwhelmed, those in the garden being exterminated to a man.

Among the Muslims also the casualties were far higher than in any previous battle. Indeed, judged by modern standards, this seems to have been the first really serious fighting in which the Muslims were engaged—a foretaste of what was to come. At Bedr, Quraish had suffered forty-nine killed out of nearly a thousand combatants. At Uhud, seventy-four Muslims had been killed out of about seven hundred. At this battle of the so-called Garden of Death, 1,200 Muslims are alleged to have been killed.[4] If we suppose Khalid to have been in command of 5,000 men, these were considerable casualties, for the figures ostensibly refer only to the dead. The wounded are likely to have been at least as numerous, which would give more than 2,400 casualties out of 5,000. It must be admitted, however, that the figures given by Arab historians are so vague as to make their statistics utterly unreliable.

Musailama the liar was himself killed by Wahshi, the same javelin thrower who had slain the Apostle's uncle Hamza at Uhud. Wahshi had transferred his allegiance to the side of the believers, as many of his betters had done. He could, however, scarcely claim to have become a good Muslim, for he remained a confirmed drunkard to the end of his life. Tradition relates that, as an old man, he used to show his visitors a short javelin which he invariably carried and say, "With this I killed Hamza and Musailama, the best and the worst of men."

The critical situation in Nejed before the Battle of Yemama, or the Garden of Death, had caused Abu Bekr to despatch particularly strong reinforcements from Medina to Khalid. Among them were many Emigrants and Helpers who were doubtless in the thick of the fighting with the result that the casualties were especially heavy among the Companions[5] of the Prophet.

[4] Tabari claims that 10,000 were killed from both sides together.

[5] Hereafter the title of Companions was used of those who had known or served with Muhammad.

Indeed, so many were killed of those who knew part or all of the Qoran by heart, that it was this battle which first gave rise to the idea of its collation into one volume. Hitherto the various portions of the Prophet's revelations had been retained only in the memories of his Companions or in notes taken down here and there on miscellaneous materials by such as could read and write.

Zeid, the brother of Umar ibn al Khattab, was among those killed at the Battle of Yemama. When Umar's son, Abdulla, returned to Medina in safety, his father reproved him for surviving the death of his uncle. "Father," the young man is said to have replied, "he asked God for martyrdom and his prayer was granted. I did the same but my petition was refused."

The next day, Khalid moved his forces up to Hajr, the "capital" of Musailama, and sent a captive Haneefa chief to demand its surrender. He promised the defenders their lives but claimed the right to all their worldly possessions. The emissary returned ostensibly bearing the reply of the defenders of the town, stating that the terms were too severe and that they would fight it out. At the same time, masses of armed men could be seen manning the walls. In reality the messenger had himself arranged for the old men, women and children to put on helmets and mount the battlements. Khalid was deceived and consented to accept their surrender, if they handed over their weapons and all their gold and silver. Several thousand of the prisoners were sold as slaves. Khalid married the daughter of the Beni Haneefa chief, an action which provoked a rebuke from the khalif, who wondered how Khalid had time to marry while the blood of the Muslim martyrs was still not dry.

The Battle of Yemama (fought in December 632 or January 633) put an end to all resistance in Nejed and the tribes allied to Beni Haneefa came in to Khalid, and made their surrender. Meanwhile Abu Bekr had sent a message to Khalid, ordering him to put all the adult males of the rebellious tribes to death. Fortunately the armistice had already been concluded. Beni Haneefa were, in the years to follow, to fight gallantly on behalf of Islam, and to have massacred many thousands of them in cold blood after their defeat would have been not only inhuman but unwise.

It is difficult for us now to analyse the motives which inspired the mild Abu Bekr to send so savage an order. The most plausible explanation perhaps lies in his utter devotion to Muhammad. We have already seen that he insisted on sending Usama ibn Zeid on his raid to the Byzantine frontier after the Prophet's death, in spite of the fact that all Arabia was in revolt. The situation was utterly different from that in which Muhammad had ordered this force to mobilize, but Abu Bekr indignantly refused to cancel the orders given by the Apostle. When, however, a new situation arose, for which the Apostle had left no instructions, he used his own discretion and acted with considerable perspicacity.

Now it was a peculiar feature of the Prophet's policy that he was generous to unbelievers and idolaters but merciless to apostates. An idolater, even if overtaken in arms fighting against the Muslims, had only to call out the profession of faith and his life must be spared. In the lifetime of Muhammad, believers had at times complained to him of the manifest insincerity of such conversions. Galloping after some fugitive polytheist, they said, they had been in the act of raising sword or lance to kill the enemy of God, when he had quickly called, "There is no god but God and Muhammad is His Apostle." Thereupon the sword must be lowered and the idolater escape. Was it just that in such circumstances their professions be accepted and the Muslims defrauded of their spoils? The Prophet, however, insisted on regarding such persons as true Muslims.

If, however, such men, having once professed Islam, subsequently recanted, Muhammad exacted extremely severe retribution, normally the death sentence. Thus if Beni Haneefa and their associates be regarded as apostates, Abu Bekr would find the Prophet's verdict already given. In such circumstances, as we have seen, the khalif was unwilling to use his discretion. The orders of Muhammad must be literally executed. Fortunately, however, the Apostle had also said that terms, once granted, must be faithfully observed. Thus the armistice terms granted by Khalid were accepted by Abu Bekr. Not only so, but when Khalid sent deputations from the defeated tribes to the khalif, he received them graciously and sent them back to their tribes unmolested.

It is interesting here to notice that, during the Wahhabi revival in the 1920's, when the tribe of Mutair rebelled against ibn Saud, orders were given that all the men of Mutair were to be put to death. Political rebellion was regarded as apostasy from religion.

This attitude finds its origin in the fact that Muhammad made himself the political as well as the religious ruler of his people, and that government has ever since been combined with religious leadership in Muslim states, at least until the twentieth century. This identification of religion with political rule has been a fundamental cause of misunderstanding on the part of Europeans in Muslim countries. Non-Muslims are inclined to be critical of the intervention of Muslim religious teachers in politics and to ask why they do not limit themselves to their proper field of spiritual teaching, leaving politics to those whose concern they are. But this separation of the religious from the political is a Christian viewpoint. To the old Muslim, if not to the modern Arab nationalist, religion and politics were inseparable. By the same token, political revolt became religious apostasy.

* * * * *

The great sand desert in the southern half of the Arabian Peninsula—the Empty Quarter—has always severed the coastal regions of Oman and Hadhramaut from the Arabs of Nejed and from the fertile northern lands of Syria and Iraq. These areas on the Indian Ocean, now as then, absorb many influences from further afield, from Persia, Baluchistan, India, Malaya and East Africa. The sand desert at their backs has made them look out over the sea to the outside world. By corollary, they have played only a minor part in the history of the Arabs further north. By his victories in Central Arabia, Khalid had subjected the strongest and the most warlike tribes to the rule of Medina. The conquests of the areas beyond the sand desert were thenceforward scarcely more than subsidiary operations, in so far as the main stream of Arab expansion was concerned.

The Beni Haneefa defeated at Yemama were only one component of the much larger tribal group of the Beni Bekr ibn Wail ibn Rabia (from which the great modern bedouin tribe of Anaza is also descended). Beni Bekr ranged over a wide area of territory from Hira and the lower Euphrates along the southern shores of the Persian Gulf. During the heyday of the Lakhmide dynasty of Hira, Beni Bekr formed a large part of their subjects, but it will be recollected that in 605 the reigning Lakhmide prince had quarrelled with the Great King and a Persian Satrap had been appointed to rule directly over the Arabs of the Lower Euphrates. Ever since then, Beni Bekr had been in almost continuous rebellion and had indeed, in about 606, gained the first Arab victory over Persian troops, perpetuated in Arab history as the day of Dhu Qar.

With the defeat of one of their branches, Beni Haneefa, Beni Bekr found themselves between two great political forces. For many years, they had been engaged in guerilla warfare against the Persians, but were in no danger from their rear, where the divided tribes of Nejed were engaged in their usual internecine feuds. But the appearance of Khalid ibn al Waleed at the head of many thousand aggressive Muslim warriors on their southern flank, suddenly placed Beni Bekr between two fires.

As is usually the case with Arab tribes, Beni Bekr were divided and uncertain. Their decision to cast in their lot with the Muslims was largely influenced by one of their principal chiefs, Muthanna ibn Haritha, of the Beni Shaiban clan, the heroes of Dhu Qar. The orthodox Arab historians, townsmen writing at a later date, tend to attribute every action taken at this period to religious motives. It is perhaps more probable that the Beni Bekr decision was influenced rather by policy than by religion. They were at perpetual feud with the Persians. Here unexpectedly was a powerful force, composed chiefly of bedouin tribesmen like themselves. Would it be wise for them to resist this new Arab power in a war of mutual extermination or to secure their support for further hostilities against the Persians? It was largely the influence of Muthanna which persuaded Beni Bekr to join the Muslims and secure their help against Persia. The principal chiefs of the tribe thereupon proceeded to Medina, where they were welcomed by Abu Bekr.

Before proceeding, however, with an account of the hostilities against Persia, it will be well to dispose of the minor operations which took place before the "apostate" rebellion was finally subdued.

* * * * *

Some resistance was offered in the vicinity of Bahrain after the battle of Yemama, but thereafter the war front was moved to Oman. In both areas, a number of Muslim pockets of influence had remained, in spite of the general apostasy. Ikrima, the son of Abu Jahal, advanced into Oman, where he was joined by Hudhaifa and Arfaja, two tribal chiefs. In a single battle, the enemy was defeated and the province conquered.

Abu Jahal, it will be remembered, had been an uncle of Muhammad and one of his bitterest opponents and had been killed at Bedr. But the situation had now changed entirely. Instead of the leaders of Mecca regarding with jealousy the activities of their poor relation Muhammad, Quraish had now realized that Islam was rapidly transforming them into a ruling aristocracy. The son of Abu Jahal had become a Muslim military leader, while Abu Sofian and his family were to rise even higher.

Hudhaifa, a tribal chieftain, was left as governor of Oman, perhaps a sign of the little importance attached to the area by Medina, or of the inability of the khalif to send a strong Muslim force so far afield. Ikrima, meanwhile, was advancing through Mahra. Nothing proverbially succeeds like success, especially among undisciplined tribes. The victories of Khalid in Nejed and the re-establishment of order in Oman resulted in large tribal contingents joining the son of Abu Jahal in his southward march.

While Oman and Mahra were thus being brought under control, anarchy had been rampant in the Yemen. Here, also, even during Muhammad's lifetime, a rival prophet had appeared under the name of Al Aswad, who, however, had been assassinated a short time before the death of the Apostle. His movement thereupon collapsed but left Nejran and the Yemen in utter chaos and confusion. As many of the tribes and chiefs of the area were later on to play a distinguished part in the Arab conquests, it may be worth while referring to them in passing.

The flourishing Christian community of Nejran [6] had concluded a treaty with Muhammad before his death, which Abu Bekr now agreed to renew. The most important tribes in revolt were Zubaid, under their chief Amr ibn Madi Kerib, of whom we shall hear more, and the Kinda, under Al Ashath ibn Qais. Another chief, Qais ibn Makshouh, had meanwhile seized Sanaa.

Jareer ibn Abdulla, on the other hand, chief of the Beni Bajeela, declared his loyalty to Islam.[7] In no case, however, does the whole of a great tribe seem to have espoused one cause or the other, but many small clans in the mountains adopted an independent line or amused themselves robbing or raiding their neighbours. Such was the condition to which the once civilized and prosperous south Arabian kingdom had been reduced. It will be remembered that, in 574, the country had been conquered by the Persians,[8] and placed under a Viceroy of the King of Kings. But as a result of the collapse of Persia after the murder of Chosroes Parwiz, communications with and reinforcements from the home government had been cut off. The sons of the viceroy and the remains of the Persian garrison were left to fend for themselves and formed another party, which, by allying itself to some tribes and fighting against others, increased rather than moderated the general chaos.

When news of the anarchy of the Yemen reached Abu Bekr, he was without men. Every available warrior had been sent with Khalid ibn al Waleed to fight against Musailama, the false prophet. Nothing daunted, the khalif sent Al Muhajir ibn abi Umaiya (the brother of Umm Salma one of Muhammad's widows) to re-establish order without troops. He was instructed to raise a levy of men from the loyal tribes between Medina and the Yemen. Mean-

[6] See page 24. [7] Map XI, page 107. [8] Page 24.

while instructions were sent to Ikrima ibn abi Jahal, who was in Oman, to hasten through Mahra and down the sea coast to Aden, to come to the assistance of Muhajir.

Fortunately the rebel tribes in true bedouin style, though all in revolt against Islam, were likewise at loggerheads with one another and acted on no agreed plan. When at last Muhajir arrived from Medina with some loyal levies and Ikrima reached Aden from Oman, Amr ibn Madi Karib of Zubaid realized that his followers would be outnumbered. Being a jovial bandit, remarkably innocent of scruples, he cast about in his mind how to make peace with the Muslims. He hit upon the idea of kidnapping his fellow rebel, Qais ibn Makshouh. This done, Amr ibn Madi Karib rode in to Muhajir to make his peace, dragging with him his fellow apostate loaded with chains, as evidence of his devotion to the government.[9] Muhajir, however, was not so easily persuaded, and placing Amr himself also in fetters, despatched both chiefs to Abu Bekr in Medina. The khalif pardoned them both and, after exacting an oath of allegiance, sent them back to their tribes.

In the spring of 633, the principal rebels of the Yemen having been thus disposed of, Muhajir and Ikrima joined forces at Mareb and moved eastwards against the Kinda tribe, under Ashath ibn Qais. This chieftain had ridden to Medina two years before with his fellow shaikh, Wail ibn Hejr (the same who made Muawiya run beside his camel). On this occasion, Ashath ibn Qais had sealed his devotion to Islam by becoming affianced to the sister of Abu Bekr. On the death of Muhammad, however, he could not resist the temptation to reassert his independence of Medina.

Muhajir and Ikrima now besieged him in his castle of Nujair. The Kinda fought back gallantly and made many desperate sorties but eventually provisions began to run out. The wily Ashath entered into negotiations with Ikrima, and agreed to surrender the town if the lives of ten men could be spared. To this the Muslim commanders agreed, the gates of the fortress were opened and Ashath rode out to the Muslim commander with the ten names written out. Muhajir gave orders for the ten to be spared, the remainder of the men to be massacred and the women and children to be sold into slavery.

Then, however, Muhajir noticed that Ashath had omitted his own name from the list of ten, which included his relatives and family. He ordered Ashath to be decapitated, but was persuaded to remand the order and to send the apostate chief in chains to the khalif. Abu Bekr not only pardoned him but permitted him to consummate his marriage with his sister.

With the reconquest of Hadhramaut, the whole Arabian peninsula was reduced once more to obedience to Islam. Its subjection was now indeed far more complete than in the days of the Prophet himself. The chiefs had then visited Muhammad and made a formal adherence to Islam, but there had been no trial of strength. Now, however, a showdown had taken place, the rebels had been utterly defeated all over the peninsula, and had everywhere been coerced into abject surrender.

The war of the apostasy had occupied one year after the death of the Apostle of God. Now all Arabia was united under one firm rule, and the Muslims,

[9] Tabari, however, does not mention this incident.

burning with zeal for religion, honour and plunder were casting their eyes around for fresh and more distant fields to conquer.

## *NOTABLE DATES*

| | |
|---|---|
| Death of Muhammad and election of Abu Bekr as his successor | June 632 |
| Usama's Raid | July–September 632 |
| Bedouin tribes dispersed by Abu Bekr at Dhu al Qassa | August 632 |
| Battle of Buzakha, defeat of Tulaiha | October or November 632 |
| Battle of Yemama and defeat of Musailama | December 632 or January 633 |
| Oman subdued | February or March 633 |
| Yemen subdued and final suppression of the Apostasy | May–June 633 |

## *PERSONALITIES*

Abu Bekr, Successor or Khalif.

Ali ibn abi Talib, Umar ibn al Khattab, Abu Ubaida } His principal supporters.

Tulaiha, Musailama } The false prophets.

Khalid ibn al Waleed, chief Muslim commander.

Muthanna ibn Haritha, chief of Beni Bekr.

Ikrima ibn abi Jahal, former enemy of Islam now Muslim commander.

Amr ibn Madi Karib, chief of Zubaid tribe in Yemen. Apostate but later Muslim commander.

Jareer ibn Abdulla, chief of Beni Bajeela in the Yemen, remained loyal to Islam; later to be a Muslim commander.

# VI

## *Pirate Strategy*

They were always a warlike people, seldom being at peace either with one another or their neighbours. Their chief excellence consisted in managing horses, and the use of bows, swords and lances. Their learning lay wholly in their poetry, to which their genius greatly inclined them.

OCKLEY, *History of the Saracens*

Nomads lead an isolated life, undefended by walls. Hence they look for protection to themselves alone. Always armed and watchful, they are ever on the look out for any sign of danger, being full of confidence in their own courage and power. For courage has become one of their deepest qualities and audacity a second nature to them.

IBN KHALDUN

[Translation from Charles Issawi, *An Arab Philosophy of History*.]

Thus much is certain; that he that commands the sea is at great liberty and may take as much and as little of the war as he will.

FRANCIS BACON

## VI

## PIRATE STRATEGY

THE successful conclusion of the operations in the Yemen and the Hadhramaut marked the termination of the so-called apostasy. The peninsula of Arabia, south of the Byzantine and Persian borders, had been cowed into submission. It is interesting to notice that the greater part of the area had, verbally at least, bowed to the supremacy of Muhammad during his lifetime, almost without the use of force. The small and, in most cases, ineffective raids carried out by the Muslims during the Prophet's life had certainly not coerced the tribes into submission. The fact that so great a part of Arabia had consented to pay taxes to the Muslims without coercion is an extraordinary testimony to Muhammad's personality. It is true that in many or most cases, verbal submission was made only by the chiefs who rode with tribal delegations to see Muhammad in Medina. But the effect on these leaders, so jealous of their independence, must have been most remarkable. Indeed, the fact that nearly all renounced their pledges as soon as they heard that Muhammad was dead, seems in itself to be proof that Islam to them meant Muhammad and nothing more. It is scarcely more than academic to wonder what would have happened if the Apostle had lived for another ten years. Could he have maintained and consolidated his control by the same peaceful means and personal ascendency as he had exercised hitherto? A prominent feature of the Arab character, today as much as then, is their extreme turbulence and dislike of authority, as a result of which they are always discontented with whatever government is over them. Thus they are nearly always ready to welcome its overthrow if only to try a new system. This constant ferment of insubordination makes the Arab countries easy to conquer, especially if the invader obtains the co-operation of the many local malcontents. But no sooner does the invader become the ruler than the very spirit which facilitated his seizure of power begins to work against him. Now he is the government and the Arabs soon tire of his rule and begin to seek for an alternative.

During the greater part of Muhammad's ministry, he was struggling desperately for his own survival. It was only in the last four years of his life that success suddenly crowned his efforts. Most of the tribal delegates visited him only in the last two years of his life. It is not conceivable that, in this extremely short period, the tribesmen all over Arabia immediately became true Muslims. If, on the other hand, there was little religious feeling in the tribal protestations of submission, then a reaction was inevitable as soon as the novelty had worn off.

The fickleness of the Arabs is perhaps well known, but they possess also another quality more rarely appreciated. Constantly turbulent and insubordinate, they are yet capable now and again of giving their complete devotion to a leader whom they respect. In Arabia, however, this personal devotion can only be won by a man whom they can actually meet. The extraordinary influence wielded by Muhammad must have been of this nature and, therefore, limited to the men who had met and conversed with him. It could not inspire the remote tribesmen of Beni Bekr, still less those of Oman or Hadhramaut. Thus, if the Prophet had lived for ten years longer, his personal magnetism would have drawn many more adherents from those who came to know him. A further use of force, however, would almost certainly have been necessary in the more remote districts. But such punitive measures would have been required at irregular intervals and in different places. The whole peninsula would not have rebelled simultaneously as it did after his death. When, however, the general "apostasy" did occur and the rebels were defeated by Khalid with great slaughter, the authority of Medina was much more firmly established than it ever had been in the days of Muhammad himself.

Nevertheless, many problems faced the khalif, whether or not he foresaw them. The nomadic tribes had their own way of life hundreds, rather perhaps thousands, of years old. Unending tribal warfare was the background of their emotional existence. The casualties in any given battle were not heavy, but, as hostilities never ceased, the total losses in manpower were very great. Although they were all desperately poor, at least by our standards, the object of their endless wars and feuds was primarily honour rather than gain. Pastoral life in these vast deserts was monotonous in the extreme. The wild excitement and glory of the raid was an emotional outlet compensating for the dullness of desert existence, just as the cinema, detective novels, drink or tobacco serve to relieve the monotony of modern industrial cities. Religion sat lightly on the nomads. Some of them were, in the seventh century, professedly Christian, a fact which did not cause them to abandon the pursuit of war. Although Islam countenanced war against unbelievers, it forbade it categorically between Muslims. Thus as soon as all the Arab tribes had adopted Islam, tribal warfare would have to cease.

In such a situation, a great statesman and conqueror might have conceived the bold idea of uniting the Arab tribes to attack and plunder the non-Arab world. But Abu Bekr was scarcely a great conqueror or statesman. Rather was he a simple man, dedicated to the memory of the Prophet and to his religion. In general, therefore, we seem justified in the conjecture that the great Arab conquests were not deliberately planned. Owing to a coincidence of circumstances, they happened as it were of their own accord.

* * * * *

Thus the first cause of the Arab expansion was the warlike spirit of the bedouins, now for the first time forbidden to fight one another by an authority which had shown itself capable of enforcing its commands. The second factor, truly a remarkable coincidence, was that just before this period, both the Byzantine Emperor and the King of Persia had abolished their local Arab dynasties and attempted to rule their frontier provinces direct. Consequently the Arabs along their borders, who for centuries had defended the marches of both empires, had become hostile to their former sovereigns. We have already seen that Beni Bekr were already engaged in desultory hostilities against the Persians, and some years before had actually defeated a Persian force at Dhu Qar.

Meanwhile, on the Byzantine side, the Emperor Heraclius, after the Battle of Mota, suddenly cut off the subsidies which had hitherto been paid to the chiefs of the frontier tribes. His action does not appear to have been caused by any dissatisfaction with the tribes but by the need for post-war economies. It is, of course, easy to be wise after the event, but no action on the part of Byzantium could, at this precise moment, have been more foolish. Thus a number of Arab tribes in the area, Gaza, Moab (the modern Kerak), Duma, Aila, was made resentful and disaffected to the empire. We have seen that Muhammad, in the year 630, on the Tebook expedition, had already concluded friendly agreements with the chiefs of Aila (the modern Aqaba) and Duma (the modern Jauf) perhaps some of those whose subsidies had just been cancelled by Heraclius.

Not only, however, had both the Persian and Byzantine empires deliberately incurred the hostility of their Arab satellites, but the twenty-six years of war between them which had terminated in 628 had left both states utterly exhausted. Byzantium, the ultimate victor, was bankrupt, or suffering from post-war depression as we should call it. Our own times are all too familiar with the mental and spiritual collapse which often follows as a reaction at the end of long years of struggle. Persia, the defeated party, was in revolution and anarchy.

Few historical coincidences can have been more remarkable than the simultaneous exhaustion of Byzantium and Persia and the sudden rise of Islam, producing an outward surge of Arab tribes, resulting from the Muslim prohibition of inter-tribal war.

* * * * *

The first incidents of the Arab conquests were to take place on the Persian front. As we have already seen, Beni Bekr had been engaged in guerilla warfare on the lower Euphrates ever since the quarrel between the Great King and the Lakhmide dynasty of Hira, which began in 605. After the battle of Yemama, the Muslims appeared on the south of Beni Bekr, who were thus between two fires. Were they to make peace with the Muslims against Persia? The Persian army had no camels and–since the abolition of the Lakhmide dynasty—no desert troops. It might have been presumed that the Persians could defend the settled areas of Iraq against the desert dwellers, but they could not possibly defend the grazing grounds of Beni Bekr in the desert against the Muslims. In the 1920's, when the Wahhabi revival occurred in Nejed, the Iraq desert tribes were in precisely the same position as Beni Bekr in 633. The Iraq government, like that of Persia 1,300 years earlier, had no troops which could operate in the desert. As a result all bedouins west and south of the Euphrates were obliged to come to terms with the Wahhabis.[1]

The majority of Beni Bekr thus found themselves compelled to ally them-

[1] See *War in the Desert.*

selves with the Muslims, though some are reported to have been aligned with Persia, at least at the beginning of hostilities. The principal engineer of the alliance with the Muslims was Muthanna ibn Haritha, chief of a sub-tribe of Beni Bekr, whom the Arab historians represent as becoming a Muslim. Meanwhile, after the completion of the pacification of Nejed, the majority of Khalid's men had returned to their homes in the Hejaz, leaving him with a force of only about nine hundred warriors. So great was the opprobrium attached to "apostates" that Abu Bekr decided that none of the tribes which had recently rebelled were to be allowed to fight on the Muslim side. Bedouin loyalty is to the tribe and they see no treachery in changing sides in so far as any supra-tribal organization is concerned. Thus many of the lately defeated tribesmen would doubtless have been quite ready to join Khalid in raiding Persian territory, had they been accepted. As it was, portions of the Beni Bekr who had neither previously professed Islam nor joined in the rebellion were the only allies available to Khalid.

Judging by the resources of bedouin tribes in the same area in our own times, it seems unlikely that Muthanna ibn Haritha can have raised more than 2,000 or 3,000 men. The combined forces of Khalid ibn al Waleed and Muthanna were therefore probably in the vicinity of 3,500 warriors. These set out to raid the Persian frontier.

The accounts of Khalid's campaign in Iraq are vague and confused. The Muslims are alleged to have collected in March 633 at Al Hafeer, a place in the desert south-west of the Euphrates. Here a contingent of Tai joined the forces of Khalid and Muthanna. The modern wells of Al Hafar are exactly in the place where such a bedouin camel force would concentrate before raiding Iraq. They would also have been the ideal place for a junction with the Tai tribe, which lived in what is now Jebel Shammar.

Thence the Arabs advanced and fought a battle with a Persian force at Kadhima, which was probably near the present site of Kuwait, or perhaps between Kuwait and the site now occupied by Basra. The Persian forces, which probably consisted of local Arab tribes with a contingent of regular Persian troops, were defeated. As the Persians could not operate in the desert, the battle, which is said to have been fought at a distance of two days march from the place where Basra was later to be built, must have been near the Bay of Kuwait.

The town and port of Ubulla were situated on the estuary of the combined Tigris and Euphrates, now known as the Shatt al Arab. It was the emporium of the Persian sea-borne trade with India and the land base of the Persian navy. Khalid advanced upon this important city but the inhabitants forestalled an attack by an agreement to pay tribute. Thence the Arabs were bold enough to cross the Euphrates and fight an action at Walaja, perhaps near the modern town of Shatra, but hearing that the enemy was again collecting to oppose him, Khalid hastily recrossed the Euphrates into the desert.

The key to all the early operations, against Persia and against Syria alike, is that the Persians and Byzantines could not move in the desert, being mounted on horses. The Muslims were like a sea-power, cruising off shore in their ships, whereas the Persians and Byzantines alike could only take up

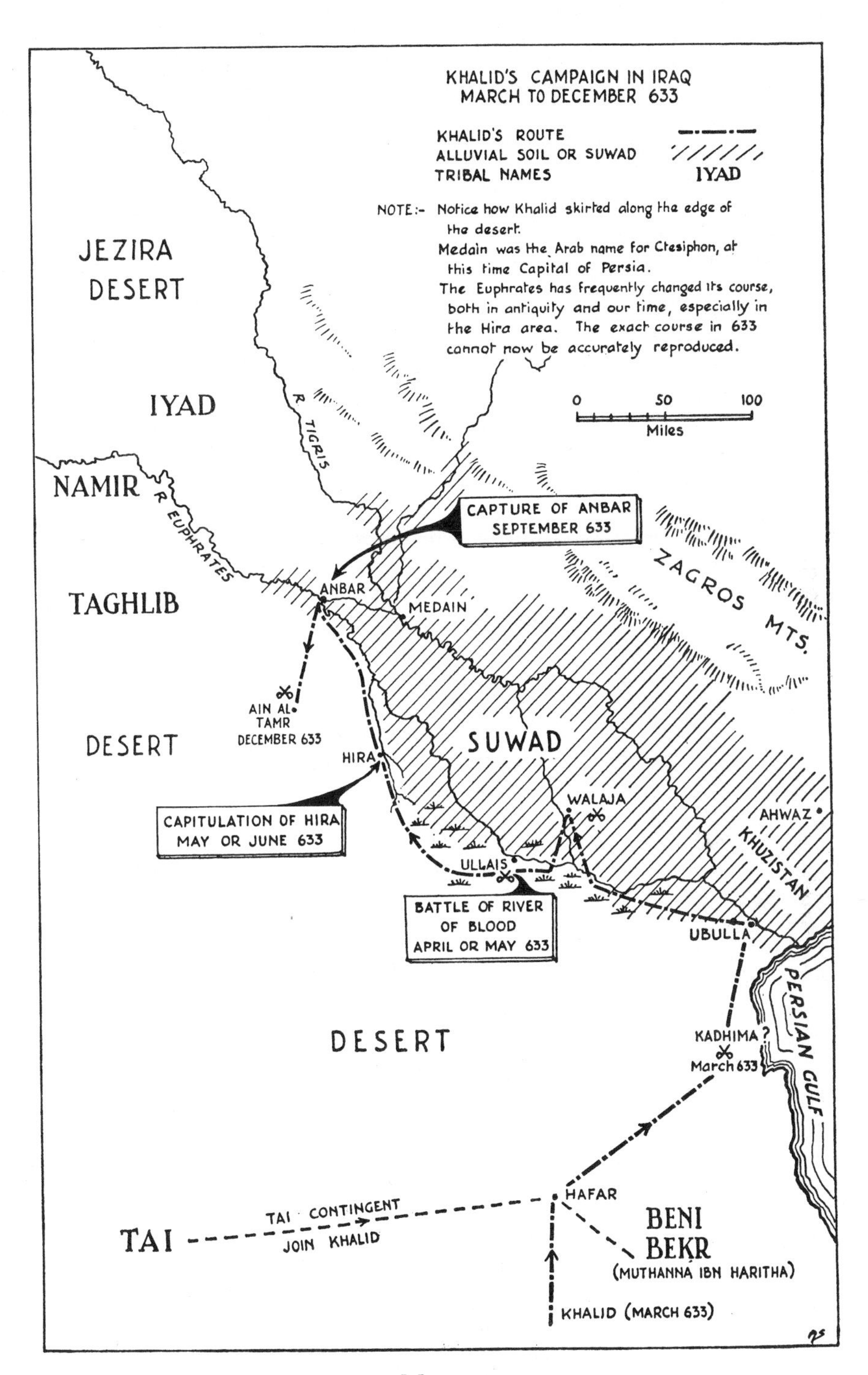
KHALID'S CAMPAIGN IN IRAQ
MARCH TO DECEMBER 633
KHALID'S ROUTE
ALLUVIAL SOIL OR SUWAD
TRIBAL NAMES
IYAD
NOTE:- Notice how Khalid skirted along the edge of the desert.
Medain was the Arab name for Ctesiphon, at this time Capital of Persia.
The Euphrates has frequently changed its course, both in antiquity and our time, especially in the Hira area. The exact course in 633 cannot now be accurately reproduced.
0
50
100
Miles
JEZIRA DESERT
IYAD
NAMIR
R TIGRIS
R EUPHRATES
TAGHLIB
CAPTURE OF ANBAR
SEPTEMBER 633
ANBAR
MEDAIN
ZAGROS MTS.
AIN AL TAMR
DECEMBER 633
DESERT
HIRA
SUWAD
CAPITULATION OF HIRA
MAY OR JUNE 633
WALAJA
AHWAZ
KHUZISTAN
ULLAIS
BATTLE OF RIVER OF BLOOD
APRIL OR MAY 633
UBULLA
PERSIAN GULF
DESERT
KADHIMA ?
March 633
HAFAR
TAI
TAI CONTINGENT
JOIN KHALID
BENI BEKR
(MUTHANNA IBN HARITHA)
KHALID (MARCH 633)

Map XII

positions on the shore (that is, the cultivated area) unable to launch out to "sea" and engage the enemy in his own desert element. Similarly the Arabs, like the Norse or Danish pirates who raided England, were at first afraid to move inland far from their "ships". Raiding the areas on the "shores" of the desert, they hastened back to their own element when danger threatened.

In this manner Khalid, hearing that a new enemy force was collecting, hastily recrossed the Euphrates on to the fringes of the desert, where he appears to have been reinforced by a contingent from Beni Temeem, under their chief Qaqaa ibn Amr, whose name will recur frequently in our narrative. A further battle was then fought at Ullais, apparently on the west bank of the Euphrates somewhere in the vicinity of the modern Samawah. Again the enemy force seems to have consisted largely of Arab tribes, under a Persian commander. The battle is alleged to have been more severely contested than any hitherto, but the Muslims were eventually victorious. The ruthless Khalid gave orders that all the enemy prisoners be beheaded. The Arab historians allege that many thousands were butchered, the executions continuing for three days. As a result the action became known to the Arabs as the Battle of the River of Blood. By contrast, however, the Arabs did not interfere with the peasants who cultivated the soil. These were required to pay tribute and their safety was then guaranteed. After every victory, one fifth of the spoil was sent to the khalif in Medina, according to the rule laid down by Muhammad himself. The remainder was divided among the Muslims, who received no other pay.

Flushed with these successes, the Muslim raiders advanced to the city of Hira, once the capital of the Arab Lakhmide dynasty, which had been suppressed twenty-five years before by the King of Persia. Had these princes still been at the height of their power, the outcome of the campaign might well have been different, for Beni Bekr had been extremely loyal to the dynasty. Now, however, on the approach of Khalid's army, the Persian governor fled to Medain.

Hira was surrounded by walls with which the bedouins were quite unable to deal. But the citizens were themselves mostly Arabs, and the tribes in the surrounding deserts had been cowed by Khalid's victory at Ullais. We have seen, in the Prophet's lifetime, that Mecca could not resist once the surrounding tribes had submitted to Muhammad. Taif also was obliged to surrender when the Hawazin went over to the Muslims. Townspeople were steadier than bedouins in a pitched battle, but such were the mobility and harassing power of the nomads that towns in the desert could not resist without the help of allied tribes.

The same situation arose at Hira. Besieged within their walls and without tribal support, the citizens were glad to come to terms, especially as the sum of money demanded by the Arabs, though it appeared large to the bedouins, was trivial in comparison with the wealth of the city. In return for this payment, the Muslims undertook to protect the town, the inhabitants of which, though Arabs, refused to renounce their Christian religion in favour of Islam. This agreement was probably signed in May 633, while the last embers of the apostasy were being stamped out in the Yemen.

It may well be asked how the Persian King allowed an important city like Hira to be captured by a force of bedouins, especially as it was less than a hundred miles distant from his capital at Medain. To understand the reason, it will be necessary to glance briefly at internal events in Persia. The overthrow of Chosroes Parwiz by the Emperor Heraclius in 627 and 628 has already been noted. In the hour of defeat, Chosroes, with eighteen of his sons, was assassinated by his son Siroes, who seized the throne and made peace with Byzantium. The better to secure his position, the parricide caused all the male descendants of the great Chosroes Anushirvan to be sought out and murdered, with the object of leaving no member of the royal family alive capable of disputing the throne with him. These savage massacres were, however, of no avail, for Siroes himself was murdered after a reign of only eight months. The whole of Persia was then abandoned to anarchy and torn between rival factions. All the male members of the royal family having apparently been put to death, no legitimate successor to the Crown could be discovered. In the ensuing four years, no less than nine claimants ascended and were deposed from the throne, several of them being princesses, for no royal princes could be found alive.

With the whole kingdom in an uproar, the most that the Persian army could do against the Arabs was to take up a defensive position south of Medain covering the capital, while Khalid and the Muslims overran the fertile Suwad, plundering, collecting tribute and driving off the inhabitants into slavery.

In the summer of 632, soon after the death of Muhammad in distant Medina, a boy of royal descent, who had been hidden during the massacres, was said to have been discovered. Yezdegird was only fifteen or sixteen years old, and thus was unable himself to assume command, though he was proclaimed king.[2] The mighty kingdom of Persia, after twenty-six years of war against Byzantium and four years of anarchy and civil wars, was utterly ruined and exhausted.

Profiting by the paralysis of the Persian government, the Arabs overran the rich agricultural country east of the Euphrates, raiding and exacting tribute up to the very banks of the Tigris. Any of the inhabitants who resisted were speedily overwhelmed and doubtless roughly handled. But to such as were willing to come to terms, the Arabs gave written agreements, stipulating the payment of tribute and promising security and protection in return. Receipts were given when the tribute money was paid. Brutal as the Muslims appear to us to have been in their massacres of those who opposed them, they were extremely scrupulous in the fulfilment of the terms of the agreements into which they entered.

While, however, the Persians were unable to operate in the desert, the Christian Arab bedouins of the upper Euphrates were not so restricted. The Taghlib and a portion of Beni Bekr who had sided with Persia were able to threaten the Muslim forces in the desert and to raid their communications with Medina. The Arab strategy was based on the fact that they were secure in the desert and could raid the settled areas as they liked. Hostile Arab

[2] Other accounts make Yezdegird's proclamation two years later.

bedouins, who could also operate in the desert, might upset this strategy and thus could not be tolerated. In this situation, Khalid was not the man to sit idle in the palaces of Hira, "playing a woman's part" as he contemptuously remarked. He hastily made his arrangements, with a view to embarking on mobile operations once more.

It is interesting to notice the comparative indifference shown at this stage by the Quraish leaders in Medina towards the operations in Iraq. All their interest, as we shall see below, was concentrated on Syria, an area with which they were familiar, and to which Muhammad himself had sent the Mota raid and Usama's force. Most of the Companions of the Prophet who had been with Khalid in the battle against the false prophet Musailama had gone home. As a result, we find Khalid's chief commanders to be, not Meccans or Medinis, but bedouins. He left Muthanna ibn Haritha of Beni Bekr to command a force confronting the Persian army south of Medain, and appointed to command at Hira, Qaqaa ibn Amr, the recently joined chief of Beni Temeem.

He then moved up the west bank of the Euphrates to the site of the modern town of Fellujah, where he crossed the river and laid siege to the city of Anbar. The Suwad, or black soil alluvial delta of the Tigris and Euphrates, ends on a line drawn east and west through Anbar. South of this line, the rich silt valley of the two rivers was inhabited by a toiling race of cultivators of mixed origin—descendants of the ancient Sumerians and Babylonians, with an admixture of Persians and, along the Euphrates, of Arabs. The black soil valley was densely populated and intersected by irrigation canals, an area extremely difficult for the operations of desert warriors mounted on horses or camels.

North of the line drawn east and west through Anbar, the country consisted of rolling gravelly desert, through which the two rivers had cut their way. In this area, the Syrian desert actually crossed the Euphrates and the Tigris almost to the foothills of the Persian mountains. The nomadic tribes of Taghlib, Namir and Iyad from the Arabian deserts had infiltrated across the Euphrates and camped in this Jezira desert between the two rivers. Thus the town of Anbar on the Euphrates was bounded by desert both on the west and on the north. Some four centuries earlier it had been founded, or perhaps merely seized, by nomadic Arabs and it was still almost as much an Arab town as Hira, though it was garrisoned by Persian troops. The city was surrounded by walls and a moat, one part of which Khalid caused to be filled in by slaughtering all the weak camels in his army and throwing their carcases in the ditch. The town was then carried by assault.

To capture Anbar, Khalid had not been obliged to plunge into the densely populated silt valley. He was still following the old bedouin principal of skirting along the fringes of the desert, attacking the "coastal" towns and villages, but always ready to vanish into the desert beyond pursuit in the event of regular enemy troops appearing on the scene. In accordance with these tactics, he turned west from Anbar back into the desert and moved to Ain al Tamr, the spring of dates, the modern oasis of Shitata. Here the Taghlib and other Arab tribes offered some resistance but were dispersed.

The oasis, inhabited by Christian Arabs but with a Persian garrison, was captured. Khalid, in one of his periodical ruthless moods, caused the garrison to be slaughtered in cold blood, the wives and children being distributed among the Muslims or sold into slavery. A leading shaikh of Taghlib was publicly beheaded. In a Nestorian monastery at Ain al Tamr, forty Arab Christian young men were captured, who claimed to be religious students. Perhaps because their standard of education made them useful to the rude Muslim community, their lives were spared and they were sent to Medina as slaves or clerks. One of them was called Nusair. In Medina he was to have a son, Musa ibn Nusair, who many years later was to be the conqueror of Spain.

We must now leave Khalid at Ain al Tamr in the autumn of 633, and consider for a while events in Syria.

* * * * *

Khalid as we have seen had not originally been sent by Abu Bekr to invade Persia, but to destroy apostasy in Arabia by defeating the false prophets Tulaiha and Musailama. Then, almost by accident, he had come into contact with Muthanna ibn Haritha and his Beni Bekr, who had made the tempting suggestion of a few raids on the Persian border. Muthanna had ridden to Medina and secured the consent of the khalif. As a fifth of all loot and slaves was sent to Medina, the khalif had no objection to these unpremeditated forays, rendered unexpectedly successful by the anarchy of the Persian Kingdom.

In reality, however, the new rulers in Medina were more interested in the Byzantine frontier. Quraish, who supplied all the leaders and commanders of the new Muslim community, had always, as traders, been familiar with Syria and Palestine. The battle of Mota and Usama's retaliatory raid had initiated hostilities. The Prophet's own expedition to Tebook had reduced the frontier tribes to submission and tribute. The Arab Christian prince of Duma had, as we have seen, made profession of Islam. His conversion was apparently insincere, for on receipt of the news of Muhammad's death he renounced his allegiance to Medina, or at least withheld the tax.

Meanwhile, as soon as information reached Medina of the defeat of the false prophets in Nejed, the khalif decided to renew hostilities on the Byzantine frontier. With this object, he appealed to Medina, Mecca, Taif and the surrounding tribes for recruits. He then appointed three commanders, to each of whom, following the precedent established by Muhammad,[3] he presented a banner.

The three column commanders were Amr ibn al Aasi, Shurahbil ibn Hasana and Yezeed ibn abi Sofian. (His father, old Abu Sofian, the victor of Uhud and Muhammad's old opponent, had meanwhile been shelved by being given a governorship in the Yemen.) It is not clear why the force available was divided into three columns. Perhaps the lack of desert water-points made it necessary to move in separate detachments, or dispersion (in the absence of any system of supplies) made it easier to live on the country,

[3] In reality by Qusai, see page 38.

or perhaps the jealous leaders were unwilling to serve under one another. Logically such a division might be taken to indicate that Abu Bekr was thinking more in terms of harassing raids than of an army of invasion, but Arab methods of warfare at this period were so haphazard that no such deduction can be made with confidence.

Abu Bekr is alleged to have instructed Amr ibn al Aasi to proceed through Aila (modern Aqaba) into southern Palestine, in the direction of Gaza, an area well known to Quraish, whose commercial caravans had often plied to that port. The second column, under Yezeed ibn abi Sofian, was to move northwards through Tebook and then up the east side of the Dead Sea, while Shurahbil ibn Hasana was instructed to keep further east and to move towards Busra or Damascus. In the event of any of the columns meeting with strong opposition, the other two were to move to its assistance. If all three columns were to come together, the supreme commander would be the one in whose area the operations took place. As the Muslim warriors returned from the various punitive columns sent to Nejed, Oman and the Yemen, the khalif collected them and sent them forward again as reinforcements to the three Syrian columns.

Amr ibn al Aasi engaged and defeated a Byzantine force at Dathin[4] on the track between Aila and Gaza, while Yezeed ibn abi Sofian drove back Sergius, the patrician of Caesarea, at a battle in the Wadi Araba. Pursuing the retreating enemy, he overtook them again and inflicted further casualties, killing Sergius himself. The Arabs then fanned out over the southern Palestine plain, probably as far north as Lydda and Jaffa.

When Abu Bekr found himself involved in major operations in Syria and Palestine, he wrote to Khalid ibn al Waleed to come from Iraq and to reinforce the Muslims on the Byzantine front. Some allege that Khalid came from Ain al Tamr to retake Duma, the Arab ruler of which, as already related, had renounced his allegiance. A force had been sent to re-establish control, but had been unable to overcome the opposition. Other historians state that Khalid was summoned to reinforce Syria and that he merely cleared up the situation in Duma on the way. Whichever may have been the principal motive, the fact seems clear that he moved from Ain al Tamr early in 634. Suffice it to say that Duma was quickly reduced, with Khalid's usual dash and energy. Its leaders were put to death, one Arab chief being crucified, and the prisoners were massacred. After appointing a Muslim governor over the oasis, and sending all women and children and impedimenta back to Medina, Khalid moved north-westward up the Batn as Sirr valley, known today as the Wadi as Sirhan. In so doing, he was within five or six days march of the Muslim forces already operating in Trans-Jordan, and could easily have joined them. He did not do so, however, because these forces themselves were held up by a Byzantine army, which was holding a defensive position in a narrow defile near the modern town of Deraa. Yezeed ibn abi Sofian and Shurahbil ibn Hasana had joined hands and were confronting this army, but had been un-

[4] Some have identified Dathin with Dothan, where Joseph's brothers grazed their flocks, but this was twelve miles east of modern Haifa, and seems much too far north.

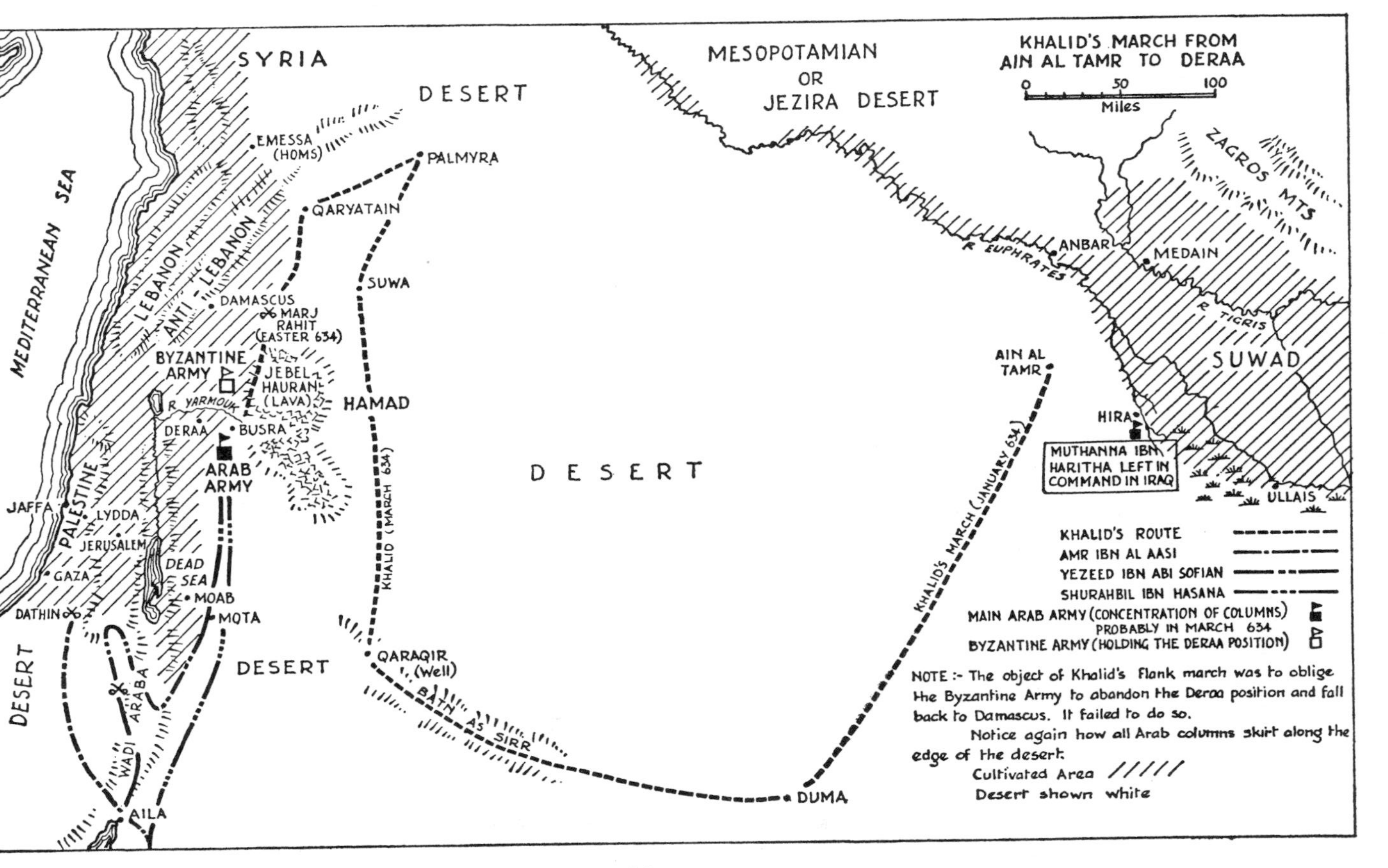

KHALID'S MARCH FROM AIN AL TAMR TO DERAA
0 50 100
Miles
SYRIA
DESERT
MESOPOTAMIAN OR JEZIRA DESERT
ZAGROS MTS
MEDITERRANEAN SEA
LEBANON
ANTI - LEBANON
EMESSA (HOMS)
PALMYRA
QARYATAIN
SUWA
DAMASCUS
MARJ RAHIT (EASTER 634)
BYZANTINE ARMY
JEBEL HAURAN (LAVA)
R. YARMOUK
HAMAD
DERAA
BUSRA
ARAB ARMY
DESERT
KHALID (MARCH 634)
KHALID'S MARCH (JANUARY 634)
R. EUPHRATES
ANBAR
MEDAIN
R. TIGRIS
SUWAD
AIN AL TAMR
HIRA
MUTHANNA IBN HARITHA LEFT IN COMMAND IN IRAQ
ULLAIS
JAFFA
PALESTINE
LYDDA
JERUSALEM
DEAD SEA
GAZA
MOAB
MOTA
DATHIN
DESERT
WADI ARABA
AILA
DESERT
QARAQIR (Well)
BATN AS SIRR
DUMA
KHALID'S ROUTE
AMR IBN AL AASI
YEZEED IBN ABI SOFIAN
SHURAHBIL IBN HASANA
MAIN ARAB ARMY (CONCENTRATION OF COLUMNS) PROBABLY IN MARCH 634
BYZANTINE ARMY (HOLDING THE DERAA POSITION)
NOTE :- The object of Khalid's Flank march was to oblige the Byzantine Army to abandon the Deraa position and fall back to Damascus. It failed to do so.
Notice again how all Arab columns skirt along the edge of the desert.
Cultivated Area
Desert shown white


Map XIII

able to dislodge it. The two armies, therefore, faced one another in a deadlock.

Doubtless with the agreement of the other commanders, Khalid decided to execute a wide flanking movement. Watering at Qaraqir, a well which still exists under the same name, he made a wide sweep northwards through the desert, involving a waterless march of nearly two hundred miles, across a flat area of desert now known as the Hamad. There are no permanent wells in this plain, though several catchment areas hold water after rain. If, as seems probable, Khalid's march took place in March 634, it is possible that no water would be found on the way if the rainfall that year had been bad. Eventually the force reached a place called by the Arab historians Suwa, possibly that now known as Seba Biyar. The raiders, before leaving Qaraqir, had adopted a bedouin device still used in our time. A number of camels had been denied water for several days and thereby had been rendered extremely thirsty. Then they had been allowed to drink their fill. Under such circumstances, camels will carry water in their bladders for several days, using it up gradually. When the march was resumed, some of these camels were slaughtered each night and the water recovered from their bladders. The problem which confronted Khalid was not only to supply water for his men but also for the horses.

At length, after five days of march, all the water was finished and all the water-carrying camels had been slaughtered. The strength of the horses and the men was failing. The guide, Rafa ibn Umair of the Tai tribe, was certain that the well must be near, but was himself perhaps too weak to seek for it, or, as some accounts say, was suffering from ophthalmia and could not see. All he could say was that the site of the well was marked by a thorn bush, which they must find. So denuded is the Hamad of vegetation that such a bush might be visible several miles away. For some hours the whole force was in imminent danger. Disasters in which whole raiding parties die of thirst in the shadeless heat of these burning plains are familiar in bedouin tradition. At last, however, the bush was found. Digging beside it the Muslims uncovered a concealed supply of water, and men and horses were saved. Khalid then went on to attack and capture Palmyra, and turning west he sacked Qaryatein.

On his march northwards from Qaraqir to Suwa, Khalid was cut off from the inhabited area of Hauran by the volcanic ranges of the Jebel Hauran, now commonly called the Jebel al Druze. His arrival in the Palmyra area would thus be a complete surprise. As, however, he moved southwards towards Damascus, his presence would become known to the enemy. An engagement ensued at Marj Rahit, about fifteen miles east of Damascus, apparently on Easter Sunday 634. From thence he turned southwards and skirting the slopes of the volcanic Jebel Hauran, he joined the remainder of the Muslim forces at Deraa. His force is alleged to have been about 9,000 strong.

The Arab historians chronicle Khalid's march as a triumph and claim that Marj Rahit was a victory. The claim, however, would seem to be of doubtful validity. The only plausible explanation of the whole operation was

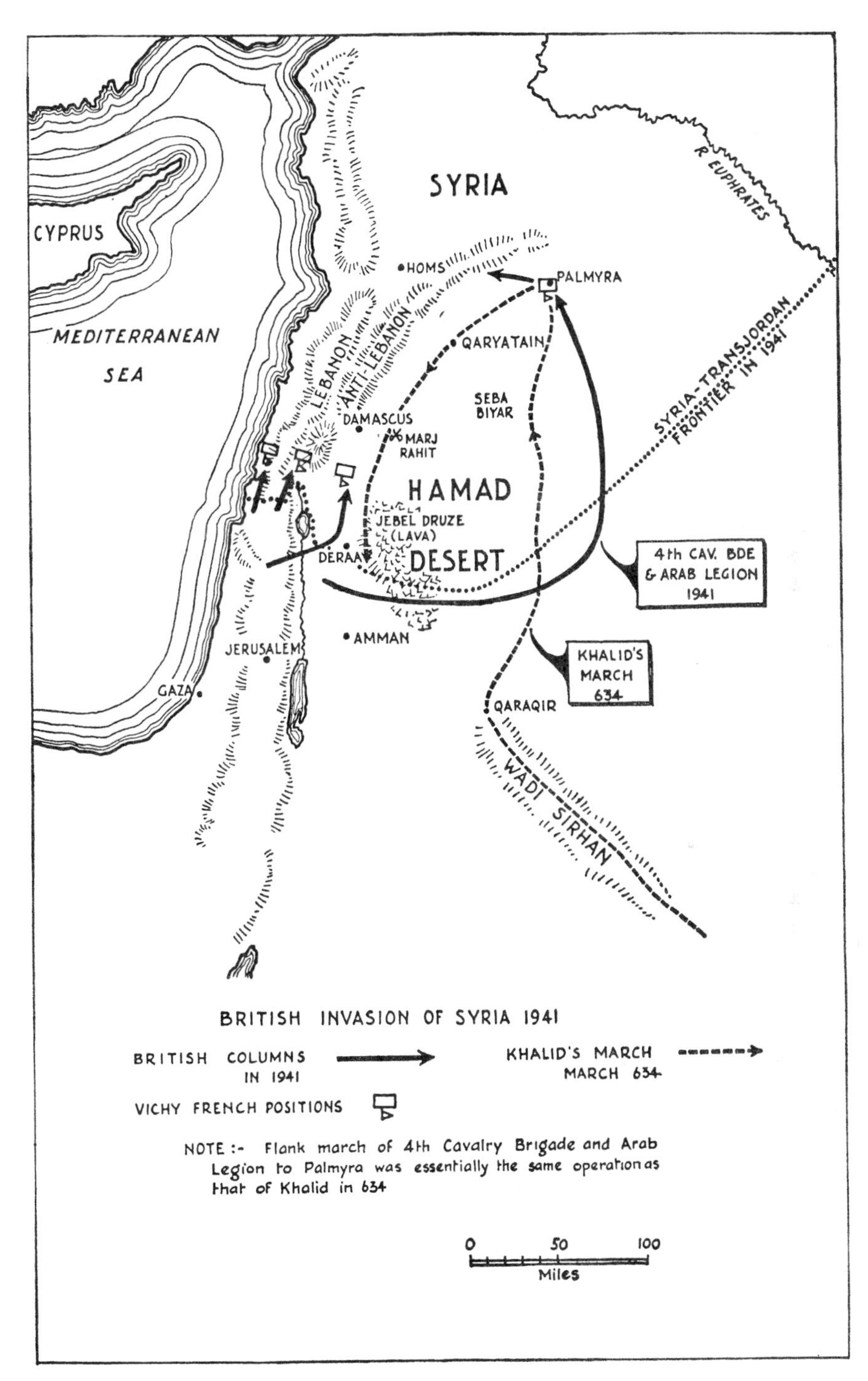
CYPRUS
MEDITERRANEAN
SEA
SYRIA
R. EUPHRATES
HOMS
PALMYRA
LEBANON
ANTI-LEBANON
QARYATAIN
SEBA
BIYAR
DAMASCUS
MARJ
RAHIT
HAMAD
DESERT
JEBEL DRUZE
(LAVA)
DERAA
SYRIA-TRANSJORDAN
FRONTIER IN 1941
4th CAV. BDE
& ARAB LEGION
1941
AMMAN
JERUSALEM
GAZA
KHALID'S
MARCH
634
QARAQIR
WADI SIRHAN
BRITISH INVASION OF SYRIA 1941
BRITISH COLUMNS
IN 1941
KHALID'S MARCH
MARCH 634
VICHY FRENCH POSITIONS
NOTE :- Flank march of 4th Cavalry Brigade and Arab Legion to Palmyra was essentially the same operation as that of Khalid in 634
0
50
100
Miles

Map XIV

as a turning movement which, by threatening Damascus, would compel the Byzantine army to evacuate its defensive position as Deraa. If Khalid had been victorious at Marj Rahit, it would have been his duty to press in more closely to Damascus and thereby force a Byzantine withdrawal from Deraa. The fact that, after the action, he turned southwards, and abandoned the operation, would seem to indicate that he must have suffered a repulse.

* * * * *

An interesting parallel can be found in modern military history. In May 1941, the British Army and the Free French invaded Syria, held by the Vichy French. Advancing from Trans-Jordan, a British column moved northwards through Deraa, but was held up by a French defensive position south of Damascus. To force the evacuation of this position, another British column, accompanied by the Arab Legion, moved up across the Hamad desert and attacked and eventually captured Palmyra, whence it turned west towards Homs. The French thereupon abandoned Damascus and retired northwards. During the course of this operation, the Arab Legion took Seba Biyar, where Khalid's raiders had nearly died of thirst and where the French had established a post.[5] This operation was an almost exact replica of Khalid's turning movement, except that it was successful, whereas Khalid's was not. The British and the Arab Legion, however, were mechanized, whereas Khalid's raiders were on camels.

## *NOTABLE DATES*

| | |
|---|---|
| Period of anarchy in Persia | 628–632 |
| Accession of Yezdegird | 632 (or 633) |
| Surrender of Hira | May 633 |
| Capture of Anbar and Ain al Tamr | Autumn 633 |
| Three Arab columns invade Palestine and Jordan | Winter 633–634 |
| Khalid ibn al Waleed crosses from Iraq to Syria via Duma | January to March 634 |
| Khalid skirmishes at Marj Rahit outside Damascus | April 634 |
| Combined Arab columns held up on the Yarmouk | May 634 |

## *OUTSTANDING PERSONALITIES*

Khalid ibn al Waleed, Arab commander in Iraq.
Yezdegird, young King of Persia.

| | |
|---|---|
| Amr ibn al Aasi<br>Shurahbil ibn Hasana<br>Yezeed ibn abi Sofian | Arab column commanders in Palestine and Jordan, all of them from Quraish. |
| Muthanna ibn Haritha, chief of Beni Bekr<br>Qaqaa ibn Amr, chief of Beni Temeem<br>Jareer ibn Abdulla, chief of Beni Bajeela | Commanders in Iraq, all bedouin tribal chiefs. |

[5] See *The Story of the Arab Legion*.

# VII

## *The Beginning of Victories*

In the victorious days of the Roman Republic, it had been the aim of the senate to confine the legions to a single war and completely to suppress a first enemy before they provoked the hostilities of a second. These timid maxims were disdained by the magnanimity and enthusiasm of the Arabian caliphs. With the same vigour and success they invaded the successors of Augustus and those of Artaxerxes; and the rival monarchies at the same instant became the prey of an enemy whom they had been so long accustomed to despise.

GIBBON, *Decline and Fall of the Roman Empire*

Thou shalt consume all the people which the Lord thy God shall deliver thee: thine eye shall have no pity upon them: neither shalt thou serve their gods; for that will be a snare unto thee.

If thou shalt say in thine heart, these nations are more than I; how can I dispossess them? Thou shalt not be afraid of them. *Deuteronomy* VII, 16

## VII

## THE BEGINNING OF VICTORIES

WHEN the leaders of the Muslims decided to engage in war with Byzantium, they were undertaking no easy task. The Roman Empire had, for four centuries, been built up and maintained by the steady discipline of its infantry—the famous legions. But the Byzantine army of the seventh century bore no resemblance to the legions. The transformation had begun after the Battle of Adrianople in A.D. 378, when the cavalry of the Goths had ridden over and utterly exterminated a Roman army of the time-honoured pattern. A complete military revolution had followed. Thereafter for more than a thousand years, cavalry was to dominate the battlefield. The legions had been armed with a pilum and a sword, and their defensive armour had been a helmet, cuirass and shield, an armament inadequate to oppose the shock tactics of the heavy cavalry charge.

After Adrianople, the Romans themselves had disbanded the legions, with their centuries of tradition and battle honours, and had made the cavalry their principal arm.[1] The pike and the sword being unable to resist the impact of the cavalry charge, they took to the bow and arrow for this purpose. Soon the cavalry were divided into light and heavy. The former, armed with the bow, could discharge their arrows in all directions at a gallop. The latter, armed with lances, were used for shock tactics. With an army of this kind, Justinian had nearly reconquered the Roman Empire (533–565). England was many centuries behind in this changeover from infantry to cavalry and bowmen. In 1066, at Hastings, the English were still fighting on foot, but the Normans used both armoured horsemen and archers. The unit of the Byzantine army was the bandum or regiment of some 400 men. Three or more regiments constituted a brigade, while three brigades formed a turma or division. Each regiment had a distinctive badge and colour in its uniform.[2] Unlike the Arabs, the Byzantines had carefully organized administrative services. Every infantry section of sixteen men, for example, was accompanied by a cart which contained picks and shovels for entrenching, a hand-mill for grinding corn and other tools. An ambulance corps, consisting of surgeons and stretcher-bearers, marched with the army. Tactical training was diligently carried out and many books on the military art were available to the student.

Against this highly organized regular army, the Arabs could bring only hordes of wild tribesmen. They had no tactical training, no organization, no

[1] It was not until the advent of firearms, that infantry became once more the "queen of battles". In our own times, the invention of mechanized armoured cavalry has again weakened the power of infantry, a revolution exactly similar to that of A.D. 378.

[2] Oman, *The Art of War in the Middle Ages*.

books, no administration, no pay, no doctors. Their weapons were inferior to those of the enemy. Yet after Mota they never lost a battle against the Byzantines. Their own hardihood and the absence of any administrative train made them far more mobile than their enemies. It was, however, to their spirit that their victories must be mainly attributed. Naturally fiery and warlike, rendered desirous of death by the belief that they would be instantly admitted to Paradise, they fought with a fury which more than counterbalanced the superior arms and discipline of the Byzantines.

* * * * *

The records of the fighting which occurred between the Arabs and the Byzantine army in Syria are extremely confusing. Our sources are virtually restricted to the Arab historians who wrote more than a century after the events which they recorded and who themselves were obviously ignorant of, or indifferent to, the course of the military operations. It was purely by accident that I discovered what appears to me now to be the key to the comprehension of the Arab campaigns in Syria, namely the narrow defile between the Yarmouk River and the Jebel Druze at Deraa. I made this discovery in the manner described below.

In July 1941, British forces had occupied Syria and Iraq. It was feared that the German army, which had seized the Balkans, would attack Turkey and thence move southwards through Syria and Palestine to Egypt, which was being simultaneously attacked from Libya on the west. There were virtually no troops in Syria or Palestine, no tanks and no efficient anti-tank weapons. If the Germans burst through Turkey with a mechanized blitzkreig, it would be difficult to stop them. It was therefore important to discover all the available narrow defiles, where armoured mechanized forces would be at a disadvantage and to put them in a state of defence, so that they could be used to hold up German mechanized columns. With this object in view, I myself was employed to examine the area round Deraa.

The Yarmouk River drains the Hauran area. In the course of thousands of years, it has cut a deep gorge down which it falls into the Jordan valley three thousand feet below the Hauran plain. This gorge begins near the town of Deraa. East and north-east of Deraa lies a large group of mountains formed by extinct volcanoes, all the slopes of which are strewn with large black boulders of lava. In places, movement in this area is difficult even to men on foot, while horses and camels are almost immobilized and wheels entirely so. These lava-strewn spurs run down into the plain very nearly to the point at which the Yarmouk becomes an impassable gorge. Through the small gap between the lava and the Yarmouk, passed in 634 (and still passes today) the main road from Damascus to Palestine, Amman and Aila (Aqaba). In 1941, we named this narrow defile the "Deraa gap". We decided to dig an anti-tank ditch across it and to build an entrenched position for an infantry brigade to close the gap.

All the European historians of the Muslim conquest of Syria complain of the vagueness and inaccuracy of the Arab records. Again and again the rival armies are reported to be facing one another on the Yarmouk. Then they

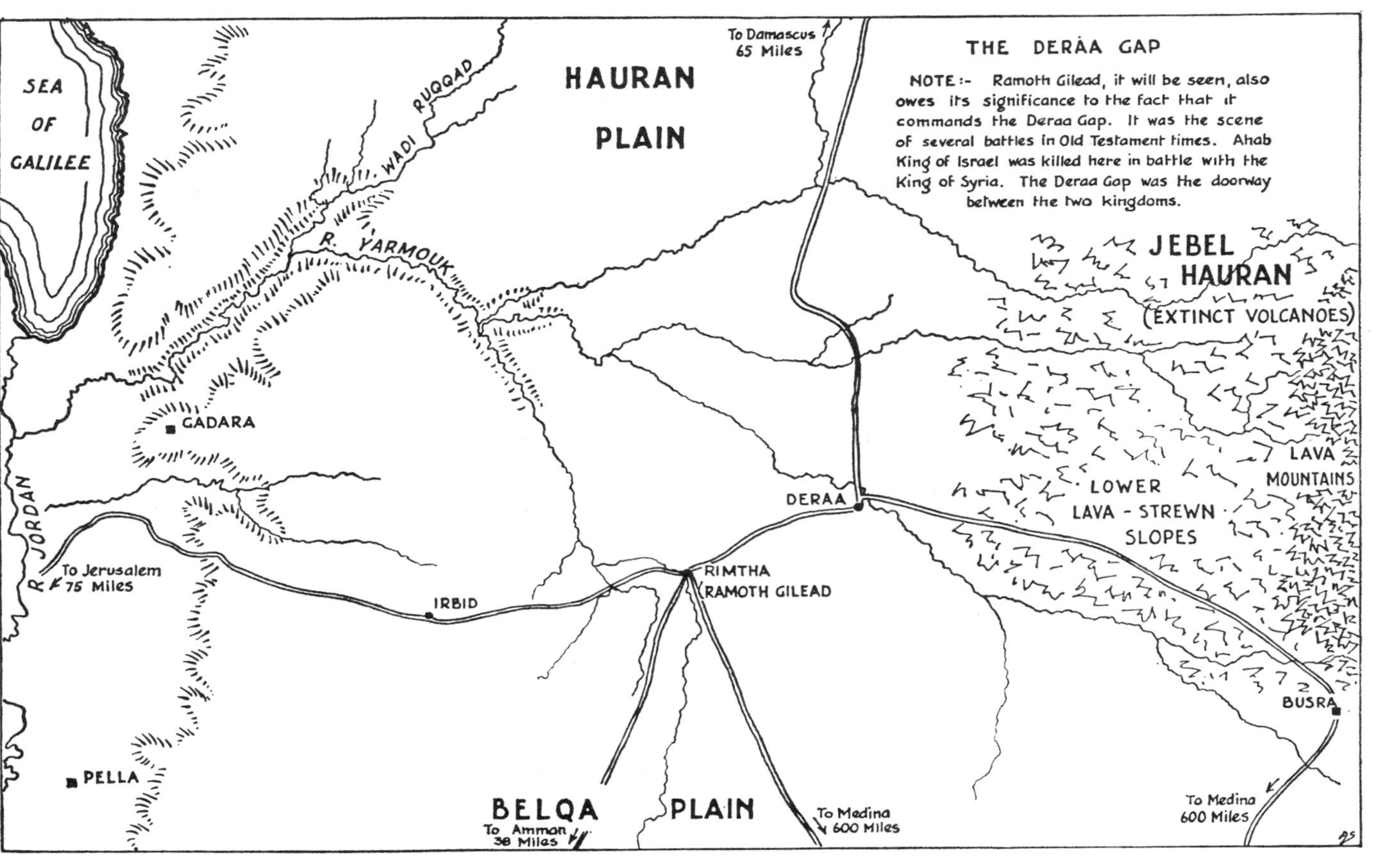
THE DERÀA GAP
NOTE:- Ramoth Gilead, it will be seen, also owes its significance to the fact that it commands the Deraa Gap. It was the scene of several battles in Old Testament times. Ahab King of Israel was killed here in battle with the King of Syria. The Deraa Gap was the doorway between the two kingdoms.
SEA OF GALILEE
HAURAN PLAIN
To Damascus 65 Miles
WADI RUQQAD
R. YARMOUK
JEBEL HAURAN
(EXTINCT VOLCANOES)
LAVA MOUNTAINS
LOWER LAVA - STREWN SLOPES
GADARA
DERAA
R. JORDAN
To Jerusalem 75 Miles
RIMTHA
RAMOTH GILEAD
IRBID
BUSRA
PELLA
BELQA PLAIN
To Amman 38 Miles
To Medina 600 Miles
To Medina 600 Miles

Map xv

disperse again without result. Were there several encounters on the Yarmouk, and why does the name keep recurring? It was only when I myself reconnoitred the area for a military purpose that, all of a sudden, the veil fell, as it were, from my eyes. Useful as this defile would be to prevent a German attack from the north, it was obvious to me that it would be of even greater importance in resisting an army coming up from the south. In so far as invasion from Arabia was concerned, the Deraa gap would be the Thermopylae of Syria.

In 1941, the Germans were invincible at their lightning mechanical warfare. A torrent of armoured and unarmoured vehicles and self-propelled guns poured across the country, overwhelming all opposition. The only way to oppose these mechanized-avalanche tactics was to fight in close country, in mountains, in passes, in narrow gaps where vehicles could only pass in single file.

The Muslims were extremely light and mobile, and their tactics consisted of a wild charge, of advance and retreat and turning movements, cutting communications and supplies. In the open plain, the heavy slow-moving Byzantine troops could not compete with this mobility. But the Arabs could not fight a close-order infantry battle, by push of pike as it were. They had not sufficient body-armour and they were not trained to fight in close, well-disciplined ranks. Moreover they had no heavy support weapons. A cloud of arrows was their only covering fire. Thus they easily overran the deserts and plains of Trans-Jordan and southern Palestine but were afraid of the mountains and defiles. Dreading the Arab blitzkrieg, the Byzantine army in 634, like the British army in 1941, established an entrenched camp near Deraa in the gap between the Yarmouk gorge and the lava beds. The Arabs would sometimes skirmish in front of this camp and sometimes withdraw, but their lack of military science made it difficult for them to assault it. Khalid's operations round Palmyra and Damascus, described in the previous chapter, would thus have had the object of persuading the Byzantines to withdraw from Deraa, a result, however, which they failed to achieve.

Meanwhile Abu Ubaida ibn al Jarrah, who had been an intimate of the Prophet himself, had been sent to Syria by Abu Bekr. The relative positions and authority of the different commanders is left doubtful by the Muslim historians. The suggestion seems to be that Abu Ubaida was appointed supreme commander over Amr ibn al Aasi, Yezeed ibn abi Sofian and Shurahbil ibn Hassana. Abu Ubaida was a middle-aged, mild-mannered man, a conscientious and devoted Muslim and a just judge and administrator, but not a great fighter. When Khalid arrived on the scene, Abu Ubaida seems to have agreed to his assumption of the supreme command.

Khalid was no man for sitting and blockading the Byzantine position on the Yarmouk, and the operations soon became both mobile and aggressive. The first enterprise undertaken was the reduction of the nearby city of Busra, one of the Decapolis, or ten Greek cities, established by Alexander the Great nearly a thousand years before. The city made terms with the Arabs and agreed to pay tribute.

Meanwhile Amr ibn al Aasi was still raiding and plundering the plains of

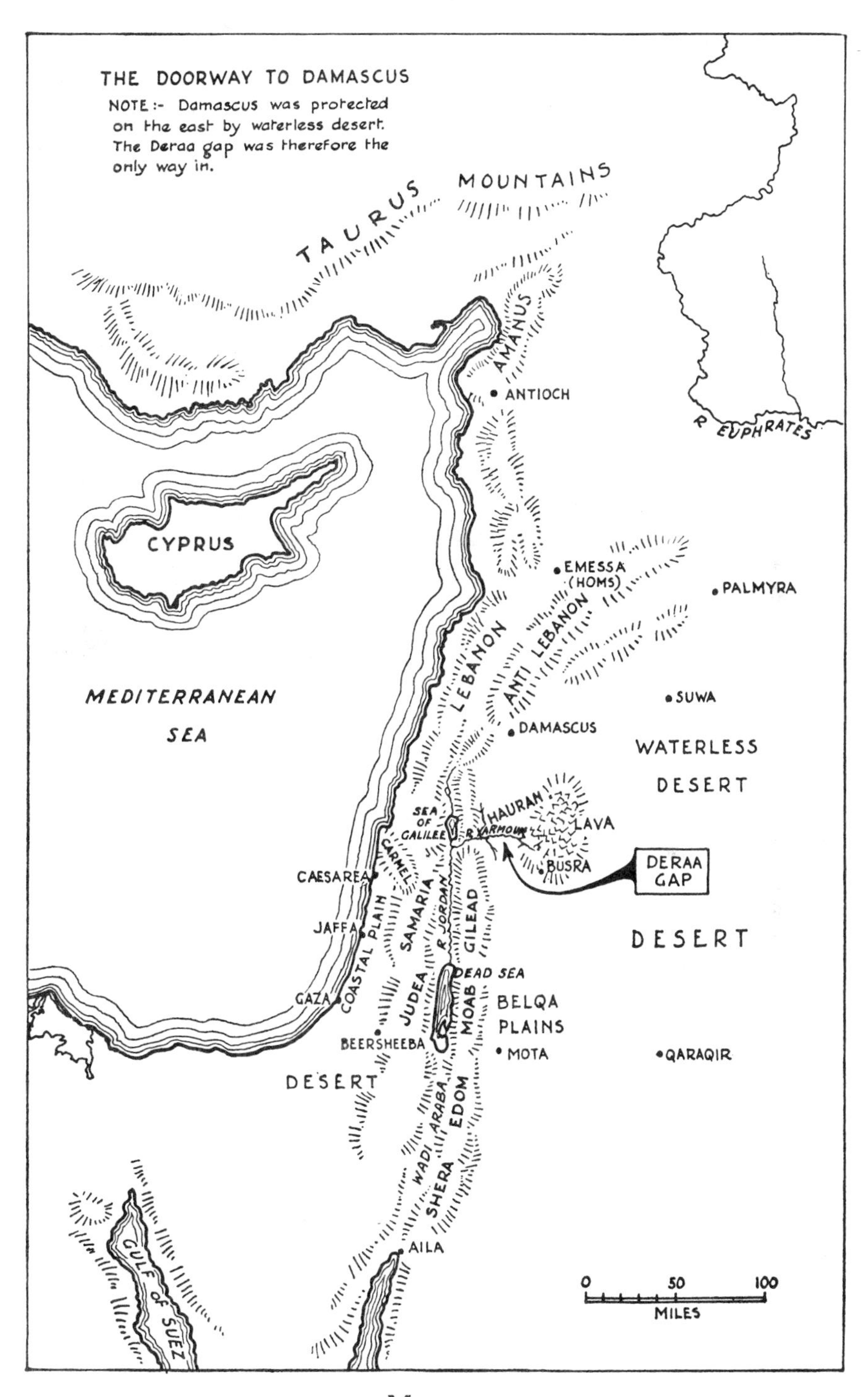
THE DOORWAY TO DAMASCUS
NOTE:- Damascus was protected on the east by waterless desert. The Deraa gap was therefore the only way in.
TAURUS MOUNTAINS
AMANUS
ANTIOCH
R. EUPHRATES
CYPRUS
EMESSA (HOMS)
PALMYRA
LEBANON
ANTI LEBANON
MEDITERRANEAN SEA
SUWA
DAMASCUS
WATERLESS DESERT
HAURAN
LAVA
SEA OF GALILEE
R. YARMOUK
CARMEL
BUSRA
DERAA GAP
CAESAREA
SAMARIA
R. JORDAN
GILEAD
JAFFA
COASTAL PLAIN
DESERT
DEAD SEA
GAZA
JUDEA
MOAB
BELQA PLAINS
BEERSHEEBA
MOTA
QARAQIR
DESERT
WADI ARABA
EDOM
SHERA
AILA
GULF OF SUEZ
0
50
100
MILES

Map XVI

Southern Palestine from his base camp in the Wadi Araba. He was unable or unwilling to venture into the mountains of Judæa, Samaria or Carmel, the Arabs, as already explained, being tactically superior only in the desert and the open plains.

The Emperor Heraclius, who was in Homs, was meanwhile engaged in raising a new army, which he proposed to send to southern Palestine. The despatch of this force seems in itself to indicate that Heraclius was confident that the Yarmouk fortifications would hold. Otherwise he would scarcely have risked sending an army so far away. By doing so, he resumed the initiative and obliged the Arabs to conform.

In Chapter III, a brief account was given of the campaigns of Heraclius against the Persians. It will be remembered that, while Chosroes Parwiz was actually besieging Constantinople, Heraclius had the courage to leave his capital, embark on the Black Sea, land five hundred miles to the east and invade Armenia. He defeated the Persians at Nineveh and was in a position to march on Ctesiphon, thereby compelling Chosroes to evacuate Byzantine territory. It is obvious, therefore, that to hold the enemy on his main line of advance and then force him to withdraw by a wide turning movement, facilitated by his command of the sea, was a strategical operation familiar to the mind of the emperor. He now proceeded to apply it once more.

Relying on the Yarmouk fortifications to halt the Arab advance on Damascus, he noted that Amr ibn al Aasi was operating alone in the Beersheba area. He accordingly sent his main army southwards into Palestine, probably through Tiberias, Nazareth and Caesarea, which could thenceforward be used as an advanced base. The Byzantines had command of the sea and could thus supply their Palestine army from Caesarea or later on from Jaffa or Gaza. The whole object of the operation was to defeat Amr ibn al Aasi in the Beersheba area, while the main Muslim forces were still occupied on the Yarmouk. If this could be accomplished, the Byzantine army could move on to Aila (Aqaba) and, from there, threaten the Muslim line of communications with Mecca and Medina, thus compelling the main Arab army to withdraw from the Yarmouk.

Most historians, considering the ultimate defeat of the Byzantines, have looked upon Heraclius as a feeble imbecile and have shown surprise that a man who could act so boldly against the Persians appeared so incapable against the Arabs. Yet, if my reconstruction be correct, we see the emperor in Syria and Palestine using precisely the same bold strategic methods as had brought him victory against Chosroes. Obviously the key to the plan was the need to overwhelm and destroy Amr ibn al Aasi in Beersheba before he could be reinforced by the main Muslim army on the Yarmouk.

Reports of the southward move of the Byzantine force from Syria to Palestine would doubtless reach the Arab commanders on the Yarmouk. They found themselves in an awkward situation. At the beginning of their invasion, they had parted company from their Beersheba column in the desert near Aila. With their instinctive desire to operate in the familiar terrain of the desert, the main or eastern forces had moved northwards to Busra and Deraa, leaving the mountains of Edom and Moab untouched to the west of

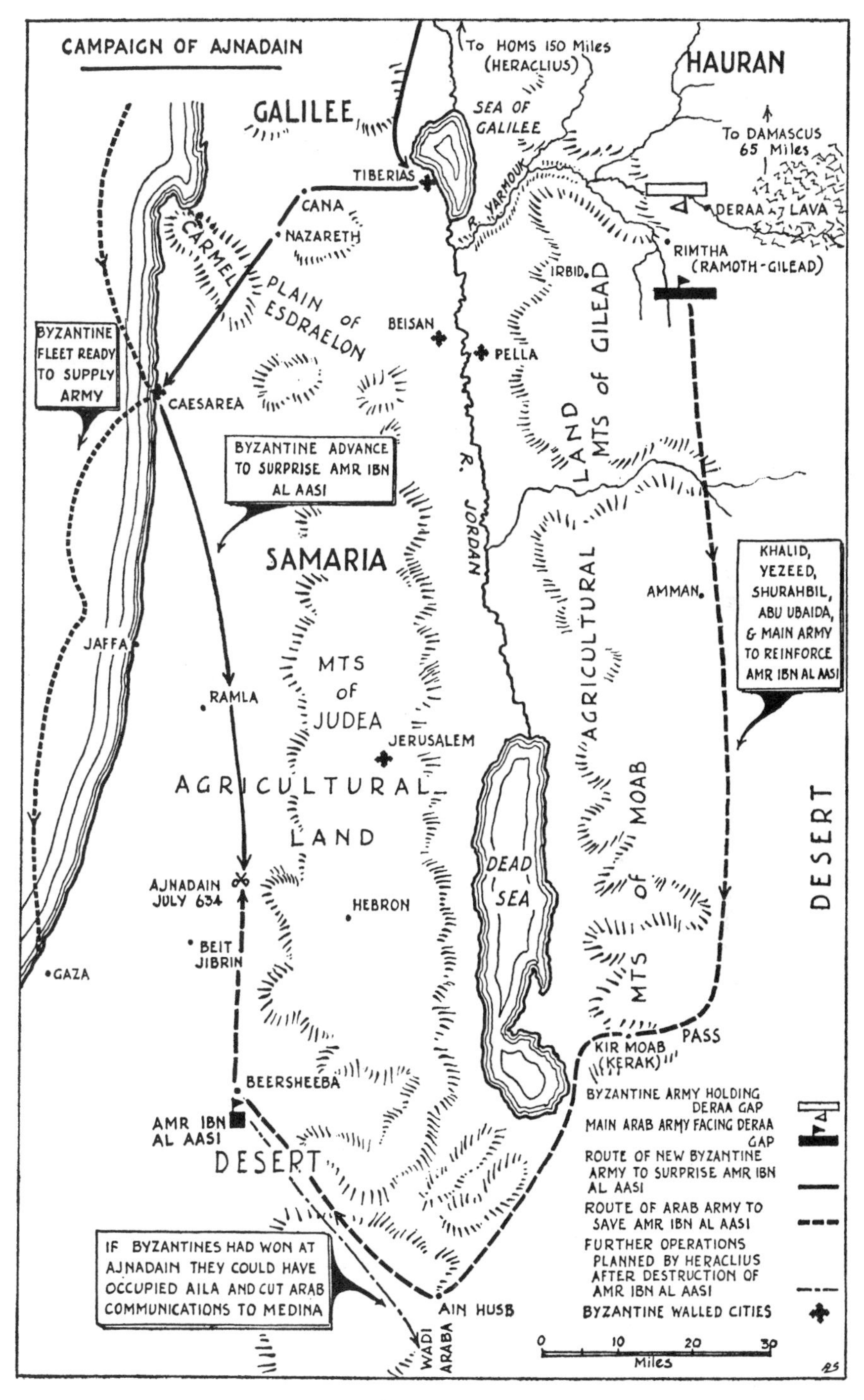

CAMPAIGN OF AJNADAIN
To HOMS 150 Miles (HERACLIUS)
HAURAN
GALILEE
SEA OF GALILEE
To DAMASCUS 65 Miles
TIBERIAS
R. YARMOUK
CANA
NAZARETH
DERAA
LAVA
CARMEL
PLAIN of ESDRAELON
RIMTHA (RAMOTH-GILEAD)
IRBID
BEISAN
PELLA
BYZANTINE FLEET READY TO SUPPLY ARMY
CAESAREA
MTS of GILEAD
LAND
BYZANTINE ADVANCE TO SURPRISE AMR IBN AL AASI
R. JORDAN
SAMARIA
AMMAN
KHALID, YEZEED, SHURAHBIL, ABU UBAIDA, & MAIN ARMY TO REINFORCE AMR IBN AL AASI
AGRICULTURAL
JAFFA
MTS of JUDEA
RAMLA
JERUSALEM
AGRICULTURAL LAND
MTS of MOAB
DEAD SEA
DESERT
AJNADAIN JULY 634
HEBRON
BEIT JIBRIN
GAZA
KIR MOAB (KERAK)
PASS
BEERSHEEBA
AMR IBN AL AASI
DESERT
BYZANTINE ARMY HOLDING DERAA GAP
MAIN ARAB ARMY FACING DERAA GAP
ROUTE OF NEW BYZANTINE ARMY TO SURPRISE AMR IBN AL AASI
ROUTE OF ARAB ARMY TO SAVE AMR IBN AL AASI
FURTHER OPERATIONS PLANNED BY HERACLIUS AFTER DESTRUCTION OF AMR IBN AL AASI
BYZANTINE WALLED CITIES
IF BYZANTINES HAD WON AT AJNADAIN THEY COULD HAVE OCCUPIED AILA AND CUT ARAB COMMUNICATIONS TO MEDINA
AIN HUSB
WADI ARABA
0 10 20 30
Miles


Map XVII

their line of advance. These mountains were not desert, but cultivated land, dotted with towns and villages, which thereby formed a barrier separating Amr ibn al Aasi at Beersheba from Khalid, Abu Ubaida and the main Muslim army on the Yarmouk. When the Arab leaders heard that the Byzantine army was marching southwards through Tiberias and Caesarea, it was already too late for them to be able to rejoin Amr ibn al Aasi by the Aila route. Yet, if they did not join him quickly, he would be overwhelmed in detail.

The Trans-Jordan mountains—the ancient Gilead, Moab and Edom—form an almost impassable barrier of cliffs. There is only one pass through them, leading to the plains of Beersheba by a route south of the Dead Sea. This route lies through Moab (the modern Kerak), skirts the southern shores of the Dead Sea and ascends through Ain Husb to Beersheba. North of this pass, the Trans-Jordan mountains fall in steep cliffs into the Dead Sea. South of it, the mountains are again so steep that riders on horses or camels are obliged to dismount and lead their animals in a dangerous scramble over rocks and ravines. The Arabs could not cross the Jordan north of the Dead Sea because the Byzantines held Jerusalem and the mountains of Judæa.

There was no time to be lost if Amr ibn al Aasi were to be saved. Disappearing from the Yarmouk, the Arabs marched day and night for the Moab pass. Suddenly confronted by a torrent of wild camel-riders, the people of Moab were glad to make terms and open the pass. These towns and villages were inhabited by half-Arab tribes, doubtless of the monophysite Christian sect, by no means enamoured of the Greeks or of the Orthodox Church. The Muslims poured down the pass, across the Wadi Araba and up on to the semi-desert plain of Beersheba, just as the main Byzantine army was marching southwards from Caesarea. The nimble bedouins on their camels, able to travel day and night with only a crust of bread to eat, had won the race against the more ponderous Byzantine army with its civilized paraphernalia. In July 634, a great battle took place at Ajnadain, between Ramla and Beit Jabrin, and the Byzantines were completely defeated. Khalid ibn al Waleed had led the campaign and commanded in the battle. Ikrima, the son of Abu Jahal, the Prophet's uncle, was killed in the action.[3]

The battle of Ajnadain had frustrated Heraclius' strategic counter-offensive. The main Arab forces returned to the Yarmouk, where the Byzantine defences were still holding up the advance on Damascus. The mountainous parts of eastern and northern Palestine were for the moment left unmolested by the Arabs, in accordance with their usual preference for operations in the desert or at least on open plains. Moreover the Byzantine force on the Yarmouk was the only enemy army still in the field. If it also could be defeated, the fortified cities could be reduced at leisure. Once again, in August 634, the main Arab forces faced the Byzantine defences in the Deraa gap.

* * * * *

Meanwhile, however, we must for the moment leave the Syrian front to consider developments in Iraq. It will be remembered that, in December 633

[3] Ikrima was the commander who had suppressed the apostasy in Oman and Hadhramaut. See Chapter V.

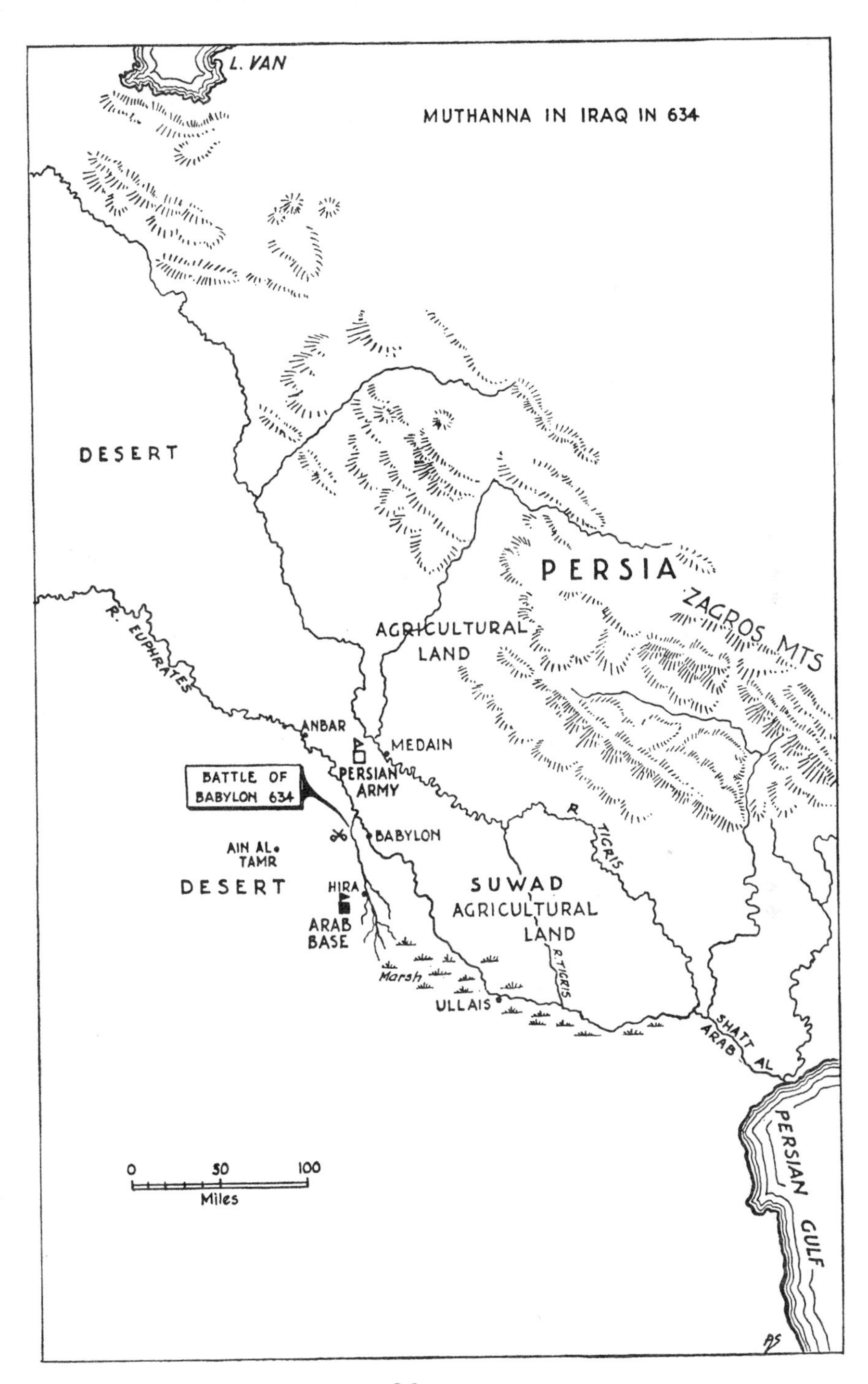

L. VAN
MUTHANNA IN IRAQ IN 634
DESERT
PERSIA
ZAGROS MTS
AGRICULTURAL LAND
R. EUPHRATES
ANBAR
MEDAIN
PERSIAN ARMY
BATTLE OF BABYLON 634
BABYLON
AIN AL TAMR
DESERT
HIRA
ARAB BASE
R TIGRIS
SUWAD AGRICULTURAL LAND
R. TIGRIS
Marsh
ULLAIS
SHATT AL ARAB
PERSIAN GULF
0
50
100
Miles


Map XVIII

or January 634, Khalid had crossed the desert with half the Muslim army of Iraq to reinforce the detachments in Syria. Muthanna, a tribal shaikh of the Beni Bekr, had been left in command in Iraq. The lack of importance attached in Medina to the Persian front is shown by the fact that, while half the force was ordered to Syria, a bedouin chief was left as commander of the remainder. For Quraish were still determined to monopolize all authority and limit high command to themselves. Even, however, if Helpers or Emigrants had been appointed, they would still have been townsmen of Mecca or Medina. The jealousy which divides tribesmen and townsmen today was already evident 1,300 years ago. Muthanna was not only not a Qurashi; he was even a bedouin. Hence the post which he was allowed to retain must have been thought unimportant.

Whatever his lineage, however, he was a man of high courage and of complete devotion, and prepared to face the King of Kings with his handful of tribesmen. The boy king Yezdegird had but recently mounted the throne of Persia and prepared to signalize his accession by driving away these desert marauders. Muthanna offered battle near to the ruins of ancient Babylon, where he awaited the Persian assault, which was led by an elephant. The Arabs had not yet learned how to deal with this early form of "tank" attack and the elephant at first caused some consternation in the ranks. In these early Arab battles it was still a point of honour for the commander to lead the hand-to-hand fighting, to challenge the enemy's general to single combat and to set an example of desperate bravery. Accompanied by a few fellow tribesmen, Muthanna himself attacked the elephant and brought it to the ground. Deprived of its help, the Persians gave way and the Arabs were left the victors in the engagement.

The delays and vacillations of the Persians in face of the feeble force of bedouins commanded by Muthanna can only be explained by the anarchy which had raged for the previous five years.

After their victory at Babylon, Muthanna and his bedouins remained in occupation of the city of Hira and of both banks of the Euphrates from Anbar to the head of the Persian Gulf. To the anxious Muthanna, however, it seemed to be only a matter of time until the enemy despatched a great army, for the civil wars were now ended. Yezdegird admittedly was still a youth but his reign was unopposed and the princes and generals of Persia were busily endeavouring to reorganize the state and the army.

Muthanna as a chief of Beni Bekr must have been perfectly familiar with the Persian government. Moreover, the capital at Medain was only eighty miles from his headquarters at Hira. Presumably aware that the Persians could not be ready for some weeks, he determined to take advantage of the lull himself to ride to Medina and to protest in person to the khalif at the indifference shown by him towards the Persian front. He determined to insist on the despatch of adequate reinforcements.

* * * * *

Abu Bekr had been born three years after the Prophet and appears, therefore, to have been fifty-nine or sixty years of age when he succeeded his master. In the first year of his khalifate, the general apostasy and rebellion of Arabia had kept him fully occupied. Indeed we have seen the aged khalif himself leading forth the people of Medina against the revolted tribes at Dhu al Qassa.[4] But in his second year of office, the tide of war had swept on to Persia and Syria, and Abu Bekr was able to conduct the pilgrimage in person. Two years before, Muhammad himself had led his farewell pilgrimage and the gentle Abu Bekr wept as he remembered his friend and master. Sitting in public in the courtyard of the kaaba as the old patriarchal custom was—and still is in Saudi Arabia—he called on any who had complaints to make to come forward and seek justice, but tradition asserts that no man with a grievance could be found.

Returning to Medina, the old khalif busied himself with the despatch of reinforcements to Syria, where the main Arab forces were held up before the fortified lines of the Yarmouk. In August 634, having apparently bathed on a chilly day, he was seized with fever, which continued to increase, so that he was obliged to delegate Umar ibn al Khattab to lead the public prayers. While he lay thus with a high fever, news was brought of the Arab victory at Ajnadain, which would therefore appear to have occurred in July 634.

The khalif continued to weaken until, after ten or twelve days, he recognized that he had not long to live. Remembering doubtless the narrow margin by which chaos had been avoided after the Prophet's death, he determined to appoint a successor. First he sent for Abdul Rahman ibn Auf, after him for Othman ibn Affan and then for Talha ibn Ubaidullah, and other Emigrants and Helpers, all old men and intimates of the Prophet, and consulted them as to the succession. Finding that the majority favoured Umar ibn al Khattab—though somewhat apprehensive of his severity and hot temper—he ordered Othman ibn Affan to write out an ordinance, appointing Umar to succeed him. Thereupon he gave instructions for this testament to be read out to the assembled people in the mosque. Abu Bekr, like Muhammad before him, occupied a small house looking on to the courtyard of the mosque. Supported by his wife, he was carried to the window, and with a final effort called out in a loud voice that Umar ibn al Khattab was the fittest to take his place, and that he ordered all to render him obedience. "We will obey, we will obey," the people called out in chorus.

When near his end, he enquired what day of the week it was, and was told that it was Monday, the day on which Muhammad also had died. "If I die tonight," he said, "do not delay my burial till tomorrow, for the dearest of days for me is that on which the Apostle of God also died."

On the very day of his death, he gave audience to Muthanna ibn Haritha, who, as already related, had hastened to Medina from Iraq to urge upon the khalif the need for reinforcements to restore the situation on the Persian front. Abu Bekr immediately ordered Umar to raise fresh levies and send them to strengthen the forces in Iraq. Then he urged Umar to restrain the violence of his temper and to use mildness and persuasion. Soon after he felt the agony of death approaching and breathed his last with a prayer on his lips. It was 23rd August, 634.

[4] Page 109.

It has been said that one of the strongest arguments in favour of Muhammad's sincerity is the life and character of Abu Bekr, one of his first converts, the companion of his flight from Mecca and his dearest and most intimate friend. For Muhammad's first successor was a man of simple character and transparent devotion. Following the example of the Prophet, the great victories and rapidly increasing wealth of the Muslims made no difference to his way of life. He lived in what we should call a hut, made of sun-dried mud bricks and roofed with palm-fronds. As ruler of a rapidly expanding empire, his clothing still consisted of a cotton shirt and a rough cloak, similar to those which he had worn fifteen years earlier, as a common citizen of Mecca. He was not above milking the goats for his little family, even while his armies were driving back the legions of Caesar and the levies of the King of Kings.

During his life, the finances of the new empire were still simplicity itself. The fifth of all plunder was sent to Medina from all the battle fronts, but no sooner was it received than it was distributed. Some might be used to acquire weapons, horses or coats of chain-mail for the armies, while the remainder was distributed to the needy among the Muslims. No accounts were kept and the constant emptiness of the treasury was as constantly remedied by the arrival of the loot of fresh victories.

It had been the practice of Muhammad himself to retain no worldly wealth for his own use. Though great sums of money passed through his hands in the form of a fifth of the plunder, all was scrupulously distributed to the needy and the widows of those killed in the wars. Abu Bekr, in this as in all else, had followed in every smallest detail the example set by his friend and master.

* * * * *

Perhaps, on the Yarmouk front, the morale of the Byzantine troops had been depressed by the news of the defeat of Ajnadain, while that of the Arabs had been correspondingly exalted. For whatever reason, fighting now became more active in the Deraa gap and eventually, at the end of August 634, the Muslims carried the position and compelled the Byzantine army to withdraw. The door of Syria had been forced open. The operations were under the supreme command of Khalid ibn al Waleed. At the height of the battle, which lasted for several days, Abu Ubaida received a despatch from Medina, announcing the death of Abu Bekr and the succession of Umar ibn al Khattab to the khalifate. The same messenger carried a letter from Umar, degrading Khalid from the command of the army and appointing Abu Ubaida in his place. The battle being at its height, Abu Ubaida concealed the order until the victory had been won by Khalid.

A personal antipathy had long existed between the new khalif and Khalid. Umar ibn al Khattab, it will be remembered, had advised Abu Bekr to dismiss Khalid at the time of the execution—or murder—of Malik ibn Nuweira,[5] but Abu Bekr had accepted Khalid's explanation of the incident and rejected Umar's advice. As a result of this and other incidents, intense animosity had arisen between Khalid and Umar ibn al Khattab, one of whose

[5] See page 112.

first actions on his assumption of power had been to dismiss the most successful of all the Arab commanders. It is easy to accuse the new khalif of mere personal spite, but Umar was to remain in power for ten years, throughout which he was to show himself a man of sincere religious convictions and of deep personal humility. Khalid was an extremely capable and aggressive commander, always ready to take the initiative and to assume responsibility, but religion was believed to sit lightly on his conscience. He had, during Muhammad's lifetime, obtained a lock of his hair which he invariably wore in his headgear and to which he attributed his safety in his many battles. This may have been superstition rather than religion but at least it seems to show a sincere belief in the Apostle.

We must, however, remember that both the Prophet and his closest companions relied for victory on divine assistance rather than on human skill. In his simple faith, the khalif might well believe that victory would be more certain under a pious commander undistinguished in war, like Abu Ubaida, but one whom God would support, rather than under a more capable soldier whose moral character would scarcely entitle him to the divine favour.

Personal jealousy is one of the principal flaws of the Arab character and a headstrong and ruthless man like Khalid might well have been expected to retire in high dudgeon at his summary dismissal after so many great victories. But nothing of the kind occurred. Khalid readily surrendered the command to the mild and pious Abu Ubaida and agreed to serve on under his command. The two men—so different from one another in character—seem to have reached an intimate personal understanding and, as far as we know, no friction or jealousy ever occurred between them. Doubtless the modest Abu Ubaida was glad to accept the advice of his formidable subordinate on all military affairs, while the astounding victories which Khalid had already won for the Arab cause must have earned for him the universal respect of the Muslims, even if he were no longer their titular commander.

## *NOTABLE DATES*

| | |
|---|---|
| Battle of Babylon in Iraq | Spring 634 |
| Battle of Ajnadain in Palestine | July 634 |
| Death of Abu Bekr | 23rd August 634 |
| First Battle of Yarmouk | End of August or early September 634 |

## *PERSONALITIES*

Abu Ubaida, new Arab Commander-in-Chief in Syria.
Umar ibn al Khattab, the new khalif.
Muthanna ibn Haritha, commander in Iraq.
Amr ibn al Aasi<br>Yezeed ibn abi Sofian<br>Shurahbil ibn Hasana } Arab column commanders in Palestine and Syria.
Khalid ibn al Waleed, dismissed by Umar.
Yezdegird, new King of Persia.

# VIII

## *The Swaying Struggle*

It is incumbent on you to fight although you may dislike it. And perhaps you dislike a thing and it is good for you, or perhaps you like a thing and it is evil for you. Allah knows but you know nothing. *Qoran* II, 216

It matters not who is our commander-in-chief if God be so.
OLIVER CROMWELL

# VIII

## THE SWAYING STRUGGLE

THE new khalif seemed in many ways to offer a striking contrast to his predecessor. Abu Bekr had been slight and stooping, modest, rather frail in his old age, and of a gentle and forgiving disposition. Umar ibn al Khattab was so tall that, as an Arab writer vividly put it, he towered above the crowd as if he were riding a horse. He was of a naturally hasty temper, inclined to be outspoken and impetuous, and more addicted to severity than to compassion. Yet the mild Abu Bekr could, in a crisis, display both firmness and dynamic energy. In the same way, the hot-tempered Umar was, on more than one occasion, to exercise no less compassion than the gentle Abu Bekr. Both had one quality in common—they were determined in every detail to follow the example of the Prophet. This determination made them both humble, for they were not seeking their own advantage or aggrandizement. Both showed the transparent simplicity which often characterizes men entirely dedicated to religion. Muslim tradition imputes to Muhammad the saying that "Verily God hath placed truth upon the tongue of Umar ibn al Khattab and upon his heart."

Both the first two khalifs, though swaying the power of emperors, remained poor, ill-clad and frugal and lived, in their modest huts, the lives of humble peasants. Umar is alleged himself to have said that he was entitled to nothing except two garments, a garment for winter and a garment for summer, and enough money to enable him to perform the pilgrimage. His food and that of his family, he claimed, was like that of a man of Quraish, neither the richest nor the poorest of them. He expected his subordinates to practise the same austerity and when he appointed a governor to some newly conquered province he was careful to warn him not to eat delicate food or to wear fine clothes or to close the doors of his house to the poor. Many witnesses record the numerous patches sewn on to the khalif's garments, while it was alleged that, when on a journey, he took no tent with him but would throw his cloak over a low bush and lie down in the patch of shade thus produced. Bedouins still do this and I have often done it myself when travelling in their company.

* * * * *

As has already been told in the previous chapter, the Muslims, early in September 634, had somehow overrun the Yarmouk position and advanced into the hitherto virgin district of Hauran, which lies immediately south of Damascus.

When the Byzantine army had marched to the plains of southern Palestine—only to be defeated at Ajnadain—it had used the road from Baalbek to

Tiberias, crossing those low hills overlooking the peaceful Sea of Galilee, where the Sermon on the Mount had been delivered.

Thence it probably climbed the steep track from Tiberias up on to the plateau of Galilee, through Cana (where the water was turned into wine), then through Nazareth and across the plain of Esdraelon to Caesarea. This route was protected from interference by the Arabs (who, it will be remembered, were at Deraa), by the fortresses of Pella and Beisan. Tiberias itself was also a fortified town. Pella was a particularly important post. It had been one of the ten Greek cities founded by Alexander the Great, of which there was a whole group in this area—Gadara (of the biblical swine), Busra which we have already seen paying tribute to the Muslims, Philadelphia, the modern Amman capital of Jordan, and Gerasa, now known as Jerash. In the seventh century, as in the days of Alexander a thousand years earlier, main roads passed through this area and it was important to defend them against desert marauders. The main military road to Palestine from the north lay through Damascus, Deraa, Pella and Beisan and was blocked by the Yarmouk position. So Heraclius had sent his column through Tiberias and Nazareth to Ajnadain.

It will be remembered that, after Ajnadain, the main Arab forces had hastened back to the Yarmouk, while Amr ibn al Aasi remained in the Beersheba plain. The remnants of the Byzantine army had perhaps withdrawn to Jerusalem and Caesarea and from thence part of it was sent to strengthen Pella, from which position it threatened the communications of the Arab army now moving northwards on Damascus. Accordingly it appears that the Muslim commanders decided to seize Pella—known to the Arabs then as now by the name of Fahel—and thus protect their communications before advancing on Damascus. Some historians allege that the matter was referred to Umar ibn al Khattab in Medina. Arab accounts include somewhat obscure references to the floods which the Byzantines had produced near Pella to hinder the Arab operations. Suffice it to say that, in January or February 635, Abu Ubaida advanced on Pella, defeated a Byzantine force outside the town, perhaps in the partly-flooded Jordan valley, and laid siege to the fortress itself. The inhabitants eventually negotiated their surrender, agreeing to pay a poll-tax and a land-tax to the victors. In return, Abu Ubaida guaranteed their lives and property, and agreed not to demolish the city or its walls.[1]

His line of communications having been thus secured, he advanced northwards on Damascus. In the last attempt to save the city, a Byzantine army offered battle at Marj as Suffar,[2] probably some twenty miles south of Damascus.

It was approximately at the same place that the Vichy French offered battle in an attempt to save Damascus in 1941, when British troops invaded Syria from Jordan through the Deraa gap. There is a natural defensive position

[1] Some accounts make the fall of Pella after that of Damascus.
[2] Pronounced like the English word "suffer".

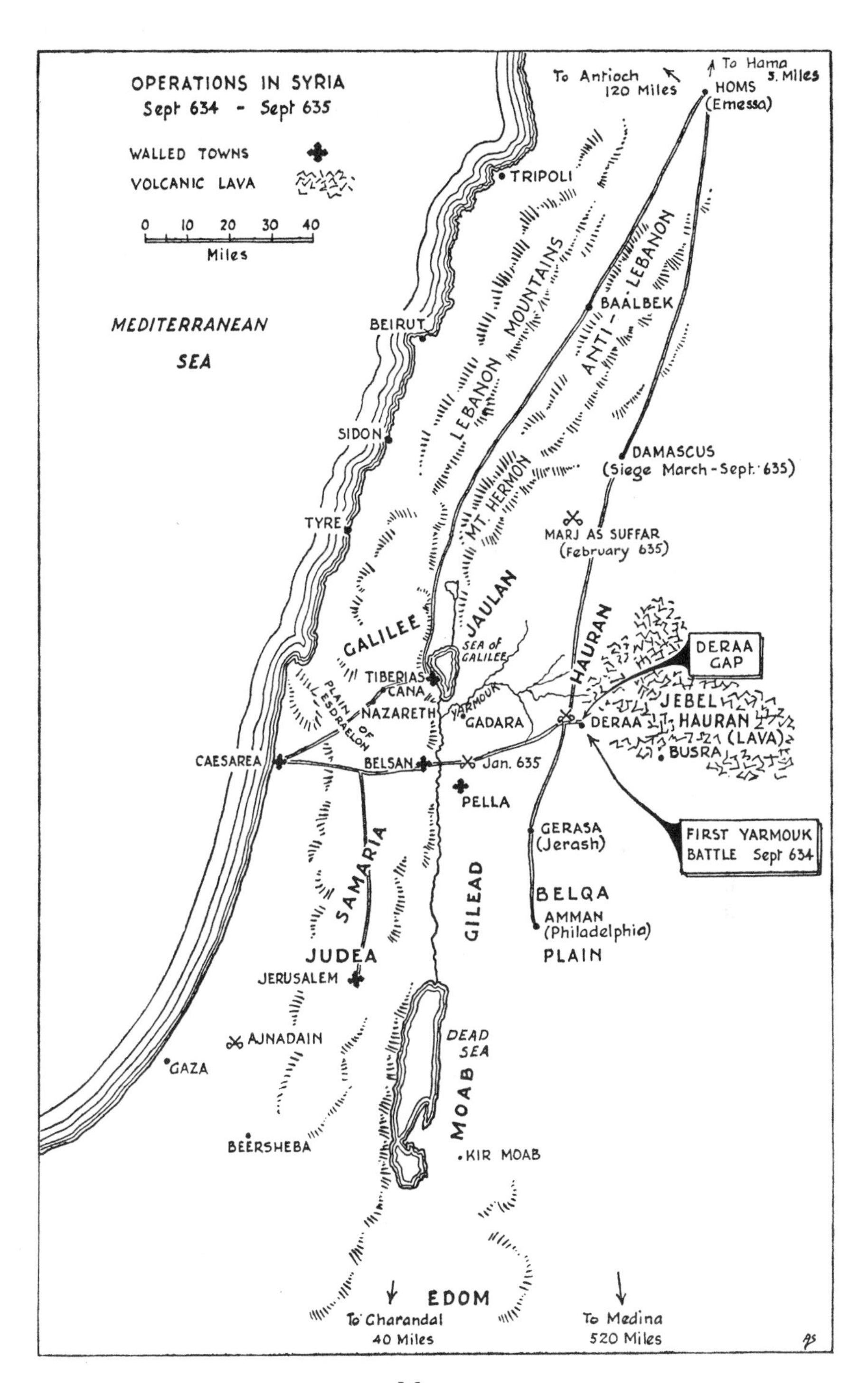
OPERATIONS IN SYRIA
Sept 634 - Sept 635
WALLED TOWNS
VOLCANIC LAVA
0 10 20 30 40
Miles
MEDITERRANEAN
SEA
To Antioch
120 Miles
To Hama
5 Miles
HOMS
(Emessa)
TRIPOLI
LEBANON MOUNTAINS
ANTI - LEBANON
BAALBEK
BEIRUT
SIDON
MT. HERMON
DAMASCUS
(Siege March - Sept. 635)
TYRE
MARJ AS SUFFAR
(February 635)
GALILEE
JAULAN
HAURAN
SEA of GALILEE
DERAA GAP
TIBERIAS
CANA
NAZARETH
PLAIN OF ESDRAELON
YARMOUK
GADARA
DERAA
JEBEL
HAURAN
(LAVA)
BUSRA
CAESAREA
BELSAN
Jan. 635
PELLA
GERASA
(Jerash)
FIRST YARMOUK
BATTLE Sept 634
SAMARIA
GILEAD
BELQA
AMMAN
(Philadelphia)
PLAIN
JUDEA
JERUSALEM
AJNADAIN
DEAD SEA
GAZA
MOAB
BEERSHEBA
KIR MOAB
EDOM
To Charandal
40 Miles
To Medina
520 Miles

Map XIX

here.[3] The battle of Marj as Suffar took place in February 635. The Arabs were again victorious and the Byzantines withdrew, though only after a well-contested and costly battle. In mid-March 635, the Arabs arrived before Damascus.

The original columns sent against Syria by Abu Bekr had, it will be remembered, been commanded respectively by Amr ibn al Aasi, Shurahbil ibn Hasana, and Yezeed ibn abi Sofian. When Khalid came from Iraq, he assumed supreme command, which, on the accession of Umar ibn al Khattab, he had surrendered to Abu Ubaida. He retained command of the force which he had brought from Iraq. The army in Syria was now, therefore, divided into four separate columns, although under the supreme command of Abu Ubaida.

Khalid, with a force of 5,000 men, now camped outside the east gate. Abu Ubaida himself lay on the south-west of the city and the other commanders were each allotted a length of the walls.

The Arabs were untrained and unequipped for the siege of a great city. We have already seen that the Prophet saved Medina from Quraish by the simple expedient of digging a single ditch. But, while they could not effectively bombard the walls, the Arabs were doubtless extremely efficient at harrying the surrounding country and cutting off supplies and communications. The siege of Damascus probably began in the second half of March 635, but it was not until late in the summer that the Arabs met with any success. Damascus was near enough to the desert to be familiar with the wayward character of the bedouins and the citizens probably hoped that a month or two of siege warfare would weary the fickle nomads, who would melt away as the army of Quraish had done from Medina.

It was noted in the previous chapter that Khalid, during his famous march from Iraq, had skirmished outside Damascus. He was rumoured to have exchanged communications on that occasion with the Christian bishop of the city. Whether he in fact had done so on the previous occasion is doubtful but now, in the summer of 635, such a correspondence appears undoubtedly to have been opened. The bishop was almost certainly a monophysite and thus probably opposed to the Byzantine government and the Orthodox hierarchy.

The reports of the fall of Damascus differ in certain details. According to that most generally accepted, the bishop sent a messenger to Khalid to inform him that on a certain night there was to be a celebration in the city and that the east gate, opposite his position, would be left virtually unguarded. There was a Christian monastery outside the walls in this area and presumably under the jurisdiction of the bishop. This monastery supplied the Arabs with two ladders and, a little before dawn, these were placed against the wall near the east gate. A number of Arabs, led by Qaqaa, the Beni Temeem shaikh who had come with Khalid from Iraq,[4] crept silently up. Two men left on guard by the garrison were quickly overpowered and the gate was opened from the inside. Just before sunrise, the Arabs poured into the city,

[3] It was at about the same place that six hundred years before, Paul had seen the vision which resulted in his conversion.

[4] Page 128.

manned the walls and, raising the cry of *Allahu akbar,* laid on with sword and dagger.

No sooner did the governor hear the sudden sounds of battle than he despatched a hasty messenger to Abu Ubaida through the south-western gate, offering to surrender the city on terms. The commander-in-chief appears to have been unaware that Khalid had already carried the east gate, a fact which, if true, would seem to indicate that a certain lack of co-operation did exist between the two leaders. On the other hand, it is possible that Abu Ubaida was aware that the Muslims were already inside the city but that, looking forward to the day when Damascus would be the Arab provincial capital, he wished to stay the bloodshed and avoid the looting of so splendid a city. Suffice it to say that the governor threw open the south-west gate to Abu Ubaida while fighting against Khalid's column was still in progress in the eastern quarter of the town.

The two commanders met in the coppersmiths' bazaar in the centre of the city. Abu Ubaida informed his perhaps excited subordinate that fighting must cease, as a capitulation had been signed. Khalid at first demurred, claiming that the city had in reality been taken by assault, but the venerable Abu Ubaida insisted that, however that might be, he had now signed an agreement, which must be respected. Thus was this great city, probably one of the oldest in the world (it is mentioned in the Book of Genesis), saved, for this time at least, from plunder and carnage.[5]

An alternative Arab account reverses the rôles of the two commanders. Khalid is alleged to have signed an agreement with the governor, while Abu Ubaida broke in at the south-west gate. The account given above seems, however, to be the more authentic and more consonant with the respective characters of the two commanders.

The terms of surrender prescribed that every non-Muslim should pay a poll-tax of one dinar and one measure of wheat per year. According to some accounts, the houses and churches of the city were to be divided in half between the Arab conquerors and the inhabitants. As a result, the great cathedral of St. John was itself bisected by a partition wall, on one side of which the Muslims prayed in their serried ranks, while on the other the Christian rites were still performed.

Ever since the Battle of Ajnadain a year before, the Arab forces had remained concentrated in their campaign from the Yarmouk to Damascus. But with the fall of the city, Byzantine resistance was thought to be at an end, and each column returned to the area to which it had originally been directed. Amr ibn al Aasi marched back to Palestine and laid siege to Jerusalem, which, however, as usual, he was unable to assault. Shurahbil ibn Hasana returned to the Jordan and accepted the surrender of Beisan and Tiberias. Abu Ubaida himself moved northward, receiving the capitulation of Baalbek, Homs and Hama. Khalid established himself in Homs, formerly the headquarters of Heraclius, who had now been obliged to withdraw to Antioch. It will be remembered that, at the time of the campaign of Ajnadain, the long line of Jordan mountains from Gilead to Edom was still un-

[5] The fall of Damascus probably occurred in August or September 635.

occupied by the Arabs, though they had broken through at Moab to go to the help of Amr ibn al Aasi in Beersheba. Yezeed ibn abi Sofian now turned southwards to remedy the omission and accepted the capitulation of all Moab, the Shera mountains and Edom, including the post at Gharandal (where, exactly 1,300 years later, I was to build a fort for the Arab Legion).[6] Only Jerusalem and Caesarea still held out in Palestine, while, further north, the coastal cities of Tyre, Sidon, Beirut and Tripoli, encouraged by the Byzantine command of the sea, still adhered to the cause of Heraclius.

Such were the events of the Syrian campaign in 635, the first year of the khalifate of Umar ibn al Khattab. Now we must turn to examine the situation on the Persian front during the same period.

* * * * *

We have already seen that almost the last act of Abu Bekr was to receive Muthanna ibn Haritha, who had ridden in hot haste from the Euphrates to beg for help on the neglected Persian front. The first act of Umar ibn al Khattab on assuming the khalifate had been to dismiss Khalid ibn al Waleed from the supreme command in Syria. The second had been, as the dying Abu Bekr had ordered, to raise a new levy for Iraq. Volunteers were at first slow in coming forward, for the Persians seem to have enjoyed the reputation of being more formidable than the Byzantines in war. As a result, recruiting proceeded but slowly, even though Muthanna himself made a speech in the mosque calling for assistance, and describing the immense plunder obtainable by those who followed the path of God and fought against the fire-worshippers.[7]

The first recruit to offer himself was a citizen of Taif, commonly known as Abu Ubaid. As the numbers increased, it was suggested to the khalif that he select a commander, either from the Emigrants or the Helpers, or at least a Companion of the Prophet. Umar, however, was perhaps indignant at the slowness with which the recruits had come forward. "What constitutes the glory of the Companions except that they should be the most eager to fight?" he asked, declaring that the first man who had volunteered was the most worthy to be the commander. Thus the apparently obscure Abu Ubaid ibn Masud[8] suddenly found himself a general.

This extraordinary incident is worthy of further emphasis, for it illustrates the fantastically haphazard methods by which the Arabs conquered a great empire. Moreover, it was not an isolated event of its kind. We have already seen how the Prophet himself had chosen Usama ibn Zeid (the son of his adopted son) to command the raid into Syria, placing Khalid ibn al Waleed, an experienced veteran, under his orders. It has indeed been well said that the Arabs were victorious not owing to, but in spite of, their commanders. In the case of Umar ibn al Khattab, it may illustrate his sole reliance on God and hence his utter indifference to the human instruments he employed, provided only that they be fervent believers. In so far as the Arabs at large were

[6] See also Map XVI, page 143.

[7] The Persians were Zoroastrians.

[8] Not to be confused with Abu Ubaida, already commander-in-chief in Syria, and one of the oldest Companions.

concerned, however, it perhaps showed their belief that battles were won by desperate courage alone, and that no skill, training or organization were required from a commander. Yet in spite of these crude ideas of war, the Arabs were almost invariably victorious.

Strange as it may seem, the Arabic-speaking peoples of today seem still to harbour the same beliefs, although war has become immensely more technical and although their soldiers are no longer fired by a passionate religious faith. In the years from 1948 to 1956, I was involved on frequent occasions in the discussions of their leaders on the subject of military operations against Israel. Again and again the opinion was expressed that a few thousand good men armed with rifles would soon dispose of the enemy, no reference being made to the need for training, organization or a competent general, any more than in the days of Umar ibn al Khattab.

Another aspect of the khalif's selection of Abu Ubaid was his neglect of Muthanna, who had been in sole command in Iraq for over a year, had recently won the Battle of Babylon and whose stirring appeals had, on that very day, produced the recruits for whom a leader was needed. But Muthanna ibn Haritha was a bedouin from Beni Bekr on the other side of Arabia. Helpers, Emigrants and Companions, citizens of Medina, Mecca and Taif, would not be prepared to serve under the command of a bedouin chief. Yet it might have been expected that veterans of Bedr and Uhud would have objected equally to service under an unknown individual from Taif. It would seem as if the general rivalry between towns and tribes was a more powerful sentiment than even personal ambition.

Meanwhile, allegedly on Muthanna's advice, the khalif removed one of the principal obstacles to Arab conquest. It will be remembered that when the "apostate" tribes were defeated in Abu Bekr's time, he had ruled that no member of the tribes which had rebelled was to be allowed again to go to war on the side of the Muslims. The ban prevented the majority of the tribes of Arabia from fighting in the Arab cause. Meanwhile Arab armies had invaded simultaneously the world's two greatest empires and the shortage of manpower was becoming a serious problem. The removal of the prohibition released the pent-up energies of hordes of war-like tribesmen. Thenceforward the Arab armies consisted less of contingents of volunteer fighters than of whole tribes, migrating en masse, accompanied by their wives, children, tents and flocks.

At length the reinforcements set out from Medina. Muthanna, anxious for his men during his absence, hastened on ahead. Abu Ubaid followed more slowly with the new volunteers, summoning all the (once apostate) tribes whom he passed on his way to join his banner for the war against Persia.

Meanwhile the renewal of Persian military activity which Muthanna had foretold was actually taking place. Yezdegird had appointed Rustem, the army commander whose support had placed him on the throne, to the chief command on the Euphrates front. The new general had urged the nobles and landlords to withhold the tribute which they had previously paid to the Arabs, and to rebel against their control. Several columns were sent out on offensive reconnaissances and behind them strong forces were despatched to drive out the Arab invaders.

Such was the situation which Muthanna found on his return from Medina. Too weak to oppose these Persian columns, he was obliged to abandon Hira and all the cultivated area of the delta, and to withdraw to the edge of the desert west of the Euphrates, to await the arrival of Abu Ubaid with the reinforcements. These eventually reached the front and Abu Ubaid assumed command of the operations. The Arabs moved forward and defeated various Persian columns in a number of minor actions. Rustem, however, was undaunted by these reverses, and concentrating his forces into a single army, sent it forward from Medain towards Hira.

Abu Ubaid followed the example of the Persian commander and, having effected a junction between his new army and the forces of Muthanna, moved up towards Hira also. The two armies, perhaps in October 634, confronted one another across the Euphrates, a short distance north of the city. (In Syria, the Arabs had shortly before overrun the Yarmouk position and were preparing to attack Pella.)

Tradition relates that the Persian general Bahman sent a messenger to Abu Ubaid, giving him the choice whether he preferred to cross the river to the Persians or whether he would rather that the latter crossed over to him. A great river offered an almost insuperable obstacle to a seventh century army. If it were too wide for archers to shoot across, it was impossible to give "covering fire" to an army attempting to cross in the face of the enemy. Thus unless the two commanders agreed as to which should cross unmolested, no battle could take place.

Gibbon mentions a similar offer regarding a river crossing made on a different occasion by a Persian commander to a Byzantine general. An even more curious example is related by Oman.[9] In 1260, Bela IV, King of Hungary, was at war with Ottokar II of Bohemia. The two armies sighted one another across the River March. Ottokar courteously requested Bela to decide which of the two armies should cross unhindered, in order that a battle in due form might take place.

In spite of the advice of his more experienced subordinates (Muthanna had been fighting the Persians for years), Abu Ubaid decided to cross the Euphrates and offer battle to the enemy on the east bank ."Shall we fear death more than they?" cried the khalif's impulsive general dramatically. Salit ibn Qais advised him to wait on the west bank so that the Arabs could use their invariable tactics of fighting with the desert at their backs. Muthanna, himself a bedouin, must certainly have given the same advice.

When they reached the east bank, thc Arabs found themselves in enclosed country unsuited to their mobile tactics. The Persians then advanced, preceded by an elephant or, some say, by numerous elephants ,which stampeded the horses of the Arabs. The battle continued for several hours, the Muslims endeavouring to attack the elephants on foot with their swords, some trying to cut the girths by which the howdahs were attached to their backs. Abu Ubaid who, if rash and inexperienced, was not lacking in courage, himself

[9] Oman, *The Art of War in the Middle Ages*.

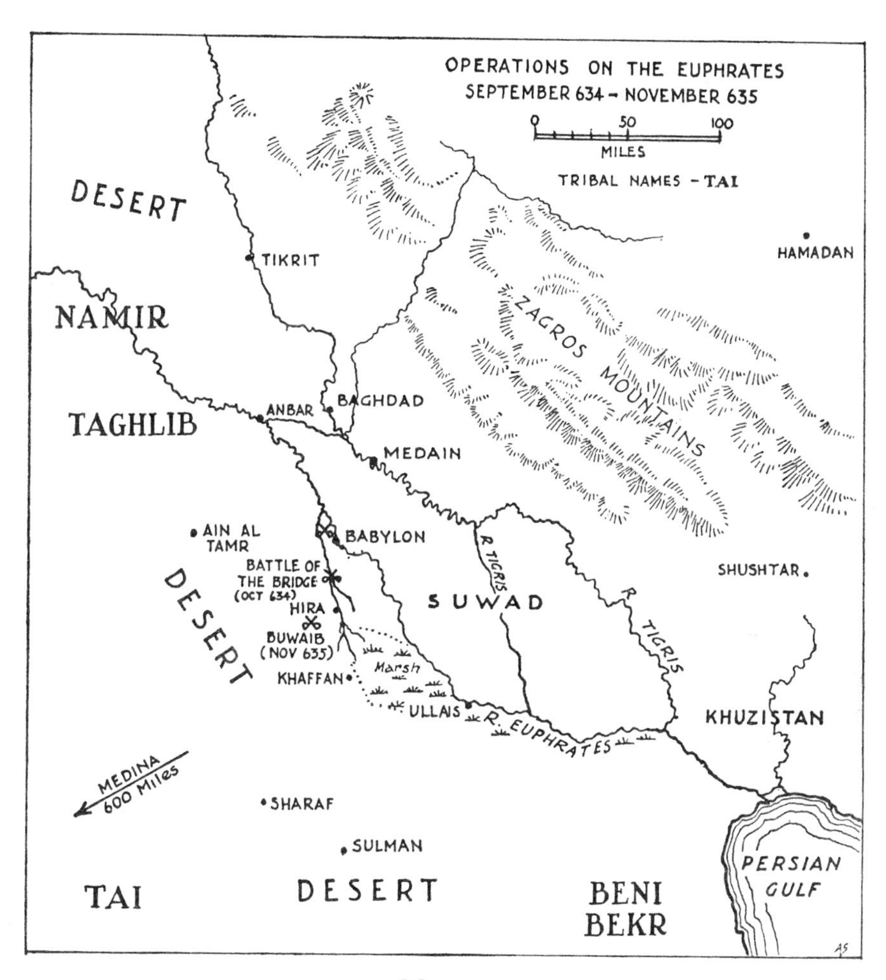
OPERATIONS ON THE EUPHRATES
SEPTEMBER 634 – NOVEMBER 635
0 50 100
MILES
TRIBAL NAMES – TAI
DESERT
TIKRIT
HAMADAN
NAMIR
ZAGROS MOUNTAINS
TAGHLIB
ANBAR
BAGHDAD
MEDAIN
AIN AL TAMR
BABYLON
BATTLE OF THE BRIDGE (OCT 634)
DESERT
HIRA
BUWAIB (NOV 635)
R. TIGRIS
SUWAD
SHUSHTAR
R. TIGRIS
Marsh
KHAFFAN
ULLAIS
R. EUPHRATES
KHUZISTAN
MEDINA 600 Miles
SHARAF
SULMAN
PERSIAN GULF
TAI
DESERT
BENI BEKR

Map xx

ran at the leading elephant. He had been told that its trunk was the most vulnerable part of the animal, and he accordingly slashed at it with his sword. The elephant, however, seized him with its trunk and, throwing him to the ground, trampled him to death beneath its feet. Seeing their commander killed, the Arabs became increasingly confused, though his brother, Al Hakam ibn Masud, seized the flag and planted it in the ground again, until he also fell.

At this critical moment, a man of Thaqeef, the tribe to which Abu Ubaid also belonged, ran to the floating bridge by which the Arabs had crossed the Euphrates, and cut the boats adrift. "Die as your commander has died or avenge him by victory," he shouted to the Arabs who were jostling one another in their efforts to escape. Instead of inspiring them thereby to a more desperate resistance, his action produced the opposite effect. Seeing their retreat cut off, they yielded to panic, many throwing themselves into the Euphrates in an attempt to swim across to safety.

Seizing the banner, Muthanna ibn Haritha rallied a handful of brave men around him and, in a desperate hand-to-hand mêlée, attempted to gain a momentary respite. Ordering that the bridge be repaired, he cried that he would hold the Persians at bay until the remainder of the now demoralized Arabs could cross. It is here perhaps worthy of note that a Christian bedouin chief of the tribe of Tai, one Abu Zubaid by name, was prominent among the heroic band who stood firm by Muthanna and covered the retreat of the panic-stricken Muslims. The fellow-feeling of bedouins fighting against Persian foreigners was presumably his incentive, and not religious enthusiasm. (Muthanna himself had only been converted to Islam about a year before.)

Eventually temporary repairs to the bridge were effected and the remnant of the Arab force, Muthanna still covering the rear, was able to withdraw across the river. Some four thousand Arabs had been killed or drowned in the Euphrates, while two thousand more deserted after the battle and returned to Arabia. Muthanna, now once more in command, was left with only some three thousand men out of an army probably about ten thousand strong before the battle. Meanwhile he himself had been seriously wounded by the thrust of a lance during his rear-guard action. The disaster was complete and was almost entirely due, it would appear, to the folly of Abu Ubaid. If the Arabs, instead of crossing the Euphrates, had fought on the west bank, no such catastrophe could have occurred. For open plains favoured their tactics and, in the event of a reverse, they could have withdrawn into the desert, their natural element and one into which the heavy Persians could not follow them. This battle is recorded in Arab history as the Battle of the Bridge or of Quss al Natif. It was fought in October 634, some three months after the death of Abu Bekr.

Muthanna withdrew through the desert, parallel with the west bank of the Euphrates, to near Ullais, meanwhile sending to all the bedouin tribes and calling upon them to join him in the war. Jareer ibn Abdulla, a chief of the Beni Bajeela tribe of the Yemen, arriving in Medina with a contingent, was persuaded by the khalif to go on to Iraq, though it is perhaps significant that, before he would do so, Umar ibn al Khattab was obliged to promise him an extra share of all plunder. The removal of the ban against the "apostate" tribes was also now beginning to bear fruit and many tribal contingents began to arrive at Medina. The majority wished to go to Syria, but the khalif was insistent that all must proceed at best speed to Iraq. (In Syria all was going well and the Arabs were advancing on Damascus.)

Another welcome reinforcement was received directly by Muthanna from the Beni Namir and Taghlib tribes of the northern Syrian desert. These tribes were Christians, led by the chief Anis ibn Hilal, and are alleged to have said that, although not Muslims, they were surely obliged to fight on the side of their own people. Thus reinforced, Muthanna, a year after the disastrous Battle of the Bridge, moved forward once again to the vicinity of Hira. The Persians thereupon concentrated their forces to meet him. Muthanna, however, was not to be enticed across the river and eventually the Persians crossed the Euphrates and the two armies, probably late in November 635, were drawn up at Al Buwaib, between the present towns of Kufa and Nejef.

Many of the tribal reinforcements from Central Arabia, which continued to pour in, had brought their flocks and families with them. These were now deposited on the edge of the desert, principally at Khaffan, a place on the right bank of the Euphrates perhaps some twenty-five miles south of Hira.

When the two armies were drawn up opposite to one another at Buwaib, Muthanna rode down the Arab lines, exhorting the Muslims to stand fast in the forthcoming battle. As he did so, he noticed a man break out of the ranks, in spite of the protests of his comrades. When he asked the reason, he was informed that the man in question had run away at the Battle of the Bridge. Stung by remorse, he now wished to atone for his fault by charging the Persian army alone and being killed. Muthanna rode on up the line in silence until he reached the scene of the altercation. Then touching the man on the shoulder with the tip of his lance, he said, "Do not just get yourself killed. You will serve God better by fighting in the ranks with your comrades." The man stepped back silently into the line and Muthanna rode on.

Before the Arabs could attack, the Persians opened the battle by advancing in three columns, each led by an elephant, which was itself escorted by a company of men on foot. The infantry and the elephants worked in tactical co-operation, as infantry and tanks have done in recent European wars. The elephants were to break through the Arab lines, while the infantry protected them from the lances and sword-thrusts of the Muslims. The Persian advance was accompanied by much noise, shouting and beating of drums.

The first brunt of the attack fell on the tribe of Beni Ijl, whose ranks were broken and who began to retreat in some confusion. Those near to Muthanna saw him stroking his beard, a sign of his anxiety. Then he hastily despatched a man to Beni Ijl with an urgent message: "The ameer[10] salutes you and says, 'do not disgrace the Muslims today'." The broken ranks reformed and the Arabs began to hold the Persian attack. Glancing towards Muthanna again, where he sat motionless on his mare, they saw that he had ceased to pull his beard and was laughing.

The mêlée swayed to and fro, amid wild cries and confusion, but the Per-

[10] The word ameer originally meant simply commander.

sian attack made little further progress. At length Muthanna, who must have possessed the flair of a great commander for knowing the decisive moment of action, determined to launch his counter-attack. For this purpose, he placed himself at the head of the Christian tribes of Namir and Taghlib and, calling upon them to prove themselves Arabs even though they were not Muslims, he led the charge against the centre of the Persian line. A desperate mêlée ensued, the whole battle wrapped in a dense cloud of dust. A Christian boy of Taghlib killed the Persian commander Mihran and at length the enemy centre was thrown into confusion. Seeing this, the whole Arab line advanced, Jareer leading Beni Bajeela, Arfaja at the head of Azd and Muthanna's brother, Masud, with Beni Bekr.

Beginning to give way, the Persian army made for the bridge over the Euphrates, which lay behind its front. But Muthanna, who had broken through the centre, had reached the bridge first and denied it to the enemy. Seeing their retreat thus cut off, the Persians turned in despair and fought their way into the advancing Arabs. The fighting on both sides became more desperate and casualties were heavy. Muthanna's brother, Masud, received a fatal wound. Seeing his fellow-tribesmen falter, he called out with all his dying strength, "Raise your banner, Bekr ibn Wail. God will exalt you. Do not be distressed at my death." Anis ibn Hilal, the Christian chief of the Namir tribe, was also killed in Muthanna's charge. The Persian army now broke in confusion and panic. The Muslims held the bridge and the terrified enemy fled here and there, some throwing themselves into the Euphrates, some seeking to hide in the undergrowth on the river bank, some turning back to be slaughtered by the triumphant Arabs. Thus was the Battle of Buwaib a bloody revenge for the Battle of the Bridge.

When the struggle was over, a coarse rug was unrolled on the bare earth and Muthanna sat down to relax from the emotions of the day. The Arab leaders came up one by one to congratulate him on the victory and, sitting in a circle on the dusty ground, began to discuss the incidents of the battle. "The Arabs have fought against the Persians in the days of the Ignorance and of Islam," said Muthanna. "In the days of the Ignorance, a hundred Persians could defeat a thousand Arabs, but now, God be praised, a hundred Arabs can put to flight a thousand Persians."

The part played by the River Euphrates in these battles is of interest. In general, there was little cultivation on the west bank of the river, but on the east bank, cultivation, gardens and irrigation ditches were continuous. The Arabs, therefore, always preferred to fight on the edge of the desert on the west bank, which meant that, if there were to be a battle at all, the Persians had to cross the river. In the event of their defeat, they were then hemmed in by the Euphrates behind them. On the occasion of the Battle of the Bridge, however, Abu Ubaid had crossed into the cultivated area, where the terrain was unsuitable for the Arabs and where they, in their turn, were hemmed in against the Euphrates when defeated. Neither side showed much originality in their strategy and the same pattern of battle across the Euphrates was repeated again and again.

So complete was the Persian defeat at Buwaib that the Arabs were able

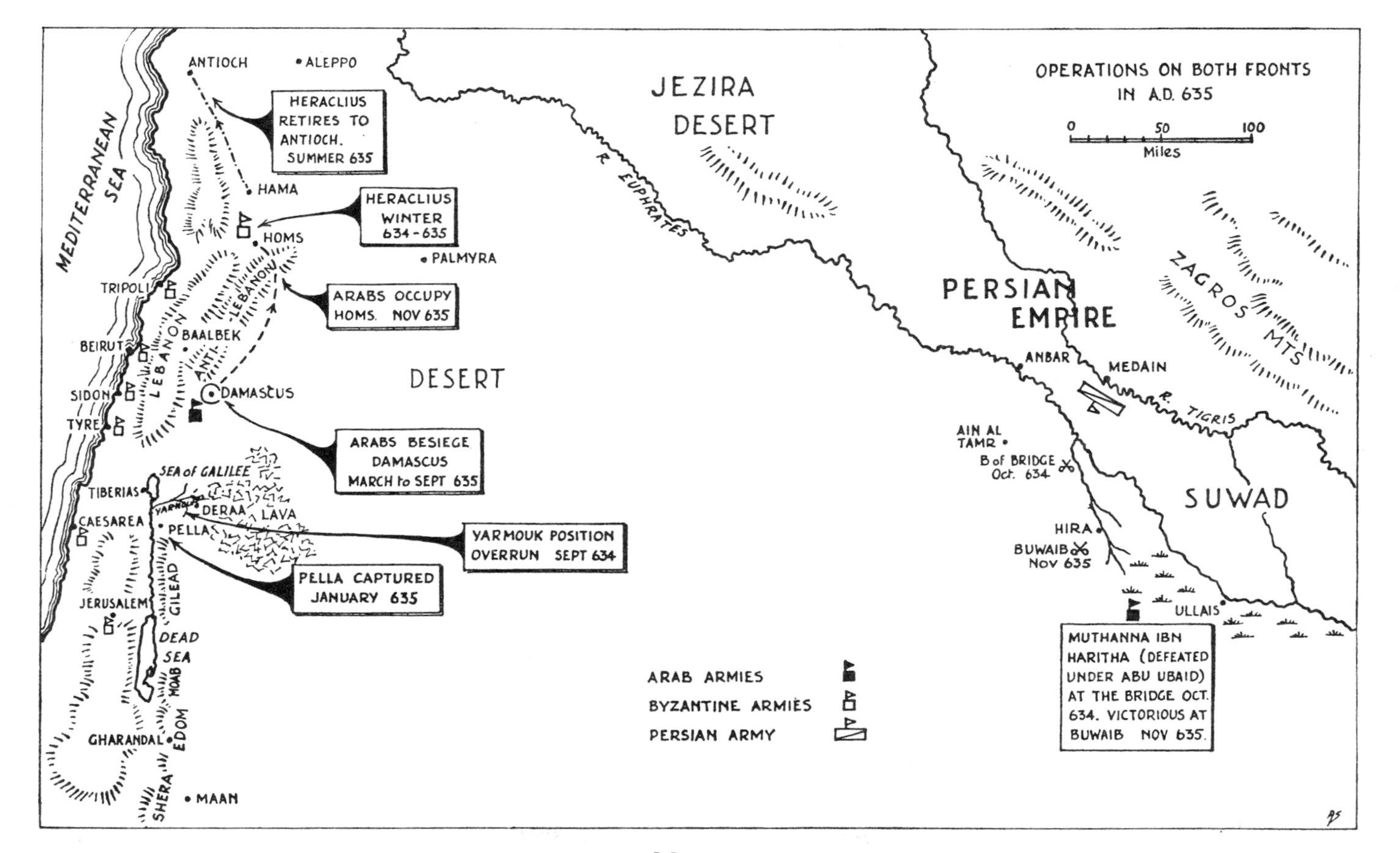
OPERATIONS ON BOTH FRONTS
IN A.D. 635
0
50
100
Miles
JEZIRA
DESERT
R. EUPHRATES
PERSIAN
EMPIRE
ZAGROS MTS
ANBAR
MEDAIN
R. TIGRIS
AIN AL TAMR
B of BRIDGE Oct. 634
SUWAD
HIRA
BUWAIB Nov 635
ULLAIS
MUTHANNA IBN HARITHA (DEFEATED UNDER ABU UBAID) AT THE BRIDGE OCT. 634. VICTORIOUS AT BUWAIB NOV 635.
MEDITERRANEAN SEA
ANTIOCH
ALEPPO
HERACLIUS RETIRES TO ANTIOCH. SUMMER 635
HAMA
HERACLIUS WINTER 634-635
HOMS
PALMYRA
TRIPOLI
LEBANON
ANTI-LEBANON
ARABS OCCUPY HOMS. NOV 635
BEIRUT
BAALBEK
DESERT
SIDON
DAMASCUS
TYRE
ARABS BESIEGE DAMASCUS MARCH to SEPT 635
SEA of GALILEE
TIBERIAS
YARMOUK
DERAA
LAVA
CAESAREA
PELLA
YARMOUK POSITION OVERRUN SEPT 634
PELLA CAPTURED JANUARY 635
GILEAD
JERUSALEM
DEAD SEA
MOAB
EDOM
GHARANDAL
SHERA
MAAN
ARAB ARMIES
BYZANTINE ARMIES
PERSIAN ARMY

Map XXI

once more to range over most of the area between the Euphrates and the Tigris, almost to the walls of the Persian capital of Medain. On the north, Anbar and Ain al Tamr were reoccupied, and the Muslims were able to raid as far as Baghdad—then a small market town—and Tikrit on the Tigris. As already explained, the "delta" area ends approximately on a line from Anbar to Baghdad, north of which the country between the two rivers is largely desert.[11]

The Arab forces, of course, had no regular system of supplies and were thus obliged to range far and wide in order to provide themselves with food and forage. The raids, therefore, combined the advantages of striking terror into their enemies, of obtaining information of Persian movements and of supplying the Muslims with food, and of course also with other plunder. The cultivated area of the Suwad appears to have been largely inhabited by non-Arabs, whether they were Sumerians, Chaldaeans or Persians. For whereas we find the Arab tribes of the Euphrates—even though Christians—fighting to some extent on the side of the Muslims, there does not appear to be any record of the populations of the Suwad between the two rivers joining the invaders. When the Arabs were victorious, these "Iraqis" paid tribute and made submission. When the Persians reasserted themselves, they reverted to their loyalty, but there does not appear to be any suggestion of treachery to Persia on their part, such as repeatedly occurred in Syria, where the monophysites at times preferred the Muslims to the Orthodox Church and the Byzantine government.

Muthanna ibn Haritha died not long after his victory at Buwaib. He had never recovered from the wounds which he had received when covering the retreat of the Arabs at the Battle of the Bridge. He seems to have possessed all the qualities of a great leader in war. The fact that, after the disastrous Battle of the Bridge, he succeeded in collecting a new army, proves the high quality of his leadership. For these were not disciplined soldiers but wild and fickle tribes, many of whom, only two or three years earlier, had been engaged in active hostilities against the Muslims at the time of the apostasy. The fact that they now rallied to Muthanna can, therefore, scarcely be attributed to religious enthusiasm. Moreover, as we have seen, both Beni Namir and Taghlib, Christian Arab tribes, fought with distinction under the command of Muthanna.

It is true that Jareer ibn Abdulla, the chief of Beni Bajeela, with typical bedouin jealousy, complained to the khalif that he, the shaikh of his tribe, should be obliged to serve under Muthanna, who was no more than a bedouin chief like himself. Yet, in fact, he did so serve and fought with courage at Buwaib. Baladhuri has a revealing sentence to the effect that Beni Bajeela still claim that Jareer was in command at Buwaib, while Beni Bekr insist that the leader was Muthanna. Indeed the jealousy of other bedouin chiefs against Muthanna provides some justification for his continual supersession by townsmen of the Hejaz, who enjoyed the distinction of having been Com-

[11] In 1941, in the operations against Baghdad, the Arab Legion crossed the Euphrates a few miles above Anbar, and likewise raided as far as Tikrit and the suburbs of Baghdad. See *The Story of the Arab Legion*.

panions of the Prophet. In practice, however, many tribal chiefs did serve under him, such as Arfaja of the famous tribe of Azd.

More remarkable, however, than his military personality or his prowess in battle—for the bedouin life automatically produced personalities full of initiative and bravery—was his apparently selfless devotion to the cause. Unlike the great Khalid ibn al Waleed, there is no mention of Muthanna marrying captive virgins on the field of battle. His wife alone is mentioned as his partner. Nor, at a time when their raids and victories were bringing the untold riches of Persia to the hands of rough and unlettered bedouins, is there any mention of his accumulation of vast wealth, such as we find attributed to many other Arab leaders. We seem obliged to conclude that this simple, tribal chieftain possessed, not only the gift of leadership in battle, but a mind and character which would have made him worthy of fame and honour in any nation and at any time. That his name was never hallowed like that of other early leaders may well be due to the fact that most of the historians lived two hundred years after these events. Many of them were not Arabs and all were city dwellers, who had no great liking for or understanding of bedouins. Moreover, under the reign of the Abbaside dynasty (during which most of the histories were written), it was, to say the least, advisable for historians to attribute heroism to the descendants of Abbas, or at any rate to Quraish, rather than to a bedouin.

## *NOTABLE DATES*

| | |
|---|---|
| Battle of the Bridge in Iraq | October 634 |
| Capture of Pella in Syria | January 635 |
| Commencement of the Siege of Damascus | March 635 |
| Fall of Damascus | September 635 |
| Battle of Buwaib in Iraq | November 635 |

## *PERSONALITIES*

Umar ibn al Khattab, the new khalif.
Amr ibn al Aasi, military commander, south Palestine.
Abu Ubaida, Arab commander-in-chief in Syria.
Abu Ubaid, appointed by Umar ibn al Khattab to command in Iraq, and killed at the Battle of the Bridge.
Rustem, the new Persian commander-in-chief.
Muthanna ibn Haritha, winner of the Battle of Buwaib, and chief of Beni Bekr.

# IX

## *The Yarmouk*

I am with you, so let the believers stand firm. I will put terror in the hearts of the unbelievers, so smite them upon their necks. . . . This is because they opposed Allah and His Messenger, and whoever opposes Allah and His Messenger, Allah will punish him severely. *Qoran* VIII, 12

The inhabitants of the desert are sounder in their minds and bodies than the sedentary people who enjoy a softer life. Their skins are clearer, their bodies purer, their figures more harmonious and beautiful, their characters more moderate and their minds sharper in understanding and readier to acquire new knowledge than those of sedentary people. Compare the gazelle, the ostrich and the antelope with their counterparts who dwell in settled countryside. The former have more shining furs, more harmonious limbs and sharper senses. IBN KHALDUN

Let the praises of God be in their mouth, and a two-edged sword in their hands: to be avenged of the heathen, and to rebuke the people: to bind their kings in chains and their nobles in links of iron. *Psalm* CXLIX, 6–8

# IX

## THE YARMOUK

IN the previous chapter we left the Arab forces in occupation of virtually all Syria and Palestine. Heraclius still retained a foothold in the district of Antioch in the north-west. In Palestine, Jerusalem and Caesarea held out, while the coastal cities of Tyre, Sidon, Beyrout and Tripoli were still encouraged to resist by the Byzantine command of the sea. The emperor set to work, after two years of unbroken defeats culminating in the fall of Damascus, to organize a new army, in the hope of reconquering Syria in the summer of 636.

This new Byzantine force appears to have been largely recruited from Armenia, which we should call eastern Asia Minor, the country east of the Upper Euphrates. It is only since the Turkish conquests in the fourteenth and fifteenth centuries that the Armenians have become scattered all over the world, and the name of Armenia limited to a narrow province at the southern foot of the Caucasus. During the six centuries of Roman-Persian rivalry which culminated in the long struggle between Chosroes and Heraclius, Armenia had played the part of a buffer state. Occasionally overrun by one empire or the other, the Armenians had nevertheless retained their national identity and, for most practical purposes, their political independence. Their warlike qualities inspired respect, particularly when exercised in the mountain valleys of their native country. Until the fourth century A.D., the sentiment of the nation had been sympathetic to Persia rather than to Rome, but their subsequent conversion to Christianity had resulted in a certain estrangement from the fire-worshipping Persians. Byzantium, however, had not reaped great political advantage from the change, for (as in the case of the Monophysite Christian Arabs), the Orthodox Byzantine Church regarded the Armenian Christians as heretics.

The fact that Heraclius was obliged to rely so largely on contingents of Armenians may indicate something of the war-weariness of the Byzantines. Moreover, the Armenians appear to have been under the command of Baanes, a general of their own nation. The imperial commander-in-chief was Theodorus, but his authority over the Armenians does not appear always to have been admitted. Moreover, the Armenians seem to have been a separate army within the army, and not intermingled with the Byzantine units.

The princes of the Beni Ghassan, once the semi-independent Arab rulers of Southern Syria and Trans-Jordan, also joined the Byzantine army with a large force of Christian Arab tribesmen. It will be remembered that, in the year 581, the Byzantines had reduced the status of the dynasty of Beni Ghassan. Moreover, the persecutions of the Orthodox Church had gone far to alienate the loyalty of the monophysite Arab Christians. Thus perhaps two-thirds of the emperor's new army consisted of either Armenians or Arabs, neither of whom were inspired by feelings of devoted loyalty to the empire. The remaining third of the imperial army was presumably recruited from those hardy peasants of western Asia Minor, who have so often been distinguished for their solid military virtues. The qualities of these varied populations are not without interest even in our own times.

Again and again in history, some conquering race will establish its rule over a subjugated territory, which will thereupon assume the name of its conquerors. In our own times, when racialism so largely dominates our thinking, we receive the impression that, thenceforward, the conquering nation had constituted the population of the territory which it had acquired. In fact, however, the invaders were more often than not a minority, which quickly intermingled with the original inhabitants. The patient peasants of Asia Minor, who fought for Byzantium under the names of Greeks or Armenians, are now designated Turks, and as such still display the stubborn qualities of their ancestors. The tribes of Eastern Syria and Trans-Jordan, largely of Arab origin, still possess considerable martial qualities. The peoples of western Syria and Palestine, however, have always displayed remarkable intellectual brilliance. As politicians, as conspirators, as demagogues, or as merchants, they reappear again and again on the pages of history. Yet as soldiers, they have few victories to record. The equal application of the name of Arab to them and to the descendants of the warriors of Khalid and Abu Ubaida serves greatly to confuse the politics of today.

* * * * *

The army raised by Heraclius in the early months of 636, was the most numerous which had yet operated in Syria.[1] No sooner did it take the field, perhaps in March or April of that year, than the Arabs abandoned all their conquests of the previous twelve months. Khalid evacuated Homs, Abu Ubaida left Damascus, and all the Muslim forces concentrated once more to the south of the Yarmouk. The Byzantines followed them and re-occupied the Deraa gap, the gateway of Syria from which they had been driven out in September 634, eighteen months earlier. The advance was led by the Arab contingents, under the command of Jabala ibn al Aiham, prince of the Beni Ghassan. Hardy, active, mobile and all mounted, the nimble Arabs formed an ideal cavalry screen in front of the main army, just as, when the Arab Legion co-operated with the British Army in operations in 1941 in Syria and Iraq, they too normally acted as advanced and flank guards.[2]

These facts are undisputed, yet I cannot avoid the impression that the historians have failed to emphasize the motives behind these military moves, some attributing to the Arabs the intention of holding the fortifications of the Yarmouk. In fact, however, as every engagement of this period proves, the Arabs always sought battle in the desert or in flat plains and they always wished to fight with open desert at their backs as a safe refuge. Far from

[1] Professor C. H. Becker, in *The Cambridge Mediaeval History*, claims that it was the first Byzantine army which had outnumbered its Arab opponents.

[2] *The Story of the Arab Legion*.

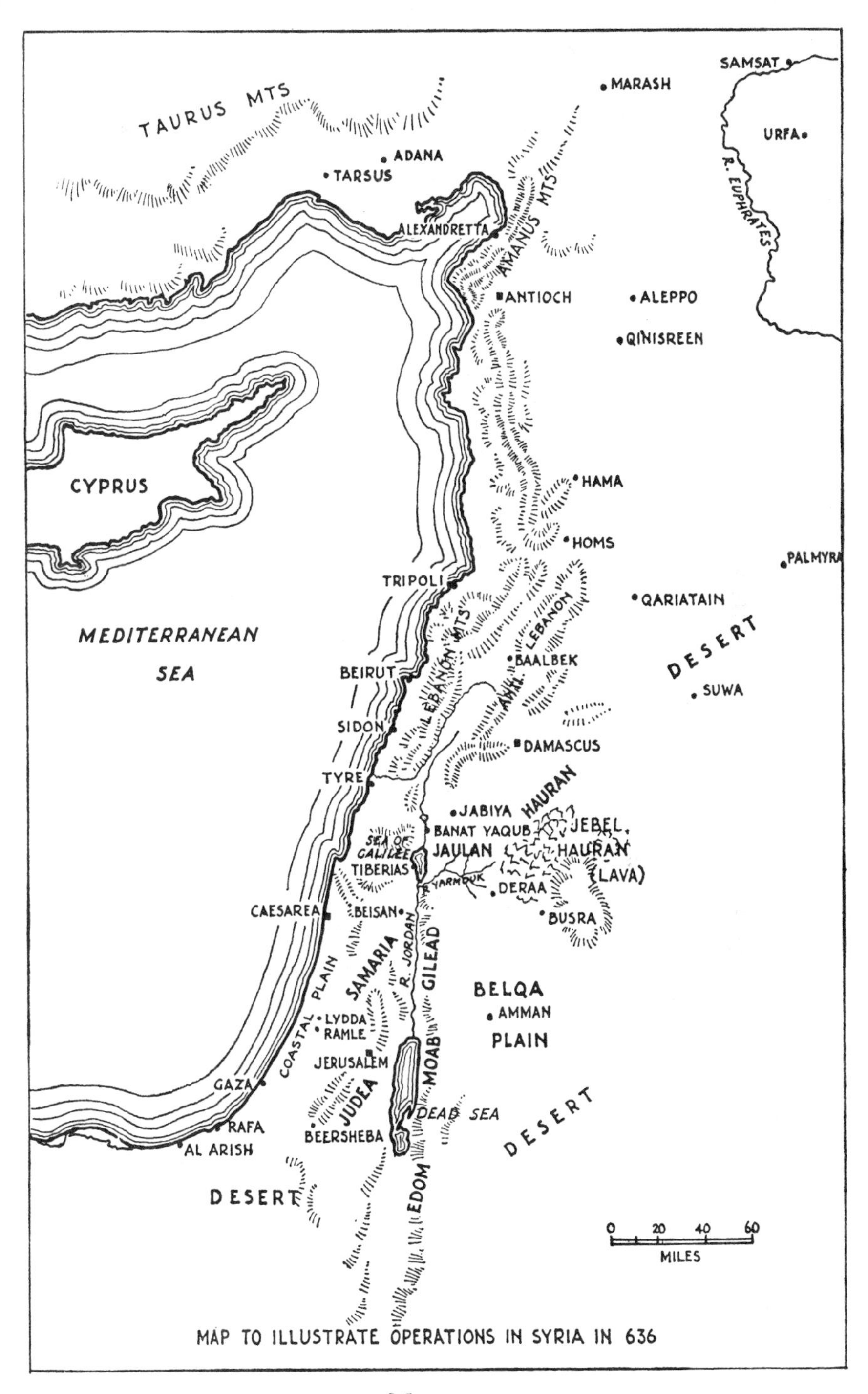
TAURUS MTS
MARASH
SAMSAT
URFA
R. EUPHRATES
ADANA
TARSUS
ALEXANDRETTA
AMANUS MTS
ANTIOCH
ALEPPO
QINISREEN
CYPRUS
HAMA
HOMS
PALMYRA
TRIPOLI
QARIATAIN
MEDITERRANEAN
SEA
LEBANON MTS
ANTI-LEBANON
BAALBEK
DESERT
BEIRUT
SUWA
SIDON
DAMASCUS
TYRE
HAURAN
JABIYA
BANAT YAQUB
JEBEL
HAURAN
(LAVA)
SEA OF GALILEE
JAULAN
TIBERIAS
R. YARMOUK
DERAA
CAESAREA
BEISAN
BUSRA
SAMARIA
R. JORDAN
GILEAD
COASTAL PLAIN
BELQA
AMMAN
PLAIN
LYDDA
RAMLE
JERUSALEM
MOAB
GAZA
JUDEA
DEAD SEA
DESERT
RAFA
BEERSHEBA
AL ARISH
DESERT
EDOM
0 20 40 60
MILES
MAP TO ILLUSTRATE OPERATIONS IN SYRIA IN 636

Map XXII

desiring to engage in static warfare in the Deraa gap, the Muslims would have been only too glad to decoy the Byzantine army out into the desert south of the Yarmouk. No sooner, however, had the Arabs passed through the gap into the wide plains beyond, than the Byzantines re-occupied their old defences and slammed the door of Syria behind the backs of the retreating Arabs. Heraclius' policy was now to stonewall. As long as the Yarmouk Maginot line held firm, Syria was safe. The Arabs, with their fear of close country and mountains, would never venture to invade Syria through Tiberias. It was true that, in the spring of 634 two years earlier, Khalid had threatened Homs and Damascus from the east, that is, from the desert. But his force had been only a small one, and even so, had nearly died of thirst. A serious invasion could not be attempted by that route, even by the Arabs. Heraclius must have heaved a sigh of relief when he heard that the Deraa gap had been reoccupied and the Arabs had pushed through it and out into the desert beyond. Syria, he must have thought, was saved.

The Arab historians leave us in doubt as to who was in command at this crisis. We may, perhaps, guess that Abu Ubaida was still the official commander, but that, in dealing with the military situation, he allowed Khalid a fairly free hand.

This second deadlock in the Deraa gap lasted for more than four months, during which the Byzantines refused to be lured from their defences, which the Arabs were unable or unwilling to attack. Battles, however, cannot be won by the passive defensive and the Muslims were both more mobile and showed more initiative than their enemies.

On the western side of the gap, the gorges of the Yarmouk and the Wadi al Ruqqad constitute almost insuperable obstacles to military movement, their sides being almost, in places quite, perpendicular. To the east, however, while the surface of the plain is strewn with lava, it is not completely impassable to riders on horses or camels, still less to men on foot. It would have been impossible to fight a seventh century battle in the lava, but the rock-strewn surface would not have prevented parties of Arabs from infiltrating round the Byzantine eastern flank into the province of Hauran. We may perhaps guess that these were the tactics which, before long, the Muslims adopted. Working their way round the eastern flank of the Byzantine position, they could cut off stragglers or foragers and even perhaps interfere with the enemy's supply convoys. The line of communications of the Byzantine army seems to have passed across the Jaulan (the Roman Gaulonitis), perhaps by the site of the present bridge of Banat Yacoub and northwards to Baalbek, and not up the main road from Deraa to Damascus.

In fact, however, disloyalty within the ranks was more fatal to the Byzantine army than were the operations of the Arabs. Theodorus was perhaps at first anxious to adopt active defensive tactics, for a number of minor actions are referred to by the Arab historians in all of which (according to them) the Byzantines had been defeated. Perhaps Theodorus would have been wiser to risk a decisive battle as soon as the two armies were face to face, for the Arabs were then considerably outnumbered. The respite, however, provided time for them to appeal to the khalif in Medina and for the latter to send up fresh

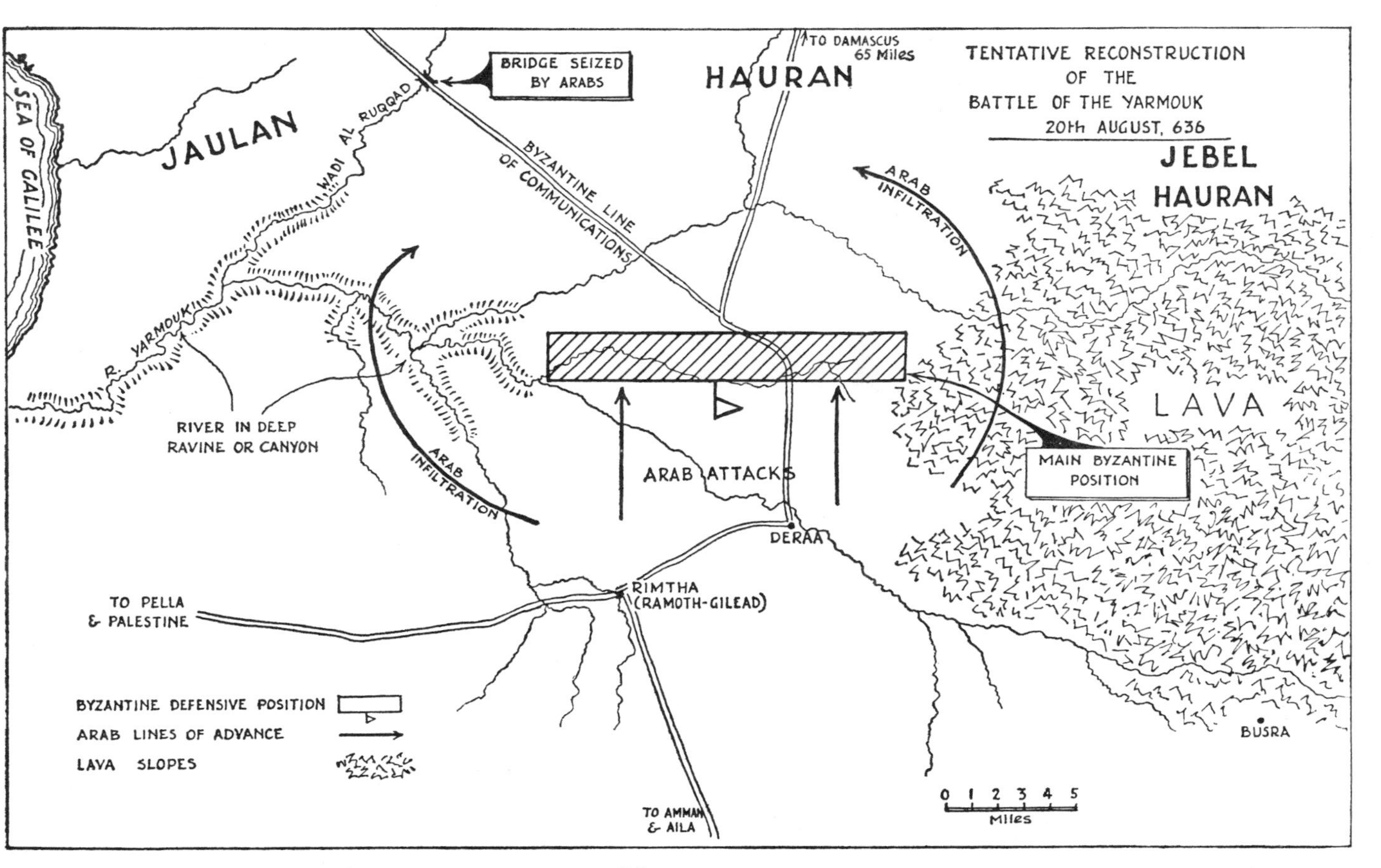
TENTATIVE RECONSTRUCTION
OF THE
BATTLE OF THE YARMOUK
20th AUGUST, 636
JEBEL
HAURAN
LAVA
MAIN BYZANTINE
POSITION
ARAB
INFILTRATION
TO DAMASCUS
65 Miles
HAURAN
BRIDGE SEIZED
BY ARABS
BYZANTINE LINE
OF COMMUNICATIONS
ARAB ATTACKS
DERAA
RIMTHA
(RAMOTH-GILEAD)
TO AMMAN
& AILA
TO PELLA
& PALESTINE
ARAB
INFILTRATION
JAULAN
WADI AL RUQQAD
R. YARMOUK
RIVER IN DEEP
RAVINE OR CANYON
SEA OF GALILEE
BUSRA
0 1 2 3 4 5
Miles
BYZANTINE DEFENSIVE POSITION
ARAB LINES OF ADVANCE
LAVA SLOPES

Map XXIII

reinforcements. The long days and weeks in the fortifications of the Yarmouk doubtless told on the morale of the defenders, especially as the Armenians were, on the one hand, accustomed to a cooler and more mountainous climate and, on the other, were virtually mercenaries, not directly defending their own homes. While the populations of the Mediterranean coast may have been loyal to the empire, the inhabitants of the Hauran were perhaps unfriendly and, at the best, indifferent, a factor liable to depress the morale of troops.

Serious friction arose between the Greeks and the Armenians, so much so that a part of the army seems to have elected Baanes as commander-in-chief in place of Theodorus. It would even seem as if Khalid had entered into correspondence with Baanes, perhaps through the medium of the Arabs in the Byzantine army, who seem to have taken little part in the fighting once hostilities became static. These constant rivalries within the imperial forces and the resulting deterioration of discipline, combined with the weeks of inaction in the fortifications, completed the demoralization of the Byzantine army. Meanwhile the Muslims, who had received further reinforcements from Arabia, were becoming increasingly aggressive and had almost surrounded the Byzantine positions, or at least had cut their communications on three sides.

On 20th August, 636, a strong hot wind was blowing from the desert from the south-east. Clouds of sand and dust swept into the faces of the Byzantine soldiers. Few experiences are more unpleasant than a really hot dust-storm in the desert. Tents are blown down, cooking is impossible, food and drink are full of grit and the blinding sand stings the face and closes the eyes. Visibility may be reduced to a few yards. To face such a wind is impossible. There is nothing to be done but to crouch on the ground, and wait miserably for the storm to blow itself out. Such winds often blow for two or three consecutive days. Perhaps it had already begun on the evening of the 19th August, enabling the Arab commanders to plan a general attack for the next morning.

While even a bedouin scarcely enjoys a sandstorm, it was to them a normal experience. Moreover the direction of the gale was from them to the enemy. Their vision was hampered, but with the wind behind them, they could attack with their eyes open, suffering little inconvenience. Such circumstances would obviously produce a soldiers' battle. An army accustomed to fight in ranks by word of command would, under these conditions, be almost helpless. The Arabs, however, were individualists. Full of daring, activity and initiative, every man was ready and eager to fight alone. Incapable of a disciplined slogging match in serried ranks, they were at their best in a wild charge, every man for himself. The battle, however, was obviously planned, for a detachment of Arabs appears to have early seized the bridge over the Wadi al Ruqqad, behind the Byzantine army and over which their line of communications passed. Then a wild horde of screaming Arabs, suddenly appearing like ghosts through the driving sand, poured across the Byzantine fortifications. If the dust-storm was really thick, it is unlikely that the imperial army succeeded in giving battle at all. With the bridge in their rear already seized by the Muslims, an immense slaughter resulted, Theodorus himself being killed in the mêlée. By the next morning, the Byzantine army, which

Heraclius had spent a year of immense exertion to collect, had entirely ceased to exist. There was no withdrawal, no rearguard action, no nucleus of survivors. There was nothing left.

A number of Arab women are said to have been present at the Battle of the Yarmouk, singing and screaming encouragement to their warriors. Old Abu Sofian, once Muhammad's arch-enemy, had come on a visit to Syria, where his two sons, Yezeed and Muawiya, held important commands in the Muslim army. His old wife, Hind, the daughter of Otba, had accompanied him. Twelve years before at Uhud, she had encouraged the warriors of Quraish by singing to the praises of Uzza and Hobal, completing her warlike exploits by tearing out and chewing the liver of Hamza. The fire of battle was still unextinguished in her ancient bosom. On the day of the Yarmouk she was well forward in the battle, calling repeatedly on the Muslims to cut off the arms of the uncircumcised polytheists with their swords. Abu Sofian is not mentioned as taking part in the battle. He was present, but was already seventy-three years old. He had lost an eye at the siege of Taif, and his fighting days were over, though he was to live on for another fifteen years, dying at the age of eighty-eight. By a curious irony of fate, this rough old couple, once the bitterest enemies of Islam, were to bequeath to the Arab race a dynasty of emperors.

* * * * *

When the aged Heraclius heard at Antioch of the utter extermination of his army, he knew that the decision was irrevocable. Bidding a sad farewell to the Holy Land, which he had fought so long to win back from the Persians, only to lose it to the Arabs, he rode slowly away across the Taurus mountains to the west.

Seventy years before, the Emperor Justinian had died in Constantinople, having apparently almost achieved his ambition of re-uniting the Roman Empire. Africa, Spain and Italy had been reconquered by his two brilliant generals, Belisarius and Narses. But it was with Justinian as with Louis XV, *après nous le déluge*. The resources of the empire were exhausted, the treasury empty. The successors of the great Justinian, Justin, Tiberius, Maurice, were unable to support the top-heavy edifice. In 603, Maurice had been replaced by the infamous Phocas. In 610, the young Heraclius had sailed into Constantinople from Africa, to be crowned emperor the next day amid the enthusiastic plaudits of the people. But Chosroes Parwiz was already at the gates, and Heraclius was to spend eighteen years in incredible military exertions before he finally triumphed over the Persian enemy. He might well have hoped that, after a life of so much hardship and anxiety, his declining years might have been passed in peace and honour. But the respite was short-lived. Four years after the conclusion of peace with Persia, the Arabs arrived in Syria, and after three years more of unremitting labour, the ageing emperor lost once again the smiling promises which he had fought for eighteen years to rescue from Chosroes. He still had five more years to live—years of further humiliation and failure.

Historians have not hesitated to blame what they have called the cowardice of Heraclius in his failure to drive the Arabs from Syria. Such criticisms seem scarcely justified. It was his misfortune to be charged with the task of propping up an empire, the resources of which were inadequate for the task. A conscientious and indeed deeply religious man, he spent his life in arduous labours, at times crowned with triumph, but ending only in failure and despair. History tells of few lives more well-intentioned, and more laborious and, at the same time, more tragic.

* * * * *

The active operations in the Arab conquest of Syria ended with the Battle of the Yarmouk. Abu Ubaida advanced northwards once again, reoccupying Damascus, Homs, Baalbek, and the other towns which had been evacuated during the Byzantine offensive. In some cases, the returning Muslims were welcomed back with singing and dancing. According to an Arab historian, the people of Homs expressed a preference for Arab justice rather than the tyranny of the Orthodox Church and the Byzantine Empire. Such statements must be accepted with reserve, firstly because our sources are Muslim writers and secondly because the pliable Syrians doubtless desired to conciliate their new, and now undisputed, masters.

There were, nevertheless, solid reasons why the east Syrians and the Trans-Jordanians should (for the moment at least) be gratified by the change. English people, living on an island, regard the sea as a natural frontier. Arriving from the West and landing in the country now called Lebanon, they expect to find themselves in "the East". Thereafter, proceeding inland to Damascus, Baghdad or Teheran, they do not expect to find any marked contrasts, such as they looked for between France or Italy and Lebanon. For France and Italy are "the West", Lebanon, Damascus and Baghdad are "the East". Even today, this clear-cut classification is misleading. In the seventh century, it was even less correct. The whole basin of the Mediterranean constituted the Graeco-Roman world. To the Romans, the Mediterranean was the highway connecting their dominions, not the frontier separating them. In classical times, a Syrian or an Egyptian was at home in Greece, Italy or Gaul, but a foreigner in Iraq or the Hejaz. The frontiers of Rome had been all land frontiers, the Rhine, the Danube, the Atlas mountains or the desert. In Syria and Palestine, the cultural frontier of Rome had been, in general, the anti-Lebanon range, the Sea of Galilee, the Jordan and the Dead Sea valley. East of this line, the desert tribes had from time immemorial infiltrated into the towns and villages. The people in this eastern district were semitic or "half-Arabs", speaking Aramaic in preference to Greek, and in general leaning towards an eastern culture. The Romans and Byzantines had failed to assimilate this area culturally, and had normally preferred to control it through local satellite rulers, such as the Nabatacans, the Herods, an Beni Ghassan. West of the Jordan and anti-Lebanon, however, the peoples tended to look principally to the west, and (though not entirely free from eastern influence) were on the whole considerably more European than "Arab". Thus the natural, cultural frontier of Byzantium approximated to the Jordan valley.

The conversion of all Syria, Palestine and Trans-Jordan to Christianity should have forged a closer link with Byzantium, but in fact the reverse had resulted. The Orthodox Church of Byzantium had persecuted Syrian and Egyptian Christians as heretics. The Arab conquerors accorded them religious toleration. The Muslims of the conquest made little or no attempt to convert Christians, but imposed upon them a different system of taxation, though this differentiation conveyed an impression of inferiority. Thus we find certain Christian Arab tribes objecting to paying taxes as Christians, but willing to pay more than Muslims on condition the taxes be called ushr or sadaqa, instead of jiziya or kharaj, the names of the taxes imposed on non-Muslims. Thus, even at first, some idea of subordination was conveyed by the payment of non-Muslim instead of Muslim taxes. The indignity, however, was slight, and, it must be remembered, it replaced actual persecution. In later years, the position of Christians was to deteriorate, but under the first Arab conquerors it was by no means onerous. It is, therefore, not incredible that the settled populations east of the Jordan and anti-Lebanon were even gratified by the Arab eviction of their former Byzantine rulers.

Most of the Christian bedouin tribes adopted Islam without more ado. To such desert warriors, the Muslim wars of conquest were entirely congenial. By professing Islam, they were able to join as equals with the tribes of Central Arabia in an intoxicating life of military glory and plunder.

West of anti-Lebanon and the Jordan, however, the position was different. Here the people had looked to Greece and Rome for many centuries. Many of them were of actual European descent, and regarded the Arabs with contempt and aversion. We do not read of these people welcoming the Arab conquerors with music and dancing. An additional complication is produced by the differences between townspeople and countrymen. This distinction, so fundamentally important in the northern Arab countries today, is difficult for Europeans to understand. It arose partly owing to differences of occupation, as in the rivalry between the towns and the bedouin tribes all over Arabia. In Syria and Palestine, however, it originated far more in military conquest. These countries had always been exposed to invasion, by Assyrians, Babylonians, Egyptians, Persians, Greeks and Romans. Each conquering nation established its rule in the cities, which were held by garrisons of foreign troops. These soon mixed and inter-married with the native city-dwellers, but few, if any, of them mingled with the tribes or the peasants. Thus, in each district, the city-dwellers tended to be more Graeco-Roman than the tribes or the peasants, both in culture and in racial origin.

* * * * *

In northern Syria, Qinisreen (the ancient Chalcis) resisted.[3] Khalid ibn al Waleed was in command of the Arab column. He inflicted a heavy defeat on the defenders and occupied the city by force. Abu Ubaida then advanced upon Antioch, the Queen of the East, with Rome, Alexandria and Byzantium, one of the greatest cities of the classical world. Augustus, Tiberius, Trajan, Antoninus Pius and Hadrian had adorned it with temples, theatres, baths and aqueducts. But the city had been partly destroyed by Chosroes in

[3] Map XXII, page 175.

the Persian wars. A battle occurred in the wooded country outside the walls—perhaps in the groves of Daphne, famous in classical times for their beauty and for the immoral orgies said to take place there. The garrison was driven within the city walls, and soon afterwards capitulated. Khalid, in a dash further northwards, reached to the foot of the mountains at Marash, Urfa (the ancient Edessa) and Samsat. As usual, the Arabs held back from operations in the mountains, thereby establishing a frontier which has constituted their northern limit ever since.

By the autumn of 636, the Arabs had overrun the whole of Syria as far as the mountains of Asia Minor, but, in the south, Jerusalem and Caesarea still held out. Meanwhile the Arabs had established a military cantonment at Jabiya in the Jaulan, a central position from which their army could operate rapidly in any direction to suppress insurrection. The idea of thus forming military cantonments in central positions in which the Arab forces could be concentrated and not be subverted by close contact with the civil populations, appears to have owed its origin to Umar ibn al Khattab. We shall hear more of these encampments later.

Since the beginning of the invasion of Syria three years before, Palestine had been the special province of Amr ibn al Aasi. At moments of crisis, such as the Battle of the Yarmouk, he had periodically rejoined the main Arab army, but as soon as the danger was passed, he had returned to his own area. As already explained, the tactics of the Arabs, which had made them irresistible in the open plain, could not be applied in mountainous or close country. As long, therefore, as there had been Byzantine armies in the field, Amr ibn al Aasi had limited his operations to the Palestine coastal plain from Beersheba to Caesarea. Now, however, no enemy field army remained. As a result, the Arabs climbed the rocky hills of Judæa and laid siege to Jerusalem. With Heraclius beyond the Taurus, no hope of prolonged resistance remained. Probably in the late autumn of 637,[4] Sophronius, the Patriarch of Jerusalem, opened negotiations and general agreement was soon reached on the terms of surrender. Sophronius, however, insisted that he would only hand over the city to the khalif, Umar ibn al Khattab, in person. A message to this effect was sent by Abu Ubaida to Medina. Umar immediately decided to visit the Syrian front in person.

Setting out in his usual patched and ragged clothing, he rode up the old caravan track to Deraa, now on the southern boundary of Syria with Jordan. (Deraa is mentioned in Numbers XXI, 33, as the scene of a battle between Israel and Og, King of Bashan.) To the horror of the puritan khalif, the people of Deraa came out to meet him with singers, sword dancers and women playing on tamborines. "Stop them! Stop them!" the old man is said to have shouted in indignation. But Abu Ubaida pointed out that such was the custom of the country, and that if they were prevented they would conclude that Umar came to them as an enemy. By these arguments, the khalif was with difficulty persuaded to overlook such frivolity. But his anger with the Muslim commanders was deeper. Abu Ubaida, Yezeed

[4] Some authorities make the surrender of Jerusalem a year earlier.

ibn abi Sofian and Khalid ibn al Waleed had ridden south to meet him, dressed in rich robes of brocade, their horses gaily caparisoned. "Do you come to me dressed like that?" he is alleged to have demanded angrily. "Have you changed so much in two years? You all deserve to be dismissed in disgrace." The abashed generals, tradition relates, replied that the change was only on the surface, and throwing open their gay cloaks, they showed their coats of chain-mail beneath. But the khalif in his patched cloak was with difficulty pacified. The future was to prove how just had been his fears.

A deputation from Sophronius waited upon Umar ibn al Khattab in the cantonment at Jabiya, and terms of surrender were soon drawn up. Crossing the Jordan valley by the ancient highway through Beisan, the khalif rode southwards through the smiling hills of Samaria, covered with cornfields, vineyards and olive groves, to the Holy City, where he was received by the patriarch, the honey-tongued defender of the Church. But if Sophronius spoke courteous words of welcome with his lips, he felt far from cordial in his heart. As the ragged, barefooted bedouin khalif walked round the church of the Holy Sepulchre, the patriarch whispered in Greek to one of his subordinates, "Surely this is the abomination of desolation spoken of by Daniel the Prophet standing in the holy place." [5]

By chance, Umar ibn al Khattab was engaged in viewing the church of the Holy Sepulchre when the time came round for the Muslim midday prayer. An attendant was about to spread his prayer mat on the floor of the church when the khalif intervened, exclaiming that he would not say his prayers there. "If I did so," he is alleged to have added, "the Muslims would want to seize the church as a mosque." He accordingly went out of the building and prayed outside the wall. A small mosque still exists, built against the wall of the church of the Holy Sepulchre, and alleged to mark the spot where the khalif performed his devotions. Jerusalem was, and still is, deeply venerated by Muslims. Muhammad had first taught his followers to face towards Jerusalem when praying, and it was from the site of the temple in Jerusalem that he had flown up to the heavens on his night journey.[6] Umar ibn al Khattab seems to have behaved with especial modesty and courtesy towards the people of the Holy City.

During the course of this visit, the khalif made arrangements for the administration of the newly-conquered provinces, dividing them also into military districts. Then, in the spring of 638, remounting his horse, the simple old Arab ruler rode away into the desert towards Medina.

* * * * *

As has already been mentioned, Jabala ibn al Aiham, prince of Beni Ghassan, had led the advance guard of the Byzantine army to the last and fatal campaign on the Yarmouk. Himself an Arab, his pride in his princely descent doubtless made him loth to bow before the ragged bedouin invaders. After the destruction of the imperial army, however, he made his peace with the

[5] Tabari says that Lydda and Ramla surrendered at the same time as Jerusalem.
[6] Page 50.

Arabs, professed Islam, and rode to visit the khalif in Medina. Becoming involved in a crowd on one occasion, however, he was jostled by an ordinary bedouin. The prince, resenting such familiarity, struck the tribesman in the face, some accounts saying that he put out his eye. The victim complained to Umar ibn al Khattab, who, summoning Jabala to his presence, ordered the bedouin to strike the prince a similar blow, according to the Muslim law of retaliation. Incensed at such an indignity, Jabala rode away, renounced Islam and accompanied by several thousand relatives and retainers, followed Heraclius across the Taurus. The dynasty of Beni Ghassan had been honoured and respected all over Arabia for centuries and there were some who criticized Umar ibn al Khattab for his clumsiness. More diplomatic counsels prevailed and messengers were sent after the prince to invite him to return. (An alternative account states that Jabala himself, pining for his native country, initiated the exchange of messages.) No agreement, however, was reached and the new Muslim Empire was denied the participation of the family which, for three and a half centuries, had been one of the most glorious in Arabia.

These lines are part of a poem, attributed to the aged Jabala ibn al Aiham, living in exile at the court of Byzantium:

'Twas the rage in my heart made us Christians once more
I resented that blow in the face.
I felt that my honour I could not restore
If I bowed to such shame and disgrace.
Ah! Would that my mother no son ever bore
Nor my name had in history found place!
How I yearn for the land of my fathers of yore,
Damascus, the home of my race!

The great and decisive battle of the Yarmouk was fought in July 636. It should not be confused with the Arab capture of the Yarmouk defensive position two years earlier, in September 634, after the Battle of Ajnadain. (It is this confusion between the two actions on the Yarmouk which has caused the despair of so many European historians of the Arab conquests.) We may, if it be preferred, call the engagement in 634 the first Battle of the Yarmouk, and that in 636, the second.

Jerusalem surrendered in the winter of 637–638. Caesarea alone, with its city and port supplied by the Byzantine fleet, maintained its resistance until the year 640. Thereafter the conquest of Syria and Palestine was complete and irrevocable.

## *NOTABLE DATES*

| | |
|---|---|
| Battle of the Yarmouk | 20th August 636 |
| Sophronius offers to surrender Jerusalem to the khalif | September 637 |
| Umar visits Jerusalem | January 638 |

## *PERSONALITIES*

Theodorus, Byzantine commander-in-chief, killed in the Battle of the Yarmouk.
Baanes, Armenian army commander, under Theodorus.
Sophronius, Greek Patriarch of Jerusalem.
Jabala ibn al Aiham, last prince of Beni Ghassan.

# X

# *Qadasiya and Medain*

O you who believe, when you meet those who disbelieve marching to battle, do not turn your backs to them. Whoever turns his back on that day—unless it be in a military manœuvre or to join another unit – he indeed incurs the wrath of Allah, his destination is hell and an evil end. *Qoran* VIII, 15

The combination of a tribal solidarity and a religious drive is overwhelming.
IBN KHALDUN

And ye shall chase your enemies and they shall fall before you by the sword. And five of you shall chase an hundred and an hundred of you shall put ten thousand to flight: and your enemies shall fall before you by the sword.
*Leviticus* XXVI, 7

# X

## QADASIYA AND MEDAIN

AT the end of Chapter VIII, we left the Muslims in November 635 once more in a dominating position on the lower Euphrates as a result of Muthanna's victory at the Battle of Buwaib. They had reoccupied Hira and were raiding the country between the Tigris and Euphrates almost up to Medain, the capital of Persia. The victorious Muthanna, however, was dying of his wounds and the Arab forces had been left without a commander.

Rustem, the Persian commander-in-chief under the boy king Yezdegird, was not discouraged.[1] The force engaged at Buwaib may have been only a covering screen, thrown out in advance while the main army was recruited and organized. Fresh levies were being raised, the nobles rallied to the royal banner, a new enthusiasm was roused and Persian troops were soon advancing once again. The Arabs were driven from the fertile plains of the Suwad and over the Euphrates into the desert, abandoning Hira, Anbar and all their other conquests.

Muthanna, on his deathbed, sent an urgent appeal to Medina. Umar ibn al Khattab was not slow to face the emergency. A call for reinforcements was issued and a new army began to assemble near Medina. The khalif himself, amid popular applause, declared his intention of leading it in person, but allowed himself to be dissuaded by his principal advisers, who recommended Saad ibn abi Waqqas as the commander of the reinforcements for Iraq. The unfortunate Abu Ubaid had been chosen by Umar alone, but the khalif now accepted the advice of his counsellors. Saad was a cousin of the Prophet and one of the earliest converts to Islam. As a young man, he was a famous archer and was reputed to have been the first man to draw blood in the cause of Islam. Short and thickset, with a large head and shaggy hair, he had the reputation of a veteran fighter. He was forty years old when appointed to be commander-in-chief on the Persian front. As a close relative of the Prophet and a veteran of the Battle of Bedr, no bedouin chief could dispute his right to command. Umar ibn al Khattab, however, is alleged to have warned him against arrogance, for Quraish were rapidly becoming the haughty aristocracy of the new empire. "God looks for virtue and good works," he admonished Saad, "and not to birth. In His sight all men are equal."

In the late autumn of 636, Saad set out from Medina with some four thousand men, of whom three thousand were from the Yemen. Many of the tribesmen were accompanied by their wives, families and flocks. As fast as further contingents arrived in Medina, they were sent on by Umar, a process involving a good deal of argument and persuasion as the majority still persisted in their desire to go to Syria.

[1] Some historians make Yezdegird only now ascend the throne.

Early in the winter of 636–637, Saad pitched his camp at the well of Zerood in Nejed, in order to collect contingents from the local tribes. The removal of the ban on former "apostates" had immensely increased the available manpower. Soon he was joined by four thousand men from Beni Temeem. Even Tulaiha, the quondam false prophet, had turned over a new leaf and arrived at the head of three thousand men of his tribe, Beni Asad.

Another former rebel, Ashath ibn Qais,[2] an "apostate" of Kinda and brother-in-law of Abu Bekr, overtook the army with a contingent from the Hadhramaut. Amr ibn Madi Kerib[3] reported to Medina at the head of the tribe of Zubaid of the Yemen and was received by the khalif, who gave to him, and to other tribal chiefs of similar importance, a sum of two thousand dirhems. Amr ibn Madi Kerib was not so easily put off. He had a reputation as a large eater. Slapping the right side of his stomach, he exclaimed in a loud voice—"A thousand for here." Repeating the process on the left, he said —"and a thousand for here." Then pointing to the middle he added dolefully—"but what is there for here?" The khalif laughed and gave him five hundred more.

The custom of making a cash present and a change of clothes to visiting chiefs survives in Saudi Arabia to this day, and when employed amongst bedouins, I found myself obliged to observe it. Knowing that, however much I gave, more would probably be asked, I of course only offered at first about two-thirds of the sum I had allotted. The little extra bit given in the end was called by the bedouins *luhaiqa*. *Lahaqa* means to overtake, so *luhaiqa*, a diminutive, may be translated "a little chaser".

When Saad advanced from Zerood he was met by Muanna ibn Haritha, the brother of Muthanna, who had already died. He bore Muthanna's war banner and a last message of advice, sent by the old warrier on his deathbed to the new commander. "Fight the enemy in the desert," was the last counsel of the dying bedouin. "There you will be victorious, or, even if defeated, you will have the friendly and familiar desert at your backs. The Persians cannot follow you there and from there you can return again to the attack." It was the summary of Arab strategy, in Iraq as in Syria, which Abu Ubaid had so disastrously neglected at the Battle of the Bridge.

Saad was determined not to commit his army prematurely to a battle which might well prove decisive. For three months the tribes and forces under his command remained scattered over a vast area of desert nearly two hundred miles square. As so many were accompanied by their families and flocks, a closer concentration would have been difficult to maintain. Moreover forage being doubtless unobtainable for such large numbers of animals, three months of quiet desert grazing would strengthen horses and camels for the coming campaign. The season being winter, there would have been sufficient water in the desert for all concerned. The most northerly points in the training area, Sharaf,[4] Sulman and Ghudhai, were divided from the Euphrates by eighty miles of waterless desert, a distance too great to be crossed by the Persians on horses.

[2] Page 117. [3] Pages 117 and 118.
[4] The accent is on the last syllable as in the English word giraffe.

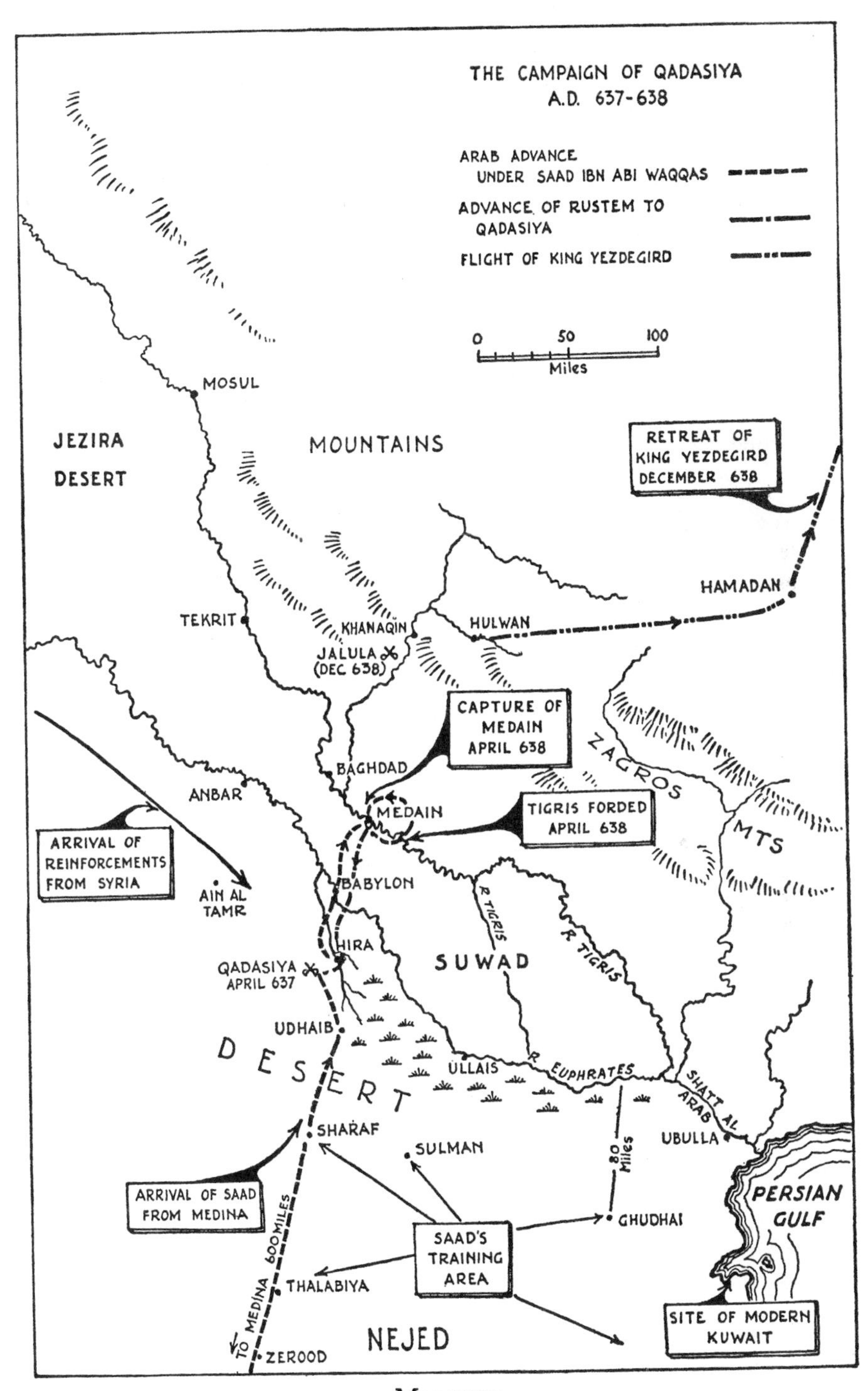
THE CAMPAIGN OF QADASIYA
A.D. 637-638
ARAB ADVANCE UNDER SAAD IBN ABI WAQQAS
ADVANCE OF RUSTEM TO QADASIYA
FLIGHT OF KING YEZDEGIRD
0
50
100
Miles
MOSUL
JEZIRA DESERT
MOUNTAINS
RETREAT OF KING YEZDEGIRD DECEMBER 638
HAMADAN
TEKRIT
KHANAQIN
HULWAN
JALULA
(DEC 638)
CAPTURE OF MEDAIN APRIL 638
ZAGROS MTS
BAGHDAD
ANBAR
MEDAIN
TIGRIS FORDED APRIL 638
ARRIVAL OF REINFORCEMENTS FROM SYRIA
AIN AL TAMR
BABYLON
R TIGRIS
R TIGRIS
HIRA
QADASIYA
APRIL 637
SUWAD
UDHAIB
DESERT
ULLAIS
R EUPHRATES
SHATT AL ARAB
SHARAF
SULMAN
80 Miles
UBULLA
ARRIVAL OF SAAD FROM MEDINA
TO MEDINA 600 MILES
GHUDHAI
PERSIAN GULF
SAAD'S TRAINING AREA
THALABIYA
SITE OF MODERN KUWAIT
NEJED
ZEROOD

Map XXIV

Thus Saad was able to organize his forces without fear of interruption by enemy action. In the same manner, in the Second World War, Britain and the United States were able to train their armies in England for the invasion of Europe, protected by the English Channel. Once again the comparison between the desert and the sea forces itself on our minds.

The learned historians to whom we are indebted for what has survived of the story of the Arab conquests were all sober citizens far removed from bedouins, deserts and battles. As a result, none of them has made any attempt to describe the training or the tactics of the all-conquering Arab armies. During this period of rest, however, we are told for the first time that Saad ibn abi Waqqas was occupied in organizing the Arab forces. He is said to have divided them into sections of ten, each under an appointed section-commander. The Arabs had now, for six years, been engaged in constant warfare with the trained troops of Byzantium and Persia, and it is only reasonable to assume that they must have acquired some ideas of the military art more advanced than those of a mere horde of tribesmen.

All the armies of this period seem to have been divided into advanced, rear and flank guards and main body, and the Arabs had now adopted the same system. The troops and commanders detailed for each of these duties often retained the same position throughout a whole campaign. The appointments made by Saad appear therefore to have included a deputy for himself, commanders for the advanced and flank guards and other formations referred to above, standard-bearers for the various tribal banners and section-commanders for every section of ten men. There is no specific mention of any appointments between formation and section-commanders, unless the standard-bearers were in reality what we should call unit-commanders.

The size of units must presumably have been extremely elastic because the Arabs fought in their tribes. Accustomed as we are to reading of incidents in the past two centuries in which primitive tribes have been routed by small detachments of regular forces, we are inclined to regard a tribal organization as utterly inefficient from a military standpoint. Yet it may perhaps have been the lack of modern weapons rather than the tribal system which was responsible for these defeats. When, however, the lance, the sword and the bow were the principal weapons, the tribes could be nearly as well armed as the regular armies. They, moreover, already instinctively possessed that esprit-de-corps which professional armies are at such infinite pains to inculcate in their soldiers. As long as the tribal system survived, tribesmen fought infinitely better among "the sons of their uncles" than in mixed groups among men of other tribes whom they regarded almost as foreigners.

That these advantages were enjoyed by all tribes, not only by Arabs, is proved by the fact that comparatively small armies of Goths, Vandals and other barbarians had sufficed to overthrow the Western Roman Empire.[5] Among Arab tribes, lack of discipline had always weakened their military

[5] The Ostrogoths who conquered Italy in the fifth century probably had only 20,000 warriors, though the population of Italy was between five and six millions. The Visigoths overthrew the Roman dominion of Spain with about the same number. Genseric, King of the Vandals, conquered North Africa from Rome with perhaps only 15,000 men. These numbers are comparable with those of the Arab conquerors. See also Henri Pirenne, *Mohamed and Charlemagne*

efficiency, but at the time of which we are writing religion had atoned for this deficiency. Obedience had become a religious obligation.

Perhaps in December 636 or in January 637, Saad moved northwards from Sharaf to the vicinity of Udhaib, a place near the Euphrates probably a few miles north of the modern Khan Ruhba. He had ordered all the scattered tribes, including those constituting Muthanna's former command, to concentrate in the same area.

Muthanna's army at Buwaib had been some 12,000 strong, of whom about 6,000 had been from Beni Bekr, his own tribe. Saad ibn abi Waqqas had collected approximately the same number by the time he had moved from Zerood to Sharaf. With other contingents still coming in, the total Arab army which concentrated at Udhaib may have amounted to some 30,000 men. In contrast to Muthanna's forces, which had consisted almost entirely of tribesmen, Saad's army included 1,400 Companions, of whom ninety-nine had fought at Bedr.

In Syria, the decisive battle of the Yarmouk had been won in August 636. No sooner did the news of the victory reach the khalif than he ordered Abu Ubaida to send back to Iraq the force which, two years before, Khalid had taken from the Persian front to Syria. Khalid did not accompany it. Six thousand strong, it was led by Qais ibn Makshouh, a former "apostate" in the Yemen and by the impetuous Qaqaa, who, with Khalid ibn al Waleed, had scaled the city walls on the day of the assault on Damascus. When Saad reached Udhaib, however, the contingent returning from Syria had not yet arrived.

* * * * *

Meanwhile the Persians had not been idle. Urged on by the youthful energy of Yezdegird, they had collected a great army under the command of Rustem, a veteran general of many campaigns. The royal banner of the Sassanian dynasty had moved out with the army to underline the importance of the occasion. No less than thirty-three elephants formed the "armoured division" destined to lead the attack. The Arab historians variously claim that the new Persian army was 60,000 or 120,000 strong. Such figures can scarcely be accepted but it is possible that Rustem's army was more numerous than that of Saad.

Probably in December 636, Rustem had moved southwards from Medain, and had camped in the vicinity of Babylon. The old general's plans differed radically from those of the young king. Rustem was most anxious to avoid a pitched battle. The Persian Empire in those days extended as far as Sind in modern Pakistan and included what we call Afghanistan. Of so vast a territory, the Arabs had scarcely as yet nibbled at one edge and indeed had now evacuated it completely and were out in the desert again. As long as Rustem's army remained in existence and undefeated, the Arabs could not cross the Euphrates except in small plundering raids, unless they were prepared to fight a great battle in the cultivated area, which would be to the advantage of the Persians. Meanwhile, thought the cautious old general, Arab enthusiasm might die down or internal dissensions might divide them. Rustem's plan therefore was to wait on the east bank of the Euphrates and see what happened.

The young Yezdegird held diametrically opposite views. With haughty impatience, he urged his general to sweep this desert scum from the frontier of his dominions and then to follow them into their own country and chastise them for their insolence in daring to molest the subjects of the King of Kings. Rustem, however, clung obstinately to his own ideas, and is said to have spent no less than four months on his march from Medain to Hira, a distance of only seventy miles.

Meanwhile the khalif had ordered Saad to send a delegation to King Yezdegird to summon him to embrace Islam. A deputation of twenty Arab warriors, selected for their eloquence and their commanding deportment, were sent to Medain. It included Amr ibn Madi Kerib and Ashath ibn Qais, both former "apostates". As the Arabs were led into the audience hall of the Great King, the crowds in the Persian capital could not refrain from contemptuous smiles when they saw their rough clothing, rude weapons and unkempt appearance. Yet the proud and fearlessly independent mien of the free Arabs of the desert did not fail to impress the smooth courtiers of Yezdegird.

Having reached the royal presence, the Muslims selected Naaman ibn Muqarrin, a Companion from Medina, as their spokesman. He informed the king of how God had sent His Prophet to them and had led them out of their former ignorance. He invited Yezdegird to become a Muslim like themselves or alternatively to pay tribute and humbly to place himself under their protection. Should he reject both courses, he would lose his kingdom.

The king, perhaps understandably, was incensed by such an address and replied contemptuously that the Arabs were but poor, half-starved desert people. In reply, they admitted the charge of poverty but added that God would enrich them. The young king, however, became further exasperated, crying out that, were it not disgraceful to kill ambassadors, he would have put them all to death. Then, calling for a sack of earth, he ordered it to be placed on the back of the leader of the Arabs as a sign of his contempt. The Muslims rode away bearing the sack of earth which they gleefully presented to Saad ibn abi Waqqas. "Good news," they cried, "the Persians have given us the soil of their country."

(A curious parallel to this scene was enacted in July 1799, when the Turkish governor of Baghdad gave audience to a representative of Saud ibn Saud the Wahhabi. Every Turkish officer, guard and soldier had been dressed up in full uniform to impress the Wahhabi emissary, who, however, proved to be a ragged bedouin. The desert ambassador, unabashed by the splendour of the Baghdad court, sat down on the floor in front of His Excellency the Governor, to whom he addressed a speech of haughty defiance and contempt).[6]

Meanwhile the Arabs began to raid the agricultural districts along the Euphrates. This they did principally to obtain food for themselves and forage for their horses. The khalif was able to send them flocks of animals to supply them (at least partially) with meat, for they travelled on the hoof from Cen-

[6] Cf. S. H. Longrigg, *Four Centuries of Modern Iraq*.

tral Arabia. But he was unable to supply them with grain for bread or forage for animals. The Persians who were the victims of these raids complained loudly to the king, demanding protection for their property. The morale of the Arabs, who were thus always attacking, continued to rise, while the Persians, helplessly watching the devastation of their country, became increasingly dejected. At length the young Yezdegird ordered his cautious general to give battle immediately to the Muslims. Unable to delay any longer, Rustem moved forward and camped on the bank of the Euphrates immediately opposite the Arabs. Perhaps in the faint hope of still avoiding a decisive battle, he despatched a message to Saad ibn abi Waqqas, asking him to send a deputation to meet him.

After consulting the Arab leaders, Saad decided that to send a delegation would show an undesirable degree of respect. An old bedouin was sent alone to meet the Persian commander-in-chief. Rustem had seated himself on a throne, surrounded by his staff and guards, the ground in front of his seat being spread with priceless Persian carpets. The Arab rode on to the carpets on his shaggy little mare. Dismounting, he advanced on foot towards the general's seat, when the guards stepped forward to take his arms. "I did not come here to be disarmed," the bedouin remarked grimly. "You invited me. I did not want to come. If you want to take my arms, I will go back." Rustem told the guards to stand back and the old tribesman, who must have been enjoying himself, walked slowly forward leaning on his lance in such a way as, at every step, to make a hole in some priceless carpet with the butt-end. In front of the commander-in-chief's chair, the ragged Arab ruined one more carpet by planting his lance through it vertically and then seated himself on the ground. To the general's enquiries, he replied with the usual offer—conversion to Islam, subjection and tribute or war. Rustem asked for time to consider these proposals and to communicate them to the king, but the old man replied that the Apostle of God had always restricted such periods of grace to three days. On the following two days, single representatives were again sent to meet the Persian commander, each in turn assuming the same defiant and aggressive manner, doubtless with the calculated object of further lowering the morale of the Persians. The last emissary was Mughira ibn Shuba, a Companion from Taif, who sat down beside the general on his couch to the horror of the courtiers and staff.

At length Rustem realized that time was no longer to be bought. The old debate was renewed as to who should cross the Euphrates. The Persians wished the Arabs to cross and fight in the cultivated area. The Arabs wanted to draw the Persians to the west bank and to fight in the desert. Whichever army crossed and fought with its back to the river, would be completely destroyed if defeated, as had twice been proved, at the Battles of the Bridge and of Buwaib.

Saad had drawn up his army on the open plain of Qadasiya, perhaps between the modern towns of Nejf and Abu Sukhair. His right rested on marshland which extended to the Euphrates. The desert lay in his rear—the river lay in his front. At length Rustem found himself obliged to comply with the king's orders and to give battle. The Persian army began to cross.

The Euphrates was then divided into several separate streams in this area, as it still is today. That which divided the two armies is called by the Arab historians the old Euphrates, presumably a subsidiary channel, the main stream having found a new course further east. The flow must have been limited for Rustem, we are told, did not use the bridge but built a dam over which to cross. The Persian army then drew up on the plain facing the Arabs.

Saad ibn abi Waqqas had found near the battlefield a small fort or building in which he had been living. When the Arabs were formed up for battle, he was sick [7] and was apparently laid out on his bed at a window or on the flat roof. From this point of vantage it appears he could see and even direct the movements of his army, but the fact that he did not appear in person among his men caused considerable unfavourable comment. As we have seen, the Arabs in war expected their commander to lead the charge, to challenge the enemy general to personal combat or to carry forward the war-banner in his own hand. Saad was a famous fighter and a veteran of many battles, so presumably the fact that he was absent from the field cannot be attributed to cowardice. Some of the men, however, hinted otherwise. During the months of waiting, he had married the widow of Muthanna. This lady, during the ensuing battle, is alleged to have repeated again and again, "O for an hour of Muthanna! Alas there is now no Muthanna," until the indignant husband slapped her face.

None of the historians suggest that Saad might have deliberately posted himself on the roof of a building behind the line, in order the better to control the battle. They probably believed, as did the men of the Muslim army, that the duty of a general was limited to charging at the head of his troops. Yet if Saad had really been ill, why did his wife Selma, the widow of Muthanna, taunt him with inferiority to her former husband? We are even told that Saad, from the roof of the house, sent written orders to the different commanders. It is tempting to think of him as a serious soldier, fighting to win and not to be deflected from his purpose by romantic ideas of single combat. His apologists, however, could think of no excuse for such extraordinary conduct. "We fought patiently," sang the Arab poet:

> "We fought patiently until God gave us victory,
> While Saad was safe inside walls at Qadisiya."

As the Persian army deployed on the plain in front of them, Chapter VIII of the Qoran [8] was recited before each Arab tribal contingent. This is the chapter which recounts the story of the Battle of Bedr and the lessons to be learnt from it.

"O Prophet, urge on the believers to battle. If there be of you twenty steadfast, they shall conquer two hundred and if there be of you one hundred, they shall conquer a thousand of the unbelievers . . ." [9] The Muslims stood in silence while these stirring passages were read; their hearts were cheered and their eyes grew bright. Thus encouraged, they prepared themselves for the alternative joys of victory or of martyrdom—direct and immediate admis-

[7] His disease is variously described as boils and as sciatica.
[8] See also page 187.
[9] Cf. Leviticus XXVI, 7, on page 187.

sion to the pleasures of Paradise. Not all, however, especially of the bedouins, fought for religious motives alone. Some called out the war cries of their tribes, boasted the names and the exploits of their forbears or recited ancient ballads of love and war.

The battle seems to have commenced with an advance by the Persians, whereupon Arab champions rode out before the lines, challenging the enemy to personal combat. Then, as the conflict warmed, the dreaded elephants emerged from the Persian line, swaying their great trunks to and fro, the howdahs on their backs crowded with warriors and waving flags. Beni Bajeela were thrown into confusion, but Beni Asad, led by Tuleiha the former false prophet, stood firm, though they suffered heavily in the struggle. At length, Asim, the leader of Beni Temeem, with a picked band of his kinsmen, concentrated on the elephants.[10] The archers attempted to shoot the soldiers crowded in the howdahs, while swordsmen endeavoured to get beneath the bellies of the great animals and cut the girth, thereby bringing the howdahs crashing to the ground. Several of the elephants having been thus disabled, or deprived of their riders, the Arabs were able to reform their ranks and repulse any further attacks. At length darkness fell and the combatants separated. The Muslims had only just succeeded in holding their ground and were disappointed at the outcome of the day. It was perhaps unfortunate that Saad ibn abi Waqqas was absent from the field, for gallant personal leadership would probably have given them fresh heart.

The morning of the second day was spent in carrying the dead and wounded from the space between the two armies. About noon, fighting began once more. The Arabs were in better form than they had been the previous day, because no elephants appeared on the Persian side, presumably owing to the damage done to them, their "crews" and their equipment on the previous day.

It will be recollected that, after the victory on the Yarmouk, Umar ibn al Khattab had sent orders to Syria for the return to the Persian front of the army which Khalid had led across the desert from Iraq to Syria two years before. Soon after noon of the second day of the battle of Qadasiya, the advanced guard of these reinforcements appeared on the scene. Messengers had doubtless been sent to inform them that a decisive battle was imminent and to urge them to hasten their march. The leading contingent was commanded by the fiery Qaqaa, who, although arriving at the end of a forced march, is reported to have found time to charge the enemy thirty times the same afternoon. A man of Beni Temeem, who had bound himself to seek martyrdom, attacked the Persian army alone in the hope of killing Rustem. Though he hacked his way deep into the enemy's ranks, he fell bleeding from innumerable wounds before he could reach the commander-in-chief. Some Arabs this day entered the battle on camels which they had disguised in hoods and draperies to frighten the horses of the Persian cavalry. Fighting went on after darkness had fallen but finally petered out. On balance the Arabs had perhaps more than held their own, but the Persians were still fighting resolutely and

[10] Reminiscent of the tank-hunting sections formed by the British army in the Second World War, before adequate anti-tank weapons were available.

the issue was undecided. All night long, the Arabs continued to dance and sing, to recite poetry and to recall the names and the exploits of their forbears.

It is interesting to note this Arab quality, which contrasts so strikingly with the conduct of British troops in similar circumstances. Before, and in the intervals of fighting, the Arabs—instead of resting—stir up their enthusiasm with poetry and song. They are too excited to eat and in every emergency seem to depend on their nerves and their emotions. British soldiers, under similar circumstances, would demand tea, and then lie down, cursing and grumbling, to rest and sleep. Yet both, after using such different methods, would be ready to fight on again the next morning.

The third morning of battle was again perforce spent in clearing the dead and wounded from the field. The Arab women were engaged, behind the fighting line, in hastily burying the dead or in doing whatever was possible to alleviate the anguish of the wounded. Just as fighting was about to recommence, the main body of the forces returning from Syria came into view and joined in the battle. While the Arabs were encouraged by this welcome succour, the renewed appearance of elephants increased their anxieties. This time it was the gallant Qaqaa who was ordered by Saad to deal with them. The tactics employed on this occasion consisted in the use of dismounted men armed with lances or long spears, for the Arab horses could not be persuaded to approach the elephants. While his followers engaged the elephant's escort and bothered the great animal with fighting all around it, Qaqaa and another man of Beni Temeem, armed with lances, watched their opportunity. Then Qaqaa with a sudden lunge pierced the elephant's eye with his lance, though it is alleged that it then seized him in its trunk and threw him to the ground. Another elephant was blinded in both eyes by the Arab lances, then, rushing round the field in panic, it stampeded all the others, which, trumpeting loudly, galloped off, trampling friend and foe alike beneath their feet. The soldiers' battle then continued, both sides standing firm, until the approach of night again put an end to hostilities.

Once more fighting ceased as darkness fell, but after a brief pause, some of the Arabs decided to harass the enemy during the night. This unpremeditated attack led on once more to a general engagement in the dark, neither Rustem nor Saad being able to exercise any control. The bedouins, then as now, prided themselves on their prowess in the darkness. They loved to compare themselves to wolves, which sleep by day and prowl by night. Indeed a community which lives half under the stars and half in frail tents, cannot but be as familiar with the night as with the day. Once men live under roofs, and shut the doors of their houses, the night becomes to them strange, hostile and alarming. The Persian troops probably consisted principally of men who normally lived in houses.

The army of the Great King, moreover, was doubtless "trained" to a greater extent than were the bedouins. To men who fight in close ranks expecting to receive frequent orders from their superiors, a night battle is always a delicate operation, for individual soldiers lose their comrades and units become separated from their commanders. Under such circumstances, it is often every man for himself and a horde of wild enthusiasts, shouting, slashing and thrusting may well have the advantage over men who hesitate, while awaiting orders from above. In this manner, the night attack at Qadasiya may have served the Arabs in the same way as the dust-storm at the Battle of the Yarmouk. The bedouin is characterized by one quality perhaps more than any other—his readiness to take the initiative in a tight corner, without paying any attention to anyone else. It is noticeable that the night attack at Qadasiya is said to have been initiated by the tribesmen themselves, without the orders of Saad ibn abi Waqqas, and that the Arabs do not appear to have made use of night attacks in other battles, though they did so for raids. This might well be explained by the fact that the commanders in the bigger battles were townsmen of Quraish, unused to movement at night.

Such was the "night of fury", the name given to the final stage of the battle.[11] When day dawned, the struggle was still in progress. It had become a battle of attrition, in which victory would go to the side which could summon that last ounce of courage and energy, for both armies were worn out. It was the Arabs who were able to mount the last daylight attack. Once more Qaqaa, not Saad, is stated to have provided the impetus, which only the incredible hardihood of the bedouins, inured to the hunger and weariness of the desert, could have carried out. One more charge and the Persians began to waver. Then the centre of their line gave way. Meanwhile a high wind had sprung up, the sand began to fly and the conditions of the Yarmouk appeared about to be reproduced.

The Arabs broke through the centre, discovered Rustem, the Persian commander-in-chief, seated on his chair, overtook him and slew him. The Persian army then collapsed. Two formations, reaching the dam by which they had crossed originally to the west bank, were able to withdraw relatively intact. The majority of the Persians scattered in flight in all directions, some were drowned in the river, some were pursued into the neighbouring marshes, some were cut down as they fled across the plain. Thirty "regiments" of Persians, however, stood fast disdaining flight and were killed to a man. No sooner was the fighting ended than the Arab tribeswomen and their children spread over the field. Carrying clubs and weapons in one hand and goatskins of water in the other, they assuaged the thirst of the wounded and dying Muslims and despatched the disabled Persians to hell-fire. According to Tabari, 2,500 Arabs had been killed during the first three days of battle and a further 6,000 during the night of fury and the final attack on the fourth morning. If Saad's original army was 30,000 strong and the contingent from Syria 6,000 men, the killed were just under twenty-five per cent. of the army. These—for there is no mention of wounded—would (if correct) be extremely heavy casualties, even in the most desperate modern battle.

Large quantities of money, jewels and weapons were captured on the field, in addition to the great banner of the Sassanids. The Battle of Qadasiya was as fatal to Persian rule in Iraq as had been that of the Yarmouk to Byzantine control of Syria. The Persian army, which only ten years before had been

[11] The word used has been variously translated, "The night of clangour", "The night of yells", etc.

hammering on the gates of Constantinople, had been destroyed beyond recovery by the rude but hardy tribesmen of Arabia. The death of Rustem added to the confusion and despair. The young King Yezdegird, now twenty-one years of age, was obviously too inexperienced to handle such a crisis alone. But the country was accustomed to look up to Rustem, the old dictator, the statesman behind the throne, as the mainstay of the kingdom. Now that he was dead, no man was left of sufficient calibre to ride the storm.

The remaining Christian Arab tribes of the north hastened to make their submission and, in some cases, to embrace the Muslim religion, by means of which their bedouin brothers of Arabia had achieved such incredible glory and wealth.[12] The settled Christians made their submission and paid the poll-tax prescribed. A problem seemed here to arise, for Muhammad had specified Jews and Christians as being people with religious books, who were to be left to practise their religion if they paid tribute. Apart from them, "heathen" were to be offered the alternatives of conversion or death. The Persians were Zoroastrians and therefore not entitled to the toleration accorded to Jews and Christians. Yet it was obviously impossible to put them all to death. Circumstances made it inevitable for them also to be accepted as "people of the book", and admitted to the status of tolerated tributaries.

Saad ibn abi Waqqas had been in constant correspondence with the khalif in Medina, who, therefore, was fully aware that a major battle on the Euphrates was impending. Tradition relates that Umar ibn al Khattab used, early every morning, to walk out of the east gate of Medina in the hope of meeting some messenger from Iraq. At last one morning he did indeed see a weary camel-rider approaching the city from the desert. To Umar's anxious enquiry, the rider (not recognizing this barefooted man with his patched cloak) replied that the Persians had been defeated. The khalif was obliged to run panting beside the messenger to keep up with the stride of his camel, while he asked him for details of the battle, until the pair reached the city. Here the people, hearing the news, crowded excitedly round him to congratulate him, to the embarrassment of the bedouin messenger who had failed to recognize him. Innumerable such anecdotes are related of Umar, some perhaps true and some not, but all, doubtless justifiably, emphasizing the humility and simplicity of this great man and leader.

Although the Persian army had been completely routed, the Arabs themselves had been too exhausted to pursue. For two months, they rested on the field of battle. Probably the delay was also partly due to the need to remain with the great numbers of wounded, who could not be abandoned nor could they be carried forward with the army. Two months would have sufficed to enable those capable of recovery to rejoin the ranks, and to allow of the performance of the last obsequies over those whom God had deemed worthy of martyrdom.

The date of the Battle of Qadasiya is difficult to fix. Historians differ in their estimates by as much as two years. If we assume the Battle of the Yar-

[12] The Taghlib, however, remained Christians for a long time to come.

mouk to have been fought in July 636, then Qadasiya must have been after that date, for the reinforcements released by the victory in Syria arrived in time for the Battle of Qadasiya. It is 600 miles from the Yarmouk to Medina and approximately the same distance from the Yarmouk to Qadasiya. Thus it would probably have taken at least a month for Abu Ubaida to inform Umar ibn al Khattab of the result of the battle and for him to receive the khalif's orders to send the Iraq contingent back. It might well have taken two months, for the Medina authorities were not a highly trained staff. This would bring us to September 636. In any case, it would have been difficult for the Iraq contingent to cross the Syrian desert before October 636. It had been two years in Syria, and must have been accompanied by women and children, while the Syrian desert is peculiarly lacking in water. If, therefore, we assume the Syrian contingent to have set out in the winter of 636–637, it could have reached Qadasiya any time between February and April 637,[13] according to whether it set out in October, November or December.

* * * * *

After two months' rest, that is, if our chronology be correct, in April, May or June 637, Saad reoccupied Hira, the tribute of which was doubled, on the charge that the city had returned to its Persian allegiance before Qadasiya. Saad ibn abi Waqqas then moved northwards and established his camp by the ruined mounds of ancient Babylon, whence the Arabs raided up to the very walls of Medain, the capital of the Persian empire.

Medain, the plural of Medina meaning cities, was a name given by the Arabs. In reality the capital consisted of two cities, Seleucia on the west bank of the Tigris and Ctesiphon on the east. Seleucia had been founded in B.C. 312 by Seleucus Nicator, one of the Greek rulers who inherited portions of the empire of Alexander the Great. (Until then Babylon had been the capital.) Seleucia was originally populated by Greeks and was, for several centuries, one of the greatest political and commercial cities of the then known world. Ctesiphon was established two hundred years after Seleucia, on the opposite bank of the Tigris, and became the capital of the Sassanid dynasty in the second century A.D. At the time of the Arab conquests, the Persian court, palaces and government were in Ctesiphon, on the east bank. The Muslims first set themselves to deal with Seleucia, the city on the west bank. Advancing from Babylon, Saad ibn abi Waqqas surrounded and blockaded the walled town.

As usual, the Arabs were unable effectively to attack the massive fortifications, though, with the help of Persian deserters, they brought up twenty mangonels as "artillery". Presumably these machines threw stones too light to damage the walls.[14] The Muslims therefore settled down to a long blockade of doubtful efficacy, for one side of the city lying along the bank of the Tigris was open to supplies and reinforcements from Ctesiphon on the other bank.

[13] Tabari states that ibn Ishaq placed the Yarmouk in September 636 and Qadasiya in February 637. Ibn Ishaq (born 704, died 768) is an early and therefore a comparatively reliable authority. Tabari was born in 838 and died in 923.

[14] Stones in any case are very difficult to obtain in the flat alluvial valley.

Meanwhile, however, the Arabs raided and subdued the whole area west of the Tigris, for no Persian army remained in the field to oppose them.

Eventually King Yezdegird proposed terms of peace. He offered to evacuate the west bank city and to abandon everything west of the Tigris to the Arabs, on condition that the river become the frontier and he be left in peaceful possession of everything east of it. Saad immediately rejected the proposal, which may have served only to encourage him by revealing the weakness of the enemy. A few days later, the Muslims noticed that the walls were no longer manned. The west bank city had been silently abandoned, all boats and ferries being withdrawn across the river. The Arabs entered the city unopposed and the hardy, ragged bedouins found themselves, to their own astonishment, free to occupy an ancient city, the product of a thousand years of commerce, wealth, art and luxury.

The River Tigris did indeed offer an obstacle, which halted the advance of the Arabs for several weeks. But the morale of the Persians had sunk too low to make possible a spirited defence of the line of the Tigris. King Yezdegird had already despatched his family to Hulwan, a fortified town at the foot of the Zagros mountains. He now followed in person, leaving Mihran, the general defeated at Buwaib, in command of Ctesiphon. A Persian informer told Saad ibn abi Waqqas of the existence of a ford across the Tigris. The chronology of these events is difficult to decide. If we were correct in estimating the time of the Battle of Qadasiya as February, March or April 637, it would be natural to suppose that siege was laid to the west bank city of Medain, that is Seleucia, in the late summer of 637, and that that part of the capital was evacuated by the Persians in mid-winter 637–638. Baladhuri states that the Arabs spent nine months on the west bank, which would fit such a timetable, but he then adds that others say it was eighteen months, because the date harvest came round twice while the army was there. He also states that, when the Persian informer revealed the ford, there was some doubt as to whether it would still be usable, because the river was about to rise. The annual rise of the Tigris takes place in the spring, when the snows melt in Anatolia. Consequently we may conclude that the affair of the Tigris ford took place in March or April 638. (If, however, the Arabs spent eighteen months on the west bank, then it would be April 639.)

Sulman the Persian, previously heard of as having suggested to the Prophet the digging of the trench of Medina, confirmed the possibility of fording. A force of horsemen made the attempt, and though a Persian detachment shot arrows at the Arabs during the crossing, the east bank was safely reached, apparently with only one casualty. As soon as the first group of Muslims was seen to be safely across, more and more horsemen dashed into the river. It is not quite clear whether the horsemen waded across the ford, or whether they swam.[15] To those who have not known them, it is sometimes surprising that bedouins, who live in almost waterless desert, are often splendid swimmers. Yet I testify myself to having seen men from Central Arabia swim the Euphrates.

[15] Chesney, quoted by Muir, says that, in A.D. 1392, Timurlane's army swam the Tigris near Baghdad.

The garrison of Ctesiphon seems to have been surprised by this daring operation. Such as had time to get away fled eastward to the mountains. The remainder submitted without resistance and agreed to pay tribute in return for protection. The luxuries of Seleucia proved to have been but a mild foretaste of the splendours of the court of the King of Kings in Ctesiphon. The immense vault of the palace of Chosroes still to this day towers above the surrounding plain, enabling the spectator to form at least some estimate of what that palace must have been in its glory.

The Arabs became possessed of immense wealth, as, on the old raiding system, the plunder was immediately distributed to the men of the army, after the subtraction of the orthodox fifth, which was sent to the khalif in Medina. The pious Umar ibn al Khattab in his patched cloak found himself the possessor of the imperial regalia of Persia, sparkling with jewels and gold, and of the immense carpet of the banqueting hall, covered with diamonds, rubies and pearls and woven with gold and silver thread. Saad ibn abi Waqqas established himself in the royal palace, the great banqueting hall became a mosque, and the ragged bedouins reclined luxuriously on the soft upholsteries of Persian nobles.

Meanwhile King Yezdegird had not been idle. From his headquarters at Hulwan, he had summoned fresh levies from far and near and was intent on creating a new army. As the work progressed and morale rose in consequence, the Persians pushed forward to the west and a strong force under Mihran occupied Jalula, where the Diyala emerges from the foothills, now called Jebel Hamreen, on to the flat plains of Iraq.[16] This enemy forward movement was reported to Saad in Medain. The cautious khalif had apparently forbidden any further advance, and Saad felt obliged to refer the matter back to Medina. On receiving permission from Umar, he sent his cousin, Hashim, with 12,000 men, to attack this advanced Persian garrison. An obstinate struggle resulted and further reinforcements had to be sent up from Medain. Eventually, however, in one day's heavy fighting at Jalula, the Persians were defeated and hotly pursued through the foothills as far as Khaniqin. King Yezdegird withdrew from Hulwan to northern Persia, and the Arabs occupied Hulwan unopposed. At the same time, another column was despatched up the Tigris. It captured Tikrit, was joined by Arab tribes from the Jezira and advanced on Mosul. By the end of 638, the whole of the great and wealthy valley of the lower Tigris and Euphrates had been surrendered irrevocably, and had become a submissive province of the new Arab Empire.

## *NOTABLE DATES*

| | |
|---|---|
| Battle of Qadasiya | February, March or April 637 |
| Occupation of Ctesiphon (Medain) | April 638 |
| Battle of Jalula | December 638 |

[16] In 1920, I was myself stationed for several months with an Indian Army battalion at the same spot.

### *PERSONALITIES*

Rustem, Persian commander-in-chief, killed at Qadasiya.
Saad ibn abi Waqqas, Arab commander-in-chief in Iraq.
Amr ibn Madi Kerib, former rebel in the Yemen, now distinguished Muslim fighter.
Mughira ibn Shuba, Companion, sent on deputation to Rustem.
Qaqaa ibn Amr, chief of Beni Temeem, distinguished Muslim leader.
Naaman ibn Muqarrin, leader of Arab deputation to Yezdegird.

# XI

## *Consolidation*

There in a portion of the lawgiver was he seated: and he came with the heads of the people, he executed the justice of the Lord and his judgements.
*Deuteronomy* XXXIII, 21

Surely We have revealed the Book to thee with truth that thou mayest judge between people by means of what Allah has taught thee. And be not one pleading the cause of the dishonest, and ask the forgiveness of Allah. Surely Allah is ever forgiving, merciful. *Qoran* IV, 105

Empire without justice is mere robbery. St. Augustine

## XI

## CONSOLIDATION

THE advance of the Arab armies in Syria and in Iraq had hitherto been effected in pursuit of the Byzantine and Persian armies. On the west, the line of withdrawal and advance had been through Damascus, Homs and Antioch to the foot of the Taurus mountains. In Persia it had led through Hira to Medain. In between these two lines of advance, a wide extent of territory had remained undisturbed.

The Christian tribes in this area had apparently been appealing for protection to the Byzantines, who, however, had already crossed the Taurus. It appears, nevertheless, that they promised to support the tribes by a landing from the fleet on the Mediterranean coast. The tribes accordingly concentrated in the direction of Homs, perhaps early in the year 638. At the same time, the Byzantines landed and reoccupied Antioch. Abu Ubaida suddenly found himself between two fires, the tribes of the Syrian desert threatening Homs from the east, while the Byzantines from Antioch and the sea coast appeared to be about to invade from the west.

The Arabs must have been considerably alarmed by this sudden counter-attack. So disconcerting was the despatch sent by Abu Ubaida to the khalif that the latter ordered Saad ibn abi Waqqas to send a column up the Euphrates immediately, to attack in the rear the tribes which were threatening Homs. Meanwhile Abu Ubaida sent Iyadh ibn Ghanm against Antioch. So anxious was Umar ibn al Khattab that he set out in person for Syria to conduct the operations. Saad sent the ever active Qaqaa with four thousand men up the Euphrates in hot haste. Hit closed its gates, but the column by-passed the town and pushed on, having obviously been impressed by the need for speed. Advancing by forced marches, Qaqaa captured Circesium (Arabic Kirkesiya) at the junction of the Khabur with the Euphrates. As this column travelled up the river valley, there was no question of shortage of water, with the result that the men were mounted on mules, not on camels. The horses were led in order to keep them fresh and were mounted only for battle.

Meanwhile, however, Iyadh ibn Ghanm had retaken Antioch and there is no further reference to the Byzantines, who presumably had re-embarked. Before Umar ibn al Khattab could reach the cantonment at Jabiya, Abu Ubaida himself had sallied forth from Homs and dispersed the insurgent tribes, and the crisis had passed. Qaqaa and the column from Iraq were turned back after taking Circesium. Iyadh ibn Ghanm was thereupon ordered to lead a force to the Jezira and to secure the pacification and settlement of that area. He appears to have marched to Raqqa, which he invested, sending foraging parties far and wide to collect supplies and bring in prisoners.

We are told that it was the time of the harvest, perhaps mid-summer 638. After five or six days, Raqqa surrendered on the usual terms. The condition of all such surrenders had now become standardized in Syria and consisted in general of the following clauses:

(1) Every non-Muslim man was to pay a poll-tax of one dinar per year, one measure of wheat and varying amounts of oil, vinegar and honey.

The Arabs had, of course, only the most primitive system for rationing their armies and the tribute in kind was doubtless intended to assist in supplying the troops. In so far as the poll-tax was concerned, the dinar today is the name used for the equivalent of a pound sterling. To endeavour to evaluate the dinar in the seventh century in terms of modern living costs would not be of great help to us, because the daily needs of people in the seventh century were so different from our own. All that can be said is that it was the gold coin of the time.

(2) The churches were to be left intact for Christian worship but no new churches were to be built, nor were church bells to be used to call people to divine service. Processions bearing crosses were not to move along the streets.

(3) As long as these terms were observed, the inhabitants would be under the protection of the Muslims and their lives and property would be guaranteed.

From Raqqa, Iyadh ibn Ghanm rode up to the gate of Edessa and parleyed from horseback with the defenders on the walls of the town. (Urfa is the modern name of Edessa. The Arabs called it Ruha.) Eventually they too agreed to surrender on the usual terms. Establishing his base in Edessa, he then proceeded to Samsat and Haran and accepted their surrenders also. Thereafter he went on to conquer Ras al Ain, Mardin, Nisibin, Amida (the modern Diyarbekr) and Sinjar, until the whole of the northern Jezira was subjugated and pacified. The operations seem to have dragged on without remarkable incident until the year 640 or 641. Iyadh was later appointed by the khalif to be the governor of the Jezira. Returning to Homs in 642, however, he died there.

It may be of interest to notice in passing that Ghanm had been an Arabian idol in the days of the Ignorance, and that the name of Iyadh's father had been Abid Ghanm, or servant of Ghanm. When he became a Muslim, Iyadh was apparently unwilling to recollect the fact that his father had been an idolater. He consequently dropped the abid, or servant, and called himself the son of Ghanm, as if that had been his father's name. Yet his fellow Arabs must have known that Ghanm had been an idol. Perhaps he wished to conceal from the Jews and Christians the fact that his parents had been polytheists. This incident serves to remind us of the extraordinary speed of the transformation which had occurred. The year 638, in which Persia and Byzantium were simultaneously defeated, was only sixteen years after the Prophet's flight from Mecca, when there were in the world just over one hundred Muslims. These wild and enthusiastic Arab conquerors were nearly all men who had grown up in idolatry. Many of them had been "apostates" only four years earlier. As only a negligible proportion of them could read and write, the majority must still have been ignorant of the details of the

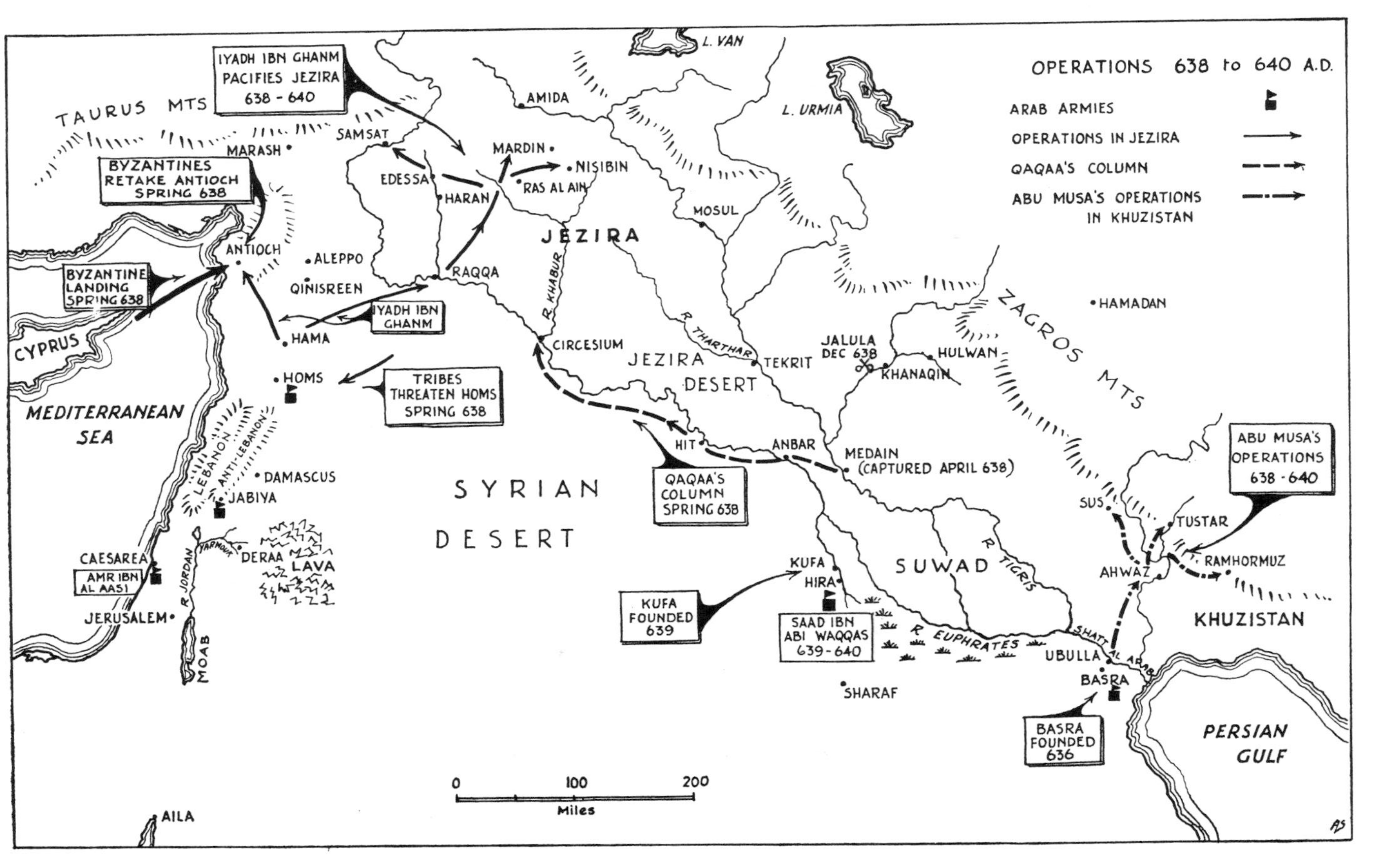
OPERATIONS 638 to 640 A.D.
ARAB ARMIES
OPERATIONS IN JEZIRA
QAQAA'S COLUMN
ABU MUSA'S OPERATIONS IN KHUZISTAN
IYADH IBN GHANM PACIFIES JEZIRA 638 - 640
TAURUS MTS
MARASH
SAMSAT
BYZANTINES RETAKE ANTIOCH SPRING 638
ANTIOCH
ALEPPO
QINISREEN
BYZANTINE LANDING SPRING 638
CYPRUS
MEDITERRANEAN SEA
HAMA
IYADH IBN GHANM
HOMS
TRIBES THREATEN HOMS SPRING 638
LEBANON
ANTI-LEBANON
DAMASCUS
JABIYA
YARMOUK
DERAA
LAVA
CAESAREA
AMR IBN AL AASI
R. JORDAN
JERUSALEM
MOAB
AILA
L. VAN
AMIDA
EDESSA
HARAN
MARDIN
NISIBIN
RAS AL AIN
RAQQA
JEZIRA
R. KHABUR
CIRCESIUM
MOSUL
L. URMIA
R. THARTHAR
TEKRIT
JEZIRA DESERT
JALULA DEC 638
KHANAQIN
HULWAN
ZAGROS MTS
HAMADAN
SYRIAN DESERT
HIT
ANBAR
MEDAIN (CAPTURED APRIL 638)
QAQAA'S COLUMN SPRING 638
KUFA
HIRA
KUFA FOUNDED 639
SAAD IBN ABI WAQQAS 639-640
SUWAD
R. TIGRIS
R. EUPHRATES
SHATT AL ARAB
UBULLA
BASRA
BASRA FOUNDED 636
SHARAF
SUS
TUSTAR
AHWAZ
RAMHORMUZ
ABU MUSA'S OPERATIONS 638 - 640
KHUZISTAN
PERSIAN GULF
0
100
200
Miles

Map xxv

Muslim faith. Yet I do not think that this proves that they were not genuinely stirred by religion. Emotional religious "revivals" often spread with great rapidity, produce intense enthusiasm and have little to do with intellectual dogma. The belief that a great spiritual Ruler of the universe not only existed but saw and was interested in them, may well have transformed their outlook on life. Moreover, the belief that death in battle would secure instant admission to paradise was calculated to ensure courage in war.

* * * * *

The great Khalid ibn al Waleed had, as we have seen, been previously deprived of his command by order of the khalif. In spite of this, he continued to serve under Abu Ubaida. His services at the Battle of the Yarmouk and at the capture of Qinisreen had been so outstanding that Umar ibn al Khattab had relented. "Khalid really is a prince among men," the khalif is said to have admitted. "Abu Bekr seems to have been a better judge of human nature than I was." He was appointed governor of Qinisreen.

Unfortunately when Iyadh ibn Ghanm set out to conquer the Jezira, Khalid is alleged to have gone with him and after the capture of Amida to have indulged in a bath of wine or some other similar orgy. Returning from this expedition to his headquarters at Qinisreen, he was visited by Ashath ibn Qais, who had been fighting at Qadasiya. The custom according to which bedouin chiefs "visit" the great men of their time, receiving gifts and suits of clothing, has already been mentioned.[1] Upon Ashath's departure, Khalid made him a gift of one thousand pieces of gold. The report reached Umar, who, claiming to suspect the misappropriation of public funds, wrote to Abu Ubaida to arrest the greatest of Arab generals and to bring him to trial. Publicly stripped of his government and humiliated, he was ordered to proceed to Medina, where Umar renewed the accusation. Khalid replied that the money was his own. There can be no doubt that he had grown rich from the plunder of many battles, but at least it was he who had won them. Some of the Companions of the Prophet were richer and had remained at home in Medina ever since the death of Muhammad.

Khalid was not a religious man. He had made a great deal of money, acquired wives and concubines, perhaps even indulged in wine. But it was largely due to him that the Byzantine Empire had been driven from Syria for ever. He was not only a great general, and a leader of genius, but he was also an extremely brave man in battle. Perhaps his reputation was too high. When justifying the treatment meted out to Khalid, the khalif was alleged to have said that the great soldier had been a cause of stumbling to the people, because they had been tempted to trust him to win victory, instead of relying solely upon God. He had defended his frequent supersession of Muthanna on the same grounds. Umar, as we have frequently observed, was a deeply conscientious man. Are we justified in suspecting that, possibly unconsciously, he was jealous of the fame and popularity of Khalid and Muthanna among the Arabs, which perhaps equalled or exceeded his own? After

[1] It was Ashath who had forgotten to include his own name in the ten to be pardoned and who had later married the sister of Abu Bekr. See page 118.

his final degradation, Khalid returned to Syria, where he died two years later in neglect.

* * * * *

While the northern Jezira was being pacified, another subsidiary campaign was necessary in order to consolidate the conquests already achieved. The main Arab army in Iraq, following in the tracks of King Yezdegird, had gone up into the mountains north-east of Medain. No major operations had taken place at the mouth of the Tigris and Euphrates, and the Persians were still holding the east bank of the combined rivers below their junction.

Four years earlier, Khalid ibn al Waleed, after his defeat of the false prophet Musailama at Yemama, had moved northwards towards the mouth of the Tigris and Euphrates and had concluded an agreement with the people of Ubulla, which was then the port of Iraq. From there, however, he had joined Muthanna ibn Haritha and had moved up to the Hira district. A chief of the Beni Bekr, a fellow-tribesman of Muthanna, had remained in command of the Shatt al Arab [2] area, in which he had continued guerrilla raids on the Persians across the river.

After the battle of Buwaib in November 635, the khalif had appointed Utba ibn Ghazwan, a Companion, to command the operations on the Shatt al Arab. When reports were received of the military preparations undertaken by the Persian general Rustem before Qadasiya, the khalif sent orders to Utba to make a diversion towards Ahwaz, in order to draw away Persian troops and detain them in that area. Some of the Beni Bekr and Beni Temeem from the deserts on the west shore of the Persian Gulf joined in these operations. Utba established his base in huts and tents on a strip of gravelly soil south-west of the Shatt al Arab, known as Al Basra. He also captured Ubulla, the port from which ships sailed to Bahrein, Oman and India. Having thus procured for himself a firm base, he proceeded to subjugate the flat delta country, and to push his raids across the Shatt al Arab into Khuzistan.[3]

Utba then obtained permission to visit Mecca and Medina for the pilgrimage, presumably in the year before Qadasiya, while Saad ibn abi Waqqas was organizing the Arab army at Sharaf. Leaving for Mecca, he appointed a bedouin chief to command in his absence. The point is of interest solely because, when Utba reached Medina and reported these arrangements, the khalif strongly disapproved. "Have you appointed a bedouin to be the superior of a town Arab?" he asked indignantly. He immediately selected Mughira ibn Shuba, a Companion of the Prophet, who had taken the oath at Hudeibiya, to assume command. Utba died soon afterwards and Mughira was confirmed in the command of the Khuzistan front. We have already heard of Mughira on a deputation to Rustem before Qadasiya, on which occasion he gave offence to the proud Persian by trying to sit down beside him.[4] As no one in Mughira's force could read or write, a youth by the name of Zayyad was appointed to be secretary to the commander. We shall hear much more of Zayyad later on.

[2] The name of the combined rivers Tigris and Euphrates below their junction.
[3] Map, page 209. [4] Page 195.

After the defeat of the Persian army at Qadasiya in the spring of 637, the situation changed. King Yezdegird had retired to Hulwan, abandoning the plains of Iraq to the Arabs, hoping to hold the line of the mountains to halt their further advance. Hormuzan, a Persian noble who had held an important command at Qadasiya, returned to his province of Ahwaz, in order to defend it against the Muslim raids from Basra. At the same time the Arab victory of Qadasiya had made Saad ibn abi Waqqas secure and thereby permitted the despatch of reinforcements to the Basra front.

At this stage an incident occurred which resulted in a change of commander and which provides also an interesting sidelight on the manners of the time. Mughira ibn Shuba was accused of adultery by four of his subordinates, one of them his secretary Zayyad. They reported their accusation to the khalif, who summoned the accused and the witnesses to Medina, even though the former was a governor and commander-in-chief. As the text of the Qoran stands today, the penalty for adultery is scourging with a hundred lashes, but tradition, from very early times, had assigned death by stoning for this offence. (This was the old Hebrew law.)[5]

When Aisha his favourite wife had been the victim of a scandalous charge, Muhammad had decreed that men who maligned innocent women were to be scourged if the charge were unproved.[6] Four eyewitnesses were needed to establish the crime of adultery. Three of the witnesses against Mughira gave evidence before Umar ibn al Khattab, leaving only the young Zayyad. When he was called forward, the khalif exclaimed, "Verily I see the face of a man through whom I hope one of the Companions of the Prophet of God will not be stoned to death and by whose testimony he will not be disgraced." After so broad a hint, Zayyad doubtless thought it prudent to modify his evidence and gave testimony that he could not be certain of what he had seen. The charge was therefore declared unproven, a result which exposed the three first witnesses to scourging, as having maligned an innocent woman. Mughira, however, lost his command, the khalif sending Abu Musa al Ashari to replace him in Basra, probably at the end of 638.

Abu Musa immediately marched against the Persians and invested the city of Sus, which he eventually captured. A certain senior cavalry commander in Yezdegird's army had been sent by the king to defend the area. This officer, seeing the continued success of the Muslims, opened negotiations with Abu Musa, offering to change sides with the cavalry under his command. It is of interest that, in the terms agreed upon, the Persian cavalry declared that they were "desirous of entering with you into your religion, on condition that we help you fight your foreign enemies, but that if there arise a difference between you, we are not to fight with some of you against others of you". In view of what was to happen in the future, it is significant to note that foreigners already foresaw the possibility of civil wars between the Arabs, even at the apparent height of Muslim brotherhood and enthusiasm. The Persian cavalry allied themselves with Beni Temeem. Other Persian communities are reported as joining the Muslims in the same area,

[5] Deuteronomy XXII, 22.

[6] Page 84.

including infantry soldiers, some of whom were even Indians. Each such group was adopted by an Arab tribe.

After the surrender of Sus and Ram Hormuz, Abu Musa pressed on to Tustar, where a considerable Persian force was assembled under Hormuzan already mentioned. Abu Musa was constrained to ask the khalif for reinforcements, receiving Jareer ibn Abdulla al Bajali, the hero of Buwaib and Qadasiya, with a contingent from the army of Saad ibn abi Waqqas. An action was then fought against Hormuzan, who was defeated and compelled to shut himself up in Tustar. A Persian deserter led a party of 240 Arabs into the city at night by a secret way. The Muslims killed the guards on the walls, and, raising the cry of *Allahu akbar*, threw open the gates to their comrades. Hormuzan was sent a prisoner to Medina.

Summoned before the khalif, the Persian noble had little hope of his life. Feigning thirst, he asked for a drink. On being handed a bowl of water he looked anxiously about him, as if fearing to drink lest someone strike off his head while he held the bowl with both hands. The khalif noticed the movement and assured him that his life would be safe until he had drunk the water. Hurmuzan immediately poured the water on the ground. A bystander, indignant at the trick played on the khalif, asked leave to strike off the head of the wily Persian, but Umar refused. A pledge, he said, must be observed and Hormuzan's life was safe. Thereafter he lived in the Holy City, as a Muslim, where he was to come to an untimely end, as will later on appear. These Persians provide the first example of non-Arabs becoming Muslims and thereafter being incorporated into the Arab race.

These operations in the Persian province of Khuzistan resulted in the capture of great numbers of prisoners, until Umar ibn al Khattab sent orders for their release. The land, he pointed out, must be cultivated if it were to remain prosperous after its conquest by the Arabs. Both in the Suwad and in Khuzistan he forbade the removal of the cultivators from the soil, but ordered that they be assessed to pay poll-tax and tribute to the conquerors.

Soon afterwards the inspectors appointed to assess the taxes in Khuzistan were charged with peculation, with the result that Umar ordered the confiscation of half their wealth, a rough and ready method, but perhaps the only one available to a man who had found himself suddenly burdened with the administration of an empire by means of a community in which scarcely anyone could even read and write.

With King Yezdegird behind the Zagros mountains and Khuzistan subdued by Abu Musa from his base at Basra, we may now turn to events elsewhere.

* * * * *

All through history, Arabia has been liable every few years to a season of drought, when the winter rains fail, no green grass or shrubs mark the return of spring and the whole country remains parched, dusty and dead. At such times sheep and camels die in great numbers and the poorer classes, in town and in tribe, are reduced to desperate straits to obtain food. Such a year was 639 in Arabia. The khalif adopted energetic measures to alleviate the public distress, and long trains of camels were summoned from Syria, Palestine and Iraq, laden with foodstuffs and grain. Umar ibn al Khattab, to set an example to others, refused all but the most Spartan diet, such as that to which the poorest of the people were reduced.

In addition to the disastrous famine in the Hejaz, the year 639 witnessed an outbreak of bubonic plague in Syria and Palestine. Many Arabs died, until great numbers sought refuge in the desert from the plague-infected cities. Before this migration to the desert could be completed, however, the commander-in-chief, Abu Ubaida, was himself struck down and died. He was buried in the Jordan valley. (In the 1940's, his tomb which had fallen into decay, was rebuilt by order of King Abdulla of Jordan.) Yezeed ibn abi Sofian, who had played a distinguished part as a column commander throughout the Syrian campaign, was also a victim.

The indefatigable khalif decided himself to visit Syria in order to reorganize the administration after the loss of so many leaders. Indeed so fatal had been the plague among the Arabs, twenty-five thousand of whom are said to have died, that it was feared the Byzantines might seize the opportunity to attempt the re-conquest of Syria.

In place of Abu Ubaida and Yezeed ibn abi Sofian, Muawiya ibn abi Sofian was appointed governor of Syria. We have already seen Muawiya as the secretary of the Prophet in Medina, running barefoot beside the camel of some arrogant little chieftain from South Arabia.[7] Muawiya, now the eldest surviving son of old Abu Sofian, was flexible and ambitious. Capable of being respectful and humble when necessary, patient enough to wait his chance, he was to prove himself a far-seeing statesman and a ruler of outstanding ability. He was also to transform the theocratic Muslim dominion, with its threadbare and dedicated khalifs, into a mighty and splendid hereditary empire.

* * * * *

With the Byzantines and the Persians simultaneously humiliated, and the Arab hold on Syria and Iraq firmly established, we may now turn for a moment to the internal affairs of this new empire, which had grown up as it were in a night. The new situation faced Umar ibn al Khattab with the need of making several major decisions.

The peoples of Palestine and Syria were not homogeneous. On the Mediterranean shore, they were a peculiar race of extremely mixed origin. The early settlers–Philistines, Canaanites, Hittites, Hebrews, Phoenicians—had for nearly a thousand years been overlaid with Greek and Latin immigrants. Many of the major cities were largely Greek. The eastern areas of Syria and Palestine, the former satellite state of Beni Ghassan, was half or more than half Arab. The language of most of the area was Aramaic, the religion was Christianity. In the course of the military operations, thousands of tribesmen from Central Arabia had arrived in the area to fight, the majority of them bringing their wives and families. Although many Arabs had died of the plague, there were still considerable numbers of them in Syria. With the

[7] Page 100.

termination of hostilities, these tribesmen had nothing to do. Moreover the end of fighting meant the end of loot.

The problem which confronted the khalif was whether to allow these Arabs from Central Arabia to mingle with the native Syrians and Palestinians, or whether intentionally to isolate them. In the former case, they would, in the course of two or three generations, have become merged in the local population. There are, of course, no reliable census figures for the populations of Syria and Palestine in the seventh century, but both had been prosperous Roman provinces for some six centuries. The population of the whole area in 1960 was probably a little under 10,000,000. In Byzantine days, though perhaps relatively more prosperous than now, the high infant mortality and the helplessness of men to prevent epidemics would inevitably keep the population down. Perhaps we may hazard a guess and accept 3,000,000 as the number of inhabitants of Syria and Palestine in 648, though this may well be an under-estimate. In the most desperate battles, when every Muslim was rallied to the banners, the Arab army rarely, if ever, exceeded 25,000. Some of these were accompanied by their women and children, and some not. Perhaps we may therefore guess that the Muslims with their families who were in Syria in 648 did not exceed 100,000. The Central Arabians after the conquest, therefore, possibly constituted one-thirtieth of the population. Thus if they were allowed to mingle with the natives, they would soon have been submerged. The Syrians had shown few martial qualities during the fighting, except for the nomadic tribes of the desert. Thus inter-mixture would probably result in the loss of the military virtues of the Arabs.[8] Finally, the puritan Umar ibn al Khattab viewed with horror the dancing and music, not to mention the soft clothing and the wine drinking of the luxury loving Syrians. As a result, he decided to segregate the Muslim Arabs, keeping them as a ruling military caste, charged only with the duties of government and war. For this purpose, he chose the site of the military camp at Jabiya to become the permanent headquarters and cantonment of the dominant race.

In Iraq, as we have seen, the Arabs, under Saad ibn abi Waqqas, had occupied the luxurious palaces of the kings and the nobles in Seleucia and Ctesiphon. Umar no doubt viewed with the deepest apprehension the possible corruption of the Muslims by over-indulgence in such luxury. The troops, moreover, themselves complained of ill-health in Iraq and of the attacks of clouds of mosquitoes. The khalif, in addition to the above considerations, had an almost pathological fear of allowing his troops to be cut off on the other side of water. The disastrous battle of the Bridge may have confirmed this obsession.

The khalif accordingly wrote to Saad ibn abi Waqqas to select a site for a main military base on the edge of the desert and on the west bank of the Euphrates. With only desert between him and his armies, Umar rightly felt that they could not be cut off from one another. After examining various areas, Saad ibn abi Waqqas selected a site close to Hira. Here, probably in 639, the main Arab forces were concentrated, at first in tents and in huts made

[8] This it subsequently did.

of reeds. Saad caused a mosque to be built and then a house for himself. Eventually other buildings were erected until the town of Kufa[9] gradually became a city, which was to play an important and sometimes sinister rôle in Arab history.

We have mentioned that the Arab forces near the head of the Persian Gulf had already camped on a strip of gravelly soil known as Al Basra. The extension of military operations in Khuzistan after Qadasiya resulted in the despatch of additional reinforcements to this area, until Basra, like Kufa, developed first into a military base camp and then into a city. Thus we see a pattern emerging. The Arab armies from Central Arabia are established in the conquered provinces, where, however, the soldiers are not "demobilized". They are forbidden to merge with the local population or to take up land and engage in agriculture. They are ordered to remain distinct and separate, a master race of rulers and soldiers, concentrated at the great military bases of Jabiya in Syria, and of Kufa and Basra in Iraq.

In one direction, however, intermixture with the local population could not be prevented. The Prophet had declared it to be permissible for a Muslim to have any number not exceeding four wives. Before his time, there had been no legal limit. In any case, the natural balance of births between the sexes had automatically prevented most men from having many wives. Muhammad, however, had also sanctioned the use as concubines of women captured in war and of course of slaves. The small scale of the Prophet's own battles and the general poverty of the Arabs had prevented the abuse of such a concession. But with the fantastically rapid conquests of the fertile and civilized provinces of Syria and Iraq, an almost unlimited supply of women captured in war became available to the Muslims, together with the necessary wealth to enable them to maintain them. As a result, an immense number of children was born to Arab fathers, mostly in the military bases, and these children were classified as Arabs, although most of their mothers were captive foreign wives or concubines. Within a single generation, the ethnological character of the Arabs who had conquered Syria and Iraq was already becoming different to that of the Arabs of Arabia.

The concentration of the Arab invaders in military cantonments made it necessary for them to be given pay, for they were forbidden to take part in agriculture or commerce. To pay an army was a formidable task for a ruler so few of whose subjects could read or write. During the years of conquests from 633 to 638, four-fifths of the plunder taken in battle had been immediately divided up between the troops, a process which not only made pay unnecessary but made almost every Muslim fighter rich. Umar ibn al Khattab did not desire further conquests until those already achieved had been consolidated. Yet the cessation of military operations meant the end of plunder, and the need to pay the army.

The Prophet himself had always refused to accumulate money or even food in his home. Various traditions refer to his dislike of anything remaining in the house overnight. God would provide the food for each day when it was

[9] Pronounced Koofa.

needed.[10] Any storing up of money or supplies seemed to him to be a lack of faith. On the same principle, in the years from 633 to 638, when the wealth of empires was pouring into Medina in the form of the statutory fifth, these riches were immediately distributed and the treasury hastily emptied. When someone suggested that a certain amount of money be retained in the treasury as a reserve, Umar replied that such a suggestion was inspired by the devil. "We trust in God and His Prophet," exclaimed the pious khalif. "They are our reserves." The Muslim cause was the cause of God and He would doubtless provide the necessary funds. Thus when Umar ibn al Khattab was faced with the necessity to pay the army, the treasury was empty.

It is true, of course, that any reduction in plunder might be compensated by the fact that the conquered provinces were bound to pay poll-tax and tribute. But even if the money could be found in this way, the difficulty of the work was increased, for revenue must be balanced with expenditure. The Arabs were certainly not able to supply a competent civil service. In fact, both in Syria and in Iraq, the old civil servants remained. In Syria, the accounts continued to be kept in Greek by Byzantine officials, in Iraq in Persian by the former employees of the Great King. Umar ibn al Khattab, of course, had no means of minting coinage, and Byzantine currency remained in circulation in Syria and Palestine, while that of Persia was legal tender in Iraq. Whatever rules the Muslims might make regarding poll-tax, jiziya, kharaj, ushr or other taxes, the real work of assessment and collection from the conquered peoples must still have been performed by the officials of the former imperial powers.

In judicial matters, other difficulties arose. The Muslims had no code of civil laws. For them, the Qoran, supplemented by the traditions of the Prophet's actions and sayings, provided an adequate answer to every problem. Obviously Christians, Jews and Zoroastrians could not be expected to accept such a system, for they did not believe that the Qoran came from God. Yet there was no attempt to compel these people to become Muslims. The Qoran itself had said that there was no compulsion in religion. The only and inevitable solution was to allow Christians and Jews to have their own separate judicial systems, administered by their own judges. This procedure has remained until our own times. The Turks took it over from the Arabs in the sixteenth century. Under the Ottoman Empire, the Christian churches and the Jews formed semi-independent enclaves within the state. The fact that the original Muslim state was a theocracy, the laws of which were believed to have been dictated by God Himself, made religion, not race or nationality, the factor which differentiated between man and man. For 1,300 years, any man living in the Middle East, if asked what he was, would reply, "a Muslim, praise God", or "a Christian", not "an Egyptian" or "an Arab". This was the logical result of theocracy. Yet, curiously enough, the immediate result of the conquests of the seventh century was to give rise, temporarily at least, to a form of Arab nationalism. Byzantium and Persia had been over-

[10] Holy Poverty has of course also been a Christian ideal. St. Teresa of Avila tells us that when the Carmelite Order was founded, the monks kept no provisions from one day to the next.

thrown by Arabs alone and by a generation of Arabs most of whom were only converted in middle life and who had been brought up in idolatry and the old Arab sagas of heroism, love and war. The immediate result of the conquests, therefore, was to produce an arrogant Arab master race. During the course of the first century of Islam, non-Arabs gradually worked their way into positions of authority. As a result, Arab race pride was gradually to disappear, to be replaced by Muslim religious superiority, a situation which remained unaltered until the twentieth century. Only in the last forty years has the theocracy been weakened or destroyed by the divorce of the state from religion in Muslim countries. The modern secular states have been modelled, not on Islamic tradition, but on the nations of Western Europe. Thus the *ad hoc* decisions taken by Muhammad and his two successors, when suddenly confronted with the administration of an empire, were to decide the framework of life in the Middle East for more than a thousand years.

* * * * *

If the collection of the taxes of the conquered provinces continued at first in the hands of Greeks and Persians, the payment of the Arabian armies had perforce to be carried out by Arabs. For this purpose, the Khalif Umar was obliged to undertake a task of fantastic magnitude; no less than the preparation of a census of the Arabs. Tribes had always taken the place of units in the army. Each tribal contingent fought under its own banner and its own chief. Consequently pay had to be issued on a tribal basis. Three considerations decided the amount of pay due to each individual—priority of conversion, relationship to the Prophet and military services rendered. Thus Aisha, the favourite wife of Muhammad, was allotted 12,000 dirhems a year, while his other widows received 10,000 dirhems each. The dirhem was the silver coin of the time. Close relatives of the Prophet received some 5,000 dirhems, the same as the three hundred warriors who had fought at the Battle of Bedr. Those who had taken the Oath of the Tree at Hudeibiya [11] were awarded 4,000 dirhems, while such as had fought in the suppression of the apostasy received 3,000 dirhems a year. Warriors who had been present at the capture of Damascus or who had fought at Qadasiya were allotted 2,000 dirhems per annum. Later on, the average soldier seems to have received some 500 dirhems a year, but men judged to have outstanding fighting records might be awarded an additional 500 dirhems, over and above what they earned by their other qualifications. Two hundred dirhems was the lowest rate of pay, issued to the last joined recruits. Widows of men killed at Bedr received 500 dirhems and the widows of Muslims martyred in later battles proportionately lesser amounts. It is remarkable that so illiterate an administration should have succeeded in operating such a complicated system. Distribution was apparently carried out by tribes, the money being paid to the tribal chiefs who handed it on to trustworthy elders and so to the individual.

The weapons used were still the lance for mounted men, the favourite Arab weapon par excellence. "Fire" was provided by bows and arrows, and slings throwing stones. The throwing javelin, as we saw at the Battle of Uhud, was

[11] Page 87.

a favourite weapon of the Meccan guards, who had been employed by Quraish as mercenaries in the days of the Ignorance. Mounted and dismounted men used swords. Defensive armour was the coat of chain-mail and a steel helmet. Armour at first was rare, but great quantities of weapons, armour and horses must have been captured from the Byzantines and the Persians.

The Arabs, especially the bedouins, had long been accustomed to the basic principles of strategy, speed, surprise, and concentration at the decisive point. In the days of the Ignorance, they lacked organization and discipline. Six years of close conflict with the Byzantine and Persian armies must have taught them many lessons, which, alas, have not been recorded for our benefit. In general, however, it may be surmised with confidence that they were still in 638 inferior to their enemies in the details of organization and equipment. While religious enthusiasm lasted, the problem of discipline, usually a difficult one with Arabs, was temporarily solved. They were fighting, not for men, but for God. Not for nothing was the commander also the leader of public prayers and the preacher at public worship. On the whole, however, there can be no doubt that their amazing victories were not gained by any superior knowledge of warfare. The Arab conquerors owed their successes principally to their enthusiastic spirit and high morale, particularly fostered by the belief that they were fighting for God's cause and that those who died would go straight to Paradise. Secondly, they possessed the immense hardihood of a race which had lived for thousands of years on the verge of starvation in the desert. Thirdly they were highly mobile, particularly in the desert, where their enemies could not move at all. As we have seen, they always (except at the Battle of the Bridge) exploited this factor to the utmost, drawing their enemies to battle on the edge of the desert.

* * * * *

The Prophet had only become a strong ruler during the last two years of his life. Abu Bekr ruled only a little more than two years, but Umar ibn al Khattab remained khalif for ten years from 633 to 643, and the greatest conquests took place during his reign. Thus he was able to leave an indelible mark on future generations.

Among his more important decisions was that which laid down that no non-Muslims were to live in the Arabian Peninsula. Muhammad himself had concluded a friendly treaty with the Christians of Nejran but Umar evicted them from their native country. The greater part of them migrated to the Euphrates. Muhammad, as we have seen, had conquered the Jews of Khaibar, but had left them in possession of their lands on payment of tribute. Umar now caused their eviction to Palestine. These harsh measures were ostensibly justified by a tradition that the Prophet himself, on his deathbed, had given instructions that the Muslim religion alone was to exist in Arabia. Had he really given such an order, it was curious that Abu Bekr made no attempt to enforce it. We have seen how conscientious he was in executing, to the least detail, everything which Muhammad during his lifetime had enjoined. In this respect also Umar laid the pattern for future generations. Although large Christian and Jewish minorities remained, and still remain, in the conquered countries of Syria, Egypt and Iraq, none survived in Central and Southern Arabia except the Jews in the Yemen.

Reference has already been made to the first collection of the Qoran in writing, commenced after the Battle of Yemama as a result of the death of so many Companions who knew it by heart. A committee had been appointed for the purpose, under the presidency of Zaid ibn Thabit, the Prophet's former amanuensis. The work was not completed until after the death of Abu Bekr, in the khalifate of Umar ibn al Khattab. A copy of the book thus compiled was entrusted to Hafsa, a daughter of the khalif and widow of Muhammad, for safe custody.

When Abu Bekr had assumed control after the death of the Prophet, he had assumed the designation of khalif, or successor of the Apostle. Umar ibn al Khattab on his election, had modestly protested that he was not the successor of the Prophet, but the successor of his successor. Such a title was obviously too cumbrous for use. By chance someone addressed him as Commander of the Believers.[12] The designation was to remain with the khalifs of Islam for thirteen centuries.

## *NOTABLE DATES*

| | |
|---|---|
| Tribal concentration and Byzantine recapture of Antioch | Spring 638 |
| In Iraq, the occupation of Medain | April 638 |
| Conquest of Khuzistan | 638–640 |
| Famine in the Hejaz<br>Bubonic plague in Syria | 639–640 |
| Foundation of Kufa | 639 |

## *PERSONALITIES*

Mughira ibn Shuba, Governor of Basra, removed for adultery.
Abu Musa al Ashari, conqueror of Khuzistan and Governor of Basra.
Abu Ubaida, commander-in-chief in Syria, died of bubonic plague.
Muawiya ibn abi Sofian succeeds him as Governor of Syria.
Zayyad, secretary to the Governor of Basra.

[12] The title has been alternatively translated into English as the Prince of the Faithful.

# XII

## *That Great Babylon*

The magnanimous Omar trusted in his God and his sword, which had shaken the thrones of Chosroes and Caesar, but when he compared the slender force of the Moslems with the greatness of the enterprise, he condemned his own rashness. The pride and the greatness of Pharaoh were familiar to the readers of the Koran; . . . the cities of Egypt were many and populous: their architecture was strong and solid: and the granary of the imperial city would be obstinately defended by the Roman powers.

GIBBON, *Decline and Fall of the Roman Empire*

Babylon the great is fallen, is fallen. Alas, alas, that great city Babylon, that mighty city! Alas, alas, that great city, wherein were made rich all that had ships in the sea by reason of her costliness! for in one hour is she made desolate.

*Revelation XVIII*

## XII

# THAT GREAT BABYLON

EGYPT had been conquered by the Persians in 617 during the long wars between Chosroes Parwiz and Byzantium. It was not abandoned by them until 627, as a result of Heraclius' invasion of Persia and his advance from Mosul on Medain. During this period of ten years, Byzantine power had of course disappeared. The Persians had committed many and terrible atrocities during their conquest of Egypt but they had not persecuted the Monophysite, that is the Coptic, Church. Peace was concluded between Persia and Byzantium in 628, and probably late in that year or early in 629, a Byzantine army arrived by sea from Constantinople to garrison the country.

Heraclius was at the height of his glory. The empire had been saved, the True Cross had been recovered from the fire-worshippers. At this moment of triumph, one great ambition remained to the victorious emperor—to reunite the Christian Church, torn for so long between Orthodox, Monophysites and Nestorians. The defeat of the heathen Persians and the recovery of the True Cross had roused all sects of the Church to enthusiasm. Now was the moment to cement once again the shattered fabric of Christendom. For this purpose, the emperor caused a committee of three bishops to draw up a new theological statement, which came to be known as the Monothelite formula. It offered ostensibly a compromise between the Orthodox and Monophysite doctrines.

To persuade the Egyptian Christians to accept the new dogma, Heraclius chose Cyrus, bishop of Phasis in the Caucasus, who was made simultaneously both Patriarch of Alexandria and also civil governor of Egypt. The news of Cyrus' appointment, far from inspiring confidence, was enough to cause Benjamin the Coptic Patriarch to flee from his palace and hide in the desert. The struggle between the Orthodox and Monophysite Churches was of too old standing to be terminated by an imperial decree. The Monophysites rejected the emperor's new formula, probably without understanding it. Perhaps, with the passage of time, they might have been won over, for the new formula was thought by some people to have been very nearly a surrender to Monophysite doctrine. The Copts, however, were not prepared to listen and Cyrus was quite ready to use force. Without waiting to observe the healing effects of the new formula, he inaugurated an active persecution of all who refused to conform. Early in 632, the year of Muhammad's death in Medina, violent measures were adopted against all heretics in Egypt. Menas, brother of Benjamin, the Coptic Patriarch, was seized, his body burned in many places with torches and his teeth pulled out. He was then put in a sack weighted with sand, and rowed out to sea. Three times he was offered his life if he would acknowledge the Orthodox formula. As he still refused, he was thrown into the sea in his weighted sack.

Parties of soldiers were sent to Monophysite monasteries to demand the signatures of their abbots to the creed of the Orthodox Church and to flog, torture or imprison the recalcitrant. Many Copts submitted, others fled, while many continued to worship in secret according to the creed of the Monophysites. On the whole, as has so often happened, the persecution probably strengthened the Coptic Church. It also severed the last strands of political loyalty and affection for Byzantium.

* * * * *

Tradition relates that when Umar ibn al Khattab came to Jerusalem to accept the surrender of the city, he discussed with Amr ibn al Aasi the advisability and the possibility of an attack on Egypt. Meanwhile, Amr ibn al Aasi was sent off to press the siege of Caesarea, the only city in Palestine or Syria which was still holding out for Byzantium. The prolonged resistance of Caesarea was itself due to the presence of the Byzantine forces in Egypt, for Alexandria was the naval base from which they were able constantly to supply the besieged city by sea. The Byzantine landing and reoccupation of Antioch in connection with the rising of the Jezira tribes, had also been executed by a naval and military force from Alexandria. Amr ibn al Aasi may well have argued that the coast of Syria and Palestine would never be safe, as long as the Byzantine fleet was based on Egypt.

The khalif, as we have seen, always tended to be cautious. He feared that some army of his would go too far afield and be cut off. He had forbidden Saad ibn abi Waqqas to cross the Zagros mountains, and had insisted that his main cantonment be at Kufa on the edge of the desert. His caution was further reinforced when the governor of Bahrain, without Umar's consent, sailed across the Persian Gulf and landed with a force in the province of Fars. The detachment was cut off from its boats, nearly met with disaster, and had to be rescued by a column from Basra. As a result, the khalif hesitated to accept the commitment of a new campaign against Egypt.

It was a dilemma which many new expanding powers have, throughout history, been called to face. As each country is conquered, the military commanders claim that the security of the new province is threatened by the country beyond it. The politician hesitates to undertake fresh commitments. Then the neighbouring country embarks upon some fruitless offensive action and another forward movement by the imperial power becomes inevitable. Seven hundred years earlier, the Roman Republic had moved forward in the same reluctant manner into Syria and Egypt.

The final arrangement between Amr ibn al Aasi and the khalif is still in doubt. Some say that, after their meeting at Jerusalem, they met again at Jabiya, and Umar ibn al Khattab gave his consent. According to other accounts, the khalif returned to Medina and there consulted his leading advisers, Ali ibn abi Talib and Zubair ibn al Awwam, and that Zubair strongly advocated an attack on Egypt, with the result that a letter was despatched to Amr ibn al Aasi authorizing the operation. Baladhuri, on the other hand, gives one

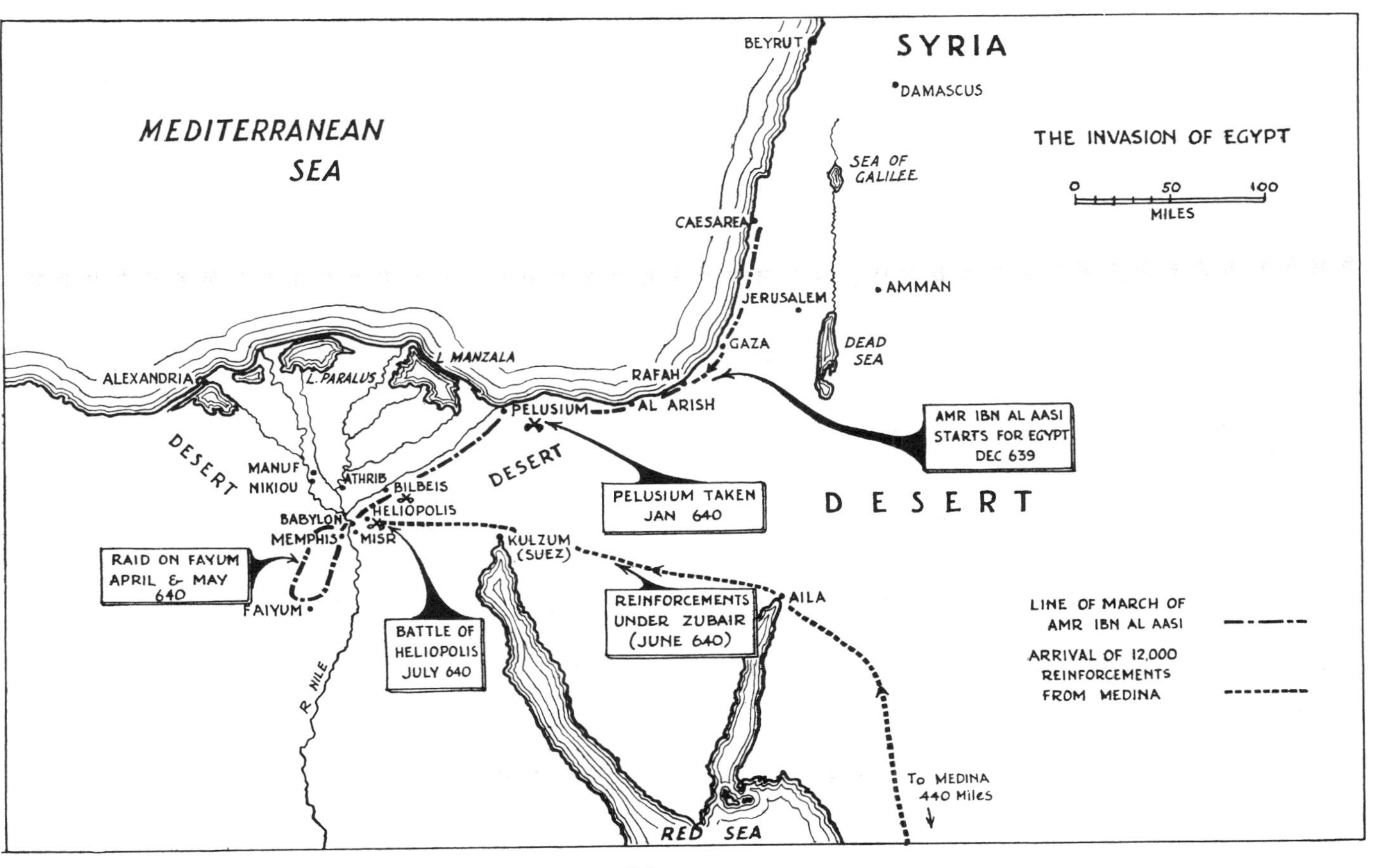
THE INVASION OF EGYPT
0 50 100
MILES
SYRIA
DAMASCUS
MEDITERRANEAN SEA
BEYRUT
CAESAREA
SEA OF GALILEE
JERUSALEM
AMMAN
GAZA
DEAD SEA
RAFAH
AL ARISH
ALEXANDRIA
L. PARALUS
L. MANZALA
PELUSIUM
DESERT
MANUF
NIKIOU
ATHRIB
BILBEIS
HELIOPOLIS
BABYLON
MEMPHIS
MISR
FAIYUM
R. NILE
KULZUM (SUEZ)
AILA
RED SEA
DESERT
DESERT
AMR IBN AL AASI STARTS FOR EGYPT DEC 639
PELUSIUM TAKEN JAN 640
RAID ON FAYUM APRIL & MAY 640
BATTLE OF HELIOPOLIS JULY 640
REINFORCEMENTS UNDER ZUBAIR (JUNE 640)
To MEDINA 440 Miles
LINE OF MARCH OF AMR IBN AL AASI
ARRIVAL OF 12,000 REINFORCEMENTS FROM MEDINA

Map XXVI

account according to which Amr ibn al Aasi went off on his own initiative and without permission, much to the khalif's annoyance. As the Arab historians say resignedly when faced with such a dilemma, "Allah knows best".

Whatever may have been the exact detail of these communications, the main facts appear to be clear. Amr ibn al Aasi was exeremely anxious for permission to make an attempt on Egypt, while Umar ibn al Khattab was cautious and vacillating. He was unwilling to make enough men available, for fear of a Byzantine attempt to reconquer Syria, and he was afraid that the enterprise would fail if Amr ibn al Aasi went without sufficient troops. Eventually Amr ibn al Aasi set out with a force of only some 3,500 men. Passing down the coastal plain by Gaza, he had reached Rafah when he received a letter sent post haste by the khalif from Medina. According to tradition, Amr ibn al Aasi suspected the purport of this despatch, and did not open it until the next day when he had reached Al Arish.[1] When he did so, he found that the khalif had ordered him, if he received the letter while he was still in Palestine, to abandon the operation. If, however, the despatch reached him when he was already in Egypt, he was to proceed. He then enquired innocently from those standing near, whether he was in Egypt or in Palestine. When they replied that they were in Egypt, he ordered the continuation of the march. Presumably, if this tradition be true, Amr ibn al Aasi knew the contents of the letter, or perhaps the messenger told him verbally.

By a fortunate coincidence, we have an accurate knowledge of the date when Amr ibn al Aasi crossed into Egypt. We are told that at Al Arish the force celebrated the feast of pilgrimage, 10th Dhu al Hijja A.H. 18, which coincides with 12th December, 639.

From Al Arish, Amr and his little force moved along the age-old caravan track from Palestine to Egypt, now the line of the railway. From Al Arish, it ran some miles inland, but parallel to the sea coast, until it reached the city of Pelusium, called by the Arabs Al Farama, where in those days the Pelusiac channel of the Nile fell into the Mediterranean. Along this track, Abraham had doubtless travelled into Egypt, and those Arab merchants who carried with them the young Joseph. Numberless Pharaohs with their armies had marched this way on their northern campaigns, while kings of Assyria and Babylon, Cambyses the Persian, Alexander the Great, and Pompey had by it invaded Egypt. The armies of Chosroes, only a few years earlier, had taken the same road. Few, if any, of these ancient kings and conquerors can have appeared outwardly so unimpressive as did Amr ibn al Aasi with his ragged 3,500 bedouins on their scraggy unkempt horses and camels. They indeed might well have deserved the title of desert rats.

Pelusium was a fortified town, which virtually commanded the road into Egypt. Amr decided that it would have to be taken, doubtless in order to keep open his communications with Arabia, from whence he hoped for reinforcements. A few years before, the Persians had captured the town without much trouble, but the Arabs, with their usual lack of skill in siege warfare and in the absence of heavy weapons, were unable to take it. They remained for a month blockading the town, until one day, as a result of an unsuccess-

[1] Pronounced Al Areesh.

ful sally by the garrison, the Arabs were able to enter one of the gates with the retreating soldiers. The shipping in the port was burnt, the churches pulled down and the fortifications dismantled. The town was probably deliberately severely damaged. Amr had not enough men to enable him to garrison it and he did not want the Byzantines to re-occupy it as a fortress when he had marched on. It was January 640 when the Arabs resumed their march from Pelusium. Following their usual strategy, they coasted along the edge of the desert in a south-westerly direction, keeping close to the boundary between the desert and the sown. The Suez Canal was not of course in existence in those days and the desert came across the present canal zone and up to the delta land actually irrigated by the Nile. Passing the site of the modern Tel al Kabir, the Arabs reached Bilbeis, where a successful action was fought against a Byzantine force under Aretion, formerly military governor of Jerusalem. The capture of the town of Bilbeis, however, delayed them for another month. Meanwhile Cyrus, the Patriarch and Governor of Egypt, had arrived on the scene accompanied by Theodore, the commander-in-chief of the Byzantine forces in Egypt, and both had established themselves in the fortress of Babylon.

It is surprising to find a place of this name in Egypt. Some have alleged that the fortress was so called by Nebuchadnezzar, who invaded Egypt in B.C. 567. Diodorus Siculus states that some Babylonian prisoners of war brought by the legendary Sesostris of Egypt gave to their place of exile the name of their native city. Josephus, on the other hand, believed that the fortress was built by Cambyses the Persian, who conquered Egypt in B.C. 525. The castle which was standing in the year A.D. 640 is believed to have been built by the Roman Emperor Trajan about A.D. 100. The truth probably is that every successive conqueror of Egypt established a fortress and garrison at this strategic place.

The name of Babylon caused the Arab historians to fall into a peculiar error. The word *bab* in Arabic means a gate, and thus Babylon seemed to them to mean Bab al Yon, or Bab al Yona, the gate of Yona. Reading that the Arabs had assaulted Bab al Yona, they received the impression that the gate of Yona had been captured, and hence that the name of the fortress was Yona.

Babylon derived its importance from the peculiar geography of Egypt. Rainfall in that country is negligible and normally the whole country would be desert. In fact, however, the Nile, bringing vast quantities of water and silt from Central Africa, has cut itself a channel across this desert to the Mediterranean. Throughout most of its course through Southern Egypt, the Nile was a narrow cut through the desert, but at this point it divided up into several streams which flowed over the flat country to the sea. The triangle or delta so formed was very nearly equilateral, each side being approximately 120 miles long. Inside this triangle, the land was flooded for several months every year. When the floods receded, the whole area was still extremely difficult to cross even on foot, being intersected by the several branches of the Nile, and by innumerable irrigation canals and ditches.

Meanwhile, however, the desert on both sides came right down to the edge of the lush cultivated soil. The farmland did not gradually peter out, through pasture and scrub lands, into desert. The desert and the sown were divided by a hard and fast line, so that a man could almost literally pass in a single stride from the dry, gravelly desert into the soft mud and vegetation. Babylon lay on the Nile at the apex of the triangle. Thus from it armies could move along the firm hard desert to Alexandria or to Pelusium, with the maximum speed and with no obstacles from canals or floods.

Babylon was the name given to the fortress which held the garrison at this strategic spot. In ancient times, the city of Memphis lay just above this fortress on the west bank. In 640, it was still in existence though much reduced and decayed. On the east bank and close to Babylon was the new city of Misr. Today the city of Cairo covers the whole area.

To besiege and capture the fortress of Babylon would have been a hopeless task for Amr ibn al Aasi and his small force without any equipment for siege warfare. He seems to have skirmished in the neighbourhood, perhaps for some weeks, without achieving any success. He appears, however, to have succeeded at last in capturing an outpost north of Babylon called Umm Dunain, which formed the harbour of the city of Misr.[2]

Amr ibn al Aasi was now in a difficult situation. He had written urgently to the khalif in Medina asking for reinforcements but had received no reply. The morale of his men, always restless and avid of adventure and plunder, would be lowered if he continued inactive and achieved nothing. Yet it was difficult to find any suitable objective within reach which he could successfully attack.

About fifty miles south of Babylon on the farther or west bank of the Nile, lay the fertile district of the Faiyum. At Umm Dunain, he had captured shipping. He accordingly ferried himself across the Nile and bypassing the remains of the old city of Memphis, he marched southwards. Strategically this operation was somewhat risky, for if the reinforcements did arrive from the Hejaz, they would be on the east bank of the Nile and Amr on the west, with the Byzantine garrison of Babylon between them. If Theodore took the initiative, he might defeat the two Muslim armies in detail. On the other hand, of course, the Arabs would still have been in the strong position of being able to retire into the desert and avoid battle. Even so, to put the Nile between himself and Arabia was a risk, for it was by no means certain that he would again be able to find boats on which to re-cross the river.

Meanwhile he marched southwards but found the city of Faiyum too strongly held. A number of flocks of cattle were driven off—perhaps shortage of food supplies had been one cause for the raid. A smaller town in the province of Faiyum was taken by storm and the inhabitants massacred, men, women and children. Meanwhile John, the Byzantine commander of the Faiyum district, had set out with an escort of fifty men to make a personal reconnaissance. Amr received a report of his presence and turning on him swiftly, succeeded in surrounding him and his guard and in killing them all. Then, receiving information that the reinforcements sent by the khalif were

[2] Misr, pl amsar, is an Arabic word meaning city, but had here become the name of this particular city. Nowadays the term is applied to the whole country of Egypt.

arriving, Amr turned northwards again. It was now the beginning of June 640.

Umar ibn al Khattab had sent a force of some 12,000 men to reinforce the invaders of Egypt. They arrived at Heliopolis on 6th June, 640, and were under the command of Zubair ibn al Awwam, one of the oldest of the Prophet's companions and a leading member of Quraish. He had been one of the inner circle of advisers who had worked both under Abu Bekr and Umar ibn al Khattab, since Muhammad's death. The other members of this "cabinet" had been Ali ibn abi Talib, the Prophet's cousin and son-in-law, Talha ibn Ubaidullah, Othman ibn Affan and Abdul Rahman ibn Auf, all of whom were to play leading, if sinister, parts in the history of the Arabs.

The situation had now arisen which might have been foreseen when Amr ibn al Aasi crossed the Nile. Theodore had built up a considerable army in Babylon. To the north of that fortress lay Zubair ibn al Awwam with 12,000 men. On the other bank of the Nile was Amr ibn al Aasi. Here was Theodore's opportunity to destroy Zubair before Amr could join him. Yet he seems to have remained inactive in Babylon until Amr ibn al Aasi succeeded in re-crossing the Nile and joining forces with Zubair at Heliopolis.

Once the famous City of the Sun, Heliopolis had already fallen from its ancient grandeur when the Arabs established themselves in it in June 640. It lay on slightly rising ground and was separated by an open plain, some six or seven miles wide, from the fortress of Babylon, which lay on the east bank of the Nile. As they stood in Heliopolis looking towards the Byzantine army in Babylon, the Arabs had at their backs the open desert which they always felt to be familiar and friendly.

The Muslim army was now perhaps 15,000 strong and included many Companions of the Prophet who had come from Medina with Zubair to join in so holy and glorious a contest, Abdulla, a son of the ruling khalif, being one of their number. The original force which Amr ibn al Aasi had brought from Palestine had consisted principally of bedouins, some of them from the tribes of what is now southern Jordan and some from Sinai.

It is impossible to decide on the strength of the Byzantine army but it is generally believed to have been more numerous than were the Arabs. Yet the morale of the Byzantines had been undermined by reports of the desperate valour of the Arabs, who had already defeated the main armies of the Byzantine and Persian Empires.

In the middle of July 640, Theodore, who had omitted to attack the different portions of the Arab forces when they were separated, decided to give them battle now that they were united. He accordingly marched out of the fortress and across the plain to attack Heliopolis.[3] Amr ibn al Aasi had meanwhile drawn up his army likewise but, before doing so, he had sent out two detachments under cover of darkness. One of these took up a concealed position near to the site of the present citadel of Cairo, the other somewhere near the present site of the Ezbekiya. Early in the morning, the Byzantine army emerged from the suburbs and gardens which lay north-east of Babylon and advanced across open desert. At the same time, the Arabs moved out of

[3] My account of the battle is taken from Butler, *The Arab Conquest of Egypt*.

Heliopolis to meet them. Amr's two flank parties had taken up their positions in the dark and had not been observed by the Byzantines.

The two main armies met head-on and a desperate hand-to-hand struggle ensued. Suddenly the eastern Arab ambush emerged and charged straight into the right rear of the Byzantines. The latter, taken in front and rear, fell into some confusion, and tended to edge away to the west to make front against both attackers. Then suddenly the western ambush appeared and streamed in a wild charge into the Byzantine left flank. At this, the whole army fell into panic and confusion. Some fled back to seek shelter in the fortress of Babylon, but great numbers were cut down and slaughtered by the exultant Muslims. Theodore, the commander-in-chief, succeeded in making his escape.

The remnants of the Byzantine army withdrew inside the fortress of Babylon and closed the gates, but the city of Misr surrendered unconditionally to the Arabs. There being no longer an enemy army in the field, the Muslims were able to scour the country, commandeer supplies and gather plunder. The Byzantine forces, which had successfully defended Faiyum against the raid of Amr ibn al Aasi, now abandoned the whole province and taking ship on the Nile, passed Babylon and took refuge in the town of Nikiou, forty-five miles north-west of the fortress. Amr immediately detached a force, which took Faiyum by assault and massacred the inhabitants. The whole province thereupon surrendered without resistance.

To the north, the Arabs occupied the towns of Athrib and Manuf, some thirty-five miles north of Babylon. Amr continued to act towards the Egyptians with considerable ruthlessness, either because there was a cruel and arrogant side to his nature or as a matter of policy, intending thereby to increase the terror of his name and to make further resistance impossible. Having thus subdued the province of Misr, which lay at the head of the Delta, in addition to that of the Faiyum, the Arabs were now in a strong position, with their supplies assured by the possession of two prosperous provinces. Meanwhile, however, August had come, the Nile was rising and a great part of the delta would soon be flooded, rendering further operations difficult. Amr ibn al Aasi accordingly decided to reduce the castle of Babylon before proceeding further.

* * * * *

This great fortress consisted of an irregular quadrilateral of walls about eight feet thick and some sixty feet high, built in alternate layers of brick and stone. Two towers rose considerably higher. In plan it was about one thousand feet long by five hundred feet wide at one end, tapering to about three hundred feet wide at the other end. The River Nile washed one of the long sides. A small harbour for river boats lay at the foot of the wall by the south gate. The whole of the castle was surrounded by a moat filled with water from the Nile. Opposite the main fortress the island of Raudha lay in midstream. It also was fortified and garrisoned, and the two fortresses were able to maintain communications by boat.

The capture of such a fortress presented a formidable task to the Muslims, who had found such difficulty in seizing even the town of Pelusium. The Patriarch Cyrus, the Governor of Egypt, known to the Arabs as Al Muqauqas, was himself besieged in Babylon. The garrison may have consisted of 5,000 or 6,000 men and the fortress was well supplied with food and warlike stores. The siege probably began in earnest early in September 640.

Cyrus himself was largely responsible for the weakness of Egypt in face of the Arab invasion. The majority of Egyptians, as already explained, belonged to the Coptic Church and had for ten years been the victims of ruthless religious persecution. Thus, when the crisis arose, the Byzantine Greeks and the comparatively small number of Egyptians who adhered to the Orthodox Church, were the only really loyal defenders of the country. The Copts were an inarticulate and subject community. It is true that, in order to stand up to the persecution of Cyrus, they must have taken their religion seriously and so could scarcely welcome the Muslims. But neither were they actively defending their own country. Hitherto they had been the victims of Byzantine oppression. If the Arabs won, they would become the servants of the Muslims. Whatever the outcome, they would still be slaves. Probably, however, they knew that in Syria, the Arabs had allowed religious freedom to the Christians, although compelling them humbly to pay tribute. Perhaps the Muslims might even be an improvement on Cyrus.

The fortress of Babylon seemed likely to be able to resist for several months, but Cyrus must have been aware of the hatred felt for his régime in the country. Perhaps also he realized that little help was to be expected from Byzantium. Accordingly, early in October 640, when the siege had been in progress for about a month, Cyrus was ferried over to the island of Raudha, from whence he sent a mission to negotiate with Amr ibn al Aasi. The negotiations were conducted secretly from the island, presumably in order not to depress the morale of the garrison of the main fortress.

The emissaries were received by Amr ibn al Aasi, to whom they delivered their message. While, they admitted, the Arabs had achieved certain successes, they could not hope to resist the power of Byzantium for long. They, therefore, proposed that, for a cash payment, they should withdraw from Egyptian territory. Amr ibn al Aasi replied by offering them one or other of the three courses which had become the standard conditions of peace for conquered territories. The first course open to them was the acceptance of Islam, which meant (in theory at least) equality with their conquerors. The second was the payment of tribute and the acceptance of a subordinate status. The third was war to a final conclusion.

While Cyrus was not prepared to accept these terms, he nevertheless thought it worth while to pursue the negotiations and he accordingly invited Amr to send a delegation to Raudha. It is perhaps worthy of note that the Muslim delegation which arrived was led by a negro of the name of Ubada ibn as Samit, who addressed the Patriarch, informing him that the Muslims lived only to fight for God and to follow His will and that they cared nothing for money. "This world is nothing," he concluded, "the next world is everything."

The Patriarch was not a little impressed by the earnestness of the Muslims, their contempt of this world and their readiness to die in order the earlier to enter into the joys of paradise. "I am afraid that God has sent these men to lay waste the world," he whispered to one of his companions. Then, replying to Ubada's speech, he admitted that perhaps the Greeks had failed, in that they did care too much for the things of this world. Now, however, he explained, they were sending immense armies to destroy the invaders. Before these reinforcements arrived, the Arabs would do well to accept a handsome payment in cash and to withdraw from the country.

"We are not afraid of numbers," replied the Arabs. "We pray that we may win martyrdom in the path of God, not that we may return safely to our wives and children. Our small numbers do not make us afraid: for it is written in the Qoran, 'Very often a small company has overcome a great army, by the order of God.' " The Muslims steadfastly refused to listen to any terms other than those already offered by Amr ibn al Aasi. Islam, tribute or war were the only courses open to the Byzantines.

Cyrus appeared to be somewhat inclined to accept the payment of tribute, but a number of officers protested strongly. They perhaps were residents of Egypt, whereas Cyrus, as we have seen, was a Greek, who had previously been a bishop in the Caucasus. Eventually they asked for time to consider the offer, but Amr allowed only three days for the purpose. No sooner was this period over than the Byzantines suddenly lowered one of the drawbridges, sallied forth and attacked the Arabs. After heavy fighting, however, the sortie was repulsed and the garrison driven back within the fortress. This reverse depressed those who had advocated resistance and strengthened the hand of Cyrus in advocating submission.

As a result, negotiations were reopened and a treaty drawn up in the usual form of tribute and submission, in return for which the Christians were to enjoy freedom of worship and to be under the protection of the Muslims. A clause was added, however, that the agreement was subject to the approval of the emperor, to whom it would be immediately submitted. Pending his agreement, the military situation was to remain unchanged.

Armed with this draft, Cyrus embarked on the Nile and sailed down to Alexandria, whence he wrote a despatch to Heraclius in Constantinople, explaining why he had been compelled to submit to the invaders and begging the emperor to ratify the treaty. Heraclius was now an old man, enfeebled in body and broken in spirit, but even he could not stomach the defeatism of Cyrus. A peremptory message was sent back to Alexandria, ordering the patriarch to report immediately to Constantinople.

The emperor received his Governor of Egypt with angry and bitter reproaches, which, it must be admitted, were not unjustified. For Cyrus had utterly alienated the loyalty of the great majority of the Egyptians by the savagery of his religious persecution, but, when the Arabs had arrived, he had been the first to despair and to advocate submission. In his defence before the emperor, he pleaded that the Arabs were invincible, that they cared nothing for wealth or comfort, and that they desired to be killed in battle that they might gain admittance the quicker to paradise. But his eloquence was unavailing and he was convicted of betraying the empire to the enemy.

After suffering many reproaches and indignities, he was dismissed from his appointment and sent into exile.

When the emperor's refusal to ratify the treaty became known, hostilities were reopened and both the attackers and the defenders of Babylon nerved themselves for a desperate struggle. At this stage also, certain Egyptians began to assist the Arabs, presumably Copts who had suffered at the hands of Cyrus. Undismayed, however, the garrison continued to carry out sallies and to inflict casualties on the besiegers.

Gradually the winter dragged on. As the Nile flood subsided, the water almost dried up in the moat. The Arabs, however, had been unable to make any impression on the walls of the castle, though they caused casualties by shooting arrows over them into the courtyard within. Once, in the late winter, Amr ibn al Aasi received news of a Byzantine force said to be concentrating in the delta. Leaving a small detachment to mask the castle, he set out to attack and disperse the enemy. The Arabs, however, became involved in the canals and irrigation ditches, were roughly handled and obliged to fall back.

One day in March 641, news reached Babylon of the death of the Emperor Heraclius.[4] The garrison was plunged in despair, the Arabs shouted for joy in their camp. The theory that Heraclius, at any rate at the end of his life, was utterly feeble and cowardly seems to be contradicted by this account. "God broke down the power of the Romans by his death," writes the Arab historian, Jallal al Deen as Suyuti.

The Muslims, encouraged by the news, prepared for an assault on Babylon. In some places they had succeeded in almost filling in the moat. Scaling ladders were prepared and Zubair ibn al Awwam, the Companion of the Prophet, declared himself ready to seek martyrdom in the lead of the assaulting column. The ladder was swiftly placed under cover of darkness and Zubair, sword in hand, climbed up it with a handful of followers, apparently unperceived. A rain of arrows was directed against the ramparts to compel the enemy to keep their heads down. In a few minutes the cry of *Allahu akbar*—God is most great—resounded from the ramparts. But only a small party had established itself on the castle wall. There was still time for a determined counter-attack to cut them down and throw them headlong into the moat. But the siege had already lasted seven months, from the beginning of September 640 to early April 641. The garrison had had enough. As day slowly dawned, the commander of the garrison offered to parley. Amr ibn al Aasi immediately accepted, and a form of capitulation was drafted. After three days, the garrison was to retire, embarking in ships on the Nile and leaving the fortress intact with all its stores. On 9th April, 641, the garrison duly withdrew and the great fortress of Babylon was occupied by the victorious Arabs.

[4] He died on 11th February, 641, in Constantinople.

## *NOTABLE DATES*

| | |
|---|---|
| Crossing of the Egyptian frontier at Al Arish by Amr ibn al Aasi | 12th December 639 |
| Capture of Pelusium | End of January 640 |
| Arrival of reinforcements from Arabia | 6th June 640 |
| Battle of Heliopolis | July 640 |
| Commencement of siege of Babylon | September 640 |
| Death of Heraclius | 11th February 641 |
| Capture of Babylon | 9th April 641 |

## *PERSONALITIES*

Umar ibn al Khattab, the khalif.
Amr ibn al Aasi, Arab commander-in-chief in Egypt.
Zubair ibn al Awwam, commander of the Arab reinforcements and leader of the storming party at the fall of Babylon.
Cyrus, the Orthodox Patriarch and Governor of Egypt.
Theodore, Byzantine commander-in-chief in Egypt.

# XIII

# *The Egyptian Surrender*

The Lord hath given you the land. Your terror is fallen upon us and all the inhabitants of the land faint because of you. . . . As soon as we heard these things our hearts did melt, neither did there remain any more courage in any man because of you.
*Joshua* II, 9

Ethiopia and Egypt were her strength and it was infinite. Yet was she carried away, she went into captivity. They cast lots for her honourable men and all her great men were bound in chains. All thy strongholds shall be like fig trees with the first ripe figs: if they be shaken, they shall even fall into the mouth of the eater. The gates of thy land shall be set wide open unto thine enemies.
*Nahum* III, 9

They came into the fight expecting a defeat and therefore earned one. . . . They were half beaten before a blow was struck.
OMAN, *War in the Middle Ages*

## XIII

## THE EGYPTIAN SURRENDER

THE surrender of Babylon in April 641 automatically led to the complete pacification of the city and province of Misr at the head of the delta and of that of the province of Faiyum fifty miles further up the Nile. The situation of Babylon was ideal from the Arab point of view, for it was on the east bank of the Nile, and from it the desert stretched unbroken to Arabia. It also dominated the delta. The Arabs were unable or unwilling to operate among the canals and vegetation of the irrigated lands. Byzantine resistance, however, was now concentrated in Alexandria, and access to that city could be obtained by marching down the western side of the delta through the desert. The Persians had followed the same route twenty-five years before when they had conquered Egypt. From Pelusium they had marched to Misr at the head of the delta and then down the western channel of the Nile to Alexandria.

Before setting off, Amr ibn al Aasi is said to have given a two-day banquet to the Egyptians—that is the Copts—of Misr. On the first day, the mixed company of Copts and some of his own Arabs were served with camels' meat boiled in salt water. The Arabs made a hearty meal, but the more delicate Copts turned with loathing from the disgusting mess. Next day, the same company was served with a delicious banquet, consisting of all the choicest delicacies of Egyptian luxury. Amr ibn al Aasi then made a speech in which he pointed the moral. It would be inadvisable, he suggested, for the delicate Egyptians to despise the Arabs for their poverty and lack of refinement.[1] The Muslims could use the good things of this world, but their very roughness enabled them to endure unlimited hardships, which the more delicate Egyptians could not stomach. It was this very toughness which had enabled them to overthrow the far greater armies of Persia and Byzantium.

An unspecified number of Copts are reported, at this time, to have embraced Islam, tempted no doubt by the opportunity of thereby becoming the social and financial equals of these redoubtable conquerors. Indeed the Muslim army of Amr ibn al Aasi is alleged to have already included a number of Syrian Byzantine converts and also some Persians from the Yemen, remnants of that army which Chosroes had sent to drive out the Abyssinians and to occupy the Yemen in the year 574. Thus the adulteration of the Central Arabian race had already begun, even at this early date.

When the tent of Amr was about to be struck at the commencement of the march on Alexandria, a dove was found to have built a nest on it and be sitting on her eggs. The tent was left behind, sooner than disturb the bird, Amr stating that she had taken refuge in his tent and was therefore under his protection. The tent has always been a place of refuge in the social system

[1] As they still do today.

of the desert. To it any man or woman in want or danger could flee for protection to afford which the owner of the tent, even if a complete stranger, was bound to devote not only his best efforts but if need be his life. I have elsewhere told the story of a man who gave refuge in his tent to a sick wolf, and even killed a fellow tribesman to protect it. To us, it may seem curious that so ruthless a soldier as Amr ibn al Aasi should give up his tent rather than disturb a nesting dove.

It was doubtless with joy and exhilaration that the Arabs crossed the Nile from Babylon to Jiza and set out once more through clean, dry desert, in search of new fields to conquer. Bedouins chafe under immobility and the dampness of the ground around the besieged fortress, especially during the months of high Nile, must have been distasteful to them.

A skirmish took place at Tarrana, some forty miles from Babylon, in which the Byzantines were driven back after a sharp engagement. Ten miles further on, the Arabs found themselves opposite the fortress and city of Nikiou, which lay on the east bank of the Nile. They were therefore obliged to cross the river in order to attack it. An active and enterprising commander might have sallied from the town and disputed the river crossing or caught the Arabs when half across and defeated them in detail. Instead of this, however, panic seems to have seized the garrison, which began to evacuate the city in confusion and to scramble into boats with a view to escaping down the river. The Arabs, hastening to the attack, killed many Byzantine soldiers on the shore and in the water. The city, though surrounded with fortifications, was not defended and the Arabs charging into it, put many of the inhabitants to the sword. This massacre took place on 13th May, 641. They then raided the surrounding villages, killing and plundering indiscriminately. It is probable that this action was taken as a deliberate act of policy. The Arabs, as we have seen again and again, were tactically at a disadvantage in close, irrigated country. They were doubtless most anxious to avoid military operations in the delta, which was here fifty miles, and, further north, a hundred miles wide. They were able to capture a number of places like Nikiou on the edge of the irrigated lands. In these places they deliberately plundered and massacred in order to terrorize the timid inhabitants of the remainder of the delta and thereby secure their submission without fighting. For this purpose time was short. It was already May 641 when Nikiou was taken and in August the Nile would rise again, making operations in the delta impossible. By that time, the Arabs might be besieging Alexandria and their communications with Babylon would be threatened if the delta rose against them. The atrocities (if such they may be called) committed by the Arabs in the country round Nikiou are perhaps worthy of notice in another direction, because they were committed against the Copts or native Egyptians. In the capture of Pelusium and of Babylon and in the battle of Heliopolis, the Byzantines had been the enemy, that is to say the Orthodox Church party. Nikiou and its villages, however, were inhabited by Copts or monophysites, previously the victims of the persecutions of Cyrus.

Recrossing the Nile to the west bank, after a few days in Nikiou, Amr ibn al Aasi resumed the march on Alexandria. A few miles to the north, the

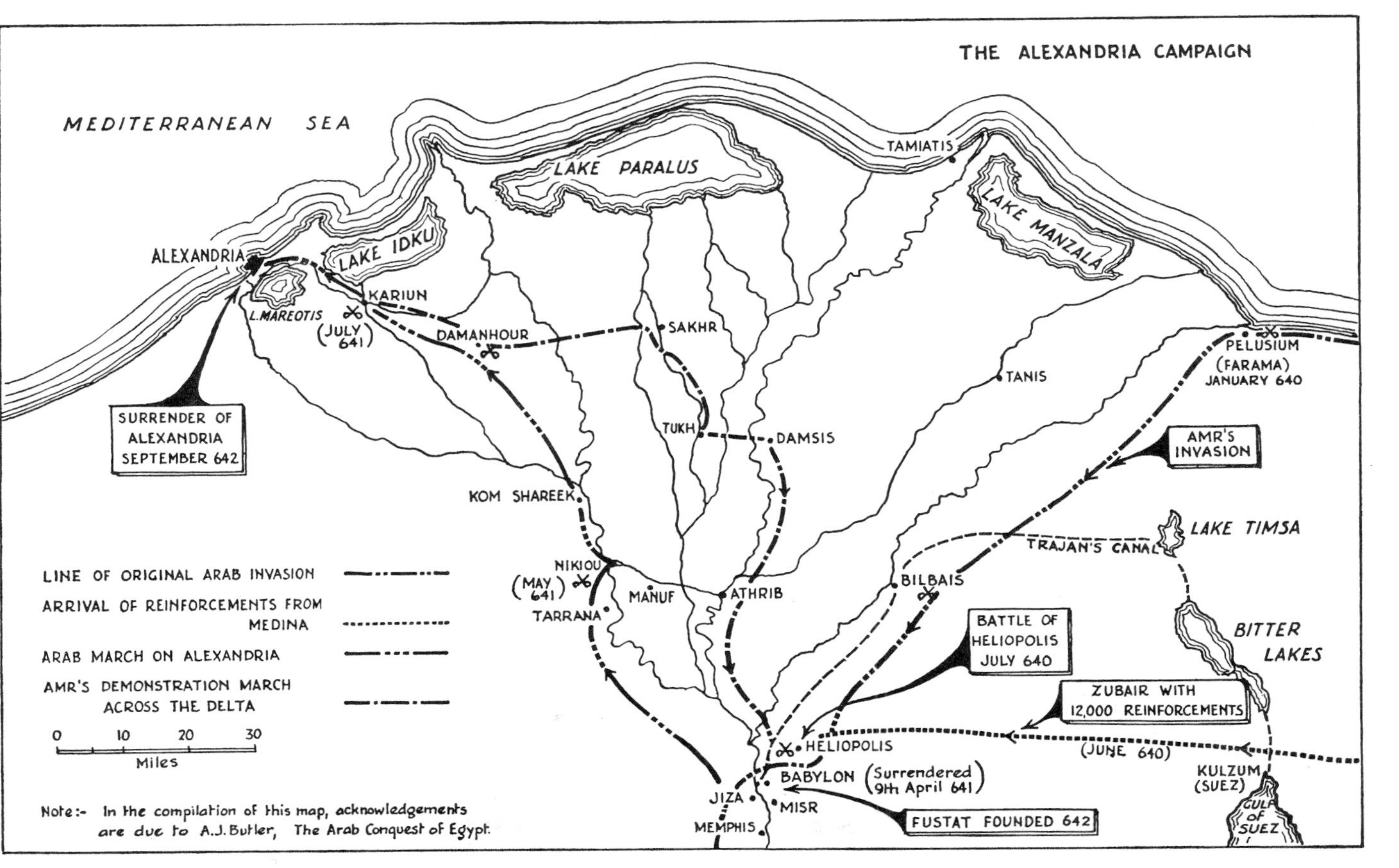
THE ALEXANDRIA CAMPAIGN
MEDITERRANEAN SEA
LAKE PARALUS
LAKE MANZALA
LAKE IDKU
ALEXANDRIA
L. MAREOTIS
KARIUN
(JULY 641)
DAMANHOUR
SAKHR
TAMIATIS
PELUSIUM
(FARAMA)
JANUARY 640
TANIS
TUKH
DAMSIS
SURRENDER OF
ALEXANDRIA
SEPTEMBER 642
AMR'S
INVASION
KOM SHAREEK
LAKE TIMSA
TRAJAN'S CANAL
NIKIOU
(MAY 641)
MANUF
ATHRIB
TARRANA
BILBAIS
BATTLE OF
HELIOPOLIS
JULY 640
BITTER
LAKES
ZUBAIR WITH
12,000 REINFORCEMENTS
HELIOPOLIS
(JUNE 640)
BABYLON (Surrendered 9th April 641)
KULZUM
(SUEZ)
JIZA
MISR
MEMPHIS
FUSTAT FOUNDED 642
GULF OF SUEZ
LINE OF ORIGINAL ARAB INVASION
ARRIVAL OF REINFORCEMENTS FROM
MEDINA
ARAB MARCH ON ALEXANDRIA
AMR'S DEMONSTRATION MARCH
ACROSS THE DELTA
0
10
20
30
Miles
Note:- In the compilation of this map, acknowledgements
are due to A.J. Butler, The Arab Conquest of Egypt.

Map XXVII

advanced guard ran into a considerable Byzantine force and was, for some time, severely handled, being driven to take refuge on some rising ground where for a time they were virtually surrounded. Amr, however, hastened up with the main body and drove the enemy back. The ridge on which the advanced guard made its stand was, ever afterwards, known as Kom Shareek, after the name of the advanced guard commander. The force which had thus mauled the advanced guard proved to be the remaining Byzantine field army, under the command of Theodore, the general defeated the year before at the battle of Heliopolis.

A few miles north of Damanhour, a further engagement occurred, in which obstinate fighting took place, the Byzantines eventually withdrawing. Reinforcements had apparently been received from Constantinople and the army was in fair shape. Amr ibn al Aasi had also doubtless received reinforcements from Arabia, though no detailed account of them seems to be available.

At Kariun, Theodore again took up a defensive position and very heavy fighting followed. It is noticeable that Baladhuri mentions especially that the Greeks and the Copts had gathered at Kariun to resist the Arab advance. Bitter as the Byzantine persecution of the Copts had been, the Arab massacres may have convinced them that they had nothing to gain by a change of masters. The battle of Kariun, like so many of the greatest Muslim victories, lasted several days, a fact which seems to prove that the Arabs made use of attrition rather than shock tactics, as more suited to their character. The successful use of the mass attack depends on training and discipline, qualities in which they were still inferior to their enemies. The Arabs, however, greatly excelled all their adversaries in spirit and initiative. We may perhaps conjecture that they first engaged the enemy everywhere in exploratory actions, until they found a weak point. As soon as any success was achieved, it was boldly exploited by the initiative of the men on the spot, without awaiting orders from above. Among modern armies, the Australians may perhaps be justifiably compared to the bedouins. Both, moreover, were produced by somewhat similar living conditions—the struggle against nature to survive in a vast, often arid, and undeveloped country. Shock troops are the product of urban civilization. The exploitation of local success by the individual fighter is the method best suited to a nation of free pioneers.

The fighting at Kariun lasted for ten days, after which, in July 641, Theodore appears to have withdrawn in good order into the defences of Alexandria.

* * * * *

Following up the withdrawal of the enemy, Amr launched a hasty and ill-advised assault on the walls of the city, and met with a bloody repulse. The Arabs were constrained to withdraw to a distance, out of range of the ballistae mounted on the ramparts and there to pitch their camp, probably on the east of the city.

In the period of which we are writing, Alexandria was one of the greatest cities in the world. Founded by Alexander the Great a thousand years earlier, it contained well over a million inhabitants. Egypt was then an immensely wealthy country and Alexandria had long been its capital. Once the granary of imperial Rome, the Nile delta now played the same part in the economy of Byzantium, and the port for this commerce was Alexandria. The lighthouse above the harbour was one of the seven wonders of the world. In the city itself, the churches, the palaces and the statues, were unrivalled even by Constantinople itself. The whole of this vast city was surrounded by massive walls and towers, against which such missiles as the Arabs possessed were utterly ineffectual. Not only so, but whereas one side of the city was defended by the sea, a great part of the landward side was protected by Lake Mareotis and by a number of canals, with the result that the only unimpeded approach to the attack was on a comparatively narrow front from the east. After his first and ineffective rush against the walls, following the Battle of Kariun, Amr ibn al Aasi appears to have appreciated his utter inability to take so great a fortress by storm, especially as the Byzantines enjoyed complete command of the sea, on which the Arabs could not boast a single vessel. Such a city could have held out for years. Byzantium itself, as we have seen, had successfully withstood attack by the Persian army, which was well equipped with the implements of siege warfare, for years on end. Alexandria, as long as the Byzantines retained command of the sea, was probably in an even stronger natural position.

Not many weeks were left before the annual rise of the Nile. Amr accordingly determined to leave a detachment in observation south-east of the city, which would suffice to prevent the Byzantines from coming out of the walls and re-establishing their authority in the delta. Then he proposed to take advantage of the low Nile to march across the delta on his way back to Babylon. He accordingly set out from Damanhour eastwards to Sakha, and then southwards to Tukh and thence to Damsis. All three towns were defended by walls and closed their gates on the approach of the Arabs. Unable as usual to deal with masonry walls, the Muslims were obliged to pass by. The open countryside and villages were plundered and the crops, now ripe for harvest, were burnt. Eventually, after this rather unsuccessful attempt to terrorize the delta, Amr ibn al Aasi returned to Babylon, just in time before the Nile began to rise.

This abortive operation provides a further illustration of the fact, already frequently emphasized, that the Arabs were only really successful in open plains. It is interesting to think what the Byzantines could have done in Egypt. Ultimately wars can only be won by attack. In the long run, they would have had to give battle to the Arabs and defeat them, and if the latter had refused to fight except in the desert, it would finally have been necessary to give them battle there. But, at the stage which we have now reached, it seems to me that the Byzantines should have remained on the defensive. The Arabs could not fight in the delta nor the Byzantines in the desert. The latter should therefore have sought to defend the delta only, remaining themselves inside the irrigated and cultivated area. Work should have been undertaken immediately to fortify the towns and villages, beginning with those nearest the desert border. The inhabitants of these settlements on the edge of the delta should have been armed and trained and encouraged to defend themselves, assisted by small groups of regular soldiers here and there. Further back, in central positions, mobile columns of Byzantine soldiers should have been located, so that, in the event of Arab raids, they could quickly have moved to the threatened area to repulse the attack. The inhabitants in the front line could have been told that they had only to hold on for twelve hours (let us say) when attacked, and then reinforcements would reach them.

The Arabs liked to travel and to fight in the desert, but there is no food there. They must needs depend on the cultivated area for food. Thus the more efficient the defence of the cultivated area, the more difficulty the Arabs would have encountered in getting supplies. By an energetic defence of this nature, the Byzantines would have gained time during which they could have built up fresh field armies, in preparation for the final struggle.

The Arabs had been wary, as we have seen, of operating in the mountains of Palestine and Syria, but the Nile delta was even more difficult for them than the hilly country. It is, however, easy for us to be wise in the light of our present knowledge. An idea is frequently obvious, once somebody has thought of it, but until that happens, the most brilliant minds continue in the use of old-fashioned methods for century after century.

The Byzantine idea of war was doubtless one of pitched battles between armies and we cannot blame them if no other methods occurred to them. The idea of organized popular resistance as a legitimate means of defence is more familiar to us than it was to the Byzantines. The principal difficulty in attempting such methods would of course have been the ill-feeling towards Byzantium produced by the religious persecutions of Cyrus. If the Egyptians had been loyal to the empire, the situation would have been very different.

* * * * *

Leaving Amr ibn al Aasi established once again at Babylon in August 641, let us look for a moment at what had been happening meanwhile in the capital, Byzantium.

The departure of Heraclius from Syria after the disaster of the Yarmouk in 636 has already been noticed. He did not return directly to Byzantium, but halted at Chalcedon, where he seems to have suffered from some mental derangement. Perhaps we should call it a nervous breakdown. Eventually he recovered and resumed control of the affairs of the state. Yet disasters continued to overtake the arms of the empire. Jerusalem surrendered, then Antioch, then Caesarea and finally the Arabs arrived in Egypt.

Even in the bosom of his family nothing but misfortunes dogged the ageing emperor, who a few years earlier had been the hero of the age. When his first wife Eudocia had died some years before, he had defied the laws of the Church and the opposition of the patriarch by marrying his niece, Martina. In his declining years, his conscience tormented him with the thought of his incestuous marriage. Constantine, his eldest son by the Empress Eudocia, had already received the title of Augustus. Now twenty-nine years old, he was of an age to assume responsibility for public affairs, had he not been afflicted by a wasting disease, possibly tuberculosis. Martina profited by the weakness of Constantine to press for the association with him of her own son Heracleonas. The Senate was summoned on 4th July, 638, to ratify in the imperial palace the equal association of Constantine the son of Eudocia and Heracleonas, a youth of thirteen years.

The old Emperor Heraclius died, as we have seen, on 11th February, 641, at the age of sixty-six, while Amr ibn al Aasi was still besieging Babylon in Egypt. Martina at first attempted herself to wield the authority but was compelled by popular opposition to withdraw from the public scene, and to content herself with supporting the pretensions of Heracleonas by intrigue. But Constantine was not destined for long to remain an obstacle to her ambition. After a reign of only 103 days, he died on 25th May, 641, from a fit of coughing, which led to an internal haemorrhage and a vomiting of blood. Before he died, he had summoned Cyrus from exile and Theodore from Alexandria to advise him on the situation in Egypt.

No sooner was Constantine dead than Martina caused her fifteen-year-old son Heracleonas to be proclaimed sole emperor. But Constantine had left two young sons, of whom the eldest, Constans, was already twelve years of age. Martina, the incestuous empress, was detested by the populace of Byzantium, who rose in revolt. Valentine, the commander of the troops in Asia Minor, marched on the capital, and forcibly crowned Constans as the partner of Heracleonas in the imperial purple.

Meanwhile Cyrus had been sent back to Egypt. Martina, presumably engrossed in intrigues to place her son on the throne, was anxious to terminate the war with the Arabs, and to surrender Egypt to them. It would appear possible that Cyrus himself persuaded both Martina and the young Heracleonas of the necessity for surrender, for he was to press this policy with an energy which seemed to go beyond the mere execution of his official instructions.

As we have seen, such a surrender was by no means inevitable. Alexandria could probably have held out for years and, before his death, Heraclius had been preparing further reinforcements, which he declared his intention of leading in person to the reconquest of Egypt. Meanwhile, however, the dissensions of the court had spread to Alexandria. The very reinforcements sent to Egypt had been divided against one another, some supporting the claims of Martina and some those of the sons of Constantine. Soon conflicts broke out in the streets of Alexandria between the supporters of the rival contestants for power in Constantinople.

On 14th September, 641, Cyrus landed at Alexandria, having been reappointed Patriarch and imperial Governor of Egypt. He was greeted apparently with great popular enthusiasm. As he had, during his previous ten years of office as governor, devoted himself principally to the persecution of the Coptic Christians, one can only assume that the majority of the people of Alexandria belonged to the Orthodox Church, of which he was the patriarch. Such a situation was to be expected, for Alexandria, being the capital, would naturally have a large proportion of Greeks, as had Caesarea and Jerusalem in Palestine. Perhaps, also with the Muslims outside the walls and factional fights in the streets of the city, the people hoped, from the presence of a dictator in their midst, an improvement in security and confidence. If so, they were indeed grievously mistaken. Little did they know that Cyrus had come back, not to defend but to abandon them.

Alexandria was in reality an international city, lacking a homogeneous spirit of its own. Like all great capitals, it had, for a thousand years, been a resort of strangers. The Jewish community was numerous and wealthy. Greeks, Italians, Jews, Copts, and African negroes mingled in the streets. The schism which divided the Orthodox Church from the Copts was not the only cause of dissension. The rival Blue and Green factions of Constantinople existed equally in Alexandria. In the absence of Theodore, the commander-in-chief, rival generals Domentianus and Menus, had respectively secured the support of the Blues and the Greens, who fought in the streets and indulged in looting and arson.

A month after his return to Alexandria, that is in the second half of October 641, Cyrus set out for Babylon to meet Amr ibn al Aasi, with the intention of surrendering Alexandria and all Egypt to the Arabs. He did not apparently reveal his intention to anyone in Alexandria, where the people still believed that he had come to save them. He had received the authority of the emperor for the surrender—but who was the emperor?—the fifteen-year-old Heracleonas, the twelve-year-old Constans or the incestuous and intriguing Martina?

Amr ibn al Aasi had returned to the fortress of Babylon after his somewhat unsuccessful march across the northern delta. Egypt, it appeared, was still only half conquered. If the aged Heraclius had lived long enough to carry out his project of landing in person in Alexandria with an army, resistance might have been prolonged, perhaps almost indefinitely. But Cyrus had come on a very different mission. Amr ibn al Aasi welcomed Cyrus amicably. Almost exactly a year had elapsed since he had negotiated the first treaty of surrender, which Heraclius had torn up so indignantly. "God has given this country to you," are reported to have been the words with which the patriarch now greeted the Muslim commander.

On 8th November, 641, an agreement was signed between Amr ibn al Aasi and the patriarch Cyrus. The treaty stipulated that the people of Egypt were to pay tribute in the same manner as those of Syria, Palestine and Iraq. The poll-tax appears to have been fixed at two dinars per man, with the usual clauses relating to measures of wheat and oil in kind and suits of clothing for the Muslim soldiers. An armistice was to last for eleven months, until the end of September 642. During this period, the Arabs were not to attack Alexandria, but the Byzantine army was, in the interval, to evacuate the city by sea, taking its possessions with it. The Byzantines were never to return or to attempt the re-conquest of Egypt. The Muslims were not to seize any more churches nor to interfere in any way with Christian worship. The Jewish community in Alexandria was to be allowed to remain. The Egyptians were, as a result of the payment of the tribute, to become a people under Arab protection.

Tabari reports a rather interesting clause to the effect that the Nubians (presumably the Sudanese as we should say) were not to be allowed to invade the country. It is also alleged by some authorities that the treaty contained a clause to the effect that the tribute was never to be increased.

When the negotiations with Cyrus were concluded, Amr ibn al Aasi sent a messenger to carry the news to the khalif in Medina. Tradition relates that the messenger asked for a letter but that Amr replied, "What have I to do with a letter? Are you not an Arab who can give a verbal report of what you have seen?" By such informal methods did the first khalifs and their commanders conquer a great empire. The messenger arrived at Medina one day at noon and made his camel kneel at the entrance to the mosque, on the courtyard of which opened the door of the khalif's house. A girl chanced to come out and seeing the marks of travel on the camel and its rider, enquired who he was. He replied that he was a messenger from Amr ibn al Aasi. The maid ran back into the house and a few seconds later summoned the messenger into the presence of the khalif. Umar ibn al Khattab enquired the news, whereupon the emissary replied, "Good news, O commander of the faithful. God has conquered Alexandria for us."

The simple khalif hastened into the courtyard of the mosque and told the mueddhin to call the people to prayer. When the news had been reported, prayers were recited and then Umar ibn al Khattab returned to his modest dwelling, where bread, oil and dates were placed before the travel-stained messenger. Thus simply was the news carried and received.

Meanwhile Cyrus had returned to Alexandria. Although Theodore had accompanied Cyrus to Egypt, he was not a member of the party which went with the patriarch to Babylon. Theodore had lost every battle he had fought against the Arabs but it is at least to his credit that, after the death of Heraclius, he pressed strongly for the continuation of resistance in Egypt. Perhaps, therefore, he was not in the confidence of Cyrus and was unaware that he had gone to Babylon in order to sign a surrender. When the patriarch returned, however, he seems to have succeeded in persuading Theodore of the impossibility of further resistance, doubtless claiming to have been instructed by the emperor to sign the capitulation.

But when the populace of Alexandria heard of the surrender, they were seized with furious indignation and the crowds ran through the streets to the palace with the object of lynching the patriarch, whom only two months before they had hailed as their saviour. For a short time, the life of Cyrus was in imminent danger. Then he was gradually able to persuade his critics of the inevitability of surrender. "The Arabs are irresistible," he said. "God has willed to give the land of Egypt to them," repeating again the phrase which he had addressed to Amr ibn al Aasi. Bursting into tears, he sobbed that he had done his best and that the object of his efforts had been to save them, their children and their churches from massacre and destruction. By such means, he appeased the indignation of the unfortunate people whom he had so cravenly betrayed.

It is no longer possible to ascertain the motives which caused Cyrus to behave as he did. The suggestion that he was a poor, weak old man seems difficult to accept in the light of the determination and ruthlessness of his persecution of the Copts. Some have speculated that he believed himself to be a friend of Amr ibn al Aasi and hoped to stay on as patriarch of Egypt under Muslim rule. If he cherished such ambitions, he was destined to be disappointed, for he died on 21st March, 642, before the city was taken over by the Arabs.

Meanwhile the treaty had been ratified by Heracleonas in Byzantium. This was one of his last acts, for in November 641 he was overthrown by a military *coup d'état* carried out by the supporters of Constans. Martina suffered the amputation of her tongue and the young Heracleonas that of his nose, after which both were driven into exile, amid the execrations of their former subjects.

While awaiting the surrender of Alexandria, Amr ibn al Aasi had founded a new garrison town outside the walls of Babylon. Alexandria, a seaport city on a sea commanded by the Byzantine fleet, was unsuitable as an Arab capital. It will be remembered, moreover, how insistent Umar ibn al Khattab had always been that Arab armies in the conquered provinces must always have their backs to the desert. He would obviously never consent to the garrison of Egypt being divided from Arabia by the delta of the Nile. No water or mountains, on the other hand, divided Babylon from the (to the Arabs) hospitable deserts of Arabia. The new Arab cantonment was named Fustat. Today modern Cairo and its suburbs covers the ancient Memphis, the seventh century city of Misr, Fustat, the fortress of Babylon and the battlefield of Heliopolis.

The unnecessary defeatism, or the calculating treachery, of Cyrus is emphasized by the fact that even after the ratification of the surrender by Heracleonas and by Umar ibn al Khattab, a number of towns in the delta refused to open their gates to the Muslims. Indeed so stubborn was their resistance, even in the hopeless situation caused by their abandonment by Byzantium, that it took the Arabs from November 641 to July 642 to subdue the northern delta. The area was one which, divided up by innumerable water channels, was peculiarly difficult for desert Arabs. In spite of this, however, it is remarkable that, in circumstances which held no hope of ultimate success, the Copts fought on so obstinately.

These factors suggest many lessons which are relevant to the events of our own times. The first of these is the manner in which the Egyptian, as a fighter, has so often in history been defeated as a result of the inadequacy of his leaders. As opposed to the Arabs, the Egyptians have always been slow of movement and lacking in initiative. Yet, when established in a fortified position, they can show determination and courage in defence, and will maintain a stolid refusal to surrender even in a hopeless situation. The bedouins of Arabia show an almost complete contrast to these qualities. Alert, mobile, ever ready to take decisions and seize the initiative, the Arab of the Arabian peninsula dislikes immobility and hates to feel himself bogged down. These characteristics of the two peoples are as distinct today as in the seventh century, a fact which seems to prove that they still constitute two different races, often possessing exactly opposite characteristics. The modern tendency to refer to them all equally as Arabs is therefore utterly misleading.

Population numbers tend to confirm the same conclusions. Today there are more people in the tiny Nile delta than in the vast area of the Arabian peninsula. In the seventh century, the population of Egypt probably exceeded that of all the peninsula. Yet, as we have seen, the people of Arabia at that time were not only engaged in Egypt, but also, and simultaneously, in Persia, Iraq, Syria and Palestine. Soon they were to spread over North Africa also and up into Spain and France. Thus, at the time of the conquest, the number of the inhabitants of Arabia was quite inadequate to effect much change in the population of a country like Egypt. Moreover, at that time the Arabs who migrated were almost entirely bedouin tribesmen, to whom the deep, muddy soil, innumerable water channels and damp enervating heat of Egypt were utterly uncongenial. Such tribes, in certain cases, turned southwards into the desert towards the Sudan, or crossing the Nile, migrated westwards into Libya. The bedouin from Arabia today will find it difficult to understand the dialect of the delta, but in Libya and the Northern Sudan will recognize many of the terms of speech in familiar use in his own tribe in the peninsula.

The principal source of intermixture of Arab blood in Egypt after the conquest would doubtless arise from the garrison of Fustat. According to the social customs of the time, the Arab troops would acquire many Egyptian wives and concubines. The offspring of such unions would, of course, claim to be Arabs as their fathers were, but would themselves marry Egyptian wives in the like manner, so that even the descendants of the Prophet's Companions would, in a few generations, be very nearly pure Egyptians.

In addition, however, the historians tell us that at the time of the ratification of the treaty concerning Alexandria, many Coptic Christians decided to adopt Islam, thereby not only securing a lighter system of taxation but also social equality with their formidable conquerors. Such as became Muslims tended to be regarded as Arabs, a confusion of thought between race and religion.

In September 642, according to the agreement, Alexandria opened its gates to the Arabs, and Byzantine control of Egypt was terminated for ever.

* * * * *

A remarkable sequel to the conquest of Egypt by Amr ibn al Aasi was a letter from the khalif, in which he informed his victorious general that it had been reported in Medina that he now owned commodities, slaves, plate and animals which he did not own when he first went to Egypt. Amr ibn al Aasi replied that he had increased his possessions by trade. "I have had enough experience of dishonest officials," replied the inexorable khalif. "My suspicion has been aroused against you, and I have sent Muhammad ibn Maslama to divide with you whatever you possess." Thus, as the seal of victory, the Khalif Umar confiscated a great part of the wealth of the victor. History can surely present few such extraordinary incidents.

When the khalif's auditor helped himself to the wealth of the victorious commander, Amr ibn al Aasi is alleged to have remarked, ill-humouredly, "An age in which the son of Hantama [2] treats us in this manner is certainly

[2] The mother of Umar ibn al Khattab. It must be remembered that all these leaders were Quraish, related to one another and familiar with each other's women.

an evil age. Al Aasi used to wear brocade garments with silk borders." "Hush," the khalif's inquisitor is alleged to have answered, "had it not been for this age of ibn Hantama which you hate, you would be today bending in the courtyard of your house, at the feet of a goat, whose abundance of milk would please you or whose scarcity would cause you dismay." "I beg you for God's sake," exclaimed Amr ibn al Aasi, "not to report what I have just said to Umar ibn al Khattab. A conversation is always confidential." "So long as Umar is alive," replied Muhammad ibn Maslama, "I shall mention nothing that has passed between us." This delightful little dialogue, 1,300 years ago, so typical of the sarcastic Arab humour, seems by its very vivacity to convince us of its truth.

Every age tends to attribute to other periods of history the mentality of its own. Our religious-minded ancestors attributed the Arab conquests to Muslim religious enthusiasm. In our own materialistic days, it has become fashionable to put down this outburst of energy to economic causes and to the pressure of famine in Arabia. This incident alone is sufficient to refute such a thesis. Admitting the worldliness of Khalid ibn al Waleed and Amr ibn al Aasi, what was it which compelled these victorious commanders at the head of their armies to hand over their wealth without a murmur to a single unarmed messenger sent by the bare-footed khalif in his patched cloak? There can be no two answers to such a question. It can only have been the high moral tone of the whole community which enabled Umar ibn al Khattab to act in such a high-handed manner with his generals. When we contrast such a situation with the selfishness, the factions and the palace intrigues of Constantinople, the reason for the Arab victories is plain to see.

## *NOTABLE DATES*

| | |
|---|---|
| Capture of Nikiou | 13th May, 641 |
| Death of Emperor Constantine, eldest son of Heraclius, in Byzantium | 25th May, 641 |
| Byzantines withdraw into Alexandria. | July, 641 |
| Return of Cyrus the Patriarch to Alexandria | 14th September, 641 |
| Meeting of Cyrus and Amr ibn al Aasi and Surrender of Egypt signed in Babylon | 8th November, 641 |
| Martina and Heracleonas driven into exile | November, 641 |
| Death of Cyrus | 21st March, 642 |
| Arabs occupy Alexandria | September, 642 |

## *PERSONALITIES*

Amr ibn al Aasi, Arab commander-in-chief in Egypt.
Theodore, Byzantine commander-in-chief.

## *SUCCESSORS OF HERACLIUS*

Emperor Constantine, son of Heraclius.
Empress Martina and her son, Heracleonas.
Emperor Constans, son of Constantine.

# XIV

## *The Victory of Victories*

Then will the Lord drive out all these nations from before you, and ye shall possess greater nations and mightier than yourselves. . . . There shall no man be able to stand before you: for the Lord your God shall lay . . . the dread of you upon all the land. *Deuteronomy* XI, 23

To the first Saracens, the call to the battle-field was like the call to a wedding feast. And these men, so terrible in battle, are eminently mild in victory. The plighted faith was rigidly kept; we hear of no indiscriminate massacres. It was no sort of disgrace to the armies of either Rome or Persia to have been discomfited by enemies like these. FREEMAN, *History of the Saracens*

The Arabians are a fierce people, their character having been thus moulded by the rough life they lead, until roughness has become a second nature to them. In fact they positively enjoy a rough life because it enables them to shake off the yoke of authority and to escape political domination. Such a character is opposed to the spread of civilization. Lastly every Arabian regards himself as worthy to rule and it is rare to find one of them submitting willingly to another. IBN KHALDUN

## XIV

## THE VICTORY OF VICTORIES

IN Chapter XI, we saw King Yezdegird's army defeated again at Jalula in 638, and Abu Musa al Ashari pressing forward in Khuzistan, where he had captured Shushan, Tustar and Ram Hormuz. The khalif, however, had forbidden Saad ibn abi Waqqas to cross the Zagros mountains, with the result that fighting died down for three years after the Battle of Jalula.

But the young king was apparently not resigned as yet to accept defeat. Messengers were despatched to the governors of all the provinces still unoccupied by the Arabs, with orders to raise the greatest possible numbers of troops and to despatch them to the king's standard. As the years 640 and 641 passed by, a new army was slowly built up in Persia. News of these activities was conveyed to Saad ibn abi Waqqas in his headquarters in Kufa, and was forwarded by him, with urgent appeals for reinforcements, to the khalif at Medina.

With his usual energy, Umar ibn al Khattab rose to the occasion. Fresh levies were summoned from the Arab tribes and the khalif declared his intention of leading them in person to Persia. Eventually allowing himself to be dissuaded, he despatched the reinforcements to Iraq, nominating Naaman ibn Muqarrin,[1] a Helper of Medina, who was commanding a column in Khuzistan, to lead the force which was to engage King Yezdegird's new army. Meanwhile the force in Khuzistan was ordered to send a detachment to reinforce Naaman ibn Muqarrin, and at the same time to press vigorously onwards itself, in the hopes of drawing Persian reinforcements to the Khuzistan front.

Naaman ibn Muqarrin then moved forward to Hulwan, where he received information that the Persian army was concentrated at Nehawand, which lay in a plain on the further side of the Zagros mountains. The Muslim army is alleged to have consisted of 30,000 men, that of the Persians being more numerous still. Nevertheless such figures can certainly not be trusted and the numbers on both sides may have been considerably less.

The descriptions which have come down to us of the Battle of Nehawand are even vaguer than those of the earlier battles. In general it would appear that the Persians were occupying a fortified position, from which they refused to emerge. Over all the ground in front of their defences, they had strewn small iron spikes which pierced the hoofs of horses, thereby making it impossible for mounted men to approach. The Arabs were baffled by this early form of minefield and a council of war was called, which was attended by many famous Arab leaders present. The khalif's own son, Abdulla ibn Umar

[1] He was leader of the deputation to King Yezdegird before Qadasiya. Page 194.

ibn al Khattab was commanding the Helpers and the Emigrants of Medina. Jareer ibn Abdulla of Beni Bajeela was there and Abu Musa, the governor of Basra, with the contingent from that area. Tulaiha, the false prophet of Beni Asad, who had performed prodigies of valour at Qadasiya, put forward a plan. Let part of the army feign to attack the Persian position, he suggested, and then simulate defeat and panic. As it fled, the Persians would be tempted out of their defences in pursuit. When they were well clear of their fortifications, the main Arab army would appear and engage them in open country.[2]

Tulaiha's plan was adopted and the fiery Qaqaa was detailed to attack the enemy position with his Beni Temeem. After a simulated battle, they turned to flee in apparent disorder. The Persians, exhilarated by the taste of victory at last, left their defences. Preceded by men who swept a lane through their "minefield" of spikes, they set out in pursuit. Suddenly they found themselves in the presence of the whole Arab army, which had hitherto lain concealed. It was too late to retreat and the Persians set their line of battle in order as best they could.

When Naaman ibn Muqarrin gave the signal to attack, the Arabs cried, "O God! make Thy religion glorious and Thy people victorious," and dashed forward. Naaman, bearing the commander's standard, led the charge but an arrow entered his groin and he fell. The standard was snatched up by Hudhaifa ibn al Yaman, who had been designated by the khalif as second-in-command, and who now took the lead. Casualties were heavy and the horses were soon stumbling over dead bodies and slipping in pools of blood. At sunset the Persians broke and fled, some of them being driven back on to the field of spikes, which they had themselves put down. Their army was utterly destroyed in the pursuit, the commander-in-chief himself being killed.

The Arabs then laid siege to the neighbouring city of Nehawand which, however, surrendered on terms. In it was found much booty, including two chests filled entirely with precious stones, which were despatched to the khalif in Medina. The messenger sent with news of the victory and bearing this fabulous treasure, related later that he found Umar ibn al Khattab wandering through the streets of Medina, asking if any travellers had arrived with information from Iraq. Seeing the emissary, the khalif asked eagerly what news he had brought. The messenger gave an account of the victory, whereupon Umar enquired about Naaman. "He was killed," was the reply. "We come from God and to God we return," murmured the pious khalif and, covering his face with his hands, he burst into tears. Embarrassed at this outburst of emotion and seeking to console his chief, the messenger added, "No one else whom you know personally was killed." "The others were just poor Muslims," interposed the khalif, "but it is no loss to them if Umar does not know them, for God knows them."

When the chests of jewels were presented, Umar ibn al Khattab caused

[2] To simulate flight seems to have been a common tactical manoeuvre of the Arabs. The Qoran specifically states that God is angry with those who turn their backs on the enemy, excepting as a tactical manoeuvre. (See quotation at the beginning of Chapter X.) William the Conqueror used the same deception to draw the Anglo-Saxon army from its defences at the Battle of Hastings.

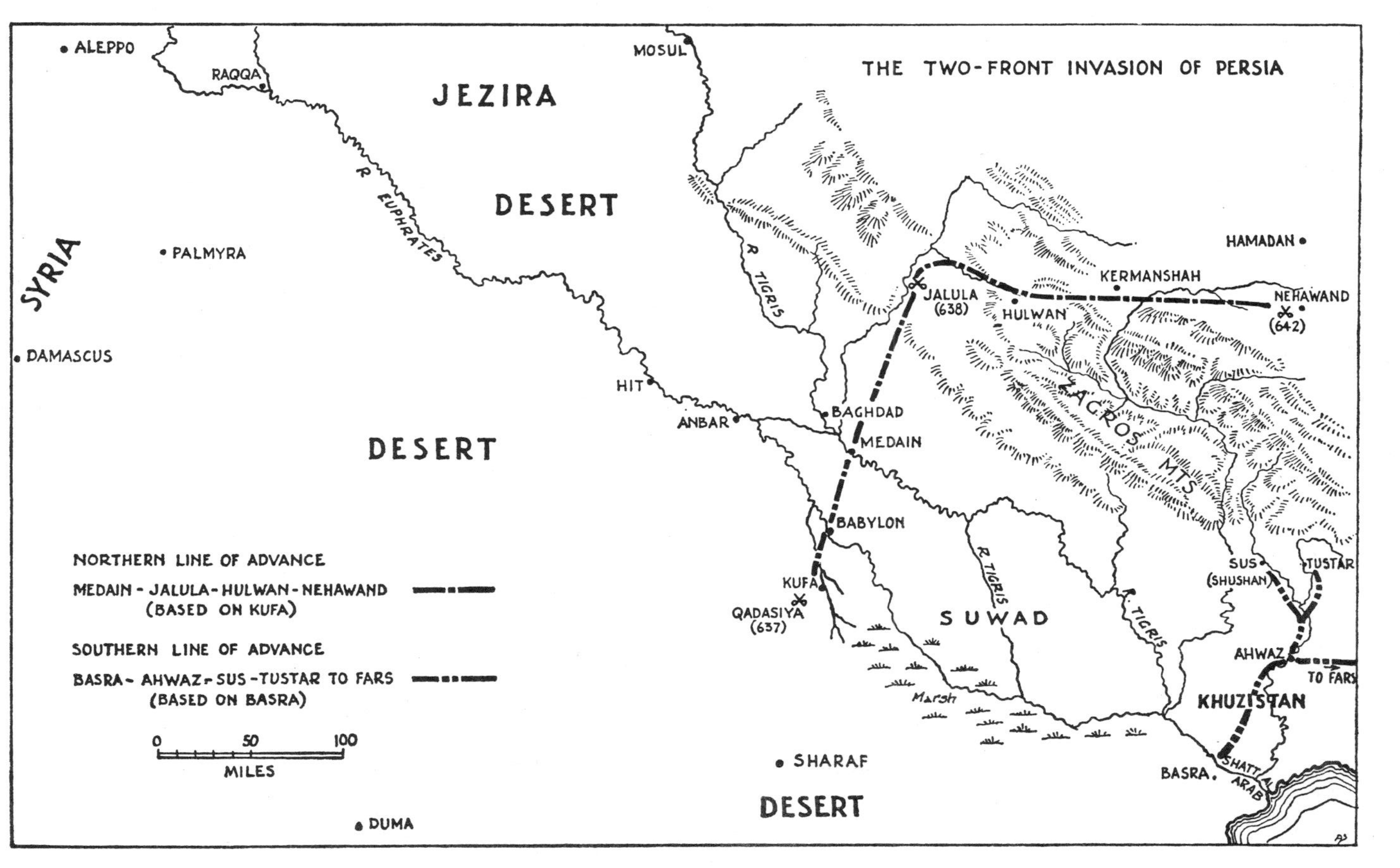
THE TWO-FRONT INVASION OF PERSIA
ALEPPO
RAQQA
MOSUL
JEZIRA
DESERT
R EUPHRATES
SYRIA
PALMYRA
DAMASCUS
R TIGRIS
HAMADAN
KERMANSHAH
JALULA (638)
HULWAN
NEHAWAND (642)
HIT
ANBAR
BAGHDAD
MEDAIN
ZAGROS MTS
DESERT
BABYLON
KUFA
QADASIYA (637)
R TIGRIS
SUWAD
R TIGRIS
Marsh
SUS (SHUSHAN)
TUSTAR
AHWAZ
TO FARS
KHUZISTAN
BASRA
SHATT AL ARAB
SHARAF
DESERT
DUMA
NORTHERN LINE OF ADVANCE
MEDAIN - JALULA - HULWAN - NEHAWAND (BASED ON KUFA)
SOUTHERN LINE OF ADVANCE
BASRA - AHWAZ - SUS - TUSTAR TO FARS (BASED ON BASRA)
0 50 100
MILES

Map XXVIII

them to be placed in the room where the public money was kept. But during the night, the presence of such vast wealth worried his conscience. In the morning he sent for the messenger saying, "Take these chests away again. Sell their contents and distribute the price among the troops." Having thus apparently successfully disposed of what appears to have been government property, the good old man (undaunted by any premonitions of queries from the audit department) doubtless returned to his duties with a lightened conscience.

This incident, if it be accurately related, is of some interest as showing how extremely simple was the administration of the new empire, even after nine years of ever-expanding victories. The financial resources of the state were still handed personally to the khalif in his mud-brick shack adjoining the mosque. There seems to have been some confusion in his mind and conscience between his own wealth and that of the state. He felt guilty at having so much treasure. Not least, perhaps, is it to be noticed that the messenger was told to take the fabulous jewels away, without any idea of giving a receipt or making an inventory. No wonder that some of the Arab commanders and governors grew rich. It is worthy of note also that the messenger returned across the whole breadth of Arabia, infested by tribes famed both before and since for their predatory habits, without any of the historians referring to an escort or any other precautions.

The messenger carried the jewels back to Kufa, where he sold them to a young man of Quraish. The purchaser re-sold one of the chests in Hira for the price which he had paid for the two, retaining the second, presumably in order to sell the contents stone by stone. The transaction enabled him to lay the foundations of a great fortune. Not all Muslims, it would appear, possessed such tender consciences as the khalif on the subject of worldly riches.

Soon after the Battle of Nehawand, the Arabs occupied Hamadan, the famed Ecbatana of the ancients. The Persians were never again able to put an army in the field to fight a major battle. The significance of this final triumph is emphasized by the fact that it was known ever afterwards to the Arabs as the "victory of victories". It had been the misfortune of Yezdegird, the grandson of Chosroes, to be raised when still a boy to the throne of an already defeated and disintegrating empire. After Nehawand he took refuge in Rei, not far south of the present capital, Teheran. A thousand years earlier, Darius III had followed the same route, when fleeing before the armies of the invincible Alexander.

Umar ibn al Khattab had wept at the news of the death of Naaman ibn Muqarrin. With that extraordinary Arab idea that his nearest relative has the right to avenge the death of a commander, the khalif appointed Naaman's brother, Nuaim ibn Muqarrin, to command of the army of Nehawand.

A striking sidelight on the spirit of the Arabs in these early years of conquest is to be seen in the casual way in which the khalif played with their seniority. We have already seen how Umar ibn al Khattab dismissed Khalid ibn al Waleed, already the most famous military commander of the age. Khalid nevertheless continued to serve under Abu Ubaida and even under

Iyadh ibn Ghanm,[3] a commander hitherto little known. If tradition be correit, Naaman ibn Muqarrin was serving in Khuzistan under Abu Musa al Ashari, before he was appointed to command the army which fought at Nehawand. Yet a contingent sent from Khuzistan to reinforce that army was apparently commanded by Abu Musa, to whom Naaman had been subordinate a short time before.

The significance of such incidents lies in the fact that personal jealousies are one of the great weaknesses of the Arab character. Even today, when the Arab states maintain "regular" armies, the rivalries and jealousies of different commanders cause constant anxiety to their governments. Not many years after Umar ibn al Khattab, these mutual jealousies were to break out once again, a development which only serves further to emphasize the enthusiastic devotion of these early pristine years of conquest. Public spirit was for a time strong enough, not only to enable the khalif to deprive victorious commanders of their wealth but completely to disregard their seniority and their past services in subordinating them to one another.

* * * * *

After the occupation of Medain, Umar ibn al Khattab had written to Saad ibn abi Waqqas ordering him not to attempt to cross the Zagros mountains The fertile plains of Iraq, he said, were sufficient for the Arabs, and the mountains would form an adequate frontier between them and the Persians (as indeed today they do). But Yezdegird was apparently no longer prepared to accept such a compromise. When he concentrated a new army, Saad reported that the king's intention was to reconquer Iraq. Thus as we have seen, a fresh Arab army was obliged to meet him and defeated his army at Nehawand. As a result, whether the khalif desired it or not, the Arabs were already across the Zagros range. It was impossible to halt in such a situation or perhaps Umar no longer desired to do so, now that the last Persian army had been destroyed. He accordingly sent new instructions to the Arab commanders in Persia, ordering them to pursue the enemy relentlessly wherever they might flee.

King Yezdegird retired to Rei, followed by Nuaim ibn Muqarrin, while Abu Musa al Ashari returned to Ahwaz and the invasion of the province of Fars. On the southern shores of the Caspian, Isfandiar, brother of that Rustem who had been killed at Qadasiya, was raising new forces to fight for the king. Nuaim advanced to meet him and a battle took place south of Rei in 643. Isfandiar was defeated and taken prisoner and his army dispersed. Despairing of the royal cause, he went over to the Arabs and thenceforward assisted their operations. King Yezdegird doubled back to the south and took refuge in Isfahan. Meanwhile, Hudhaifa ibn al Yaman, who, as we have seen, had taken over command during the Battle of Nehawand, was instructed to invade Adharbaijan.

The name of Roman, of which the Byzantines at this time still made use, is associated in our minds with the stern virtues of the republic, whereas we visualize the kings of ancient Persia as oriental despots driving into battle

[3] Page 210.

tens of thousands of unresisting slaves. The course of Arab conquest does not confirm the accuracy of this over-simplification. For once the Byzantine regular armies were defeated, the populations of Syria, Palestine and Egypt bowed submissively to the Arab yoke. The Byzantine Empire, it would appear, had been over-centralized in Constantinople. Once the emperor ceased to resist, the provinces went limp. No virile communities maintained a local resistance to the loss of their independence. In Persia the situation was different, for although the Great King was officially supreme, the system of government was partly feudal. Local Persian nobles held such authority in their provinces that they were, in many cases, able to prolong resistance, even when the king was already a fugitive.

Admittedly other factors also contributed to the continuation of the struggle in Persia, long after Arab rule had been unquestioningly accepted in the eastern Mediterranean states. First of these, perhaps, was the fact that Persia contained mountains, which everywhere halted, or at least delayed, the Arab advance. Then again the age-long infiltration of Arabs from Arabia into Syria, Palestine and Iraq had provided the first Muslim invaders, if not with a fifth column, at least with half-hearted enemies. The Persians, however, east of the Zagros mountains, had no racial relationship at all either to the Arabs, or to that even wider group of peoples sometimes classed as Mediterranean. Thus the Persians were the most difficult to conquer and the earliest to reassert themselves against the dominance of the Arab race.

But whereas local Persian resistance was to continue for many years, the Great King was never again able to put a formidable army in the field. The Arab pacification of Persia took henceforward the form of slow relentless pressure in many widely dispersed areas, but without decisive battles or dramatic campaigns, such as might focus the attention of the historian or evoke the enthusiasm of the patriot or the poet. Each year the Arabs advanced a few miles further, a number of towns were besieged, surrendered or rebelled, a few local chieftains went over to the victors. Suffice it to say that in 643 Isfahan was taken, and its people agreed to pay poll-tax and tribute.

Before Qadasiya, the Arab lines of communications, though already six hundred miles long, lay entirely across their own deserts. Now, however, they extended over distances of a thousand or twelve hundred miles, and passed through hostile territory, across great rivers, through mountain ranges and over passes at times blocked with snow. As a result, we find that surrender agreements of this period included clauses obliging the Persians to supply food and accommodation to passing Arabs. Anyone who assaulted an Arab was liable to the death penalty. Persians who had concluded an agreement with the Arabs had secured a charter of their rights. If, however, they were guilty of aggression against the Muslims, they risked repression by force and the cancellation of the agreement, becoming thereby exposed to unconditional slavery. By these measures the Arabs ensured the safety of their communications without military detachments to guard them.

Before the fall of Isfahan, Yezdegird retired southwards to Persepolis, called by the Arabs Istakhr, which Abu Musa al Ashari from Ahwaz was endeavouring in vain to subdue. Hudhaifa ibn al Yaman appears to have

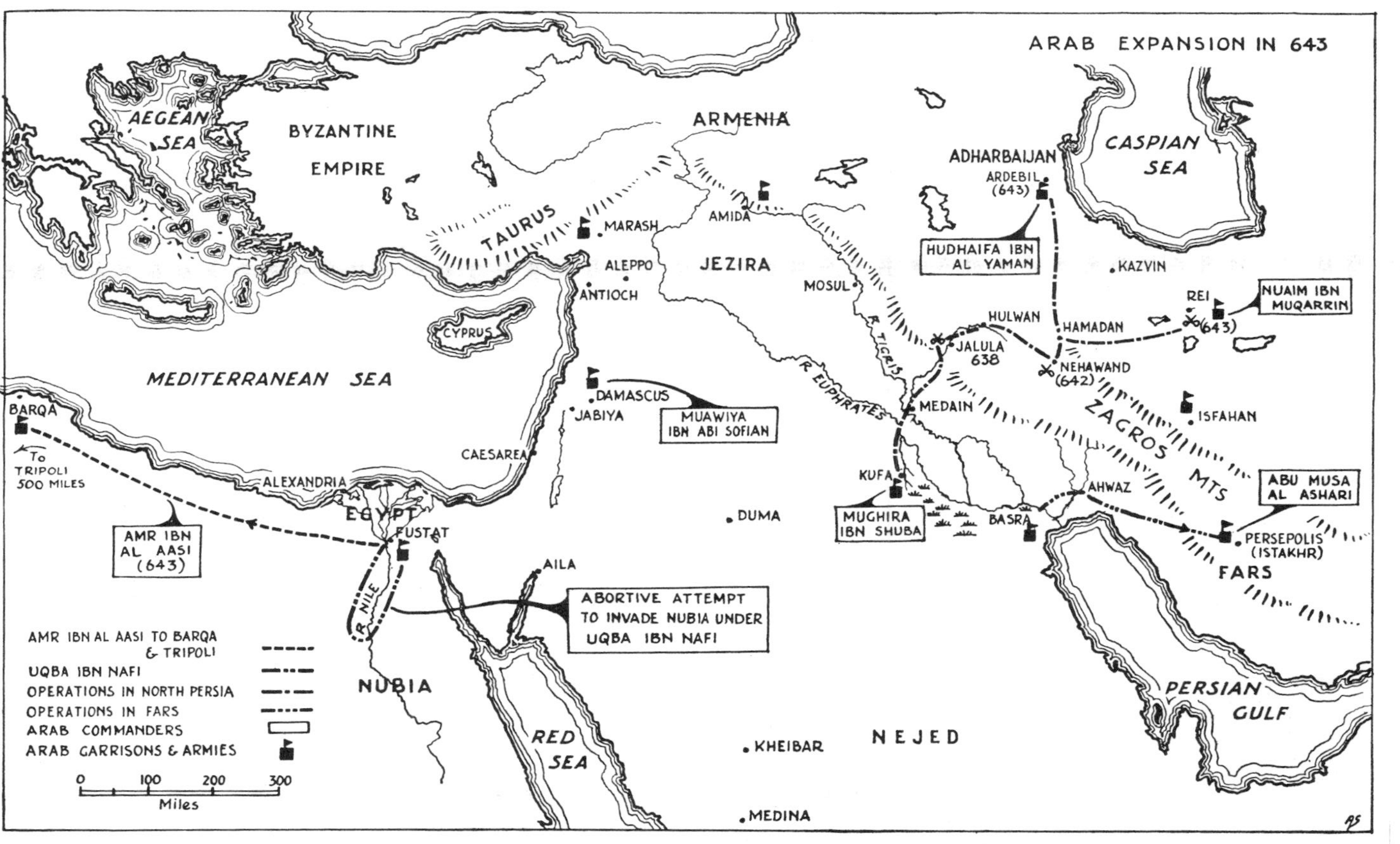
ARAB EXPANSION IN 643
AEGEAN SEA
BYZANTINE EMPIRE
ARMENIA
TAURUS
MARASH
AMIDA
ALEPPO
ANTIOCH
JEZIRA
MOSUL
CASPIAN SEA
ADHARBAIJAN
ARDEBIL (643)
HUDHAIFA IBN AL YAMAN
KAZVIN
REI
NUAIM IBN MUQARRIN
(643)
HULWAN
HAMADAN
JALULA 638
NEHAWAND (642)
CYPRUS
MEDITERRANEAN SEA
R. TIGRIS
R. EUPHRATES
MEDAIN
ZAGROS MTS
ISFAHAN
DAMASCUS
JABIYA
MUAWIYA IBN ABI SOFIAN
BARQA
To TRIPOLI 500 MILES
CAESAREA
ALEXANDRIA
EGYPT
FUSTAT
AMR IBN AL AASI (643)
KUFA
MUGHIRA IBN SHUBA
BASRA
AHWAZ
ABU MUSA AL ASHARI
PERSEPOLIS (ISTAKHR)
FARS
DUMA
AILA
R. NILE
ABORTIVE ATTEMPT TO INVADE NUBIA UNDER UQBA IBN NAFI
AMR IBN AL AASI TO BARQA & TRIPOLI
UQBA IBN NAFI
OPERATIONS IN NORTH PERSIA
OPERATIONS IN FARS
ARAB COMMANDERS
ARAB GARRISONS & ARMIES
0 100 200 300
Miles
NUBIA
RED SEA
KHEIBAR
NEJED
MEDINA
PERSIAN GULF

Map XXIX

achieved better success on the western shores of the Caspian. Invading Persian Adharbaijan, he met with resistance from the local forces, under the satrap of the province, but defeated them in a battle and occupied the capital, Ardebil. Thereupon the satrap came to terms, agreeing to pay taxes and tribute. An alternative report attributes this conquest to Mughira ibn Shuba, who, as we shall shortly see, had been made governor of Kufa. The two accounts are, however, reconcilable, for Hudhaifa's army was based on Kufa, and he therefore was doubtless under the orders of the governor. The first pacification seems, however, to have been superficial, for Adharbaijan rebelled in 645, and had to be conquered a second time.

* * * * *

While the Arab armies were thus slowly fanning out over Persia, all was not well at their main base of Kufa. We have already seen that, when the Arabs almost unexpectedly found themselves the rulers of Syria and Iraq, Umar ibn al Khattab took a major decision of policy. He ruled that, in every conquered country, the peasants were to remain in occupation of their lands, which they were to continue to cultivate and on which they were to pay taxes. Arabs were not, in general, to settle on the land, but were to be retained as an imperial, military race, concentrated in their cantonments, ever ready to fight against the unbelievers. As a result, military cities were founded at Kufa and Basra in Iraq, at Jabiya south-west of Damascus, and at Fustat on the site of modern Cairo.

But military cantonment life has many drawbacks, as other imperial powers have found. The troops are isolated from the people of the country and the narrow world of the camp leads to parochial cliques and jealousies. In the Arab army depôts, the demoralization was accelerated by the naturally free and turbulent character of the bedouin and by the laxity bred by the immense wealth which they had acquired. The hardihood of the desert Arabs was sapped by indulgence in great numbers of captured women as concubines, and by the idleness in which the men lived, in an age when no military training was considered necessary.

The most turbulent and insubordinate of the Arab military bases was Kufa, the cantonment founded by Saad ibn abi Waqqas, on the orders of Umar ibn al Khattab. When Saad wrote to the khalif complaining of the mosquitoes in Medain, the commander of the faithful is alleged to have replied, "Arabs are like camels. Nothing is good for them except what is good for camels. So find them a healthy place and do not let any sea intervene between them and me." It was in accordance with these instructions that Kufa had been selected. The eastern half of the cantonment was allotted to the tribes from the Yemen, the western half to those from the north.[4] The former are alleged to have numbered 12,000 men, the latter 8,000, for what such figures are worth.

While the Arab armies based on Kufa were scattered far afield in the

[4] See page 37, footnote, regarding the northern and southern halves of the Arab race.

deserts and mountains of Persia, intrigue was spreading among the troops at the base. Informers from Kufa went to Medina to complain against the governor and commander-in-chief, Saad ibn abi Waqqas. The latter had built himself a house round which the camp of Kufa had been laid out. But the camp had now become a town. Not only did the clamour of the crowds in the streets disturb the governor but visitors, petitioners or the merely curious jostled one another in and out of the house. Saad complained that it was impossible for him to discuss public business with his officers, owing to the noise and confusion. He accordingly erected a fence to enclose a small courtyard which interposed between the front of the house and the street crowds. Soon, however, the intriguers were with the khalif in Medina. The governor, they protested, had built a fence to separate himself from the people —evidence of worldly pride in the opinion of these puritan levellers. Others claimed that, when he led the prayers, the outward and visible sign of command, he prayed in an unorthodox manner. The khalif sent Muhammad ibn Maslama to investigate the complaints, the same man whom we have already seen confiscating the riches of Amr ibn al Aasi, the conqueror of Egypt. The inspector removed and burnt the fence surrounding Saad's yard and handed to him a letter from the khalif which read as follows. "I hear that you built yourself a mansion called the mansion of Saad and have erected a door between you and the people. It is not your mansion but the mansion of folly. Come out of it and close it and do not erect a door to keep the people out and to banish them from their rights, so that they have to wait until you receive them or until you go out."

Apart from the fence and its door, Muhammad ibn Maslama seems to have found little foundation for the intrigues against Saad, though the charge that he sheltered in a building behind the line at Qadasiya seems to have periodically cropped up again. Although no serious charges appear to have been proved, however, the khalif in 642 dismissed Saad from his post, appointing a certain Ammar ibn Yasir to replace him. One Arab historian relates that when Umar ibn al Khattab was asked how he had succeeded in ruling the Arabs, he replied that he frequently changed their commanders. He appears to have been constantly haunted by the fear that a successful military leader would become too strong with the result that every efficient Arab general was dismissed by him, soon after his greatest victory.

But if the dismissal of Saad was remarkable, the appointment of Ammar ibn Yasir might almost be called ridiculous. It will be remembered that when Muhammad first began to make converts in Mecca, Quraish attempted to oppose him by forcible methods. Tribal feeling was too strong to permit them to persecute fellow tribesmen, even if they accepted Islam, but they vented their indignation on slaves and anyone unprotected by a powerful tribe. Ammar ibn Yasir was a slave, one of the Prophet's earliest converts, and the victim of Quraish persecution. The well-to-do Abu Bekr had rescued the slave by buying him and then setting him free. Ever since he had lived in rigid piety, until now he had attained extreme old age. His respected sanctity and his prestige as one of the earliest converts entitled him, in the eyes of the khalif at least, to the governorship of the province of Kufa.[5] The Kufans, who had disposed of the formidable Saad ibn abi Waqqas, made short work of the feeble old slave, who had never before occupied a position of responsibility. Deputations to Medina proved to Umar the weakness of his nominee, who was consequently dismissed. "What am I to do to the people of Kufa?" complained the khalif. "If I set a strong man over them, they complained of his tyranny. If I appointed a weak one, they insulted him."

It will be remembered that Mughira ibn Shuba had been governor of Basra, but had been removed for the crime of adultery, even though it had not been proved against him by four witnesses. Mughira was of an uncouth and rough disposition, unkempt, one-eyed and fat, but ruthless. "If I send you to govern Kufa," enquired Umar ibn al Khattab, "will you repeat what you did before?" "No," replied the other curtly. He was appointed and succeeded in retaining the post for two years until the death of the khalif, when the people of Kufa were once more to assert their turbulent character.

Provincial governors and military commanders alike had a good deal to endure during the khalifate of Umar, who was always ready to listen to the voice of informers and intriguers, who hurried to Medina to undermine the position of anyone in authority in the provinces. These methods sowed the seeds of discords which, after Umar's death, went near to wrecking the still growing Arab Empire.

* * * * *

Syria and Palestine were quiet in the years 642 and 643. Desultory hostilities were to continue on the borders of Armenia and in the Taurus mountains for many years to come, but in reality the Arab expansion to the north-west had already almost reached its ultimate limits. The populations of Syria and Palestine had resigned themselves to Arab domination, under the capable rule of their new governor, Muawiya, the son of Abu Sofian.

In Africa, however, the Arab conquests continued. As soon as the Muslims were established in Alexandria, the restless Amr ibn al Aasi set out over the Western Desert for Libya. The whole of North Africa from the Atlantic to Egypt had been included in the Roman Empire at the time of its power. With the collapse of the Western Empire in the fourth century, however, the Vandals, a tribe of northern barbarians, had crossed from Europe and occupied Carthage. Here they had established an independent kingdom, which extended from modern Algeria to Libya, and included Majorca, Minorca, Corsica and Sardinia. In the year 532, however, the Byzantine emperor Justinian sent an army to Carthage. Under the command of the famous Belisarius, one of the few great soldiers of the decline of the empire, the Byzantines had defeated the Vandals and North Africa had returned to the empire of Constantinople. The population of these territories was extremely mixed. The early Carthaginians, the Romans, the Byzantines and the Vandals had occupied only the coastal plains. The mountains of the interior were the home of the

[5] About this time we begin to find records of the appointment to provinces of a treasurer, a tax-collector, a land surveyor and a judge instead of only a commander-in-chief. Thus the elements of an administration commence to emerge.

Berbers, the real natives of the country, who had resisted absorption into the successive races which had conquered the coast. It was from this province that Heraclius, as we have seen, had started on the campaign which had resulted in the overthrow of the execrable Phocas and his own elevation to the purple.

In the year 619, the armies of Chosroes Parwiz, after completing the conquest of Egypt, had penetrated to the west as far as Tripoli, apparently without encountering any serious opposition. Egypt was one of the bulwarks of the Byzantine Empire, the supplier of its food and of much of its revenue. It supported a population of perhaps six or seven millions, and was provided with a number of fortified cities. The many canals and branches of the Nile made military operations difficult, while Alexandria itself, if resolutely defended, was capable of defying any army of the period, probably for several years. Thus any invader who had conquered Egypt would find the occupation of Libya little more than child's play. To this rule, Amr ibn al Aasi proved no exception. In the spring of 643, he appears to have occupied Barqa without opposition, the people agreeing to pay poll-tax and tribute. Curiously enough, a clause seems to have been included in the agreement to the effect that the tribute would be voluntarily sent to Egypt, no Arab tax collector coming to Barqa to fetch it.

No sooner, moreover, was the agreement signed than we find Amr ibn al Aasi reporting to the khalif that he had assessed tithes on land owned by Muslims and the usual tribute on the property of non-Muslims. The report is elucidated by Yaqut, who states plainly that most of the people of Barqa adopted Islam. The point is of considerable interest. The apparently ready welcome offered to the Arabs in the Western Desert and Barqa seems to suggest that the people of this area were themselves partly Arabs. Such an idea is by no means far-fetched. The Western Desert resembles the deserts of Arabia and offers a complete contrast to the damp climate and alluvial soil of the Nile delta. The Arabs indeed had, as far as we know, never reached here before as conquerors, but it is by no means improbable that tribes from Arabia had infiltrated into the Libyan deserts before this date. As a result it may well be that the conquering Muslims recognized some signs of kinship in the Libyans, and that the latter, as a result, readily came to an understanding with these distant cousins. This possibility seems to be further strengthened by early classical writers such as Diodorus Siculus, Ptolemy, Strabo and Pliny, who refer to Arab races in the deserts of Egypt. If, however, such peoples were indeed descended from natives of Arabia, they appear to have lost their language and identity before the Muslim conquest.

At Tripoli,[6] however, the situation was different. The city was fortified, contained a Byzantine garrison and closed its gates to the Arabs. It was open to the sea, which was commanded by the Byzantine fleet, and could perhaps have resisted for a long time, if it had been replenished and reinforced. But Constantinople, as we have seen, was torn by intrigues and palace rivalries and cared nothing for these distant provinces. After a siege of several weeks' duration, during which the Arabs could make no impression on the walls, a gap was discovered between the fortifications and the sea, probably in June 643. A

[6] For the position of Tripoli in Africa, see map inside front cover of this book.

few brave men were able to enter the city along the shore, and, suddenly raising the cry of *Allahu akbar,* took the town by assault.

After storming another town called Sabrah, Amr returned to Barqa. Some historians suggested that Amr ibn al Aasi would have pressed on to Carthage, but that he was recalled by the khalif, a not unlikely eventuality for we have already seen that Umar was constantly anxious lest his armies go too far, or be cut off from Medina by intervening mountains or rivers. On his return to Barqa, Amr ibn al Aasi received the submission of a Berber tribe called the Luwata, in whose capitulation he included the clause, "you have to sell your children and your wives in order to pay the poll-tax." It is impossible now to ascertain why so remarkable a condition should be inserted in an agreement. It can only be presumed that the Berbers expressed their inability to pay the poll-tax owing to their extreme poverty and that Amr replied that they must certainly pay, even if it meant selling their wives and children.

During the life of the Prophet, we noticed many instances of Arabs of both sexes, taken prisoners in their tribal wars, being made slaves by other Arabs. It was only during the khalifate of Umar ibn al Khattab that this practice was prohibited. For during the ten years of his rule, the Arabs had been transformed into a conquering and imperial race, or rather perhaps into an aristocracy, ruling a subject empire. This newly found pride of race grew up side by side with the (entirely different) conception of Muslim brotherhood. The Arabs all through history have been slave traders and slave owners. But never since the days of Umar ibn al Khattab (to the best of my knowledge) have they enslaved one another. The fact that the enslavement of Berbers was specifically recognized seems to prove that they were not regarded as Arabs.

Amr ibn al Aasi returned from Tripoli to Alexandria laden with spoils and slaves. Another expedition had meanwhile been sent up the Nile towards the Sudan, under the command of his cousin Uqba ibn Nafi. This enterprise met with little success. The Sudanese, then called Nubians, were famous as archers and received the invading Arabs with such showers of arrows that most of them were wounded and many blinded. So many indeed lost their sight that the Sudanese were nicknamed the archers of the eyes. It is interesting to note the fighting qualities of the Nubians thirteen hundred years ago, and which they have retained until our own time. The Arab column was obliged to retreat as best it could to Egypt.

Umar ibn al Khattab had ordered Amr ibn al Aasi to establish his headquarters at Fustat, the new cantonment adjoining the fortress of Babylon. Here, in the spring of 644, the conqueror of Egypt preached a sermon which has been rendered famous by the Arab historians. He began, in the orthodox manner, by giving praise and thanks to God. He then urged his hearers to observe the ordinances of religion, to give alms, and to eschew avarice, ostentation and gossip. Idleness and frivolity, he claimed, were the chief sources of vice and sin. Then, changing his tone, he embarked on a panegyric of spring. "The Nile floods," he said, "have fallen, the spring grazing is good. There is milk for the lambs and the kids. Go out with God's blessing and enjoy the land, its milk, its flocks and its herds. And take good care of your neighbours the Copts, for the Messenger of God himself gave orders for us to do so."

It is perhaps also worth while to quote something of the report sent by Amr ibn al Aasi to the khalif. "Egypt," he is alleged to have written, "is a dusty city and a green tree. Its length is a month's journey, its breadth ten days. The Nile traces a line through the midst of it: blessed are its early morning voyages and its travels at eventide.[7] The Nile has its seasons for rising and falling. It causes milk to flow and brings cattle in abundance. When the springs and fountains of the land are loosened, it rolls its swelling and sounding waters till the fields are flooded. Then there is no moving from village to village save in frail boats, light as fancy or the evening mist. The people, who are devout in worship, and our allies, have learnt to plough the earth well, trusting that God Most High will give the increase. At one season Egypt is a white pearl; then golden amber; then a green emerald; then an embroidery of many colours."[8] Amr ibn al Aasi seems to have been a poet, in addition to his many other accomplishments.

Whatever the Egyptians may have thought of their Arab conquerors, they received at least one benefit at their hands—the end of religious persecution. The Coptic Patriarch Benjamin, a fugitive in the desert since the first appointment of Cyrus twelve years earlier, was now summoned from his concealment by Amr ibn al Aasi, and resumed the official leadership of the Coptic Church. A new Orthodox Patriarch was also appointed but, without imperial support, he was no longer in a position to persecute his fellow Christians.

When, as far as we can judge, he had rendered such extraordinary services to the Muslim cause, it is distressing to find that Amr ibn al Aasi seems to have received nothing but rebukes from the khalif. This time the latter complained bitterly that he had not received as much money from taxes in Egypt as the Byzantine emperor had been accustomed to extract. He was astonished, wrote Umar ibn al Khattab in 644, that in the preceding year Egypt had not produced half the revenue which it formerly transmitted to Byzantium. "I shall certainly not accept less than was formerly paid. I had hoped that you would do your duty but I now see that your bad administration has prevented your doing so. With the help of God, I have means to compel you to render what I demand."

These harsh threats come unexpectedly from the pious khalif, whom we have learned to regard as indifferent to worldly wealth and who seemed so ready to distribute the public funds to the community. Moreover, we know that, not Umar himself, but many of the leading Muslims of Medina had grown immensely wealthy on the plunder sent home from the conquered provinces. Were interested persons urging the khalif to demand more? Had he found that his system of paying a salary to every member of the Arab race was costing more than he foresaw? Yet if the state were in financial straits, it was not necessary to write to his commander-in-chief in such crude and threatening language. This is especially true when we remember that the

[7] Anyone who has experienced the dawn and the cool of the evening in an Arab country will appreciate this phrase.

[8] I have adopted the translation given by Butler, slightly abbreviated.

whole plan to conquer Egypt was due only to the initiative of Amr ibn al Aasi, rather against the wishes of the khalif, who now berated the conqueror for not doing more. Or was Umar ibn al Khattab afflicted by personal jealousy of his most successful commanders? His treatment of Khalid ibn al Waleed, of Muthanna, of Saad ibn abi Waqqas, and now of Amr ibn al Aasi, would almost seem to suggest such an explanation.

"I have served the Messenger of God himself," Amr ibn al Aasi replied to the angry khalif's threats, "and also his successor Abu Bekr. I have, praise God, answered to the trust which they reposed in me. You can take back the governorship which you have given me, for God has kept me free from the avarice and the meanness of which you have accused me. You could not have said more to a Jew of Kheibar. God forgive you and me."

It is impossible, on the slender evidence available, to form a final opinion on the subject of this controversy. The khalif, as we have already seen, had accused Amr ibn al Aasi of himself growing too rich. Yet it is disappointing to read these harsh and exacting words from the ageing khalif, of whom one would prefer to retain the picture of humble simplicity in the path of God.

## *NOTABLE DATES*

| | |
|---|---|
| Saad ibn abi Waqqas, conqueror of Iraq, dismissed | 642 |
| Battle of Nehawand | 642 |
| Capture of Isfahan | 643 |
| Capture of Rei | 643 |
| Capture of Tripoli in Africa | June, 643 |

## *PERSONALITIES*

Naaman ibn Muqarrin, Arab commander, killed at Nehawand.

Abu Musa al Ashari, governor of Basra and military commander in Fars.

Mughira ibn Shuba, dismissed from governorship of Basra for adultery, then appointed governor of Kufa.

Amr ibn al Aasi, conqueror of Egypt.

Uqba ibn Nafi, cousin of Amr ibn al Aasi, commander of the unsuccessful invasion of the Sudan.

# XV

## *Abu Lulu*

Confusion now hath made his masterpiece!
Most sacrilegious murder hath broke ope
The Lord's anointed temple.
. . . Prophesying with accents terrible
Of dire combustion and confused events.

SHAKESPEARE, *Macbeth*

The golden age of the Saracens was the twelve years, A.D. 632 to 644, comprised in the reigns of Abu Bekr and Omar. This was a period of uninterrupted internal harmony and external conquest. Once granting the principle of aggressive conquest, there is comparatively little to condemn in the conduct of the conquerors. FREEMAN, *History of the Saracens*

## XV

## ABU LULU

IN October 644, Umar ibn al Khattab led the annual pilgrimage to Mecca, as he had done ever since his elevation to the khalifate. Except for sporadic fighting against the still unsubdued provinces of far-away Persia, the empire was triumphant and at rest. The old khalif—he was probably about sixty years of age—had ruled for just over ten years. In those ten eventful years, the two greatest empires of the world had been simultaneously overthrown, and the khalif had become the despotic ruler of an immense empire, erected on the ruins of its predecessors. It is doubtful whether any monarch in all history had ever conquered so great an area and left it to remain intact after him for many generations.

Mughira ibn Shuba, as we have seen, had two years before been appointed by the khalif as governor of Kufa, in spite of the charge of adultery brought against him previously when he was governor of Basra. Mughira had a slave known to the Arabs by the nickname of Abu Lulu. A Persian by birth, he had been carried off a prisoner by the Byzantines in his youth and brought up as a Christian. Later he was captured by the Arabs and bought as a slave by Mughira. It appears to have been the custom for the Arabs to allow their slaves to go to work and to earn wages, on condition that they paid a proportion of their earnings to their owners. Mughira seems to have left Abu Lulu to work in Medina on these terms. He was a skilled carpenter, of which probably few were to be found in Medina, where he as a result could doubtless earn good wages. When the Persian prisoners from the Battle of Nehawand were driven into Medina, Abu Lulu was alleged to have wept bitterly. Some even said that he had been brought up as a child in the city of Nehawand.

This man, meeting the khalif one day in the street (a fact illustrating the unguarded simplicity of Umar's way of life), cried out to him for justice against his owner Mughira. He claimed that he was obliged to pay his master two dirhems a day, which did not leave him enough to live on. Being told that he was a carpenter, the khalif replied that the sum did not seem excessive, as so skilled a craftsman must be earning good wages. Abu Lulu gave a surly reply and passed on.

Next morning, shortly after sunrise, the people were assembled in the great mosque of Medina for the early prayers. As the congregation formed up rank behind rank, Abu Lulu slipped into the first row. The khalif walked to his place in front, with his back turned to the serried ranks of worshippers. Scarcely had he raised his hands and cried for the first time *Allahu akbar*, when Abu Lulu rushed upon him from behind and stabbed him in the body in six different places. As the old man fell to the ground, the Persian burst into the crowd in a frenzy, stabbing right and left, finally plunging the knife into his own body.

The aged Umar was carried into his house, the door of which opened on to the courtyard of the mosque, and was laid upon his bed. He was perfectly conscious and called for Abdul Rahman ibn Auf, one of the earliest of the Prophet's Companions. The dying man asked Abdul Rahman if he would agree to be his successor, but the latter begged to be excused. The khalif then summoned Ali ibn abi Talib, the Prophet's cousin, Othman ibn Affan, one of the earliest converts, Zubair ibn al Awwam, the man who had led the storming party up the walls of Egyptian Babylon, and Saad ibn abi Waqqas, the conqueror of Iraq, and appointed them as a selection committee to choose the new khalif. We shall hear more of their deliberations shortly.

Later the old man rallied his strength once more and asked who it was who had stabbed him. When told that it was Abu Lulu, he praised God that it had not been a Muslim, for being killed by an unbeliever would entitle him to the martyr's reward of immediate admittance to Paradise. He took a drink of milk, but the liquid flowed unchanged straight out of a gaping wound in his stomach. "I charge my successor," he murmured, "to be kind to the men of Medina, for they gave a home to us and to the faith. Let him make much of their virtues and deal lightly with their faults. And let him treat the bedouins well, for they were the raw material of Islam."

Thinking for a few minutes, he called to his son Abdulla to go and ask Aisha, the Prophet's favourite wife, if he might be buried with Muhammad and Abu Bekr under the floor of the former's bedroom. Then, on the morning of 3rd November, 644, repeating again and again the Muslim witness—"I bear witness that there is no god but God and I bear witness that Muhammad is His Messenger"—he quietly passed from this life.

It is impossible to deny to Umar the title of greatness. In his youth, he was known for his impetuosity and his hot temper. After the Battle of Bedr, it was he who urged that all the Quraish prisoners be massacred in cold blood. But with age and responsibility, his character matured and he became patient and tolerant. He was adamant in the service of God, but easy going and accommodating where his own interests were concerned and always full of sympathy and pity for the poor. Although, however, the traditionists delight to enlarge on his humility, his poverty and his compassion, there can be no doubt that he was the complete and undisputed master of the great empire which had grown up in so short a time under his rule. We have already seen that 639 was a year of famine in the Hejaz. In spite of the immense wealth accumulated by many Muslims, there was little to eat until caravans of food could be brought from Syria and Iraq. During these desperate weeks, the historians describe the khalif going forth at night through the dark streets of Medina, accompanied by one servant. The two carried between them a sack of flour and a goat-skin of oil, with which to supply the needs of the poor whom they might encounter. Sometimes the sack of flour would prove inadequate and the servant would be sent back to fetch another load. On one occasion, the khalif seated himself on the ground beside some hungry old woman, and helped her to light her fire and to cook the meal which he had supplied.

In the centuries to come, the Arabs and the Muslims were more than once to suffer idle, frivolous, luxurious khalifs, some profligate and others cruel. In those days, the traditionists would delight to repeat, and perhaps to embroider upon, the tales of the first two khalifs, who, though uniformly victorious in the field, were so humble, simple and compassionate in their private lives. Perhaps the stories of Umar's nightly sorties to feed the poor may have become exaggerated, but of his simplicity and democracy there can be no doubt, for indeed the same qualities have been visible in Central Arabia until our own times. Prisoners of war from Persia or Byzantium arrived in Medina expecting to see palaces and imperial pomp such as they were accustomed to in Medain or Constantinople. Instead, in the glaring, dusty square of the mud-built town, they would see a circle of Arabs sitting on the ground. One of these, a tall, lean man with a bald head, barefoot and wearing a coarse and patched woollen cloak, would prove to be the world's most powerful emperor.

A pleasant anecdote is recorded of one of Umar's visits to Syria, when, while journeying northwards, he spent a night as the guest of the Christian bishop in Aila, the modern Aqaba. When going to bed, the khalif removed his shirt and, handing it to his host, pointed to a tear on the shoulder and asked if it could be patched before the morning. At dawn the bishop returned to his guest and presented him with his old shirt, which had been not only patched, but carefully laundered and folded. Underneath it, a new shirt had been tactfully concealed. The bishop put down the parcel and was leaving the room when Umar noticed the second garment. "What is this?" he enquired. The good bishop was embarrassed. "We thought you might need a second shirt on so long a journey," he stammered. "My old one will be more comfortable," replied the old khalif, handing back the new one to his host.

Tabari recounts how Umar said in a public speech that he never sent governors to the provinces that they might beat people or seize their goods, but that they might instruct them in their religion and in the practices of the Prophet. On another occasion, he was reported to have said that if he were able, he would wish to tour all the provinces, spending in each place two months, so that he could be certain that every man in all the Arab dominions had been given the opportunity of personally presenting to him his complaints. The story is related of a plaintiff coming to Medina and asking of one of the citizens how it would be possible for him to obtain an audience of the khalif. "There is no door between him and the people," was the reply. "You can speak to him every day in the streets and in the mosque."

His invariable readiness to hear any and every complaint, and to act upon them against his own subordinates, undermined at times the discipline of the troops and the prestige of his governors in distant and often turbulent provinces. The worst results of these methods were to become evident after his death.

Yet the fact that the ruler of such extensive dominions could spend his day gossiping in the market place or taking bags of flour at night to poor widows, serves also to emphasize the still primitive condition of the empire. The twentieth-century administrator may well regret the happy days when a man could rule an empire without putting pen to paper. Even if the modern administrator were as simple and as democratic as Umar ibn al Khattab, he would be unable to pass his day chatting with the public in the streets. But the early khalifs were not pursued by auditors, compelled to submit monthly reports, or harassed by questions in parliament. No in-tray loaded with files confronted them each morning in the office. We have already seen how Amr ibn al Aasi, after the capture of the Egyptian Babylon, had contented himself with the despatch of a verbal message to Medina to announce the victory.

Romantic as the stories of the barefooted khalifs may appear, the system obviously had serious disadvantages. In the absence of any trained Arab officials, the administration of the Byzantine provinces, as we have already seen, continued to be handled by Greeks, that of Persia by the employees of the former government in that country, and for many years to come, the public accounts were kept in Greek and in Persian, which few if any of the Arabs could read. Indeed the drop in the revenues of Egypt, which roused the anger of the khalif against Amr ibn al Aasi, may well have been at least partly due to the dishonesty of the Byzantine officials who collected the taxes and kept the accounts. At the same time, however, we know that many of the Arab conquerors accumulated great fortunes. This, in the absence of a competent civil service, was impossible to prevent. Umar, as we have seen, dealt with the problem in a rough and ready manner. As soon as he heard, from popular report, that a commander or a governor had become rich, he sent a representative to confiscate half his possessions.

This indeed brings us to the most remarkable quality which Umar must have possessed. The Muslim historians dwell justifiably on his piety, humility and dedication to his task, but none of them comment on his powers of command. Yet he repeatedly sent a message to a victorious general at the head of his army in a remote province, ordering him to surrender his command and to give up half his wealth to the treasury. Never did one of them hesitate to submit instantly. This unquestioning obedience cannot be entirely attributed to religion for, as we shall see, Umar's successor in the khalifate was to meet with open insubordination, and eventually to be overthrown by it.

* * * * *

Abu Lulu, the murderer of Umar, was a Persian. The most prominent man of that nation then living in Medina was Hormuzan, the Persian noble who had saved his own life by pouring on the ground the water which he was about to drink.[1] Scarcely was the Khalif Umar dead than his son hastened to the house of Hormuzan and killed him in vengeance for the murder of his father. As an Arab, the son of the victim had thought of revenge before all else. Tabari alleges that someone had said that he had once seen, in the possession of Hormuzan, the dagger used by Abu Lulu to murder the khalif. Yet it would seem most unlikely that Hormuzan would plot to kill Umar, who had saved his life and allotted him a pension. Moreover, Hormuzan

[1] Page 213

was a solitary Persian noble living in the Arab capital. Umar had been brutally assassinated by a Persian—the foul act must be atoned for by the blood of another Persian.

* * * * *

One of the most difficult problems in human government is the discovery of a peaceful method of selecting a successor to a dead ruler. It was one which the ancient world never solved and which, in our own day, presents one of the strongest objections to dictatorship. It was a difficulty regarding which the Prophet had left no instructions. During his last illness, he had nominated Abu Bekr to lead the prayers but even so, it will be remembered, the appointment of the first successor had very nearly led to internal strife.

Abu Bekr had actually nominated Umar, and the latter had been strong enough to assume power unopposed. Abdul Rahman ibn Auf, who had refused the succession offered to him by Umar, would doubtless have been the best candidate, for his very refusal had proved him to be free from personal ambition, greed and lust for power. As it was, the electoral committee named by Umar assembled to choose the new ruler. Since all the members of this body were to play leading parts in the ensuing years, it is perhaps worth while to examine them more closely.

Ali ibn abi Talib was the Prophet's cousin, and had been brought up by Muhammad and Khadija as if he had been their son. He had married their daughter Fatima. He had played a prominent part in the Prophet's battles, being an extremely efficient swordsman, particularly in single combats. Since the death of Muhammad, he had remained in Medina, where he had acted as an adviser to both Abu Bekr and Umar. He had now grown rich, middle-aged and somewhat portly.

Othman ibn Affan was the second member of the committee. He was of the Beni Umaiya clan, which formerly included the richest merchants of Quraish and of which old Abu Sofian had been the chief. He had married in succession two of the Prophet's daughters. It was he who, from Hudeibiya, had been sent by Muhammad to negotiate in Mecca with Quraish, but he was alleged to have run away at the Battle of Uhud.

Zubair ibn al Awwam was the third member. He also was a close relative of the Prophet. It was he who had led the 12,000 reinforcements sent by the khalif to Amr ibn al Aasi in Egypt and who had subsequently led the assault up a ladder on to the walls of Babylon.

Saad ibn abi Waqqas, the fourth member of the committee, was the conqueror of Iraq. Abdul Rahman ibn Auf, who had already refused the khalifate for himself, was still a member of the board charged with the election.

The board had assembled while Umar was still alive and had retired to an adjoining room to begin their deliberations. Soon their voices rose in animated argument, until the dying khalif asked them to postpone their discussions until after his death. No sooner had he been buried under the floor of Muhammad's room than the electors reassembled. A guard was placed on their door, in accordance with the orders of their late master, and they were told that Umar had prescribed a maximum of three days for their deliberations. At the end of that period, they must willy-nilly unanimously choose a khalif. In the event of the decision not being unanimous, the majority candidate was to be adopted, the members of the minority being all immediately put to death. Umar had not been prepared to give a defeated candidate the opportunity to plunge the country into civil war. This provision seems to prove that the likelihood of internal strife was already apparent, a fact which may account for the manner in which Umar always dismissed a victorious general. He may have dreaded the possibility of a military revolt.

It soon emerged that, of the five electors, Othman ibn Affan and Ali ibn abi Talib were the only two serious candidates. Both had been the Prophet's son-in-law. Both were among the earliest converts. Saad ibn abi Waqqas and Zubair ibn al Awwam were both great fighters, but do not appear to have been regarded as serious rivals to the first two.

Between Ali and Othman the debate waxed hot, each loudly supporting his own claim. Two days passed thus without progress. On the third morning, the commander of the guard at the door of the council chamber warned the electors that their decision must be reached on that day. The principal responsibility rested upon Abdul Rahman, himself the most worthy candidate had he been willing to accept. On the third morning, he declared his readiness formally to withdraw any claim he might have, on condition that the other four bound themselves loyally to accept the candidate whom he might choose. After some hesitation on the part of Ali, all agreed.

There can be little doubt that, during the previous two days, Abdul Rahman had already been sounding public opinion in the town. Now he interviewed each of the other four electors separately. It will be remembered that, long before the preaching of Islam, family rivalries had appeared among the descendants of Qusai, the chief who had established the power of Quraish in Mecca. Eventually the privileges of chieftainship had been divided. Beni Abdul Dar had retained the honour of carrying the war banner in battle and of keeping the keys of the kaaba. Beni Umaiya received the hereditary right to command in war, while Beni Hashim were charged with the duties of hospitality. By this settlement, the clan rivalries seemed to have been ended. But it was no accident that, when Muhammad began to preach, he was protected by his relatives of Beni Hashim, while the principal opposition to Islam was led by Abu Sofian, the chief of Beni Umaiya. The family jealousies kept cropping up again and again.

Now once again it was no coincidence that, of the two prospective candidates, one was from Beni Umaiya and one from Beni Hashim. The old pre-Islamic feud threatened to break out once more. All were now of course good Muslims but—*plus ça change plus c'est la même chose*—tribal rivalries still stirred deep and ancient loyalties.

At length the fourth morning dawned and the people of Medina flocked to the Prophet's mosque to hear who had been chosen as the new khalif. Meanwhile, however, nothing had been decided. Abdul Rahman hesitatingly mounted the pulpit and invited the public to express their opinion. Voices immediately called out of the crowd, some in support of Ali and some of

Othman. Soon the rival supporters turned upon one another and loud altercations gave rise to an increasing hubbub. Before long swords and daggers would be drawn, and the blood of the faithful would flow in the Prophet's own mosque. It was a moment for decision. To delay any longer was more dangerous than to take the plunge. Saad ibn abi Waqqas whispered to Abdul Rahman—"Finish your task quickly or the flames of dissension will break out."

Abdul Rahman pulled himself together, and called for silence. "The decision in this matter now rests with me," he cried. Calling upon Ali to stand forth before the crowd, he addressed to him a question. "Do you pledge yourself to abide by the covenant of God, to act according to God's book, to the practice of the Prophet and to the precedent set by his two successors?" "I hope," replied Ali, "that I should do so. I would act for the best, according to my knowledge and capability." Abdul Rahman then called out Othman and addressed to him the same question. "Yes," he replied without hesitation, "I do." Taking Othman by the hand, Abdul Rahman offered a short prayer to God and then saluted him as khalif, the people in the mosque following his example without more ado. It was twenty-four years almost to a day since Muhammad had arrived in Medina, accompanied only by Abu Bekr, fleeing from the persecution of Quraish in Mecca. In those twenty-four years, the world had been turned upside down. The two greatest known empires had been routed and a mighty new world power had occupied their place. No such sudden and unforeseen appearance of a new empire has ever occurred in history. Yet on this, the twenty-fourth anniversary of its inception, the seeds of the dissolution of this empire were already appearing. Quraish had built that empire and Quraish were to destroy it.

* * * * *

The first year of Othman's khalifate passed quietly. In spite of the violent rivalries momentarily roused in Medina on the occasion of his election, the provinces accepted his nomination without protest.

Othman was seventy years old when called to supreme power. Tradition alleges that he had been the fourth male convert to Islam; Abu Bekr, Ali and Zeid ibn Haritha (the Prophet's adopted son killed at Mota) had alone preceded him. During the first persecution, he had been one of those who fled to Abyssinia. Returning to Mecca, he had then joined in the flight to Medina. Of middle height, and well built, he is reputed to have been extremely handsome, though his face was marked with small-pox. His hair, which was slightly wavy, fell to below his ears, while a full beard covered his throat. The Prophet is supposed to have said that Othman resembled the Patriarch Abraham. Although himself of Beni Umaiya, his mother had been the great grand-daughter of Hashim and thus, even if remotely, he was connected with both the rival clans of Quraish, the hostility of which to one another was to tear the Muslim world apart.

When, as a young man, he first became a convert, his uncle had abused him and, tying him up with a rope, had vowed that he would never let him go until he renounced the new-fangled notions which Muhammad was putting about. But Othman endured the persecution with fortitude, repeating that he would never forsake or abandon the faith he had adopted, until his uncle eventually released him.

When the Prophet undertook the summer raid on Tebook [2] and the Muslims were in distress for means of transport in the great heat, Othman from his own resources provided no less than 960 camels and 50 horses, an immense contribution in the early penurious days. Muhammad is alleged to have promised him Paradise as a reward for his generosity. On another occasion the Prophet promised Othman that he himself would meet him in heaven, a promise which the old khalif was to recall in poignant terms immediately before his death. In the critical days at Hudeibiya,[3] when the Muslims were hourly expecting an attack by the people of Mecca, it was the kind and generous Othman who was sent into the city to negotiate with Quraish. Perhaps the highest praise of all bestowed on him by the Apostle was the remark that even the angels stood abashed before Othman, a statement which seems to suggest a native innocence, a lack of sophistication, perhaps a certain naïveté in relation to the selfish and greedy purposes of men.

The surviving anecdotes and traditions give an impression of the new khalif as a pleasant, handsome and venerable figure, a man sincerely religious, modest and amicable. At the beginning, he was more popular than the stern and rigid Umar had been, for Othman was genial, lenient, and affectionate in his manners, when dealing with his friends and subjects.

It was his misfortune, however, to come of the house of Umaiya, which, prior to the rise of Islam, had been the wealthiest and most influential clan of Quraish. In addition to the hereditary leadership of the Meccans in war, the family included most of the big merchants, accustomed to money and comfort, in so far as such things existed in seventh-century Mecca. His contribution to the Tebook campaign proved that Othman himself was rich, even before Islam. The prosperity of Beni Umaiya perhaps made them worldly and materialistic. They were, as we have seen, under the leadership of Abu Sofian, the bitterest opponents of Muhammad, until Mecca itself surrendered to him. Then the Umaiyids quickly changed sides. The sons of Abu Sofian obtained important positions. Yezeed was a military commander. Muawiya, his second son, became Muhammad's secretary. Abu Sofian fought in the Muslim armies as a volunteer. Many of Beni Umaiya moved to Medina, in order to be at hand to secure lucrative positions in the now rapidly expanding empire. Yezeed, the eldest son of Abu Sofian, had been appointed governor of Syria by Umar after the death of Abu Ubaida. When Yezeed also died, he had been succeeded by his brother, Muawiya. In spite of the admission of some Umaiyids to important posts, however, the prestige attaching to Beni Hashim, as the Prophet's family, still gave them the first place. Now with the rise of a member of their own clan to the khalifate, Beni Umaiya might hope to regain once more the position which they had occupied before the appearance of the Apostle of God.

[2] Page 99. [3] Page 87.

## *NOTABLE DATES*

Assassination of Umar ibn al Khattab — 3rd November, 644

## *PERSONALITIES*

Umar ibn al Khattab, the second khalif.
Abu Lulu, the Persian, his assassin.
Othman ibn Affan, elected the third khalif.

## *THE ELECTORAL COMMITTEE*

Ali ibn abi Talib, Muhammad's cousin.
Othman ibn Affan, elected khalif.
Zubair ibn al Awwam, the hero of Babylon in Egypt.
Saad ibn abi Waqqas, the conqueror of Iraq.
Abdul Rahman ibn Auf, who was offered the nomination by the dying Umar but refused it.

# XVI

## *Othman*

Othman was the first who embellished the mosque at Medina, the first who established a constabulary. The first occasion in which dissension fell among the people and some accused others of error, was in his time. I note that there remain of the things in which he was foremost, that he was the first of his people who emigrated with his family for the sake of God, and the first who united the people upon one text in the reading of the Qoran. That the first laxity that showed itself in Medina when the world waxed prosperous and the fatness of men reached its height was in his time.

JALLAL AL DEEN SUYUTI, *History of the Khalifs*

# XVI

# OTHMAN

WHEN Umar ibn al Khattab was assassinated in 644, the new Arab Empire was almost everywhere at peace. Only in Persia was fighting still going on, in the form of slow expansion on a number of different and widely separated fronts. For although King Yezdegird's last army had been destroyed at Nehawand, local resistance continued in a number of different, chiefly mountainous, areas. According to Suyuti, Rei in Persia was taken in the first year of Othman's khalifate, having apparently been captured by the Arabs after the Battle of Nehawand, then lost and then retaken once more.

The passes through the Taurus mountains, which now separated the Byzantine dominions from the Arab province of Syria, do not appear to have been the scene of major operations at this stage. Indeed Heraclius, at the time of his abandonment of Syria, ordered the evacuation and destruction of a number of towns in the area, in order to establish a belt of no-man's land between the two empires. Further north, however, heavy fighting took place in Armenia, where rebellions had broken out on receipt of the news of Umar's assassination. Muawiya, governor of Syria, was instructed to send a column of 6,000—some say 8,000—men into Armenia under Habib ibn Maslama. Shortly afterwards, the governor of Kufa was also ordered to send a force of 6,000, who duly set out north-westwards from Mosul. The columns established contact but some friction occurred between the two commanders, concerning the chief command and the division of the loot. As a result, the columns separated again, that from Syria continuing northwards to the borders of Georgia. Many towns and villages came to terms with the invaders, agreeing to pay tribute and poll-tax on the usual terms. The city of Tiflis concluded an agreement of the same nature and the Arabs found themselves confronted by the snow-covered barrier of the Caucasus.

Meanwhile the column from Iraq had fought its way northward to the eastern end of the Caucasus, just south of the modern Baku. Somewhere in this area, however, they suddenly found themselves confronted by the Khazars. The Muslim force, 4,000 strong, was exterminated. Surrounded by overwhelming numbers, they fought on until one by one all were killed, crying *Allahu akbar* and "There is no god but God" until their last breath.

In spite of such set-backs and regrettable incidents, the Arabs in the years 644, 645 and 646 had established a considerable measure of control, almost up to the Caucasus, and continued regularly to appoint governors to Armenia and Adharbaijan. The frontier position, however, continued to be somewhat precarious, particularly in so far as the Khazars were concerned. These last were a race of Turkish origin, who, early in the seventh century, had controlled the whole area from the Crimea to the Caspian. The Khakan of the Khazars had assisted Heraclius with a contingent of 40,000 men in his campaigns against Chosroes Parwiz.[1] When the Arabs arrived in Armenia after Nehawand in 642, the Khazars co-operated with the Byzantines in an attempt to defend Armenia. The war between the Arabs and the Khazars was to last for nearly a century with many ups and downs, until, in 737, the Khakan submitted and professed the Muslim faith. Thereafter all the peoples of the Caucasus were subject to the Arab Empire until its collapse.

* * * * *

While operations continued in Armenia and Persia, a dramatic crisis suddenly arose in Egypt. We have already noted that Umar ibn al Khattab had severely rebuked Amr ibn al Aasi, the conqueror of Egypt, and had demanded of him that he extort more taxes from that country. One of the khalif's last acts before his assassination had been to send a certain Abdulla ibn abi Sarh to Egypt to supervise the collection of taxes, thereby emphasizing his suspicions of Amr ibn al Aasi.

This Abdulla ibn abi Sarh had already a dubious history. He was the foster-brother of Othman, had been a comparatively early convert and had migrated to Medina during the Meccan persecution. Apparently better educated than most of Quraish, he had been employed by the Prophet to transcribe passages of the Qoran. For reasons which we do not know, however, he fled from Medina back to Mecca, where he apostasized, and made derogatory remarks about Muhammad, casting doubts on the divinity of his mission. In one who had been so intimate as to receive the Prophet's confidences, such treachery provoked intense resentment. When the Muslims took Mecca, Abdulla ibn abi Sarh was one of the few people whom Muhammad excluded from the amnesty. He lay in concealment for a time and was eventually pardoned through the warm intercession of his foster-brother, Othman, though the Apostle himself admitted that he had delayed his pardon in the hope that one of the Muslims would kill him. This was the man sent by Umar ibn al Khattab to extract more taxes from the Egyptians. Undoubtedly a capable man, he was probably an efficient tax collector, though suspect from the religious angle. It was remarkable that Umar ibn al Khattab should appoint such a man, for he had removed various commanders-in-chief from their posts on the grounds of religious laxity. Presumably ibn abi Sarh was a man of quite outstanding ability, particularly at what we should call "office work", a quality rare indeed among the early Muslims.

Shortly after making this appointment, the Khalif Umar was assassinated, with the result that the prospects of ibn abi Sarh changed immediately. For Othman, the new khalif, was his foster-brother, one of whose first actions was the summary dismissal of Amr ibn al Aasi, and the appointment of ibn abi Sarh to be sole governor and commander-in-chief of Egypt. The new governor had been appointed with instructions to get more money out of the Egyptians and he set to work with a will. Soon the cries of distress arose from the victims. A group of leading citizens of Alexandria wrote secretly

[1] Page 77.

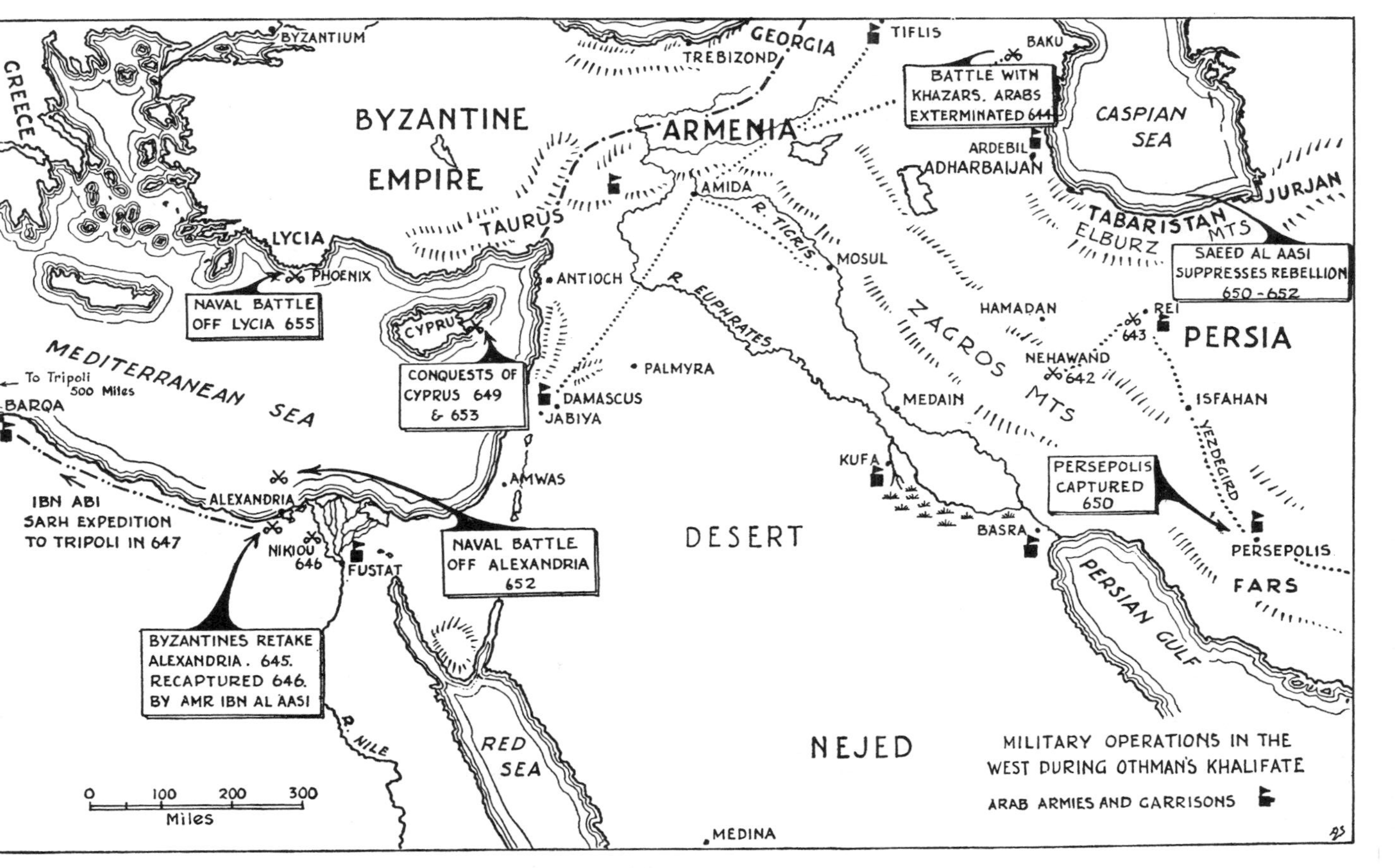

BYZANTIUM
GREECE
GEORGIA
TREBIZOND
TIFLIS
BAKU
BATTLE WITH KHAZARS. ARABS EXTERMINATED 644
CASPIAN SEA
BYZANTINE EMPIRE
ARMENIA
ARDEBIL
ADHARBAIJAN
AMIDA
JURJAN
TAURUS
LYCIA
TABARISTAN MTS
ELBURZ
R. TIGRIS
PHOENIX
MOSUL
SAEED AL AASI SUPPRESSES REBELLION 650 - 652
ANTIOCH
NAVAL BATTLE OFF LYCIA 655
R. EUPHRATES
HAMADAN
CYPRUS
REI
643
PERSIA
MEDITERRANEAN SEA
ZAGROS MTS
NEHAWAND
642
To Tripoli 500 Miles
CONQUESTS OF CYPRUS 649 & 653
PALMYRA
DAMASCUS
JABIYA
ISFAHAN
BARQA
MEDAIN
YEZDEGIRD
KUFA
AMWAS
PERSEPOLIS CAPTURED 650
IBN ABI SARH EXPEDITION TO TRIPOLI IN 647
ALEXANDRIA
BASRA
DESERT
PERSEPOLIS
NIKIOU 646
FUSTAT
NAVAL BATTLE OFF ALEXANDRIA 652
PERSIAN GULF
FARS
BYZANTINES RETAKE ALEXANDRIA. 645. RECAPTURED 646. BY AMR IBN AL AASI
R. NILE
RED SEA
NEJED
MILITARY OPERATIONS IN THE WEST DURING OTHMAN'S KHALIFATE
ARAB ARMIES AND GARRISONS
0
100
200
300
Miles
MEDINA


Map xxx

to the Emperor Constans at Byzantium, begging him to reconquer the country and save them from the oppression of the Arabs.

The Byzantines held command of the sea and the task of invading Egypt was therefore not an impossible one. A large fleet was accordingly prepared with the greatest possible secrecy. No Arab vessels sailed the Mediterranean and no warning reached Egypt of what was afoot. Suddenly one morning in the autumn of 645, a fleet of three hundred ships was seen bearing down upon the harbour of Alexandria. The troops were soon disembarked, and the Arab garrison, only 1,000 strong, put to the sword. The Byzantines manned the walls and Alexandria once again acknowledged its allegiance to Caesar. Not content with awaiting the inevitable Arab counter-attack, the Byzantine forces emerged from the town and overran a large part of the lower delta. Having thus triumphantly achieved his first objective, Manuel, the Byzantine commander, seems to have had no definite plan for the second stage of the re-conquest. The Arab historians refer to him as Manuel the eunuch. Was he perhaps some palace favourite rather than a professional soldier? (Yet in the time of Justinian, Narses the eunuch had shown himself a great general.) However that may be, the Byzantine army scattered over the delta, plundering and requisitioning supplies, instead of preparing for the coming struggle. Perhaps their intention was to provision Alexandria for a siege, though this would best have been done by sea.

No sooner did this crisis arise in Egypt than Othman immediately re-appointed Amr ibn al Aasi as commander-in-chief and despatched him post haste to Egypt. If the Byzantines had marched straight to Babylon and Fustat at the head of the delta, they might have conquered the new capital of Egypt before Amr could reach the seat of war. Alternatively, they might have established a fortress at Alexandria which could have been constantly reinforced from the sea and made impregnable, until the opportunity arose to reconquer Egypt.

Again and again in all the early Arab campaigns, we have seen how anxious they always were to fight in open country and how skilfully they drew their enemies from their fortifications or out of close country and defeated them in the desert. Amr ibn al Aasi was an efficient exponent of these tactics. If the undefeated Byzantine army had remained behind the walls of Alexandria, the city could never have been taken, or not at least until the Arabs could gain command of the sea. Accordingly Amr appears to have delayed in Babylon, in order to draw the Byzantines southwards. Eventually when they reached Nikiou, nearly 100 miles from Alexandria, they encountered Amr ibn al Aasi at the head of perhaps some 15,000 Arabs. A sanguinary battle followed, the outcome of which remained long in doubt. Eventually the Byzantines gave way. As soon as they commenced to retire, their retreat became a rout and they eventually reached Alexandria in complete confusion after fleeing for 100 miles with the Arabs in pursuit. Nevertheless they succeeded in re-entering the city and closing the gates. Amr was obliged to camp on the east side, the only direction free from lakes and canals, and impotently to survey the walls and towers of the city.

The exact manner in which Alexandria was taken on this second occasion

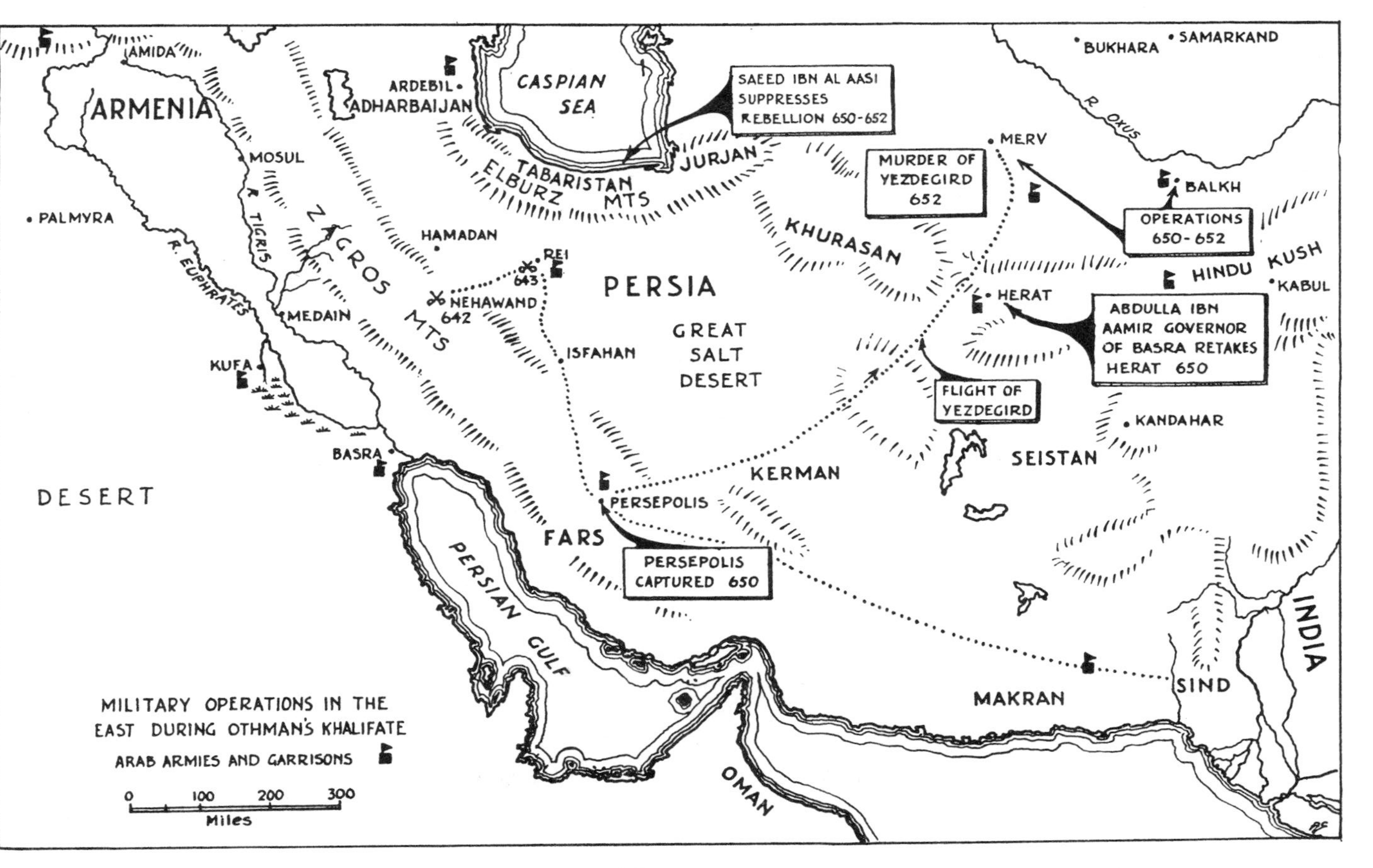
AMIDA
ARMENIA
ARDEBIL
ADHARBAIJAN
CASPIAN SEA
SAEED IBN AL AASI SUPPRESSES REBELLION 650-652
BUKHARA
SAMARKAND
R. OXUS
MERV
MURDER OF YEZDEGIRD 652
BALKH
OPERATIONS 650-652
MOSUL
TABARISTAN
ELBURZ MTS
JURJAN
PALMYRA
R. TIGRIS
ZAGROS MTS
HAMADAN
REI
643
KHURASAN
HINDU KUSH
KABUL
R. EUPHRATES
NEHAWAND 642
PERSIA
HERAT
ABDULLA IBN AAMIR GOVERNOR OF BASRA RETAKES HERAT 650
MEDAIN
ISFAHAN
GREAT SALT DESERT
KUFA
FLIGHT OF YEZDEGIRD
KANDAHAR
SEISTAN
BASRA
KERMAN
DESERT
PERSEPOLIS
FARS
PERSEPOLIS CAPTURED 650
PERSIAN GULF
INDIA
SIND
MAKRAN
OMAN
MILITARY OPERATIONS IN THE EAST DURING OTHMAN'S KHALIFATE
ARAB ARMIES AND GARRISONS
0
100
200
300
Miles

Map XXXI

is still open to doubt. The most probable account seems to be that the commander responsible for one of the gates communicated secretly with Amr, offering to open the gate to the Arabs. Such an act of treachery might conceivably have been perpetrated by a Copt, whose relatives, or who himself, had been a victim of the religious persecutions carried out by the Byzantine government. The Arabs burst into the city which was given up to massacre, plunder and arson. When half the city had been destroyed, Amr ibn al Aasi gave the order to halt the carnage. A portion of the Byzantine army reached their ships and put out to sea, but many were killed, including Manuel, their commander. This second capture of Alexandria took place some time in the summer of 646. The campaign had lasted about nine months.

The fact that Alexandria was taken twice, the first time as a result of the negotiations with Cyrus, the second time by assault, has confused historians almost as much as the two battles of the Yarmouk. The question whether any place submitted to the Muslims by agreement or by conquest was to be of great legal importance for generations to come. Where any country or city submitted to the Arabs voluntarily, an agreement was signed prescribing the conditions and the amount of the tribute. These terms were observed with scrupulous honesty by the conquerors. Where, on the other hand, a place had been taken by assault, the inhabitants retained no rights but were the slaves of the victors. Even centuries later, when the whole empire had long been consolidated, the rights of a certain city or province could only be ascertained if it were known whether it had originally submitted through negotiation or been conquered by armed force. The question was often by no means easy to answer. At the time of the conquests, the Arabs kept few records and were not interested in history. Many places had submitted by negotiation but had afterwards rebelled and been reconquered by force. The consequent disputes were to keep Muslim jurists busy for centuries to come.

The Copts appear, to some extent if not completely, to have remained neutral during this second capture of Alexandria by the Arabs. Their patriarch, Benjamin, is said to have secured an interview with Amr ibn al Aasi, and to have emphasized to him the fact that Manuel had been supported only by the Orthodox or Byzantine Church and not by the Copts.[2] Amr caused the walls of Alexandria, at least on the eastern side, to be destroyed, to prevent the city ever again closing its gates upon the Arabs.

An interesting incident is here worthy of mention. After the Arab recapture of Alexandria, a number of Coptic villages complained to Amr ibn al Aasi that they had not joined in the rebellion but that, on the contrary, the Byzantine army from Alexandria had plundered them and had requisitioned food from them without repayment. The original treaty signed with Amr after the first surrender of Egypt had, they pointed out, imposed tribute upon them, but the Arabs had in return undertaken to protect them. They had not, however, been protected during Manuel's invasion, and, in consequence, they had suffered heavy losses. Amr immediately admitted the justice of their complaint and ordered compensation to be paid for their losses. It is just to record that the Arabs, at this period, were extremely conscientious

[2] I have followed Butler in this matter.

about the mutual obligations of their surrender treaties with the conquered peoples. They demanded the full payment of tribute and poll-tax, but they also recognized the obligation which rested on them to protect the people who thereby came under their guardianship.

It is extraordinary to record that Othman, having dismissed Amr ibn al Aasi soon after he became khalif and reinstated him when the Byzantines re-invaded Egypt, dismissed him again as soon as the victory was won and the danger past. It is true that he first suggested to Amr that he remain as commander-in-chief only, Abdulla ibn abi Sarh being responsible for financial control and taxation. Perhaps to the modern European this may seem a legitimate division of functions. It must be remembered, however, that Amr had previously been sole governor and had himself fixed and collected the taxes; that he had been blamed for not extorting enough money and that ibn abi Sarh had been sent with the avowed object of extracting more. With Amr's immense prestige, as having twice conquered Egypt, it is obvious that the Copts, when obliged to pay more taxes than Amr had imposed on them, would have hastened to complain to him. It would seem inevitable, therefore, that friction would have arisen between ibn abi Sarh and the commander-in-chief. The answer given by Amr ibn al Aasi to the khalif's suggestion is typical of the pungency of bedouin wit. "If I accepted your proposal," he wrote to the khalif, "I should be like a man who was told to hold on to the horns of a cow while somebody else milked her." On receipt of this reply, Othman dismissed his victorious general from all his appointments, and for the second time nominated ibn abi Sarh governor and commander-in-chief. It will be remembered that the new governor was the khalif's foster-brother. Butler is perplexed by what he considers to be the contradictory estimates of the character of ibn abi Sarh which have come down to us. Nawawi, he notices, called him the most intelligent and the noblest of Quraish. Tabari, on the other hand, said that "of all the agents of Othman, the worst was Abdulla the governor of Egypt." Yet the two descriptions are not necessarily contradictory. For ibn abi Sarh was undoubtedly an extremely capable man, and, at the same time, of the tribe of Quraish, the family of Umaiya and foster-brother of the ruling khalif. Such qualifications might well entitle him to be called the noblest of the Arabs. Yet his extortion of ever heavier taxes from the unfortunate Egyptians might well justify Tabari in calling him the worst of the provincial governors appointed by Othman.

Finally it will be remembered that the former khalif, Umar ibn al Khattab, had accused Amr ibn al Aasi of making money for himself and had sent a representative to confiscate half the property of the conquerer of Egypt. In view of these suspicions of the honesty of the soldier, the despatch of a more educated secretary and accountant might be thought a wise measure. Yet Butler quotes Severus, an outside and non-Arab historian, as saying of ibn abi Sarh that "he loved money and collected treasure for himself in Egypt." Perhaps neither the general nor the civilian was entirely innocent of lining his own pocket. Nevertheless the very conquest of Egypt had been due to the initiative of Amr ibn al Aasi. Moreover, he had twice conquered it, in both cases largely through his personal leadership. The Arabs were not as yet familiar with the more subtle methods of modern governments, who remove an unwanted official by giving him an honourable and well-paid sinecure in some other department. The summary dismissal of Amr ibn al Aasi was to cost the Arabs a heavy price.

Desirous perhaps to achieve a military reputation equal to that of his ousted rival, the new governor of Egypt prepared in 647 for a campaign in North Africa. His foster-brother the khalif despatched a contingent of 20,000 men from Medina, including many of the Prophet's surviving companions, together with such noble volunteers as a son of Abu Bekr, a son of Umar the late khalif, a son of Abbas, the Prophet's uncle, and a son of Zubair, one of the inner council which had elected Othman to the khalifate. This army was joined at Fustat by an equal contingent of 20,000 men from the army of Egypt and ibn abi Sarh swept across the Western Desert (as we have learned to call it) with 40,000 warriors. The Greeks and the Romans had complained of the difficulty of communications in the deserts of North Africa, as did the British, the Germans and the Italians in the Second World War, but to the Arabs, with their great military ally the camel, the crossing of the Western Desert presented few problems. On the march they rode their camels, leading their mares by long leading reins. The camel was able, in addition to its rider and his kit, to carry both forage and water for the horse.

After the first surrender of Alexandria, Amr ibn al Aasi, it will be remembered, had carried his arms into North Africa and had accepted the surrender of Tripoli. After his departure, however, the city seems to have returned to its Byzantine allegiance, for on this expedition, ibn abi Sarh is reported to have laid siege to it once more.

The capital of North Africa was the ancient city of Carthage, where Gregory, the Byzantine governor, held his court. His jurisdiction extended, at least in theory, from Tripoli to Tangier. Assembling an army, he marched to the relief of Tripoli. The Arab historians, who were addicted to exaggeration, particularly in the numbers of their enemies, claim that he led a force of 120,000 men. To move, water and feed an army of such size in North Africa, with the means of transport available in the seventh century, would seem an impossible task. We might perhaps be nearer the truth if we were to estimate both armies as consisting of between 20,000 and 30,000 men.

The Arabs, still unskilful at siege warfare, were doubtless delighted at the prospect of an open battle in a desert plain, precisely the kind of engagement which had won for them all their greatest victories. As the Byzantines were still in command of these seas, they could doubtless have maintained themselves in Carthage, Tripoli and the coastal cities. But the Arabs were ravaging the plains south of Carthage, and the Berbers, who formed the bulk of the country people who suffered from these raids, doubtless insisted on an immediate battle. As we saw in an earlier chapter, the Arabs on the Euphrates had regularly used mosquito raids to compel an enemy, who wished to act on the defensive, to come out and fight.

The battle, which took place at Sufetula, the modern Sbeitla, lasted for several days. Romantic stories are told of how Gregory sought to fire the enthusiasm of the young men of his army by promising the hand of his beautiful daughter to the soldier who should kill ibn abi Sarh, the Arab commander. We should perhaps be mistaken to think of the latter as merely an efficient financier, for he is said also to have been an excellent horseman. He may, however, have been a rationalist who, like Saad ibn abi Waqqas at Qadasiya, did not believe it to be the duty of a commander-in-chief to lead the charge in person. He is alleged to have retired to his tent when he heard that Gregory had offered so tempting a prize for his head.

Zubair will be remembered as one of the Apostle's earliest converts, the man who had been first up the assault ladder at the taking of Babylon, and a member of the committee nominated by Umar ibn al Khattab to elect his successor. Abdulla, the son of Zubair, is alleged to have been present at this battle, to have protested at the absence of ibn abi Sarh from the front line, and to have urged him to turn the tables on Gregory by promising the hand of the latter's daughter to any Muslim who killed the Byzantine commander.

Eventually the Arabs resorted to a stratagem. It is remarkable how often the Arab historians mention such manoeuvres, which always seem to have succeeded. The Arabians were—and are—an extremely intelligent people, of particularly nimble wit. Moreover they were not an old army hidebound by tradition, but rather fought by the light of nature. The commanders of the Byzantine and Persian armies may well have had rigid ideas of how war should be conducted, and may thus have been incapable of adapting their tactics to a new enemy and different terrain.

The two armies had already been engaged for several days. The mornings and the evenings were daily passed in what must have been skirmishing, individual combats and manoeuvres, but during the noon heat of the day both sides withdrew to their lines. One day the usual procedure was followed at midday, both armies retiring to their camps to rest and to water their men and their horses. The Byzantines had as usual removed the bridles of their horses and had taken off their own armour, when the Arabs delivered a sudden and unexpected charge. The enemy was thrown into confusion and a disastrous rout ensued, during which Gregory himself was killed, possibly by the hand of Abdulla ibn Zubair. Ibn abi Sarh appears to have made the mistake of sending the son of Zubair to carry tidings of the victory to Medina, thereby enabling him to attribute the victory to the advice which he had given and to claim to have himself killed the Byzantine general. Unfortunately accounts differ as to the ultimate fate of Gregory's beautiful daughter.

Ibn abi Sarh returned in triumph to Egypt, laden with loot and leading into slavery many thousands of captives. Yet the conquest was not consolidated, nor does any attempt appear to have been made to establish an administration in Tripolitania. The campaign, however, did not add to the prestige of Othman, the new khalif, but rather the reverse. It will be remembered that Muhammad himself had ruled that one-fifth of all loot taken in battle should belong to the treasury, the remainder being divided among the troops. The khalif now permitted ibn abi Sarh to retain for himself one-fifth of the treasury's fifth, the remainder being sent to Medina. Not only so, but when the remainder reached that city, the misguided Othman handed it all over for disposal to Merwan, his cousin. These unsavoury transactions were to play an important part in the troubles to come.

* * * * *

Muawiya, the son of old Abu Sofian, had, it will be remembered, been appointed by Umar ibn al Khattab to be governor of Syria. Muawiya was a man of quite extraordinary capabilities. Faced with the problem of defending Syria from the Byzantines, he realized that there was little to be feared from an invasion by land. But many of the wealthiest cities and the most fertile provinces lay on the shores of the Mediterranean. The inhabitants of the coastal districts, moreover, had never been infiltrated by Arab influence, as had the peoples along the fringes of the desert. The Mediterranean had, for many centuries, been the principal highway of the Roman and then of the Byzantine Empire. All the Roman provinces had lain on its shores, with the sole exception of Northern France (as we call it) and Britain. For six centuries, Roman power had been based on naval command of the Mediterranean. No Arab sail had yet been seen on the middle sea. As long as the Byzantine fleet could sail that sea unopposed, the coastline of Syria, Palestine and Egypt would never be safe from raids, or even from invasion.

Muawiya had been one of the first to appreciate these facts and to write to Umar ibn al Khattab for sanction to build an Arab fleet. The old khalif, who, as we have seen, believed that whatever was good for a camel was good for an Arab, had been taken aback by this novel proposal, and had written to the conqueror of Egypt, Amr ibn al Aasi, for a description of naval operations. Ibn al Aasi, with his usual pungency, compared in his reply a party of men at sea on a ship, to a group of insects clinging to a twig which swung to and fro in the wind. The cautious khalif was horrified at the idea of placing his noble Arab warriors in so precarious, not to say undignified, a position, and wrote immediately to Muawiya categorically forbidding him to embark any Arabs upon the sea.

Now, in the khalifate of Othman, ibn abi Sarh, his foster-brother, likewise wrote urging the formation of a fleet. Muawiya, also an Umaiyid, returned to the charge and Othman, after some hesitation, gave his permission. Ibn abi Sarh and Muawiya, both men of practical and penetrating intelligence, appear to have co-operated in the task. The proposal for the first combined operation had come from the latter. Cyprus, he claimed, was so near to the Syrian coast that it was almost possible to hear the barking of the dogs. It is interesting to note that when Othman's approval was solicited, he replied that he had seen the refusal which Umar had previously sent to Muawiya concerning naval operations. If Umar, in his later years, kept copies of his correspondence, we have already progressed from the days when orders regarding major political events were delivered verbally. Othman, then, having read the previous correspondence, gave his half-hearted consent. The expedition, he said, could proceed, on condition that all the men be volunteers and that Muawiya take his wife with him. Presumably this quaint stipulation was intended to deter Muawiya from undertaking too rash an enterprise. In 649, ibn abi Sarh joined the Syrian armada with a fleet which he had organized in Egypt, the sailors of which were Egyptians but the fighting men Arabs. (Apparently the task of the sailors was merely to row and to navigate but not to fight.) No sooner did the Arabs land on the island than the Byzantine governor offered to surrender, before any fighting had taken place. A curious agreement was signed between the two parties. The Cypriots agreed to pay the Arabs an annual tribute of 7,200 dinars, the same amount which they were already paying to Byzantium. A clause was included, however, which left to the people of Cyprus the right to continue payment to the Byzantine government at the same time. Thus, after the signature of the treaty, the Cypriots were paying tribute simultaneously to Byzantium and to Medina. Other conditions recognized the neutrality of the island in the event of hostilities between the Arabs and Byzantium, but laid upon the Cypriots the duty of keeping the Arabs informed of the naval movements of the Byzantines. Presumably the complete surprise achieved by Manuel in his attack on Alexandria had impressed the Arab leaders with the need for intelligence regarding the movements of the enemy's fleets.

Let us for the moment continue the account of the naval operations, even if they be out of strict chronology. In 652, three years after the conquest of Cyprus, the Byzantines put a large fleet to sea and appeared off Alexandria, presumably with the object of once more capturing the city. On this occasion, however, the Arabs had obtained prior information, and ibn abi Sarh had collected every available ship in Egypt or along the neighbouring shores of North Africa. In the evening the wind dropped, and both fleets passed the night at anchor off shore. The next morning a furious battle took place. The fleets intermingled, the ships grappled one another and a desperate hand-to-hand struggle ensued with swords and daggers. At length the Byzantines broke off the action and, unable to make a landing, were obliged to sail away baffled to the north. The Arab fleet, however, made no attempt to give chase. The days were past when the Byzantine fleet could ride the sea unchallenged, and make descents on the coast wherever it wished. Ibn abi Sarh may well have been avaricious in accumulating private wealth and extortionate in his taxation of the unfortunate Egyptians, but both in his battle with Gregory in North Africa, in the building of the fleet and in the naval action off Alexandria, he had shown himself to be a capable leader and an able man.

It will be remembered that when Muawiya conquered Cyprus, he signed an agreement with the Cypriots to the effect that the latter would remain neutral in the event of renewed hostilities between the Arabs and Byzantium. They now appear to have been accused of having given assistance to the Byzantine fleet. As a result, Muawiya, in 653, invaded Cyprus for the second time with a large armament. The country was treated as hostile, an unspecified number of the people were killed, while many more were carried away into slavery. After this punitive action, however, the treaty was renewed on the original terms, but a garrison of 12,000 Arabs was left behind on the island.

In 655, another decisive naval battle took place at Phoenix on the coast of Lycia, at which the Byzantine emperor himself was present. The Arabs called this engagement the Battle of the Masts. After heavy fighting, the Byzantines were worsted and drew off. By these actions, the principal credit for which must be given to Muawiya, Byzantine naval supremacy was destroyed. Their loss of the command of the sea was perhaps the most grievous blow suffered by the feeble successors of Heraclius. If the old emperor had been still alive, he could scarcely have accepted it so tamely. It was his naval command of the Black Sea which had enabled him for four years to maintain an army in Armenia while the Persian army was actually outside Constantinople. As long as the Byzantine Empire enjoyed command of the Mediterranean, the reconquest of Syria, Palestine and Egypt remained possible. With the establishment of Arab naval supremacy, the loss of the conquered provinces became final, as Muawiya had so clearly foreseen.

* * * * *

The whole conquest of Persia had been effected during the khalifate of Umar. Just as a general rebellion in Arabia had followed the death of Muhammad, so the murder of Umar ibn al Khattab was the signal for popular risings all over Persia. Although Yezdegird was still alive, his government and authority had vanished, with the result that the local insurrections were unco-ordinated for lack of any central authority. In spite, however, of this lack of co-operation, the rebellions for several years challenged the whole structure of Arab domination. Throughout the years from the accession of Othman in 644 until 649, confused fighting continued all over Persia, the Arabs for the time failing to achieve much success.

The governor of Kufa was responsible for the conduct of military operations in North Persia from Jurjan to Adharbaijan, while the governor of Basra controlled South and East Persia up to the Oxus. In 644, 10,000 men of the Kufa army were on active service in North Persia, 6,000 of them in Adharbaijan and 4,000 in Rei. The total strength of the Kufa army at the time was 40,000. Every man did one year of active service in every four years. Thus by a system of rotation, a force of 10,000 men was always maintained at the front. The pacification of Persia was doubtless delayed by the vicissitudes experienced by the governors of Kufa at the commencement of the khalifate of Othman.

It will be remembered that Umar ibn al Khattab had appointed Mughira ibn Shuba, formerly charged with adultery during his governorship of Basra, to be governor of Kufa. In 645, a year after his election to the khalifate, Othman removed Mughira and reinstated Saad ibn abi Waqqas, the conqueror of Iraq and one of the electors who had made Othman khalif. A year after his appointment, however, Saad quarrelled with Abdulla ibn Masud, one of the oldest of the Companions, who was acting as treasurer of the government funds in Kufa. Saad had apparently borrowed money from the state treasury and was unable, or unwilling, to repay it. An unseemly scandal ensued and Saad was recalled. In his place, the khalif appointed in 646 a half-brother of his own, Waleed ibn Uqba. His father Uqba had been taken prisoner at Bedr fighting for Quraish and had been condemned to death by the Prophet himself. To his anguished cry, "Who will take care of my little children?" Muhammad had replied coldly, "Hell fire." The new governor of Kufa was one of those little children whom the Apostle of God had himself consigned to the infernal regions. Unfortunately also Waleed had a reputation for insobriety. Criticism of Othman's appointments was growing in volume. His foster-brother, ibn abi Sarh, had been made governor of Egypt, though the Prophet had pronounced him worthy of death for apostasy. His half-brother was governor of Kufa, although Muhammad had committed him to hell fire. Muawiya, a cousin of the khalif, was governor of Syria, though it is true that the appointment had been made by Umar and that Muawiya had shown himself remarkably efficient. Yet it was already being said with some bitterness that no one who was not an Umaiyid and a close relative of Othman could any longer hope for high office.

Abu Musa al Ashari, it may be remembered, had long been governor of Basra and had been active in his campaigns against Persian resistance in Fars. But Othman's weakness and nepotism were becoming increasingly apparent and discipline was everywhere breaking down. The troops in Basra now threatened to mutiny and sent a deputation to Medina to demand the removal of their commander-in-chief. Othman weakly consented, Abu Musa was recalled and, after an interlude during which the troops tried to select their own leader, a young man by the name of Abdulla ibn Aamir was appointed. The new governor was not only an Umaiyid and a cousin of Othman, but he was also only twenty-five years old. Soon afterwards Waleed ibn Uqba had to be removed from Kufa on a charge of drunkenness and was replaced by a youth called Saeed ibn al Aasi,[3] who likewise was of Beni Umaiya and whose father had been killed at Bedr fighting against the Muslims.

In spite of the discontent aroused by Othman's appointments, the Arabs began at last to get the better of the rebellions in Persia. The two young Umaiyid governors, Abdulla ibn Aamir in Basra and Saeed ibn al Aasi in Kufa, both raised large armies and marched east. Abdulla ibn Aamir, having first reduced Fars to obedience, advanced through Kerman to Khurasan and, in 650, reconquered Herat and Merv. He then crossed the Oxus, defeated the local insurgents in a great battle, and occupied Balkh. Another column from his army crossed the Hindu Kush and captured Kabul, while others marched through Makran until they reached the banks of the Indus in modern Pakistan.

Meanwhile Saeed ibn al Aasi, not to be outdone, had passed through Rei with the army of Kufa and had suppressed the insurrections in the provinces of Tabaristan and Jurjan at the southern end of the Caspian Sea. Not until 652, eight years after the accession of Othman, was the situation in Persia completely re-established and the frontiers pushed forward to the east and north, beyond those established during the khalifate of Umar ibn al Khattab.

* * * * *

As has already been mentioned, King Yezdegird after the Battle of Nehawand had retired to Rei. When that town was threatened by Nuaim ibn Muqarrin in 643, the king had doubled back to Isfahan, and thence to Istakhr, the ancient Persepolis, in the mountains of Fars. When that city was attacked

[3] No relation of Amr ibn al Aasi, conqueror of Egypt.

by Abu Musa, Yezdegird fled through Kerman and Khurasan to the River Oxus, whence he addressed to the Emperor of China an appeal for help to reconquer his kingdom. The king is alleged to have been well received in Khurasan, the local satrap professing his devotion. Nizak, the khakan of the Turks, visited him and offered him gifts and supplies. But no misfortune seems to have been sufficient to reduce the arrogance of the fugitive monarch. The Turkish chief, after remaining for a month in attendance on the king, asked him for his daughter in marriage. Yezdegird is alleged to have replied, "You are nothing but one of my slaves. How then do you dare to ask for the hand of my daughter?" With an equal want of tact, the king had likewise offended the satrap who had at first received him with honour. The latter accordingly wrote to the Turkish chief, saying, "This is the man who came here as a hunted fugitive. You have helped him in order to have his kingdom restored to him. Now see what he has written to you." In 652, the indignant Turk marched against Yezdegird, whose forces were defeated and scattered and his camp plundered. The king fled to the city of Merv,[4] which closed its gates and refused to admit him. At his wit's end, the unhappy monarch dismounted at the house of a miller, on the banks of the river outside the city. Some accounts allege that the king was killed by the miller, who coveted his crown and ring, which he still carried with him. Others state that the enraged satrap sent some of his men to assassinate him. All agree that his body was stripped and thrown into the river. His son, Fairuz, is believed to have been carried away by the Turks who gave him a wife and among whom he passed his life. Thus miserably ended the last king of the Sassanid race, which had ruled Persia for more than four centuries. The body of the grandson of Chosroes the Conqueror, who had thundered on the very gates of Byzantium, was cast contemptuously into a river. Zoroastrianism, the state religion of the Sassanids, has disappeared except among a remnant of Parsees in Bombay, who still date their calendar from the death of Yezdegird, the last of the Great Kings, on whom rested the Royal Glory of Ormuzd.

With the death of Yezdegird in 652, resistance in Persia virtually came to an end. More than eight centuries were to elapse before Persia again crowned an emperor of her own. Not until 1499 was Shah Ismail, the founder of the Safari dynasty, once again to assert the sovereign independence of his country.

* * * * *

It will be remembered that the sudden expansion of Arab power over Syria, Iraq, Persia and Egypt had confronted the previous khalif, Umar, with a major decision of policy. Was he to allow the victorious Arabs to acquire land and property in the conquered provinces and to intermarry with, and become submerged in, the subject peoples of Iraq, Syria and Egypt? Or was he to keep the Arabs separate and distinct, a herrenvolk, a master race, lording it over defeated and servile peoples? He chose the latter alternative. The agricultural land was left in possession of the conquered, whose duty it was to be to work and to pay taxes. The noble Arab nation was to devote itself solely to the task of fighting against the unbelievers, supported by the taxes paid by the subject races. We have seen Umar's insistent demands for more taxes from

[4] Merv is now in Soviet territory.

the conquered Egyptians. "Milk the camel of the Muslims," he exclaimed, when referring to his policy towards the defeated.

Racially, it was impossible to keep Arab blood undiluted. The Prophet himself had given the right to the Muslims to use women captured from unbelievers as concubines and thousands upon thousands of captive women and girls had been distributed among the conquerors. Many were promoted to the status of wives, and those who presented their owners with sons achieved the position o*f umm walad* or mother, on an equality with free women. Thus within a generation, the "Arabs" in Persia, Syria and Egypt were already racially almost half non-Arab. Socially, however, the Arabs remained an entirely distinct military aristocracy, living in their great cantonments, where, according to Umar's regulation, they were supported by state pensions.

On military expeditions, they still exhibited the patience, the endurance and the reckless bravery which in a quarter of a century had made them lords of a great empire. But during times of idleness, the cantonments seethed with intrigue, faction and turbulence. These schisms arose from three different causes. First, the rank and file of Muslim Arabs and tribesmen were beginning to resent the arrogance of Quraish. This feeling grew rapidly during the khalifate of Othman, largely because he appointed his own relatives to every important post. It is true that, in the days of Abu Bekr and Umar, most of the senior commanders had been Qurashis, but outstanding leaders of other tribes had nevertheless been given commands.

Secondly, Quraish themselves were divided into two parties, Beni Umaiya and Beni Hashim, to one or other of which most of the remaining clans adhered. This rift was greatly widened by Othman's nepotism in favouring his fellow Umaiyids for every position of importance. Religion came powerfully to the aid of Beni Hashim in this matter, for they were the kinsmen of the Prophet himself, whereas Beni Umaiya had been his most bitter opponents. Not only so, but the morals of the Umaiyids still often left a good deal to be desired. Waleed, the khalif's brother, appointed by him to be governor of Kufa, had attempted to lead public prayers when he was drunk.

Thirdly, the basic allegiance of the pre-Islamic Arabs had been to their tribes. Religious enthusiasm had, for a time, caused old loyalties to be forgotten, but among the idle soldiery in the cantonments these schisms began to reappear. Not only was every tribe potentially hostile to every other tribe, but all the tribes were divided into the two great groups of north and south,[5] Adnan versus Qahtan, or under the various other names by which the two divisions were known from time to time.

The seeds of the now increasing indiscipline had, it must be admitted, also been watered by the late khalif, for Umar had set the example of removing his provincial governors or army commanders, merely as the result of complaints from the rank and file. It is difficult to avoid the impression that Umar himself was often jealous and suspicious of his subordinates, and rather welcomed complaints which seemed to justify him in dismissing them. Umar's own personality was so strong, and his probity and self-dedication so obvious that he was able to behave thus without seriously undermining discipline.

[5] Page 37, footnote.

Nevertheless the practice of dismissing commanders, as a result of the complaints of soldiers, was a dangerous precedent, which the unfortunate Othman inherited. And Othman was neither a strong personality nor did his motives always appear entirely disinterested. In addition to his nepotism, he lived like a rich man and was believed to be willing to accept gifts from his provincial governors.

These factors were soon to rend asunder the enthusiastic theocracy founded by the Apostle of God and to place the very existence of the Arab Empire in jeopardy.

## *NOTABLE DATES*

| | |
|---|---|
| Accession of Khalif Othman | 3rd November 644 |
| Byzantine landing in Alexandria | Autumn 645 |
| Recapture of Alexandria by Amr ibn al Aasi | Summer 646 |
| Invasion of Tripoli in Africa by Abdulla ibn abi Sarh | 647 |
| Conquest of Cyprus | 649 |
| Capture of Persepolis | 650 |
| Naval battle off Alexandria | 652 |
| Death of King Yezdegird III | 652 |
| Pacification of Persia | 652 |
| Second invasion of Cyprus by Muawiya | 653 |

## *PERSONALITIES*

Othman ibn Affan, Third Khalif.

Abu Musa al Ashari, Arab commander in Fars.

Abdulla ibn abi Sarh, new Governor of Egypt.

Manuel, Byzantine commander in reoccupation of Alexandria.

Merwan, cousin of the Khalif Othman, received one-fifth of the spoils of Africa.

Muawiya, son of Abu Sofian, Governor of Syria.

Abdulla ibn Aamir } Young Umaiyid governors<br>
Saeed ibn al Aasi } who pacified Persia.

# XVII

## *The Fires Burn Low*

O, what a fall was there, my countrymen!
Then I, and you, and all of us fell down,
Whilst bloody treason flourished over us. . . .
O judgement, thou are fled to brutish beasts,
And men have lost their reason!

SHAKESPEARE, *Julius Caesar*

Othman was slain unjustly, and he who slew him was a wrongdoer, but those who forsook him are to be excused.

JALLAL AL DEEN SUYUTI, *History of the Khalifs*

The feeble temper and declining age of Othman were incapable of sustaining the weight and conquest of empire. . . . The Caliph had lost the only guard of his predecessors, the esteem and confidence of the Moslems. . . . Forsaken by those who had abused his simplicity, the helpless and venerable caliph expected the approach of death.

GIBBON, *Decline and Fall of the Roman Empire*

## XVII

# THE FIRES BURN LOW

IN 654, Othman reached the age of eighty. Ten years earlier, when he had been elected to the khalifate, he had been more popular than his predecessor Umar. There could be no doubt of his genuine piety, or of his devotion to Islam and the Prophet. Moreover, he had, in various ways, proved his religious zeal. The Qoran had been written down in the khalifate of Umar, but subsequently a number of different texts had appeared. Othman gave orders for a fresh revision of the text. When it was completed, such was his energy and diligence that he succeeded in calling in all the other versions in circulation. By this means, the text of the Qoran has come down to us, with scarcely any differences or variations, since the seventh century.

The rising popular indignation was not directed so much against Othman personally as against the governors whom he had appointed. Accused of nepotism, he had replied that God Himself had commanded men to assist their families and that this was precisely what he had done. He even went so far as to criticize Abu Bekr and Umar, who, during their khalifates, had neglected to provide for their relatives. The point is not without interest, for even today it has not been entirely settled. In Britain, doubtless, we consider that loyalty to the state should direct all the actions of its officers, even if such dedication react to the disadvantage of a man's own family. An officer will go abroad for several years' service, perhaps leaving his wife at home neglected, and the education of his children unsupervised. But in the East it has sometimes been claimed that a man's first duty is to his family. Does he not owe a greater obligation to his wife and children, and even his brothers' and sisters' children, than to a remote and impersonal organization? The point may be a moot one, but such arguments could scarcely be applied with equal cogency to the early Islamic theocracy, in which the state was not an impersonal organization but (in theory at least) the chosen instrument of God. No sophistry could justify a man preferring the material interests of his relatives to the service of God Himself.

The manifest impiety of many of Othman's nominees, and the fact that they or their fathers had been the bitterest opponents of the Prophet, offended the many sincerely religious Muslims in Mecca and Medina. The Companions were still fairly numerous, not to mention the men who had fought at Bedr and Uhud, or who had sworn the oath of the tree between the hands of the Apostle of God at Hudeibiya. All these now saw the theocracy of Islam ruled by the Prophet's enemies, who likewise enjoyed those earthly rewards which were the proper guerdon of the faithful believers.

We have already had occasion to mention Abdulla ibn Masud, who had been involved in an altercation in Kufa with Saad ibn abi Waqqas, resulting in the removal of the latter from the governorship. Ibn Masud had been the personal attendant of the Apostle of God in Medina. As a result, he prided himself that he could recite the Qoran exactly as he had heard it recited by Muhammad himself. The revision of the Qoran executed by order of Othman differed in some respects from the version retailed by ibn Masud, who was consequently displeased. To his protests, Othman was alleged to have returned a curt answer, thereby making yet one more influential enemy. At the same time, the khalif's action in ordering all alternative versions to be destroyed was denounced by the factious as sacrilege. The word of God, they alleged, had been committed to the fire.

An example of what the strict Muslims felt about the age of Othman is provided by the case of Abu Dharr. This man had been an early convert and had lived out his life as a genuine ascetic. He now, first in Damascus and then in Medina, began to preach sermons denouncing the demoralization of the times. In Syria, in Iraq, and even in Medina, the leading Muslims lived in marble palaces, surrounded by slaves and concubines, clad in luxurious clothing and indulging in sumptuous food. There can be no doubt that Abu Dharr was right in his charge that all this wealth and luxury was undermining the former hardy and frugal Arab virtues. But the rulers of the empire alleged that his words were inciting the people to revolt, and Othman decreed his banishment to a lonely oasis in Central Arabia. There, two years later, he died in want, and his memory was soon venerated as that of a saint. His tribe, Beni Ghifar, were ready to rise in revolt in order to avenge him.

Othman appears to have been not only weak but perhaps also obstinate and tactless. Though he had been ready to remove many governors and commanders at a hint of dissatisfaction by the public, no pressure was sufficient to persuade him to dismiss his Umaiyid nominees. In some cases, indeed, he seems to have been justified in refusing the demands made upon him, and some of his measures appear to have been beneficial. He devoted much care and expense to the task of enlarging and beautifying the mosques of Mecca and Medina. But in the latter part of his khalifate, nothing he could do seemed to gain public approval.

Meanwhile, sedition was rising fast in Kufa, where, it will be remembered, a young Umaiyid by the name of Saeed had been made governor. The rank and file accused him of arrogance and of supporting the claims of Quraish against the common people. One day, Saeed was alleged to have referred in public to the Suwad, or the rich alluvial plain of Iraq, as "the garden of Quraish", a remark which provoked intense resentment among the veterans, who claimed to have won it with their swords. As a result of a complaint by the governor, the khalif ordered the banishment to Syria of Malik al Ashtar, ringleader of the disaffection, with nine of his associates. At the same time, sedition was rife in the camp of Fustat in Egypt, where ibn abi Sarh, the khalif's foster-brother, was widely hated. Soon messengers and agitators were passing secretly to and fro between the conspirators in Iraq and in Egypt.

It is a remarkable tribute to the personality of Muawiya that while Egypt, Iraq and even Mecca and Medina were seething with revolt, everything was quiet and peaceful in Syria. Muawiya was himself an Umaiyid and the son of old Abu Sofian. Most of the abuse lavished on the other Umaiyids, on the subject of their previous opposition to the Apostle of God, had been true also of him and of his father. But the Arabs, turbulent and democratic as they have always been, are yet amenable to personal rule. When they find a leader whom they judge to be worthy to command them, they will render to him ungrudging loyalty and service. The whole picture of the rising sedition amongst the Arabs against Othman is one with which our own age has become all too familiar, the bazaar rumours, the violent demagogues, the infiltration of agitators, the distortion of every action taken by the government, just or oppressive, wise or foolish, into propaganda material against the authorities.

Alarmed at the rapid spread of disaffection, Saeed, the governor of Kufa, rode, early in 655, to Medina to consult the khalif. In his absence, Malik al Ashtar, released from his banishment in Syria, suddenly appeared once again in Kufa, where he lashed the people into fury with his speeches. A banner was hoisted, the insurgents rallied round and vowed that the governor would not be allowed to come back. When Saeed returned, the rebels rode out of the city a thousand strong, met him on the battlefield of Qadasiya and threatened to kill him if he attempted to enter Kufa. The governor was glad to escape with his life and return post haste to Medina. Othman, now eighty-one or eighty-two, was terrified by the revolt and decided at once to give way. Saeed was dismissed and the veteran Abu Musa, whom he had previously himself de-graded from the governorship of Basra, was now sent to allay the ferment in Kufa. Meanwhile, a deputation arrived from the army in Egypt, to lodge complaints against ibn abi Sarh. Othman is alleged to have written to the latter a letter threatening him with dismissal and ordering him to behave better. But the governor took no notice, and on the contrary arrested those who had gone to complain and put their leader to death.

The leaders of Islam in Medina had been lavish in their advice to the khalif, either to hear and relieve the public grievances, or to suppress the rising sedition by force. Now they seem to have despaired of the poor, irresolute old man, and abandoned him to his fate. The very inner council who had elected him, Ali the Prophet's cousin, Zubair who had scaled the walls of Babylon, Talha, Aisha the favourite wife of the Apostle—all, if they did not encourage the revolt, at least did nothing to oppose it. Amr ibn al Aasi, twice conqueror of Egypt, who had been so summarily dismissed by Othman in favour of his foster-brother, was busy spreading disaffection in Medina.

Othman attended the pilgrimage of 655 in Mecca. The opportunity was taken to summon all the provincial governors, in order to consult them on the deterioration of the situation. As has occurred again and again in our times, everyone could sense the general feeling of disaffection, but no actual rebellion had yet occurred and the conspirators had hitherto been working underground. At the conference of provincial governors, ibn abi Sarh, the "tax-collector" of Egypt, gave it as his opinion that all men love money. "Use the wealth which is at your disposal to win over the malcontents," he advised. Muawiya expressed the view that the fault lay with the provincial governors. "There is no disaffection in my province of Syria," he claimed, doubtless to the annoyance of the other governors. The young governor of Basra, Abdulla ibn Aamir, had justified his appointment by triumphantly carrying the Muslim war-banners over the Oxus and the Hindu Kush. "My advice, O Prince of the Faithful," he said, "is to send the armies off on a holy war against the unbelievers. When the troops are on active service, a man is fully employed in looking after himself, in treating his horse's sore back or picking the lice out of his sheepskin cloak. They would then have no time for agitation and intrigue against you." Amr ibn al Aasi, when consulted, replied brutally, "You have subjected the whole nation to Beni Umaiya. You have gone astray and so have the people. Either make up your mind to be just or give up the job." When the conference had broken up, Othman expostulated to Amr. "I did not expect you to speak to me like that," he said. "I respect you deeply, O Prince of the Faithful," said Amr cynically, "but I knew that every word we said would become public knowledge and I wanted the people to hear that that was my opinion." The old khalif was utterly bewildered. He announced, rather gratuitously, that he would never use force against other Muslims, thereby convincing the disaffected that they had nothing to fear. "The Lord is my defence," pathetically exclaimed the old man, "and that is sufficient for me."

While the provincial governors had been assembled in Mecca, the mutineers in Fustat, Kufa and Basra had matured and concerted their plans. It was agreed that contingents should set out from all three cantonments and proceed to Medina. There they would clamorously demand the redress of their grievances. If the khalif failed to give them satisfaction, they would press for his abdication or even insist on it by force. As Muawiya is said to have remarked at the time, the Arabs were returning to the anarchy of the days of Ignorance.

Early in 656, the various insurgent contingents set out on their march to the capital. Suddenly terrified, ibn abi Sarh fled from Egypt and sought asylum in Palestine, which was within the province of Muawiya. When they arrived at Medina, the three contingents camped separately outside the city. Threatened with open violence, the citizens donned their armour and refused admission to the rebels. Thus far foiled, they then sent deputations to lay their grievances before three of the surviving members of the inner council which had originally elected Othman—Ali, Zubair and Talha.[1] (Abdul Rahman ibn Auf had meanwhile died.) The three councillors rebuked the mutineers for their unruly conduct. At the same time, however, Ali visited Othman and demanded of him the dismissal of ibn abi Sarh from Egypt, while Aisha sent him a message to the same effect. The old khalif agreed and begged his advisers to nominate the new governor of Egypt.

It is sad to record that Muhammad, the son of Abu Bekr, had been one of the ringleaders of the sedition in Egypt. The difference between this violent and ambitious agitator and his firm but gentle father, the most intimate Companion of the Apostle, serves to illustrate the degeneration in morals of the new generation, brought up in the midst of wealth and luxury.

[1] Talha had been nominated by Umar but happened to be absent from Medina when the council elected Othman.

The representatives of the army of Egypt demanded the appointment of this young man to be their commander and the khalif obediently complied.

The three contingents then agreed to depart, the men of Medina unbuckled their armour and the crisis appeared, for the moment at least, to have passed. At the end of the third day's march, however, the Egyptian contingent stated that they had captured a negro slave, himself riding post haste to Egypt. On him they claimed to have found a letter purporting to be from the khalif and ordering ibn abi Sarh (of whose flight, if it had already taken place, the news had presumably not yet reached Medina) to seize and kill Muhammad ibn abi Bekr and his companions when they got back to Egypt. Thereupon the insurgents returned to Medina to demand an explanation. By what appears to be, to say the least of it, a remarkable coincidence, the Kufa and Basra contingents also returned to Medina at the same moment, although they did not claim to have intercepted any letters. Indeed Ali ibn abi Talib is alleged to have asked them how the discovery made by the Egyptian contingent on its way back to Fustat had been communicated to the Kufa and Basra parties, who had left in an entirely different direction, in such a manner as to bring all the detachments back to Medina simultaneously. An alternative theory was that the letter was a forgery and that the three parties had agreed, before leaving Medina, to meet again there in six days' time. On the previous occasion, warning of their coming had preceded them and they had found the citizens of Medina on the walls in full armour. If they pretended to go home, the rebels may have thought, the people of Medina would relax their vigilance and the city could be surprised.

Ali, who appears to have acted as a go-between at this stage, went in to Othman and recounted to him the story of the letter. The khalif vigorously denied any knowledge of the affair, but consented to receive a deputation of the mutineers, who burst into his presence without ceremony and began to shout and threaten. The slave whom they had captured, they claimed, was one of the khalif's household and the letter was sealed with his seal. The unfortunate Othman admitted that both statements were true, but swore by God that he had not written the letter, nor commanded that it be written, nor had he sent the slave in question to Egypt.

At this the mutineers began to shout once more. Some called him a liar, others abused him for a weak nonentity, and demanded his resignation. Whatever errors the khalif may have committed during his twelve years of authority, his last days were not unworthy of his high office. An old man of eighty-two, deserted by all his supporters, he calmly faced the crowd of insolent and mutinous young men. He promised to redress their grievances but refused to surrender the position to which God had raised him. His promises, shouted the insurgents, could no longer be trusted. He had promised before and done nothing. They would recognize him as khalif no longer. If he refused to abdicate, they would fight against him or kill him. Death, replied the old man, was preferable to him. If he had wanted to fight against other Muslims, he could have called an army to his defence. (Muawiya indeed had offered to send an army from Syria.)

At length, the rebel deputation withdrew to consult their comrades. Ali, who had witnessed this violent scene, retired to his house. But meanwhile the mutineers had achieved their first object, for they had gained entrance to the centre of the city, and had settled themselves all around Othman's house and in the courtyard of the Prophet's mosque. The mystery of the letter to Egypt has never been elucidated. Most Arab historians have accepted the oaths of Othman and acquitted him of any knowledge of the letter. Many have accused Merwan, the cousin to whom he had entrusted the government share of the loot from North Africa, who had access to his house and often acted as his amanuensis. Subsequent party strife and propaganda has confused the issue, with the result that the truth can now never be known.

Many undoubtedly of the Companions of the Prophet still living in Medina viewed with fear and horror these violent attacks on the successor of the Apostle of God, but Othman himself was unable or unwilling to organize any resistance and the more prudent citizens had no leader. Ali, Zubair, Talha and Saad ibn abi Waqqas, the conqueror of Iraq, were the leaders of the Muslims and had been members of the commission which had elected Othman twelve years earlier. But none of them came forward to take command of the situation. Meanwhile the malcontents demanded the surrender of Merwan, who was in the house of the khalif, but Othman refused to hand him over. The remainder of Beni Umaiya, cowed by the insurgents, were either in hiding or had fled to the protection of Muawiya in Damascus.

The Friday following the riot in his house, Othman ascended the pulpit in the great mosque to preach the Friday [2] sermon. He appealed to the reputable citizens not to be cowed by the threats of the disorderly soldiers. Then he reminded the mutineers themselves of the wickedness of attacking the successor of the Apostle of God. Several loyal citizens rose to support the khalif's appeal, whereupon the rioters set upon them and drove them from the mosque. Stones were thrown, one of which struck the octogenarian khalif. He fell to the ground and was carried unconscious into his house.

Soon the mutineers established a regular siege of Othman's residence, so that he was unable any longer to lead the prayers in the mosque, which was one of the duties of his sacred office. In a few days, the khalif's household was unable even to procure water to drink. The old man himself is described as looking down upon the rebels, perhaps from the flat roof of the house, and calling out, "Is Ali among you?", to which they replied, "No." Then he asked if Saad (ibn abi Waqqas) were there, and they said "No." "Will not anyone inform Ali that he may give us water to drink?" cried the old khalif. As a result of this message, Ali sent three goatskins full of water, which were delivered, not without a skirmish with the besiegers, by a party of freed-men of Beni Umaiya and Beni Hashim.

The Khalif Abu Bekr had belonged to the clan of Beni Taim, a branch of Quraish somewhat remote from the Prophet's family. Muhammad, the son of Abu Bekr, now appealed to his fellow clansmen to assist in the siege of the khalif. Truly the Arabs were returning to the tribal anarchy of the Days of Ignorance. There were not wanting among Quraish in Medina those who

[2] The Muslims had adopted Friday as their weekly day of public worship, as opposed to the Jewish Saturday and the Christian Sunday.

raised their voices in warning to their leaders. Quraish, they pointed out, had hitherto lived in honour and safety, looked up to with reverence by all the Arabs. Now they were standing idle, while a crowd of mutinous bedouin soldiery were attacking their leader. The sanctity of all Quraish in the eyes of the Arabs would thus be destroyed. Stung by such reproaches, Ali, Zubair, Talha and a number of other Companions sent their sons to guard the door of Othman's house. Even so, however, they did not come out openly in opposition to the mutineers, whom they were apparently unwilling to offend. While placing a guard on the khalif's house, they joined the rebels in demanding the surrender of Merwan.

Meanwhile a secret message had been despatched to Damascus, informing Muawiya of the situation and urging him to send immediate help. A force accordingly set out by forced marches from Syria, while Abdulla ibn Aamir, the governor of Basra, also despatched a contingent. News of the coming relief columns, however, reached the mutineers, who only drew the net tighter round their victim. The water supply was again cut off and the khalif and his household were once more obliged to suffer the extremities of thirst. It was the month of May 656, and the heat of the Hejaz was already oppressive. Umm Habiba, one of the widows of the Apostle of God, who must have remembered Muhammad's deep affection for Othman, actually endeavoured to lead a mule carrying water to the khalif's door. She thus exposed herself to insult by the mutinous soldiers, hoping doubtless that they would at least show respect to a widow of the Prophet. But her hopes were disappointed. She was roughly handled by the insurgents and failed to deliver her precious load. An increasing number of the citizens of Medina, the Helpers and the Companions of Muhammad, although they had bitterly criticized Othman's incompetence, were disgusted and alarmed at this outbreak of violent bedouin anarchy. Yet none made any attempt to resist. Ali, Zubair and Talha themselves remained secluded in their houses, whether from fear or from jealousy of Othman, we shall never know.

At length the mutineers, alarmed at the approach of the relief army from Syria, which had reached Wadi al Qura only 120 miles north-west of Medina, decided that it was necessary to make an end. The attack was pressed forward and flights of arrows were directed at the house. Merwan was wounded. Hasan, the eldest son of Ali, was covered with blood, as also was Muhammad the son of Talha.

At this sight, Muhammad the son of Abu Bekr, one of the most violent of the insurgents, feared that Beni Hashim would rally against the mutineers to avenge the blood of Hasan their kinsman (so strong still was tribal feeling in spite of Islam). Meanwhile, the khalif's household had replied to the arrows of the attackers and one of the latter had been killed. The sight of their dead companion further excited the rioters, who attempted to rush the door of the house. But Muhammad the son of Abu Bekr, collecting two or three others, climbed up a neighbouring building and thence, it would appear, through a window into the interior of the house of Othman. The khalif's supporters had all hastened to defend the front door, against which the mutineers were hammering. The din of battle was deafening. The old khalif was left alone, seated in his room, quietly reading the Qoran, which was spread upon his knees. Suddenly Muhammad ibn abi Bekr burst into the room from behind the house. Sword in hand, he dashed at the octogenarian khalif and, shouting loud abuse, seized him by the beard. In his last moments, the old man behaved with dignity and calm which even to this day provokes our admiration. "By God, O son of my brother," he said quietly, "what you are doing would indeed have been hateful to your father. But I take refuge from you in God." The savage young man was momentarily shamed by the calm dignity of the old khalif and perhaps by his reference to his father, the gentle and dedicated Abu Bekr. Releasing the khalif's beard, he stepped back. But his two accomplices were less sensitive and dashing past Muhammad they fell upon the old man with their swords. Othman fell forward. In his last moments he gathered up the leaves of the Qoran which he had been reading and pressed them to his breast, while his blood saturated the pages. Seeing her lord struck down, his wife Naila threw herself over him to defend him with her body. The murderers, still slashing with their swords, cut several fingers from her hand. Everything was now in wild confusion. Some of the khalif's slaves ran into the room to his rescue and struck down the first murderer. Naila was screaming hysterically for help, but no one heard owing to the din of battle below, where the rebels were battering in the gate. So she ran up on to the roof, and screamed again and again, "They have killed him! They have killed the Prince of the Faithful."

Meanwhile the mutineers had smashed in the door and a wild, yelling mob burst into the house. Breaking into the room where the aged Othman lay gasping for his last breath, they slashed him with their swords, stabbed him with their daggers, trampled upon his body and were about to cut off his head when the sobbing, screaming women of the family threw themselves on his body. At length the heartless and brutal soldiers withdrew and the khalif's dead body was left lying in silence in a pool of blood on the floor of his room. It was 17th June, 656.

Ali, Zubair and Talha, when they heard the news, went round to the khalif's house, expressed their sorrow and indignation, and reproved the defenders for their neglect to preserve the old man's life. Such words sound hollow indeed when we remember that the siege of Othman's house had lasted for forty days, during which the three leaders had done virtually nothing to save him.

The body of the murdered khalif lay for three days in the room in which he had been killed, while the mutineers lorded it in the sacred city of the Prophet. No one dared to take the body out for burial. In the evening of the third day, a small procession emerged from the house, carrying the bier on their shoulders. It consisted of Zubair, Hasan the son of Ali, and a few relatives and servants of Othman. Even so, the party was observed by the insurgents, who threw stones at the little procession. The Prince of the Faithful was buried on a small piece of land adjacent to the public cemetery outside Medina.

Othman had been a failure as khalif. He had proved too weak to control the turbulent and factious spirit of the Arabs, especially at a time when an almost unbroken succession of victories had rendered them more than usually intractable. He was of limited mental outlook, unable to grasp the big issues and dominated by his greedy relatives. He himself lived comfortably and accepted presents, though doubtless his primitive luxuries were negligible in comparison with those of the former rulers of Byzantium and Medain. Yet his predecessors, the Prophet himself, Abu Bekr and Umar ibn al Khattab had scorned all worldly possessions and had gone barefoot in rough woollen cloaks, even after the attainment of political power. In comparison with them, Othman appeared worldly. Yet he was so genuinely religious that Muhammad himself had promised him Paradise. He was so modest and innocent that the Prophet declared that the very angels were abashed in his presence. If he had not been elected to rule a great and turbulent empire, he would have ended his life as a kindly, pious and respected patriarch. Like Charles I of England, he would have been a worthy and virtuous citizen, if fate had not called him to a throne.

In brief, the times were difficult. The momentum of victory was slowing down, the white-hot enthusiasm of religion was cooling. But if Othman had been another Umar he would have weathered the storm.

* * * * *

Everything among the Arabs, and indeed in Islam, was changed by the murder of Othman. For twenty-five years, since Muhammad by taking Mecca had established a kind of theocracy on earth, they had lived in an idealistic dream. God had chosen them to conquer the world and had reserved for them the unimaginable joys of Paradise. First the Apostle of God, and then his two successors Abu Bekr and Umar, had been divinely appointed instruments to fulfil God's plan of victory for the Arabs. Nothing could mar their happiness and their triumph. If they gained fresh victories on earth, they were able to enjoy more of those worldly blessings—riches, women, horses, glory—which God lavished upon them, his chosen servants. If, on the other hand, they fell as martyrs in battle, then they passed instantly to the even greater delights of the gardens of Paradise, where they would recline on soft couches by cool fountains, their every need attended to by beautiful virgins, immortally young. But now—the dream was shattered. The Prophet's successor on earth had been represented, by the propaganda of the mutineers, as a wicked, greedy old man. Sacrilegious hands had been laid on his person and his brother Muslims had hacked him to death and left his corpse unburied on the floor of his room, adjoining the mosque and the burial place of the Apostle of God. Quraish, hitherto the nobility—I had almost said the sacred nobility—of Islam, had become divided against one another, inspired by jealousy and greed. Muhammad the son of Abu Bekr had been the first to lay violent hands on the third successor of the Prophet, and Beni Taim of Quraish, crying—not God is most great—but their tribal war cries, had attacked Beni Umaiya. The twenty-five-year dream was over and the bloody, plundering days of the Ignorance had returned.

Modern Western historians may question whether the religious enthusiasm ever existed, and point to the poverty of the bedouins and the Malthusian pressure of increasing population, as the real causes of the great Arab conquests. To some extent this, of course, is true. If the people of Central Arabia had been wealthy and luxurious, they would never have broken out of their country at all. It is certainly true that many of them as a result made great fortunes and that, as we have seen, peculation and misappropriation on the part of provincial governors was not unknown. But in all great religious or political movements, it is the principal leaders who are exposed to such temptations. Probably also the most successful military commanders were automatically the most ruthless characters, such as Khalid ibn al Waleed. But during the first twenty-five years, many even of the great leaders remained uncorrupted. In any case, the fact that some of the leaders gave way to worldly ambitions should not be allowed to obscure the genuine piety and idealism of many of the rank and file.

An illuminating insight into the first twenty-five years of Muslim enthusiasm is provided by a comparison with later outbreaks in Central Arabia. From 929 to 969, for example, the fanatical sect of the Carmathians conquered all Central Arabia and the Yemen, occupied Mecca and Medina and threatened the khalifate itself. After forty years of wild religious enthusiasm, the outbreak subsided. At the end of the eighteenth century, the Wahhabi sect appeared, conquered all Arabia and threatened Syria and Iraq. Again after some forty years, the Wahhabis were defeated and the enthusiasm petered out. In 1912, a Wahhabi revival occurred and dominated Arabia until 1930, when the flood subsided once more. It would appear, therefore, as if the Central Arabians are liable, from time to time, to be swept away by an impetuous outburst of religious enthusiasm, lasting for a period of between twenty and forty years, after which the enthusiasm subsides.

Sir Thomas Arnold, one of the greatest Arabists of our times, has the following passage. "One of the most illuminating discoveries made by modern historians is the recognition of the fact that the enormous expansion of Islam in the second half of the seventh century was not the result of a great religious movement. . . . This expansion of the Arab race was rather the migration of a vigorous and energetic people, driven by hunger and want . . . to overrun the richer lands of their more fortunate neighbours." Other modern historians and professors have declared their belief in the "discovery" of the same "facts".

I personally believe that these "discoveries" are only half the truth and are indeed largely subjective. At the point of time in which we live, the ideas of Europeans are largely concentrated on economics, with the result that we attribute the same motives to other races at different epochs. In these psychological days, we should surely appreciate the mistake of attributing the actions of men or of nations to one sole cause. Human motives and human emotions are far too complicated for mathematical analysis. The motives of the Arabs who shared in the conquests of the first twenty-five years were doubtless mixed. Ambition, hardihood, poverty and greed all played their part. But the bedouins had always been in want and hunger, for thousands of years before and after Muhammad. Why then were they invincible only for twenty-five years after the Prophet's death?

I lived many years with tribesmen still little changed from those who fought in the great Arab conquests. I "discovered" that a deep vein of enthusiastic altruism lies hidden beneath the rough exterior and rapacious actions of the Arabian tribesman. I believe that the Apostle touched that chord of Arabian idealism and that, once it had been touched, there was nothing which these men could not do. Pressure of population or economic necessity could not alone have produced so volcanic an explosion. Some deep, emotional and idealistic fire was needed to produce an outbreak of such violence. The very passion of the devotion engendered made it necessarily short-lived. Already thirty-five years had elapsed since Muhammad's flight to Medina and twenty-four since his death. The first passionate enthusiasm was beginning to cool. After the murder of Othman, disillusionment spread, the fires of religious devotion sank low, the passionate exaltation of the great conquests subsided.

## *NOTABLE DATES*

| | |
|---|---|
| Murder of the Khalif Othman | 17th June 656 |

## *PERSONALITIES*

Malik al Ashtar, agitator and mutineer of Kufa.

Muhammad, the son of the Khalif Abu Bekr, one of the murderers of Othman.

| | |
|---|---|
| Ali ibn abi Talib<br>Zubair ibn al Awwam<br>Talha ibn Ubaidullah<br>Saad ibn abi Waqqas | The khalif's most intimate advisers who did not intervene to save him. |

# XVIII

# *Let God Decide*

Ambition, the ruling motive, was mistaken for the desire of a just revenge. In the whirl of passion and intrigue, party-cry too often takes the place of reason; and we need not doubt that both leaders and followers had wrought themselves up into the belief that punishment of the high treason enacted at Medina was their real object. SIR WILLIAM MUIR, *Annals of the Early Caliphate*

# XVIII

## LET GOD DECIDE

FOR a few days after the murder of Othman, Medina was in anarchy with the mutineers in complete control. The contingent from the army of Egypt was the most violent and its leader usurped the position of the khalif and led the daily prayers in the great mosque. The Beni Umaiya had fled, some to Damascus and some to Mecca. Saad ibn abi Waqqas and a number of other respected citizens also stole away to Mecca. Amr ibn al Aasi, even before the murder, had retired to a farm at Beersheba. One of Beni Umaiya collected the bloody shirt of Othman and the severed fingers of Naila his wife, and bore them to Damascus where he presented them to Muawiya.

Eventually a reaction set in. Even some of the mutineers were now horrified at what they had done. Others of them began to realize that the whole empire was now without a head and without a government, and that, unless some central authority were quickly constituted, the conquered provinces would soon disintegrate in chaos. They accordingly summoned the people of Medina to elect a new khalif. The insurgents from Egypt favoured the candidacy of Ali, the Prophet's cousin. Those of Kufa were inclined to support Zubair, who had led the storming party up the ladders in the assault on Babylon. The men of Basra favoured Talha, whose right hand had been crippled when he thrust it forward to save the Apostle of God from a sword cut at the Battle of Uhud.[1]

To accept the khalifate, five days after the murder of the previous incumbent and when the capital was still in the hands of a mutinous soldiery, might have been thought to be an action requiring no little courage. And Ali at first appears indeed to have hesitated and offered to swear allegiance to either Zubair or Talha. But he was pressed to accept both by the Companions of the Prophet—the now venerable elders of Medina—and by the insubordinate troops who virtually controlled the city. Six days after the murder of Othman, Ali was proclaimed khalif in Medina. The majority of the citizens, including Talha and Zubair, paid to him the oath of allegiance. At last the groups of mutineers departed, returning to boast of their exploits in the great military bases of Fustat, Kufa and Basra.

The old rivalry between the Beni Umaiya and Beni Hashim clans of Quraish had originated, as we have seen, before the birth of the Prophet. In the years to come it was to rend the great Arab Empire into shreds, and it divided Islam into rival parties which still exist today. In this persistent and tragic feud, nearly all the Muslim historians have been involved, and their records and interpretations of historical events have been warped by their

[1] Page 72.

devotion to one side or the other. To the neutral student, their often contradictory reports present a now insoluble problem. I have endeavoured to the best of my ability to steer a moderate course through these stormy conflicts.

Ali ibn abi Talib, it will be remembered, was the son of Muhammad's uncle. Abu Talib being poor, however, the Prophet, after his marriage to the wealthy Khadija, had undertaken the upbringing of Ali, who was thus virtually his adopted son. When he was grown up, he had married Fatima, the daughter of the Apostle, who had given birth to two sons, Hasan and Husain, to whom Muhammad had been devotedly attached. Ali had become a Muslim at the age of ten. Some claimed that he was the first convert to Islam. Others allotted the priority to Khadija or to Abu Bekr, but he was, at the worst, in the first three. He himself was alleged to have said that Muhammad received his prophetic mission on Monday and he, Ali was converted on Tuesday. On the grounds of relationship to the Prophet or of seniority in conversion, he was therefore by far the most prominent Muslim alive in 656.

In his first youth, he had been a great champion in battle. Both at Bedr and at Uhud, he had been the first to step out between the armies and challenge the enemy to single combat, and in both cases he had killed his man. The Prophet more than once gave him the standard to carry in battle. But during the years of the great conquests he had remained in Medina, where he had acted as councillor and consultant to both Abu Bekr and Umar, for he was said to be of quick intelligence. One tradition attributed to Umar ibn al Khattab the statement that "Ali is the best of us in judicial decisions."

Inevitably he had become rich in Medina, for he was not a deliberate ascetic like Abu Bekr and Umar. Fatima, the Prophet's daughter, had died long since and Ali had taken to himself wives and concubines. He was a good speaker and learned in the customs and tenets of Islam. When he was acclaimed khalif in 656, he was already middle-aged, rather short and fat, with a large beard.

He was confronted with an alarming situation. During the years of the great conquests, tens of thousands of captured slaves of various nationalities had been sent to Medina, either as part of the government fifth of the loot or as the private property of different warriors. Many or most of them had professed Islam, which enabled them to improve their status in the Holy City. A number of these slaves or freedmen who possessed some personal skill were allowed to practise it independently in Medina, paying, in the case of slaves, a proportion of their earnings to their masters. We have seen that Abu Lulu, who murdered the Khalif Umar, was a slave-artisan of Mughira ibn Shuba. Many of these non-Arab slaves and freedmen had been taken into the households of the leading Muslims, some being armed and equipped to act as the personal bodyguards of their masters. While the empire remained strong and discipline severe, these slaves and retainers remained a pliant and submissive body. But in the anarchy which arose during the siege of Othman's house, many foreign slaves had roamed the streets fully armed, committed crimes and become insolent and insubordinate.

From the days of the Prophet's capture of Mecca until the murder of Othman, no one had ever dreamed of insurrection at home. There were no soldiers in Mecca or Medina. The Arab warriors were in their cantonments on the frontiers or in the conquered provinces. Thus a handful of mutineers —probably not more than 2,000 altogether—had laid siege to and killed the undefended khalif in his own house. Now that the insurgents had gone, the foreign slaves had the capital of the empire almost at their mercy.

The surrounding Arab tribes constituted a third danger threatening Medina. While the bedouins had formed the mass of those Arab armies which had conquered Persia and Byzantium for the faith, the instinct for plunder was ineradicably implanted in their nature. The disorders in the city had suggested to the tribes of the Hejaz that the authority of the government might be on the verge of collapse and a return to the freebooting days of the Ignorance might be at hand. Parties of armed camel-riders appeared here and there, awaiting the opportunity to loot the town or to drive off the herds of some rival tribe. To meet this disorganization, no troops were available. The armies of Egypt and Iraq were of doubtful loyalty. Those of Syria had not joined the mutiny but were commanded by Muawiya, an Umaiyid. Although the people of Medina, whether owing to fear or to parochial jealousy, had done nothing to defend Othman, they were now alarmed at the apparently imminent dissolution of all authority. Indeed the situation in Medina was almost as critical as it had been at the time of the Apostasy, immediately after the death of the Prophet. Zubair, Talha and many former Helpers and Companions of the Prophet, urged upon Ali the necessity of restoring discipline by punishing the murderers of Othman.

The new khalif found himself faced with a momentous decision. If all Quraish, supported by the Helpers and Companions, had rallied to the new khalif to avenge the murder—not of old Othman but of the sacred authority of the Prophet's successor—the growing spirit of insubordination might have been suppressed. Moreover, in this case, Muawiya, who stood at the head of a loyal army, would have been drawn in to support the new Commander of the Faithful. A Hashemite khalif avenging the death of an Umaiyid might have healed the breach between the rival clans. But Ali, while professing deeply to lament the murder of Othman, took no steps to avenge it, pleading apparently his inability to do so, the absence of adequate troops and the general disorganization.

Zubair and Talha and Saad ibn abi Waqqas, the leading Muslims and members of the unofficial advisory council, continued to urge the need to avenge the murder, although they had done little or nothing to oppose it. While Othman had been under siege in his palace, the annual pilgrimage season had come round and the old khalif had sent Abdulla the son of Abbas [2] (Muhammad's uncle) to preside over the ceremonies. Returning from Mecca after the murder, ibn Abbas added his voice to that of the other advisers. But Ali still remained unable or unwilling to take action against the murderers of Othman.

Meanwhile, a second problem presented itself. The provincial governors were, of course, still the nominees of Othman and in many cases Umaiyids. Many of his advisers seem to have suggested to Ali that he leave these persons

[2] Quraish Genealogical Table, page 36.

in office, at any rate for the moment. It is true that the discontent in Othman's time had largely taken the form of complaints against these very governors. But, by the murder of the old khalif, Beni Umaiya had become the injured party instead of being the oppressors. Ali could not have been accused of nepotism if he had left the Umaiyid nominees in office, at any rate for a time, or if he had dealt with them one by one on their merits. Mughira ibn Shuba, ibn Abbas and others seem to have pressed him to go slowly, or at least not to antagonize Muawiya, whose province was the only one which was still quiet and well-behaved, and who, after all, had been appointed by Umar ibn al Khattab.[3]

Ali, however, rejected all advice on the subject and insisted on the immediate dismissal of all Othman's nominees and also of Muawiya, although Ali himself in Medina had no army and Syria was solidly behind Muawiya. He immediately despatched his own nominees to the provincial governorships. The men whom he chose were, in some cases, capable and honourable, but a revulsion of feeling was now running strongly all through the empire. The demand for the punishment of the murderers of the khalif was everywhere growing and, with it, murmurs accusing Ali of complicity with the assassins. Ali's nominee to Basra secured his office, merely because Abdulla ibn Aamir, Othman's governor, voluntarily withdrew. In Egypt, where apparently there was a vacancy caused by the flight of ibn abi Sarh, Ali's candidate barely secured admission. But the men whom he sent to Kufa and Damascus were refused admittance and were glad to get back to Medina alive. Thus rebuffed, the new khalif belatedly attempted diplomacy. He addressed letters to Muawiya, and to the governor of Kufa, Abu Musa (formerly commander in the invasion of Fars), calling upon them to express their allegiance. Abu Musa, who might be called a professional soldier for he was not of Quraish, replied in loyal terms but warned Ali that sedition was rife in Kufa. But Muawiya, for the moment, sent no answer at all.

It will be remembered that, immediately after the murder of Othman, his blood-soaked shirt and the severed fingers of Naila his wife had been smuggled out of Medina and transported to Muawiya in Damascus. Here they were nailed to the pulpit in the great mosque, a pathetic appeal for the avenging of innocent blood. Apart from this skilful piece of propaganda and from the assumption of a sorrowful expression at the evils of the times, Muawiya did nothing. Syria, however, differed materially from Iraq and Egypt. At the beginning, it is true, Umar's policy of racial segregation (apartheid we might call it) had been applied in Syria as elsewhere, and a great army base had been established at Jabiya. But gradually, presumably as a result of Muawiya's policy, segregation had been abandoned. The capital had been established in Damascus, not in Jabiya, and the leading Arabs and the Companions of the Prophet lived in the city and mixed in familiar intercourse with the conquered peoples. In Iraq and Egypt, the Arab armies, idle in their cantonments, had become insolent praetorians always ready for revolt, while

[3] The wisdom of Umar ibn al Khattab in frequently dismissing his principal generals is illustrated by the case of Muawiya who had now been fourteen years in Syria and could not be dislodged.

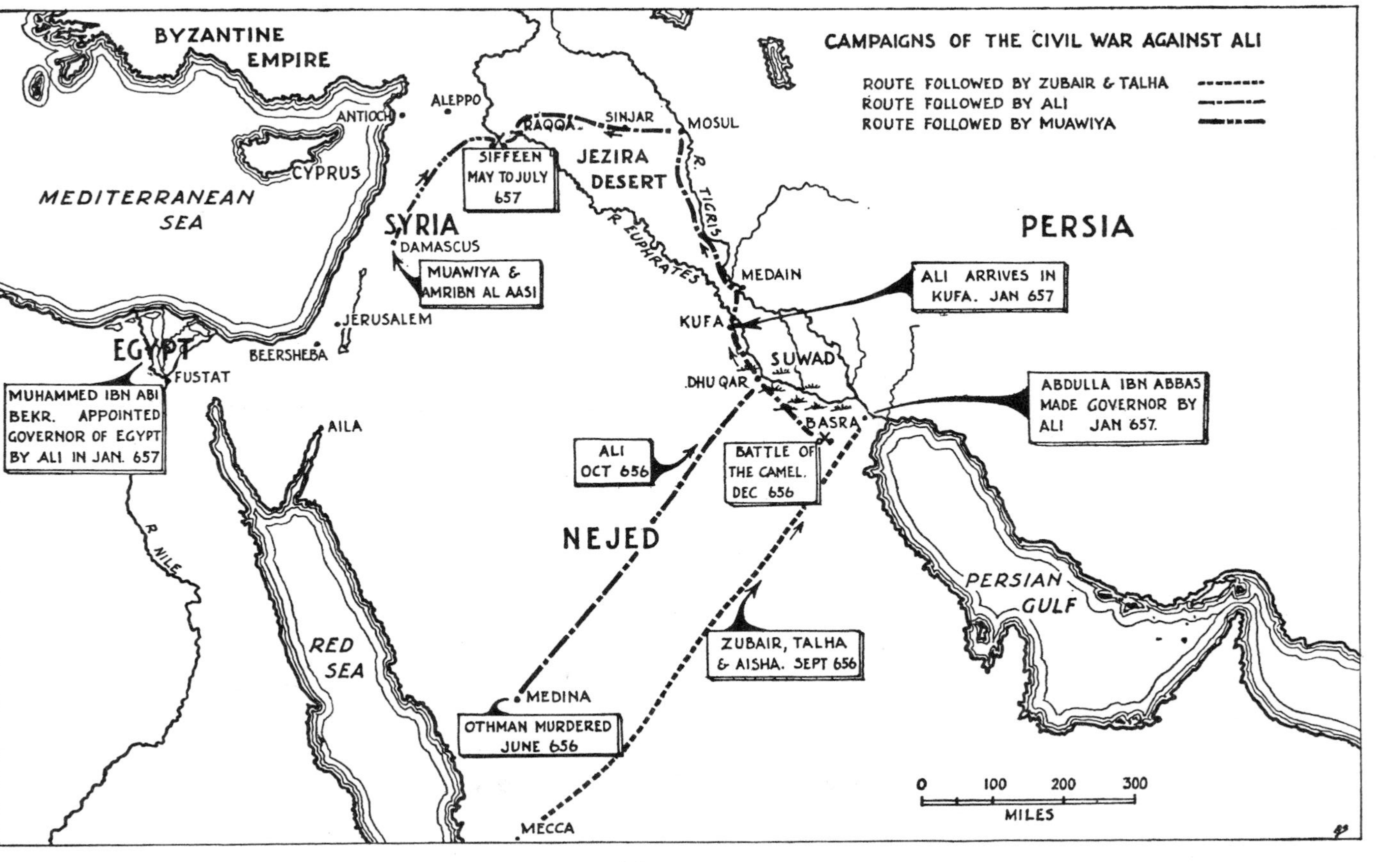
CAMPAIGNS OF THE CIVIL WAR AGAINST ALI
ROUTE FOLLOWED BY ZUBAIR & TALHA
ROUTE FOLLOWED BY ALI
ROUTE FOLLOWED BY MUAWIYA
BYZANTINE EMPIRE
MEDITERRANEAN SEA
CYPRUS
ANTIOCH
ALEPPO
RAQQA
SINJAR
MOSUL
SIFFEEN MAY TO JULY 657
JEZIRA DESERT
R. TIGRIS
R. EUPHRATES
SYRIA
DAMASCUS
MUAWIYA & AMRIBN AL AASI
PERSIA
MEDAIN
ALI ARRIVES IN KUFA. JAN 657
KUFA
JERUSALEM
BEERSHEBA
EGYPT
FUSTAT
MUHAMMED IBN ABI BEKR. APPOINTED GOVERNOR OF EGYPT BY ALI IN JAN. 657
SUWAD
DHU QAR
ABDULLA IBN ABBAS MADE GOVERNOR BY ALI JAN 657.
BASRA
AILA
ALI OCT 656
BATTLE OF THE CAMEL. DEC 656
R. NILE
NEJED
PERSIAN GULF
RED SEA
ZUBAIR, TALHA & AISHA. SEPT 656
MEDINA
OTHMAN MURDERED JUNE 656
0 100 200 300
MILES
MECCA

Map XXXII

the civilian populations lived their own lives, divorced from all affairs of state. In Syria, however, the state and the army were becoming integrated with the public and thus, instead of a crowd of idle and insolent soldiery, the people of the province and the army stood together behind Muawiya.

As the weeks went by, and Ali took no apparent steps to avenge the murder of the khalif, the blood-stained shirt of Othman still hung on the pulpit in Damascus. At last, in September 656, three months after the murder, Muawiya felt himself strong enough to reply. The letter which was delivered to the khalif in Medina bore the inscription "from Muawiya to Ali", with no titles of respect. Inside was a blank sheet of paper. The khalif, perplexed, enquired the meaning. The envoy replied sternly that sixty thousand warriors in Damascus were weeping over the bloody shirt of the martyr and were bent on avenging on the head of Ali, the innocent blood of Othman, though Ali swore by God that he was innocent. For the first time in the annals of Islam, the word civil war had been spoken. Ali saw that the time for action could no longer be postponed. He gave orders for war-banners to be unfurled for an expedition against Syria and wrote orders to Egypt, Kufa and Basra to call out their troops.

Zubair and Talha had been advising Ali to proclaim his intention of avenging Othman but had seen their advice repeatedly disregarded. The storm of accusation against Ali continued to grow louder. His inaction served only to strengthen the suspicion that he had been in collusion with the murderers of his predecessor. In reality, Ali seems only to have been vacillating, unable to take a decision. He had not been an accomplice of the murderers but he had not attempted to defend their victim. Now, in the same manner, he drifted, waiting for something to turn up.

Zubair and Talha, the two nearest to Ali in seniority and prestige, left Medina for Mecca under pretext of performing the lesser pilgrimage. Aisha, the Prophet's favourite wife, was already there. Ever since the affair of Safwan,[4] she had nursed her resentment against Ali, who had recommended the Prophet to divorce her, and she had never forgotten the injury. (Aisha was a daughter of Abu Bekr and thus the sister of Muhammad ibn abi Bekr who had first laid hands on Othman in his room. But she had previously tried to deter her brother from violence.) Many Umaiyids also had fled from Medina to Mecca, so that when Zubair and Talha arrived, they found sedition already well established. Soon the banner of revolt was raised in the Holy City also, and Zubair and Talha prepared to take the field against Ali, their former colleague.

It will be remembered that, of the three contingents of mutineers who had killed Othman, the party from Kufa favoured Zubair as their candidate for the succession, while Talha enjoyed the support of the men from Basra. Only the detachment from the army in Egypt had favoured Ali. As a result, Zubair and Talha decided first to raise the standard of revolt in Basra. They marched out of Mecca with 3,000 men, with the object of crossing Arabia to Iraq. They were accompanied also by Merwan, the cousin and secretary of Othman, whom the latter had refused to surrender to the mutineers.

[4] Page 84.

Aisha, riding in a camel-litter, went with them. The people of Mecca accompanied the army on its first day's march. When at length they said good-bye to the warriors and turned back, the whole concourse, which included many women, burst into loud sobs. That tragic day was long remembered in Mecca as "the day of tears".

* * * * *

The great Arab Empire had come into existence as if by magic, in the fantastically short period of twenty years. Now it looked as if it might collapse and disappear once more in a bedouin orgy of tribal war and mutual blood feuds. As long as men were inspired by passionate devotion to the Prophet or to his two dedicated successors, Abu Bekr and Umar ibn al Khattab, the weaknesses of the empire had been concealed. Now the first enthusiasm of the new faith had subsided. The Apostle of God had been dead nearly twenty-five years. A generation was growing up who had never known him or felt the magnetism of his charm.

The mighty Arab Empire was profoundly imposing to the onlooker. But it had been built too quickly. Ominous cracks were already appearing in the foundations. To begin with, there was no constitution and above all, no recognized method of choosing a successor to the khalifate. The laws of the state were based solely on the Qoran and on what the Prophet had said or done, and he had never discussed this subject.

The real weakness, however, was much more profound because it was spiritual. When the Apostle had migrated to Medina, he and the small party of his adherents had been virtually destitute, and a burden on the hospitality of the Medina Helpers. They had accordingly, by raiding, obtained the means of livelihood. Thus to fight for religion had meant wealth and plunder. The loot obtained during the lifetime of the Apostle had been derived from Quraish or the bedouin tribes, all of whom were themselves relatively poor. Moreover, Muhammad and his two successors were indifferent to money or luxury, and had maintained until their deaths the original simplicity of their peasant lives.

The overthrow of the Byzantine and Persian Empires, however, had made many Muslims fantastically rich. The idea still persisted that Muslims should enjoy the best of both worlds, money, comfort and women in this and Paradise in the next. There is no profounder truth than that man cannot at the same time serve God and mammon. Not that wealth is wicked but that it is so much nearer and more engrossing than God. To seek both at once is almost inevitably to devote oneself principally to mammon.

The Arabs had been victorious too quickly. The intoxicating lure of luxury, money and women, which they had come to regard as the just rewards of the faithful, had caused their minds to be preoccupied with worldly success rather than with the pure service of God. Christians have at times been criticized for denouncing the whole world as evil. To the early Arab Muslims, the world was too good.

Once worldly ambition had established its pre-eminence, the Arab customs of the Ignorance were ready instruments to hand. Tribal rivalries and the lust for revenge bred by the blood feud throve on minds in which love of wealth and women had weakened religious devotion, just as epidemic diseases lay hold on bodies previously weakened by indulgence.

* * * * *

It seems difficult now to justify the apparent treachery of Zubair and Talha, who had been close collaborators with Ali as advisers both to Umar and Othman for some twenty-four years, and who only three months earlier had sworn allegiance to him. Moreover, in so far as collusion with the murderers of Othman was concerned, they too had been in Medina when the khalif was besieged in his house and had done nothing to save him. As one actor in these disturbances remarked, one-third of the blame for Othman's death had rested on Ali, one-third on Zubair, and one-third on Aisha.

As soon as Ali heard that Zubair, Talha and Aisha had left Mecca, he decided to follow them, but found considerable difficulty in raising a force for the purpose. Only some three months before, the Companions and the people of Medina had begged him to be khalif. Now few would support him although the apparently unscrupulous Zubair and Talha had raised 3,000 men from Mecca and the surrounding tribes. The cause for the change must presumably have been the mounting tide of propaganda to the effect that Ali had secretly instigated the murder of Othman. At length, in October 656, four months after the murder, Ali set out after Zubair and Talha. He had with him only seven hundred men. Too weak to proceed, he camped on a desert well in Nejed. It was only on his arrival here that he learned definitely that the malcontents had gone on to Basra. Resting for a few days, he sent Muhammad ibn abi Bekr on ahead to Kufa, to persuade the troops at that base to join him in marching on Basra.

Meanwhile, Zubair and Talha had arrived outside Basra. It will be remembered that Ali had already sent a governor to Basra, who had assumed command in his name. This man now met the malcontents and their force at the entrance to the town. A confused discussion ensued, some accusing Zubair and Talha of perjury, because they had sworn fealty to Ali and then rebelled. They defended themselves with two arguments. Firstly they claimed that they had been compelled under duress to swear allegiance. Secondly that only after Ali had assumed office did it appear that he did not intend to punish the murderers of Othman. If mutinous soldiers could murder the Prince of the Faithful and then go unpunished, the Muslim state, they said, could not survive. From words, the two parties passed to blows and fighting ended only with the fall of darkness. During the night, the malcontents seem to have infiltrated further into the town. At dawn, fighting recommenced and by evening the streets were strewn with dead and wounded, struck down by the fury of their fellow Muslims. At length a truce was concluded. Both sides agreed to send a neutral messenger to Medina to ascertain the facts. If he returned to say that Talha and Zubair had sworn under duress, they would take over the town. If it proved that they had sworn voluntarily to Ali and then betrayed him, they would withdraw and leave Ali's nominee in command. The messenger in due course reached Medina, stood up in the Prophet's mosque at the time of prayers and asked the people to tell him whether or not Zubair and Talha had sworn under duress. The only result had been a riot in the mosque, some crying 'Yes' and others 'No'. Meanwhile an uneasy truce had been observed in Basra. When, however, the messenger returned without a clear answer, fighting recommenced, Ali's party was defeated, his governor ill-treated and driven out and the insurgents established themselves in Basra. To prove their devotion to the murdered Othman, they put to death all the members of the party from Basra who had joined in his assassination.

* * * * *

While these events were in progress, Ali had crossed the desert to Dhu Qar—the site near the Euphrates where Beni Bekr had first defeated the Persians in the days of the Ignorance.[5] Successive messengers to Kufa had failed to produce any recruits owing to the opposition of the governor, Abu Musa, who insisted that he had himself heard the Apostle say that, when seditions arose, believers should not join them. Ali's emissaries included Muhammad ibn abi Bekr, who actually took part in the murder of Othman, ibn Abbas the son of the Prophet's uncle, and Malik al Ashtar, the original instigator of the sedition in Kufa and the leader of the mutineers who had gone from that town to Medina.[6] The employment of the murderers themselves as leaders of his forces must have greatly strengthened the charges of collusion in the murder which constituted the principal accusation directed against Ali. The latter at the same time declared Abu Musa to be dismissed from his post and appointed a new governor to assume command in Kufa. The old soldier withdrew without protest, perhaps without regret. He had been a soldier for thirty years to fight against unbelievers, he said, but never to kill his Muslim brothers.

Indeed, whatever may have been the rival ambitions of the leaders in their struggles for power, there can be no doubt that great numbers of deeply religious veterans of the wars were utterly perplexed. They were profoundly distressed by the apparent collapse of the theocratic brotherhood which had formed the inspiration of their lives and which they had trusted would conquer the whole world and bring all mankind into subjection to God. But there were now three rival parties in the field, disputing the succession to the Apostle. Firstly, Ali with a handful of followers, at Dhu Qar. Secondly, Talha and Zubair, who were in Basra and thirdly, Muawiya, who was biding his time in Damascus. The "enemies of God", in the shape of the Byzantines and the Persians, were forgotten.

Hearing that his first emissaries had met with little success, Ali then sent his eldest son Hasan to Kufa, while he himself remained camped at Dhu Qar. Hasan and Husain were the grandsons of the Prophet and had been the darlings of his heart. He had never tired of playing with them and many of the Companions had seen them sitting in the Apostle's lap or climbing, with shouts of laughter, upon his shoulders. The arrival of Hasan in Kufa turned

[5] Page 116. [6] Pages 298 and 299.

the tide. The many Companions who had settled in the town were deeply moved at the sight of the Prophet's grandson appealing for their help. Soon a force of nearly ten thousand men answered the call and set out from Kufa to join Ali.

As the khalif's army approached Basra, the rebels marched out to meet it, led by Zubair and Talha. Not all Basra was with them. Beni Bekr, the tribe once led by the gallant Muthanna, joined the army of Ali. Beni Temeem decided to remain neutral. Ali's army was now slightly the stronger. In the Days of Ignorance, women mounted in litters on camels, frequently accompanied their tribes into battle, to urge on the warriors. Aisha, "Mother of the Faithful",[7] accompanied the rebel army in her camel-litter.

But Ali did not want a battle. Halting at a distance from the rebels, he sent forward the fiery Qaqaa, veteran of the early conquests, to urge negotiation. He did not deny, the new khalif said, that the murderers of Othman should be punished, but he asked for time. Many of these very men were in the force which he himself commanded. To massacre them wholesale would only lead to fresh feuds. Let order and discipline be re-established, and then the guilty could be brought to trial in a regular manner. The case was plausible, the argument was convincing. Perhaps indeed Ali had not been in collusion with the murderers. If the question were merely whether to kill them now or first to restore peace, and then bring them to punishment, the matter could be discussed. Talha and Zubair agreed to negotiate.

Ali was elated at the prospect of negotiation in place of civil war, and moved his camp close to that of the rebel army, in order to facilitate communication. He had with him, however, in the Kufa contingent, nearly all the former mutineers from that town who had joined in the killing of Othman, the very men whose punishment Zubair and Talha were demanding. As a result, he gave orders for these men to remain camped out of sight in the desert, while the negotiations were proceeding. Malik al Ashtar, the most fanatic of the anti-Umaiyid rebels, remained with them.

Negotiations between Ali, Talha and Zubair were then opened in earnest. Ali himself rode out from his army and was met between the lines by Zubair and Talha. The latter declared their determination to punish the murderers of Othman. Ali replied that he was in complete agreement, exclaiming, "God curse the murderers of Othman." But proper vengeance could not be achieved at this moment. Time was needed.

Zubair was a first cousin of the Prophet. His mother had been the sister of Muhammad's father. Zubair and Ali had known one another and worked together all their lives. When they now met between the lines of their respective armies, Ali asked Zubair if he remembered this and that occasion when they had both been young, and when both were filled with passionate religious zeal and personal devotion to Muhammad; how the Apostle of God had said this and Ali or Zubair had said that. What wonderful times those had been! Zubair was moved to tears and swore that he would never oppose Ali with force. Ali had the reputation of being a persuasive speaker.

The negotiations promised well, the tension was relaxed and the two armies

[7] Mother of the Faithful was a title bestowed on all the widows of the Apostle.

lay down to sleep, perhaps neglecting something of the vigilance which they had hitherto exercised. The last thing which suited the murderers of Othman, however, was that peace be made, for a compromise would almost certainly mean that Ali had undertaken to punish them. Although they had been left behind in the desert, they doubtless had friends who reported to them the progress of the peace talks. They met in the evening to discuss the action to be taken. It was agreed that an agreement between Ali and the dissident chiefs would be fatal to them. It was decided unanimously that, if they were to survive, a battle must somehow be engineered. The whole night was passed in these discussions. Just before dawn, they mounted and scattered silently into the darkness. The murderers of Othman came from every tribe. In the same manner, different tribes were represented on both sides in the armies of Kufa and Basra. The fanatics had decided that each one of them would steal quietly into the ranks and join his own tribal contingent in one or other army.

In the first grey light of dawn, a sudden hubbub arose in both armies. Cries of stand to, prepare for battle, the enemy has betrayed us, were heard on all sides. As Zubair and Talha ran forward asking what had happened, voices replied, "Ali is determined to exterminate us in a blood bath. The negotiations yesterday were only treachery." When Ali awoke with a start and asked the reason for the noise, a man, standing beside him but invisible in the grey dawn, cried, "Talha and Zubair are determined to massacre us. We are being treacherously attacked." The same cries ran through both armies, as the soldiers feverishly donned their armour and drew their weapons. In vain Ali called at the top of his voice, "Stand fast, nothing has happened, false alarm." It was too late. Arrows began to fly, the opposing ranks closed in on one another and soon all was in confusion. The rebels thought naturally that they had been betrayed by Ali, while Ali's troops imagined the same of the rebels. By the time day dawned, the two armies were inextricably locked in battle. In the confusion, Ali's efforts to stay the conflict were ineffectual. The sense of betrayal by the other side made both armies fight more bitterly than ever. As so often happens in civil wars, the contest was more envenomed than in the former battles with the unbelievers. This was not only a struggle of Arab against Arab and Muslim against Muslim. The tribes had been divided up in the course of the wars with Persia, some clans of a tribe settling in Basra while others established themselves in Kufa. Now fellow tribesmen found themselves slaughtering one another on opposite sides.

When the fighting was joined, Zubair, in compliance with his oath the previous day, withdrew from the battle. Wandering in a desert valley a little way from the battlefield, he was apparently encountered and killed by some passing straggler. Thus futilely and ignominiously died one of the great early heroes of Islam. Meanwhile Talha had been wounded by an arrow and was carried back to Basra, where he died soon after. The rebel army, losing sight of its two leaders, began to give ground.

Aisha, the Mother of the Faithful, had been led into battle on her camel, and had been engaged in rousing the fury of the fighters by calling out shrilly, "Kill the murderers of Othman." As the rebels began to give ground, she and her camel were being left behind to the advancing enemy until word was passed that the Mother of the Faithful was in danger. A group of brave men gathered round her, ready for her sake to surrender their lives. The battle, which had been cooling off, flamed up once more. A standard was set up beside the camel, brave fighters rushed forward to seize it by the bridle. The slumbering embers of the passionate devotion to the Apostle which had once possessed these men was suddenly kindled into flame anew by the thought that his favourite wife was in danger. The ranks reformed round the Mother of the Faithful. Seventy brave men, one after another, fell dead holding the bridle of her camel. At last Ali, seeing that the camel was the rallying point of the Basra army, sent a man to hamstring it. With a horrible scream, the camel fell to the ground, the litter was overturned, its defenders' ranks were broken and the defeated army retired to the city of Basra. Aisha's litter, perhaps by a pardonable exaggeration, was said to have been bristling all over with arrows like a hedgehog, though its fair occupant was unhurt.

The Arab historians attribute terrible casualties to this battle, which has ever since been known to history as the Battle of the Camel. For twenty-five years these Arabs had never been defeated. They had grown as accustomed to victory as the armies of Alexander or Napoleon. Now, for the first time since the Prophet had announced his mission, Muslim was pitted against Muslim in a deadly fight. To them death was familiar and involved no fear. Several cases have already been cited of men vowing themselves to martyrdom before a battle and deliberately seeking death when the fighting began. It was the custom for those who found themselves seriously wounded to stagger or crawl further into the thickest of the fighting in order the more rapidly to win martyrdom. Yet this spirit had grown up in the wars against unbelievers, for the promise of immediate admission to paradise was made only to those killed fighting against non-Muslims. But the Qoran had said that any man who intentionally killed another believer would be punished in hell. Yet the habits of thought contracted by the soldiers in twenty-five years were not so easily changed, and many were to die in civil strife with the word paradise on their lips.

The Battle of the Camel was fought in December 656. As soon as the enemy withdrew, Ali gave orders that there should be no pursuit and that killing should immediately cease. It is probable that some fifteen thousand men were engaged on each side and that perhaps six thousand dead were buried on the field. When the sword of Zubair was brought to Ali, he cursed the man who had killed him, and reminded those present of the great deeds of the deceased hero in the wars of Islam. The site is marked to this day by the modern town called after him—Zubair. When Ali entered Basra, he endeavoured to conciliate all parties. Merwan and a number of other Umaiyids made away, some to Medina, which was henceforward neutral, and some to Muawiya in Syria. Otherwise the defeated army was treated with generosity. Ali urged that bygones be bygones, for he was of a mild and generous, perhaps an easy-going, nature and wished to reunite the empire rather than to revenge himself upon his enemies.

After spending a fortnight in Basra he appointed his cousin Abdulla the son of Abbas to be governor, and marched out with his army to Kufa. He had treated Aisha with courtly respect and had sent her back to Medina, accompanied by her brother, Muhammad ibn abi Bekr, the murderer of Othman, and guarded by an escort of men and maidservants. She was to live for twenty-two years longer, henceforward renouncing politics and devoting herself to her long vigil by the grave of the Apostle. She seems to have become garrulous with age and was always ready to retail long anecdotes of the Prophet to such visitors or pilgrims as came to pay their tribute of devotion at the tomb of the Messenger of God.

Ali entered Kufa in January 657, seven months after the murder of Othman, and thereafter made the city his capital.

* * * * *

Ostensibly the revolt against Othman owed its origin to indignation at his nepotism and at the alleged corruption of his relatives whom he had made governors. But it was not merely a revolt against the Umaiyids—the Arab tribesman was, and is, profoundly democratic. He accorded a certain respect to the families of his chieftains, but, having recognized the primacy of the tribal leader, he was always ready to disobey and defy him. He was no respecter of titles or privileges, and had a rough contempt for all people who lived in houses and in towns. These men had risen against the Umaiyid aristocracy, because the latter was in power. But they had no desire to see them replaced by a Hashimite aristocracy and here was Ali appointing Abdulla ibn Abbas to govern Basra and others of Beni Hashim surrounded his person.

In addition, however, to this element of bedouin disrespect for people who gave themselves airs, there was a far more menacing and profound religious communism at work, typified by such fanatics as Malik al Ashtar. These men favoured neither Beni Umaiya nor Beni Hashim. They dreamed of a state ruled by God, of a dictatorship of the saints. Englishmen may remember that the execution of King Charles I was followed by the appearance of the Levellers and the Fifth Monarchy men in the army. Thomas Harrison, the leader of the latter, was a remarkably brave soldier, who wished England to be ruled by God, through the instrumentality of seventy godly men (the number was chosen as being that of the Jewish Sanhedrin). These worthies were to introduce the Kingdom of God and the saints. To such fanatics, Oliver Cromwell himself soon became the Dragon and the Man of Sin. These Arab dissenters were to Ali something of what Harrison and the Fifth Monarchy men were to Cromwell.

Meanwhile trouble was brewing in Egypt. When the mutineers from Fustat had set out the year before (early 656) to besiege Othman in Medina, a certain Muhammad abu Hudheifa had seized control of that province, while ibn abi Sarh, Othman's foster-brother, fled to Palestine. Abu Hudheifa himself fled to Syria when Ali became khalif. After the Battle of the Camel, Ali appointed Muhammad ibn abi Bekr as his governor of Egypt. Muhammad was himself one of Othman's murderers and the appointment therefore furthered Muawiya's propaganda to the effect that Ali had himself planned the murder in order to obtain power.

Amr ibn al Aasi, the conqueror of Egypt, had been living in Medina since his dismissal by Othman, and had been among the most acid critics of the old khalif. When, however, the mutineers had arrived in Medina and besieged the Prince of the Faithful, Amr had slipped away to a farm which he owned in Beersheba. Always an acute politician, he decided to keep out of harm's way until it became apparent who was going to win. When informed that Ali had been proclaimed khalif, he consulted his two sons as to the best course to follow. One recommended him to remain in retirement in Beersheba, the other to join Muawiya in Damascus. Amr is alleged to have answered that the first course was that recommended by religion but that worldly ambition constrained him to adopt the second. Suffice it to say that when he heard of the Battle of the Camel and Ali's march to Kufa, Amr ibn al Aasi rode from Beersheba to Damascus and threw in his lot with Muawiya. It may perhaps have been that Amr disliked Ali for some reason of which we are ignorant. The interesting aspect of the question, however, is that he was an extremely shrewd observer and bent on his own advancement. He would not openly have opposed Ali at this stage, when the latter had just won a major battle, unless he foresaw that Muawiya would eventually win. There was obviously something about Ali which made intelligent onlookers predict his failure. We can only presume that the weak quality of Ali was indecision, compromise, perhaps a certain lethargy. He did not possess the ruthless energy needed to ride the storms of the turbulent society which he aspired to lead.

Still anxious to avoid war with Muawiya, Ali sent him a further letter, written from Kufa, inviting him to fall into line with all the other provinces and to recognize his khalifate. The governor of Syria, however, replied that he would tender his allegiance to Ali as soon as the murderers of Othman had been punished. Seeing that further negotiation was useless, Ali left Kufa at the head of 50,000 men. He moved up the Tigris from Medain to Mosul and then, turning west by Sinjar, arrived at Raqqa on the Euphrates. Crossing the river, he moved on up the west bank. A little way above Raqqa, he met the Syrian army led by Muawiya at Siffeen.

The Euphrates in this area runs between low gravelly desert hills. In most places the valley is narrow, perhaps only a few hundred yards wide, but here and there it widens out, leaving an area of flat plain on one side of the river or the other. It was on such an open space by the river, and between the gravelly deserts on either side, that the two armies met in April or perhaps May 657. Tradition relates, possibly with the usual exaggeration, that each army consisted of some 50,000 men.

As he had done before the Battle of the Camel, Ali began by offering to negotiate. Muawiya, himself even more temperamentally cautious than Ali, was loath to risk everything on a pitched battle. He asked merely that punishment be meted out to the murderers of Othman. Ali, however, had already gone too far to make this possible. He had already sent Muhammad ibn abi Bekr to be governor of Egypt. The fanatic "leveller", Malik al Ashtar, was one of the principal leaders of his army. Any attempt to arrest Malik would cause a mutiny in the army of Kufa, which constituted the greater part of his force. There seemed to be no way out of this impasse. It must be remembered that to Arabs, even now, family revenge is a sacred duty. Even the Prophet himself, in general of a mild and forgiving disposition, had recognized revenge as legitimate. This is not to suggest that Muawiya was not fired by personal ambition, but it means that his supporters believed him to be right in insisting on revenge and they would quite possibly have abandoned him as a coward if he had compromised.

When the negotiations thus reached a deadlock, Ali challenged Muawiya to settle the issue by single combat. He had been a great Muslim champion in the years of Muhammad's wars and his mind still ran on these lines, though it is interesting to speculate on how the rivals would have demeaned themselves, for both were now rather portly and middle-aged. From the political angle, moreover, the challenge, though in harmony with the old chivalry of the Days of Ignorance, may have been of doubtful wisdom. For Ali's claim rested on the fact that he was the lawful Successor of the Apostle of God. Thus his quarrel was not, or should not have been, a personal one but a struggle between religion and the world. In any case, Muawiya, a cold-blooded statesman less impetuous than his rival, excused himself from the challenge.

Meanwhile constant skirmishing and challenges to single combat were in progress. Surprisingly perhaps, there were more Companions on the side of Muawiya than on that of Ali, whose forces consisted rather of bedouins. Thus Ubaidullah,[8] the son of the Khalif Umar, who was fighting on the side of Muawiya, challenged Muhammad, the son of Ali. In general, however, casualties appear to have been light during the months of May and June, while the armies lay opposite to one another. This was doubtless largely due to the fact that men of the same tribes, and even of the same families, were some on one side and some on the other. For these were not hostile nations, nor even Syrians and Iraqis, but different corps of the same army. Virtually all the men on both sides were natives of Arabia, for although many had now married Persian, Syrian or Greek wives, the time which had elapsed since the conquests had not been enough to enable a new and hybrid generation to grow up.

In the middle of June began the month of Muharram, which in the Days of Ignorance had been observed as a month of truce. This was seized upon as an excuse for further delay by two armies unwilling to fight. In the middle of July 657, at the end of Muharram, the fighting became hotter, until eventually both armies drew out opposite to one another for a pitched battle. The first day's fighting was indecisive but both sides seem to have got their blood up and on the second morning the battle began in deadly earnest. Ali posted himself in the centre of his line, with the men who had come with him from Medina. The army of Kufa held one wing, that of Basra the other. On the side of Muawiya, Amr ibn al Aasi, the conqueror of Egypt, was in the forefront of the battle, and drove back the men of Kufa in confusion. Ali himself, sword in hand, rallied the ranks, fighting with the same courage as had distinguished him thirty years before at Bedr and Uhud.

But the hero of the day was the leader of the fanatics, Malik al Ashtar. Whether inspired by religious enthusiasm or aware that Muawiya, if victorious, would order his execution as one of Othman's murderers, he was

[8] The same who had killed Hormuzan after the murder of Umar.

everywhere in the van. At the head of 400 devotees, all of whom knew the whole Qoran by heart, he charged so deeply into the enemy's ranks that he nearly overtook the person of Muawiya himself. Then the army of Syria rallied, the situation was restored and the mutual carnage continued through the dust and glare of a long July day.

It will be remembered that Umar ibn al Khattab had once sent, as governor of Kufa, Ammar ibn Yasir, now an old man but one of the earliest converts to Islam. More than thirty years before, when the first Muslims in Medina were threatened by Quraish, whom they repelled by digging a ditch,[9] Ammar had been staggering along with a great load of earth. The Prophet himself had noticed him and come to his assistance, relieved him of his load and dusted his head and clothes. With that kindly paternal spirit which was one of the reasons for the devotion of his followers, he had said, "Poor Ammar! A cruel and unjust people will certainly be the death of you." It seems probable that the remark was made jokingly, blaming his companions for overworking the willing disciple. But the phrase was remembered as a prophecy. Now on the second day of this bitter battle, Ammar was killed fighting for Ali and calling aloud, "O Paradise, how close thou art." Such was the veneration entertained by both armies for the memory of the Apostle that the death of Ammar inspired as much ardour in the army of Ali as it induced depression in that of Muawiya. For the implication of the prophecy was that the men who killed Ammar would be fighting in an unjust cause. Amr ibn al Aasi, however, hastily cried out that it was Ali who had killed Ammar by bringing the old man out to battle.[10]

The second day, like the first, ended indecisively and fighting was continued all through the hours of darkness. The night, like the last night at Qadasiya, was named also the night of fury. Malik al Ashtar, fighting with the intensity of puritan fanaticism, was forcing the Syrian army back foot by foot. It was on the morning of the third day of battle that Amr ibn al Aasi received another of his inspirations. He suggested to Muawiya that the mounted men attach the Qoran to their lances. At the worst, he pointed out, this would sow confusion in Ali's army for some would wish to fight on and others to stop. At the best, it might bring an end to the battle, victory in which seemed to be going to Ali. Muawiya immediately saw the value of the ruse and orders were given for a force to move forward with Qorans on their lances, calling, "The word of God. Let the word of God decide."

No sooner was the cry heard than it was taken up by Ali's army also. "Let the word of God decide" was repeated in loud shouts by both armies. The pious Qoran readers were the most vociferous of all. Ali expostulated on the grounds that it was all a trick. Malik al Ashtar, who felt victory to be within his grasp, protested vigorously. In true Arab style, everybody shouted at once. Al Ashtar yelled that they were all cowards, the others shouted back that they could not refuse God's word. Ali himself was pushed and jostled by the angry troops. At length it became evident that Ali's army refused to fight any

[9] Page 84.

[10] Amr ibn al Aasi always had a ready answer. The Khalif Umar, during the conquest of Egypt, once said that Amr ibn al Aasi made war with his tongue as much as with his sword.

more. A message was sent to Muawiya to ask him to elucidate the proposal. He replied that both sides should return to the decision of God's word. Each should appoint an arbitrator and the decision should be binding.

Willy-nilly, the Khalif Ali was obliged to agree, for the soldiers would no longer fight. On the contrary, they raised a cry that Abu Musa should be their arbitrator. It will be remembered that old Abu Musa had long been fighting in Persia, that before the Battle of the Camel he had been governor of Kufa. When Ali had wished to raise recruits in Kufa, he had refused to fight in these civil wars of Muslim against Muslim and had been dismissed by Ali. Presumably he had been admired and loved by the men of Kufa. Ali protested that Abu Musa was neutral and not a supporter of his at all. He suggested Abdulla ibn Abbas, the son of the Prophet's uncle, or even Malik al Ashtar, but the troops, now quite out of hand, shouted him down, insisting on Abu Musa. Muawiya chose the resourceful Amr ibn al Aasi, who had suggested the ruse of putting the Qoran on the lances.

The Battle of Siffeen was over without a victory.

* * * * *

Reference has already been made to the lack of available historical information on the tactics employed by the first Arab conquerors. But in their accounts of the hostilities between Ali and Muawiya, the Arab historians here and there drop a passing allusion which can be seized upon with gratitude. Before Siffeen, for example, Ali is reported as addressing his troops and urging the infantry to stand "as firm as a masonry wall". Elsewhere the infantry are mentioned as having been drawn up in eight ranks, or, in another place, in eleven. Some of these ranks were armed with spears, some with swords and some with bows and arrows. Although descriptions of individual challenges and single combats still occupy the principal place in accounts of the fighting, we are nevertheless led to conclude that a regular tactical system, necessitating discipline and training, had now been evolved. We no longer see a wild horde of tribesmen sweeping to victory or Paradise but are led to infer the existence of steady, disciplined armies, self-reliant and long accustomed to victory.

## *NOTABLE DATES*

| | |
|---|---|
| Murder of the Khalif Othman | 17th June, 656 |
| Ali chosen as khalif | 23rd June, 656 |
| Battle of the Camel | December, 656 |
| Battle of Siffeen | May to July, 657 |

## *PERSONALITIES*

*Claimants to the Khalifate:*

Ali ibn abi Talib, acclaimed khalif in Medina.
Zubair ibn al Awwam, killed at the Battle of the Camel.
Talha ibn Ubaidullah, killed at the Battle of the Camel.
Muawiya ibn abi Sofian, Governor of Syria.

Aisha, widow of the Prophet, Mother of the Faithful.

Abu Musa al Ashari, veteran soldier, Governor of Kufa, refused to join in the civil war.

Malik al Ashtar, fanatical puritan leveller, one of the leaders of the mutineers who killed Othman, now a supporter of Ali.

Amr ibn al Aasi, twice conqueror of Egypt, dismissed by Othman and now the chief supporter of Muawiya.

Muhammad ibn abi Bekr, son of the first khalif and one of the leaders of those who killed Othman. Now appointed by Ali governor of Egypt.

# XIX

## *Heresy and Schism*

The mischiefs that flow from the contests of ambition are usually confined to the times and the countries in which they have been agitated. But the religious discord of the friends and enemies of Ali has been renewed in every age. . . . The temptation was indeed of such magnitude as might corrupt the most obdurate virtue. The ambitious candidate no longer aspired to the barren sceptre of Arabia: the wealthy kingdoms of Persia, Syria and Egypt were the patrimony of the commander of the faithful.

GIBBON, *Decline and Fall of the Roman Empire*

That the khalif of the Prophet was the lawful lord of the world, no true believer thought of doubting; but who really was the khalif of the Prophet was a question on which opinions might differ widely.

FREEMAN, *History of the Saracens*

# XIX

## HERESY AND SCHISM

THE fighting having been stopped, Amr ibn al Aasi, representing Muawiya, presented himself in the khalif's camp with a view to concluding a written agreement. When Ali's representatives began to draw up a draft, they started it with the words: "This is what has been agreed between the Commander of the Faithful and . . ." but here Amr loudly protested that Ali was the Commander of his own army but not of that of Syria. The weakest aspect of Ali's case was that no official procedure existed for the selection of a khalif. Abu Bekr, Umar ibn al Khattab and Othman had been appointed, more or less, by the acclamation of the people of Medina, and Ali had been chosen in the same manner. But there was no tradition, no saying of the Prophet, no verse in the Qoran, which stated that this procedure was sufficient. As Amr ibn al Aasi refused to subscribe to any document which referred to Ali as Commander of the Faithful, the latter was obliged to give way. The agreement was drawn up between Ali and Muawiya. The text stated that both parties agreed to bind themselves by the decision of God's word, and where the Qoran was silent, by recognized Muslim precedents. All concerned would be obliged to accept the decision of the two arbitrators, who bound themselves to judge righteously. Fighting was to cease until the arbitration took place. Malik al Ashtar resolutely refused to witness the document.

Thus, ironically enough, Ali, who a day or two earlier had been on the verge of a complete victory, was worsted in the result. Claiming to be the duly-elected Successor of the Prophet, chosen by God, he had been obliged to lower himself to the same level as Muawiya. It boded ill for him that the whole manœuvre had been the work of Amr ibn al Aasi, who was now to be Muawiya's arbitrator, while his own representative was to be Abu Musa al Ashari, a man who loudly proclaimed his neutrality. Abu Musa, moreover, was a pious soul, a simple veteran soldier, with no skill in debate or political acumen. The débâcle had been the result of indiscipline in Ali's army, which had ceased to fight when the Qoran was raised on the lances and which had insisted on the selection of its pious old former general as arbitrator. Yet this very indiscipline arose basically from the falsity of Ali's position, for he had himself largely been the cause of the prevailing anarchy by allowing Othman to be murdered. The odour of sanctity which had hitherto surrounded the khalifate had been blown away. Perhaps, with the mutineers in possession of Medina, he could not have saved Othman's life, but he need not have exposed himself to further criticism by employing the murderers, Muhammad ibn abi Bekr as governor of Egypt and Malik al Ashtar and his company in his army. Quite apart from the characters of the two rivals, it is difficult to avoid the impression that the outcome was to prove utterly disastrous for Islam. If Ali's army had pressed on to complete victory at Siffeen, Beni Umaiya might have sunk into obscurity and Islam remained undivided. As it proved, the struggle between them and Beni Hashim was to split Islam from top to bottom. The resulting rift is still with us today.

* * * * *

The agreement signed, Ali returned to Kufa and Muawiya to Damascus. The casualties in the last two days of desperate fighting at Siffeen had been peculiarly heavy. Kufa and Damascus alike were filled with mourning. The fact that Ali had been worsted, politically if not militarily, increased the dissatisfaction in Kufa. To have lost so many men might have been endurable if peace and victory had resulted. But now everything was still in the melting pot. In the excitement of the moment, the soldiers had been carried away with enthusiasm by the slogan "let the word of God decide". But they now realized that the arbitration would merely decide whether Ali or Muawiya was to be khalif. In the former case, they would be ruled, or exploited, by Beni Hashim, in the latter by Beni Umaiya. In so far as the ordinary tribesman or soldier was concerned, there was little to choose between them. The Prophet and the Qoran had said that all Muslims were brothers. Yet the Arab Empire, which had been won by their swords, had become the private property of Quraish, whose princes monopolized the provincial governorships, oppressed, exploited and devoured the people of Muhammad. It was to destroy this worldly Quraish empire that they had murdered Othman. What they sought was a theocratic republic, in which all true Muslims should be equal, as God's word had said they should.

As they marched disconsolately back from Siffeen, the men of Kufa discussed such topics as these. As a result, before they reached their base, 12,000 men of Ali's army, about one-third of the whole force, separated themselves from the main body. They marched parallel to the rest of the army, and when the latter entered Kufa, they camped a few miles away at a place called Harura. They now bitterly regretted that they had agreed to an arbitration which could only result, whichever way it went, in the elevation of another Quraish tyrant, supported by a crowd of greedy relatives. They determined to work for a theocratic state to be ruled by God alone. Ali sent one of his chief supporters, Abdulla, the son of the Prophet's uncle Abbas, to persuade them to rejoin the army. A few did so, but the majority, electing their own leader, refused to compromise. Eventually Ali himself went to Harura and reasoned with the malcontents, persuading most of them, at least for the moment, to return to their homes.

The arbitrators met at Udhroh in Trans-Jordan,[1] thirteen miles north-west of Maan in January 658, six months after the signature of the Siffeen Agreement. Each was accompanied by 400 supporters, while a number of religious worthies and Companions attended as observers or witnesses, among them Abdulla ibn Zubair and Muhammad ibn Talha, sons of the two pretenders killed at the Battle of the Camel.

The proceedings opened with a private conference between Amr ibn al Aasi, representing Muawiya, and Abu Musa al Ashari, representing Ali.

[1] Alternatively the meeting is said to have taken place at Duma.

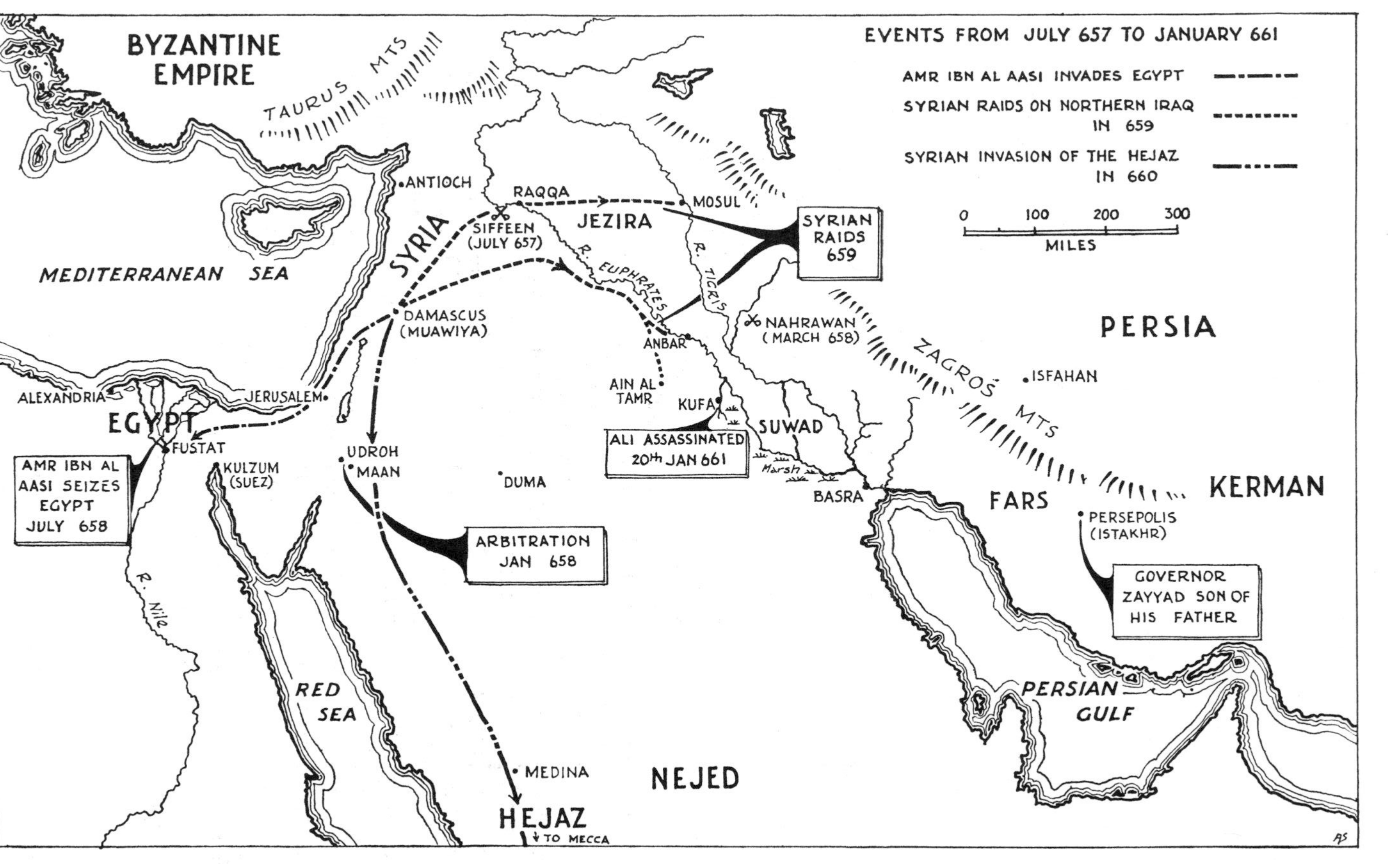
EVENTS FROM JULY 657 TO JANUARY 661
AMR IBN AL AASI INVADES EGYPT
SYRIAN RAIDS ON NORTHERN IRAQ IN 659
SYRIAN INVASION OF THE HEJAZ IN 660
0 100 200 300
MILES
BYZANTINE EMPIRE
TAURUS MTS
ANTIOCH
MEDITERRANEAN SEA
SYRIA
RAQQA
MOSUL
JEZIRA
SIFFEEN (JULY 657)
R. EUPHRATES
R. TIGRIS
SYRIAN RAIDS 659
DAMASCUS (MUAWIYA)
NAHRAWAN (MARCH 658)
PERSIA
ZAGROS MTS
ISFAHAN
ANBAR
AIN AL TAMR
KUFA
SUWAD
ALI ASSASSINATED 20th JAN 661
Marsh
BASRA
ALEXANDRIA
JERUSALEM
EGYPT
FUSTAT
AMR IBN AL AASI SEIZES EGYPT JULY 658
KULZUM (SUEZ)
UDROH
MAAN
DUMA
ARBITRATION JAN 658
FARS
KERMAN
PERSEPOLIS (ISTAKHR)
GOVERNOR ZAYYAD SON OF HIS FATHER
R. Nile
RED SEA
PERSIAN GULF
MEDINA
NEJED
HEJAZ
TO MECCA

Map XXXIII

From the brief summaries given by the Arab historians, the following general outline of their deliberations seems to emerge. Abu Musa, the simple pious old soldier who claimed to be neutral, expatiated on the need for unity among Muslims and the responsibility of the arbitrators to put an end to civil war, sentiments in which Amr heartily concurred. They then discussed whether, in view of the hostility between Ali and Muawiya, it would not be better to set both aside and to choose a new candidate. Several names were mentioned, but to each some objection arose, causing his name to be discarded. Abu Musa is then said to have suggested that Ali and Muawiya be both set aside, and that the people be left free to choose the new khalif, by what method the historians do not tell us. Amr immediately agreed to this wise suggestion of his colleague. It seems obvious that the subtle Amr was flattering his simple companion, deferring constantly to his opinion and leading him on, ready to take advantage of any false move he might make.

Having agreed to depose both Ali and Muawiya and allow the people to elect a new khalif, the two arbitrators emerged from their tent, in front of which a large crowd was waiting in breathless suspense. Abu Musa announced in a loud voice that the two arbitrators had agreed on their verdict. Amr confirmed the statement and, standing aside, begged Abu Musa, as the senior and the more venerable of the two, to speak first. The old man, flattered by Amr's complaisance and innocent of guile, then stepped forward once more and cried that they had agreed that the best way to restore peace among the Muslims was to set aside both Ali and Muawiya. They, the people, would then be asked to choose the man most fitted to be Commander of the Faithful. He accordingly agreed to set aside his candidate Ali.

Abu Musa then stepped back and Amr took his place. "You have heard the decision of Abu Musa," he cried. "He has decreed the deposition of Ali, and I confirm his decision. As for Muawiya, my chief, I confirm him as the true khalif, the heir of Othman and the avenger of his blood."

Thus by a disgraceful trick, Amr won another point for Muawiya. Ali's supporters surrounded Abu Musa, crying aloud their vexation and indignation. "But what could I do?" wailed the old soldier. "He promised to say the same as I said, but then he betrayed me." Overwhelmed with reproaches, the old man fled to Mecca, where, after a life spent in fighting for God and His Apostle, he passed his last days in religious devotions and obscurity.

This extraordinary arbitration produced little result except further to exacerbate relations. Ali and his supporters naturally refused to be bound by a "decision" which was no more than a shady verbal trick, though in Damascus Muawiya caused the people to swear allegiance to him openly as khalif. Thereafter in the daily prayers in Kufa, God was begged to curse Muawiya, Amr ibn al Aasi and their principal supporters, while in the great mosque of Damascus similar imprecations were invoked against Ali and the two grandsons whom the Apostle had loved so dearly, Hasan and Husain.

* * * * *

No sooner was the result of the arbitration announced than the levellers of Kufa seceded once more. They were disgusted, they announced, by these unseemly struggles for worldly power between unscrupulous princes. They would acknowledge no ruler but God. "*La hukm illa lillah*," they adopted as their motto—no rule but that of God. Ali, with his usual patience, attempted to conciliate and persuade them, but in vain. A month after the arbitration, they stole away one by one from their homes in the cantonments of Kufa and Basra, and concentrated at an agreed rendezvous under a leader elected by themselves. Their intention was to establish a community ruled only by God, though for the purposes of day-to-day administration, they proposed to elect a council of godly men. An attempt to seize the city of Medain was foiled, so they moved on up the Tigris to near the site of modern Baghdad, where 4,000 of them assembled at Nahrawan.

Ali now decided, in March 658, to raise a fresh army and to carry the war once more into Syria. But the dissenters meanwhile had commenced to harry the surrounding countryside. It became impossible to march to Syria, leaving Iraq exposed to the depredations of the heretics. He accordingly marched first against them, easily defeating them at Nahrawan, for he outnumbered them by more than ten to one. Nearly two thousand of the dissenters were killed, almost without loss to Ali's army. Crying "Paradise, Paradise," they ran forward on to the lances of the Muslims.

The threat of the fanatics' concentration at Nahrawan having been removed, the army returned to Kufa, ostensibly to conclude the final preparations for the invasion of Syria. But enthusiasm for Ali's cause had so far cooled that during the days of delay a great portion of the men deserted to their homes. Ali's sermons and appeals no longer met with any response. At length, seeing the public indifference, he resigned himself to the inevitable and the expedition was abandoned. Muawiya remained the undisputed ruler of Syria, while Ali governed Iraq, harassed by dissenters, and regarded with increasing coldness by the fickle soldiery of Kufa and Basra.

Meanwhile, as has already been related, Muhammad ibn abi Bekr had been sent by Ali as governor of Egypt. The prospect of two warring khalifs fighting for the throne had gone far to destroy the sacred idealism of Islam and to relax respect for authority. The Arabs in Egypt were divided in their loyalties, some favouring the side of Ali, others leaning to Muawiya and demanding vengeance upon the murderers of Othman. In these circumstances, Ali showed doubtful wisdom in sending one of the leaders of those murderers to be governor. Even so, if Muhammad ibn abi Bekr had shown discretion, all might have been well. Instead, however, he hastened to use force, sending troops to punish a community believed to be sympathetic to Muawiya. Not only so, but the troops were defeated. Thus the governor incurred the hatred of the people without inspiring them with respect.

Realizing that Muhammad ibn abi Bekr was incapable of restoring order, Ali in despair sent the fanatical Malik al Ashtar, a man of great personality and fighting spirit, to take over the governorship. Soon after crossing the border of Egypt, however, he died mysteriously in Suez, some said of poison administered by an emissary of Muawiya. The latter was at the time in Palestine, where he had caused himself to be proclaimed khalif in Jerusalem.

Muawiya was more concerned over Egypt than over Ali's control of Iraq and Persia. If Egypt were solidly behind Ali, he thought, it could be used as a base for the invasion of Palestine and Syria. Moreover, the revenues of Egypt were so large that whichever of the rival khalifs received them would gain an immense advantage. The misgovernment of Muhammad ibn abi Bekr gave Muawiya his opportunity. He entrusted Amr ibn al Aasi with 6,000 troops to enable him to conquer Egypt for the third time. Twice he had won it from the Byzantines and now he was to seize it from his fellow Muslims.

Muhammad ibn abi Bekr, hearing of the proposed invasion, wrote in alarm to Ali begging for reinforcements. The khalif summoned the people to a meeting in the great mosque of Kufa, read out the letter from Egypt and appealed for recruits to gather on the open space outside the town the next morning. But the following day when Ali rode out to the rendezvous to enrol volunteers, not one single recruit presented himself. After waiting alone for several hours, the unhappy khalif returned to his house, and invited the principal men of the city to visit him. He was profoundly dejected and complained bitterly of the lack of support of the Muslim community. "Is it not extraordinary," he asked, "that the rabble will follow Muawiya when he calls them out, even on two or three expeditions every year, though he does not care for them or pay them, while I treat you with every consideration and yet in an emergency not one man of you will come forward?" Ali was justified in his surprise. Indeed the lack of support for him is astonishing even to us. He had more right to the khalifate than Muawiya. He was by far the most prominent Muslim, pious, learned, conscientious, always anxious to compromise, to be reasonable, to avoid shedding the blood of the Muslims. But these respectable virtues must have lacked the spark of genius, the magnetism of leadership, which were needed in those heroic but turbulent days.

Meanwhile Amr ibn Al Aasi had invaded Egypt with six thousand men. Muhammad ibn abi Bekr could raise only two thousand supporters, whom he led out to meet the invaders but who were defeated and dispersed almost without a fight, leaving him alone and deserted on the field. Fleeing on foot, he endeavoured to conceal himself in a ruined village but was dragged from his hiding place. The supporters of Muawiya were particularly enraged against Muhammad ibn abi Bekr, who had been the first man actually to lay sacrilegious hands on the martyred Othman. After sating their revenge by taunting their wretched victim, they struck off his head. His body was sewn into the skin of an ass and thrown on to a bonfire. Amr ibn al Aasi thereupon established himself once again as governor of Egypt, recognizing the overlordship of Muawiya as the legitimate Prince of the Faithful.

Ali's cause was now everywhere on the decline. Even in Basra there was a revolt in favour of Muawiya, which was only suppressed after some local fighting. Then a party of kharijis [2] or levellers raised the standard of revolt in Fars, not indeed in favour of Muawiya, but demanding the rule of God alone. The Persians of Fars had been some of the last, a few years before, to submit to Arab rule. Although not Muslims, they assisted the fanatics who were in rebellion against the conquerors of their country and the revolt was

[2] Khariji, the Arabic name for the dissenters, literally means "outsider".

only suppressed with extreme difficulty. But the suppression of the revolt was only partial, and rebellion soon broke out in Kerman. The name of Zayyad has already been mentioned as that of a capable administrator. It was he who, being the fourth witness in the charge of adultery against Mughira ibn Shuba, had failed to give evidence.[3] Zayyad was the son of Sumaiya, a woman of Taif whose legal husband was a Greek slave. But the woman's morals were notorious in Mecca, and Zayyad's father was unknown. Thus deprived of a patronymic, he was generally known as Zayyad the son of his father. Appointed by Ali governor of Kerman and Fars, he rapidly restored order and, establishing his capital in Istakhr, the ancient Persepolis, he governed Southern Persia as efficiently as Muawiya ruled Syria.

The scales were weighted down ever more heavily in favour of Muawiya, who now went over to the offensive. In the second half of 658 and in 659, a series of raids from Syria threatened Ali's hold even on Iraq. Some of these inroads reached Ain al Tamr and Anbar, only 170 miles north of Kufa, driving off loot and taking prisoners. The men of Kufa were so unwilling to fight that Ali found it impossible to take effective counter-action. Muawiya himself led a raid right across the Jezira from Raqqa to Mosul unopposed. In 660, even worse befell. An army from Syria marched to the Hejaz, occupied Mecca and Medina and even moved down to the Yemen. Everywhere the people were obliged, at the sword's point, to swear allegiance to Muawiya. Ali's governor of the Yemen abandoned his post and fled to Kufa. It is true that, when the Syrian army had returned to Damascus, a force of 4,000 men was sent from Kufa, which compelled the people once more to reverse their oaths and swear allegiance to Ali, but his weakness nevertheless became more and more patent.

But the unkindest cuts of all were still in store. Abdulla the son of Abbas, Muhammad's uncle, has been several times mentioned as Ali's most enthusiastic confidant and supporter, and the governor of Basra in his name. Asked by Ali to answer certain complaints made against his administration, Abdulla ibn Abbas took offence, and abandoning his post, departed in high dudgeon to Mecca. Soon afterwards, Ali's own brother, Aqil ibn abi Talib, went over to Muawiya.

Many years later, the house of Beni Umaiya was to become nearly extinct. The followers of Ali, however, and the descendants of Abbas were to continue for many centuries. History, it is said, is the propaganda of the victorious party, or at least of that which survives. By the time that the Arab Empire had reached that maturity which produces an interest in the past and hence gives birth to historians, Beni Umaiya had almost ceased to exist. As a result, Arab history in general gives us a picture which represents Ali in some cases as a saint, at least as a man immensely superior to Muawiya in religion, morals and learning. To accept these records at their face value is to be unable to account for the general desertion of Ali's cause in favour of that of Muawiya. We are driven to the conclusion either that the characters of both of the contestants have been distorted or else that the violent and turbulent character of the Arab tribesmen could only be impressed by strength. Ali

[3] Page 212.

may have been pious and sincere, anxious to find compromise solutions and to avoid bloodshed, but, for those very reasons, inclined to be hesitating and weak. The cold and capable Muawiya and the unscrupulous but commanding character of Amr ibn al Aasi were more suited to the age and the people. Perhaps they possessed the mysterious power to command, where the hesitating Ali could only argue and implore.

At the end of 660, as a result of an exchange of correspondence, a kind of truce was agreed to between the rival khalifs. Active hostilities ceased. Ali remained in possession of Iraq and Persia, while Muawiya's rule was unanimously acknowledged in Syria and Egypt. The line which divided them, perhaps significantly, was the frontier which formerly divided Byzantium from Persia. Muawiya was the heir of Caesar while the mantle of the Great King had fallen upon Ali.

* * * * *

While this worldly compromise might be satisfactory to the rival rulers, it could scarcely commend itself to conscientious Muslims. The empire had been shattered and the great Arab conquests had come to a standstill, since Muslims had turned their swords against Muslims. Worse still, in order to be free to confront his rival, Muawiya had concluded a truce with Byzantium under which he had agreed to pay an annual tribute to the emperor. But if sincere Muslims like Abu Musa retired from so unhappy a scene to end their lives in religious studies, the levellers were of sterner stuff. They determined to end the schism by action.

Three of these kharijis met in Mecca late in 660, and were lamenting the ruin of the true faith, when one of them suggested a remedy. The three men responsible for the misfortunes of God's people must be put out of the way. Each of the three conspirators undertook to kill his man. Abdul Rahman ibn Muljam promised to murder Ali. Burak ibn Abdulla al Temeemi made himself responsible for Muawiya, while Amr ibn Bekr agreed to dispose of Amr ibn al Aasi. All three were to be assassinated at Friday prayers on 14th Ramadhan, in the fortieth year after the Prophet's flight from Mecca, 20th January, 661. Having pledged themselves to one another with solemn oaths, and dipped their swords in poison, the three fanatics set out, each on his journey. In Fustat, on the day appointed, ibn Bekr attended midday prayers, which, in every Muslim country, were led by the governor. Falling upon the man who was leading the congregation, he killed him instantly. But it so chanced that Amr that day was sick and that his place had been taken by a substitute. When led before the real Amr, the fanatic said boldly, "It was for you that my sword stroke was intended." "You intended me to die, but God intended you," replied Amr dryly, ordering his instant execution. In Damascus, Burak al Temeemi wounded Muawiya but the blow failed to kill him.

In Kufa, on the appointed day, when the mueddhin cried out the call to prayers, Ali emerged from his house to walk into the mosque. As he passed the door, ibn Muljam struck him on the top of his head with his sword, cleaving the skull. The murderer was seized, and later executed and his body burned. Ali lingered until the following evening and then died.

Tradition has added a romantic touch to this horrible crime. Ibn Muljam, it is said, loved a woman named Qatam who belonged to the levellers, and many of whose relatives (including her father and brother) had been killed by Ali's army at Nahrawan. As the dowry of her marriage, she had demanded from ibn Muljam three thousand dirhems and the murder of Ali. Al Farazdaq, the poet of Beni Temeem, the tribe to which many of the levellers of Kufa belonged, celebrated the crime in the following lines:

"Ne'er have I seen so fine a dowry paid
As that of Qatam, as the world has heard.
Three thousand dirhems, a black slave and a maid,
And Ali's head, cleft by a flashing sword."

Ali was about sixty years old when he was assassinated. The site of his grave is uncertain. Some say that he was secretly buried by his followers, for fear that his enemies might desecrate his tomb. As a young man he had been married to Fatima, the Prophet's daughter, as his sole wife. By her he had Hasan and Husain, children with whom the Apostle of God loved to play and laugh. Fatima had died not long after her father, and Ali then married other wives, by whom he had eleven sons and fifteen daughters. Suyuti says that, when he was killed, he left nineteen concubines in addition to his wives. Of a mild and kindly disposition, he was perhaps not ruthless enough for the violent times in which he lived.

* * * * *

The poisoned sword of ibn Muljam eventually accomplished that which the various Arab armies had failed to achieve—it reunited the empire under one ruler. Meanwhile, however, no sooner was Ali dead than the men of Kufa swore allegiance to his eldest son, Hasan, the Prophet's grandson by his daughter Fatima. He was thirty-seven years of age when his father was assassinated. Tradition relates that he resembled the Apostle in his physical appearance. The intense affection of Muhammad for his two grandsons has already been referred to and is the subject of many traditions. Eye-witnesses related how they saw the Prophet himself carrying Hasan on his shoulder and exclaiming, "O God, verily I love him. I pray Thee to love him." On another occasion, he was giving Hasan a ride, sitting on the back of his neck, when he met a man who smiled and called out, "That is a fine horse you are riding my boy." And the Apostle called back "and he is an excellent rider," as he "cantered" away. Another testified that he saw the Apostle of God sitting with Hasan in his lap, and saying, "He who loves me, let him surely love this boy, and let him who is present, tell him who is absent."

Hasan inherited the milder virtues of the Prophet, without his dedication, his perseverance or his moral courage. He was gentle, grave, reserved and dignified. Generous with his money, he disliked strife, war or violence. His chief pleasure was in the female sex. According to the law of Islam, he was not allowed to have more than four wives at any one time. But no limit had been set to the number of times which a man might divorce, and Hasan was alleged to have made use of this method ninety times, in order to obtain a sufficient variety of spouses. Yet curiously enough, if tradition speak the truth, nearly all his wives liked him and continued to speak well of him, even after they had been divorced. (In contrast, although the Prophet's wives gave him much trouble, he could never harden his heart to divorce any one of them.)

In some ways he was religious, and it is related that he performed the pilgrimage to Mecca twenty-five times and that he would walk the two hundred and fifty miles from Medina to Mecca on foot, to obtain greater religious merit, his horses being led behind him. He was a charming conversationalist and never spoke evil of any man. When, on one occasion, a man abused him in the most opprobrious language, he was said only to have answered that he would not retort in the same vein but that he would meet his traducer one day before God, and "the Lord is terrible in vengeance."

Muawiya, however, was not the man to let slip so great an opportunity. With all possible speed, he set himself to prepare an army, with which to invade Iraq. When the news reached Kufa, the men of that town appear to have come forward willingly for service, in spite of their previous reluctance to fight for Ali. Perhaps the assassination of the latter, or a natural sympathy for a young and blameless prince, stirred, for a short time, their emotions. Doubtless also there was a certain feeling of rivalry with Syria. It will be recollected that when the armies of Syria and Iraq had met once during operations in Armenia, co-operation had been found difficult and eventually the two columns had separated and each had engaged in its own individual operations.

It would of course at this stage, in the year 661, be deceptive to refer to them as Syrians and Iraqis. Little intermixture had yet taken place with the civil population and both armies were still tribesmen from Central Arabia. But they were drifting apart as rival military groups. For the moment, however, an army of 40,000 men stood to arms in Kufa and a covering force was despatched northwards to obtain intelligence and to check the advance of the enemy.

While, however, his supporters were thus preparing for battle, Hasan himself was increasingly unwilling to engage in armed conflict. When he was taunted with being a shame to Islam, he replied, "Shame is better than hellfire." On another occasion, he claimed that he had abandoned worldly ambition, "Seeking the favour of God, and to spare the blood of the people of Muhammad." Whether Hasan's unwillingness to fight be attributed to a lack of spirit or to a conscientious reluctance to shed blood, it failed to impress the troops who had rallied to his defence and who now showed signs of insubordination. An unworldly spirit of gentleness was perhaps insufficiently esteemed among the warlike and turbulent Arabians.

It was Hasan himself who put an end to the crisis by writing to Muawiya and offering to abdicate, on condition that he be allowed to remove the money to be found in the treasury of Kufa, and that the revenue of a Persian province be allotted to him as a pension for life. Some accounts state that he also stipulated an amnesty for those who had supported his father against Muawiya. The latter promptly accepted the terms asked for by his rival and Hasan, accompanied by his younger brother, Husain, left Kufa for Medina. He had been khalif for six months, his abdication taking effect in July 661. Muawiya then entered Kufa and accepted the oaths of allegiance of the armies of Iraq. Thereafter Hasan, the son of Ali and the grandson of Muhammad, disappeared from the pages of the turbulent history of Arabia. He lived in retirement with his wives and concubines in Medina. But he did not achieve domestic, as he had political peace. For he died eight years later, as the result of poison administered by one of his wives, presumably owing to some family jealousy. The enemies of Beni Umaiya have claimed that Muawiya, or his son Yezeed, persuaded the woman to commit the murder. But the charge would appear far-fetched, for Hasan had himself refused to compete for power and never showed any signs of regretting his decision. The accusation, however, has been sufficient to cause his adherents to claim for him the crown of martyrdom.

* * * * *

Muawiya, the new and universally recognized khalif, was, it will be remembered, the son of Abu Sofian and of his vindictive wife Hind. Both he and his father had bitterly resisted the Apostle of God and only rallied to his side on the day on which the Muslims occupied Mecca. Muawiya, however, only a few days later, fought on the side of the Muslims at Hunain.[4] The Prophet was most anxious, after the capture of Mecca, to conciliate the leaders of the town. In pursuance of this policy, he appointed Muawiya as his secretary and took him with him to Medina, a fact which seems to indicate that he was above the average level in his standard of education. One traditionist reported that he had heard Muhammad pray, "O God, instruct Muawiya in writing and accounts and preserve him from eternal punishment." The first part of the prayer seems to have been granted, for he was an able administrator.

Muawiya is described as tall, light-skinned and handsome and of a commanding mien. Umar, the former khalif, is reported as having said that he "was the Caesar of the Arabs". He presumably meant that he was of majestic carriage, but the remark is striking, for he became indeed the first temporal ruler of the Arabs whose claim was not based on religious pre-eminence. Another tradition reports the saying that when men speak of great rulers like Heraclius or Chosroes, they are wrong to omit Muawiya from that category.

Yet he was no haughty dictator. He was less autocratic than the humble and pious Umar ibn al Khattab, who ruled with a high hand. Muawiya was less the God-appointed successor of the Prophet than the prince of the Arab nation. He nevertheless made active and constant use of religion to maintain his rule and was, as will appear, active in wars against non-Muslims. In actual fact, the pride of the Arab race was already a powerful factor, even in the days of the pious Umar ibn al Khattab. It was Umar who formulated the policy of keeping the Arabs as a conquering, military caste, living on the

[4] Page 97.

produce of the toil of conquered races. It was he also who decreed that no Arab could ever more be a slave. This Arab pride did not entirely accord with Islam, which stipulated that all Muslims were equal. Nevertheless in the days of Abu Bekr, Umar and Othman, religion was so evidently predominant that Arab racial feeling passed almost unnoticed. All we can say of the reign of Muawiya is that in it Arab race pride gained in influence in comparison with pure religion. But the change was only one of proportions. Both influences had been at work from the days of Abu Bekr, and both were at work still.

But Muawiya's Arabism did not concern only relations with races other than the Arabs or with religions other than Islam. The change was also internal. The first khalifs had been implicitly obeyed because they were the Prophet's successors. The sanctity of the office had been undermined by the murder of Othman and the civil war between Ali and Muawiya. It was obvious that the latter had become khalif because he was the most powerful personality and the most capable leader. The Arabs have always, in spite of their tendency to anarchy, been willing to serve any man whom they considered to be fit to lead. They have never been willing to pay respect to pomp, rank or hereditary privileges or titles. But to a real man, they have always been ready to submit, not only with alacrity but with enthusiasm. It was as such that they gave their allegiance to the new khalif.

Muawiya, on his part, assumed the rôle of the democratic Arab chief of tradition, the first among his peers but no more. Later generations, who had perforce grown to expect in their khalifs the pomp and arrogance of oriental despots, have expressed their astonishment at the manner in which Muawiya was addressed by his subjects. Soon after his assumption of the khalifate, a man accosted him with the words, "By Allah, thou must surely act uprightly with us, O Muawiya, or we will assuredly set thee right." "How?" enquired the khalif. "With a stick," shouted his interlocutor, to which Muawiya answered, doubtless with a twinkle, "Very well then, I will act uprightly." This brutal yet humorous frankness is typical of the Central Arabian tribesmen even to our own day. Anyone who has had intimate dealings with them cannot but recognize, with that thrill of pleasure which is produced by a perfect picture, that the Arab historians are describing the bedouins of today as accurately as those of 1,200 years ago. It is noticeable, moreover, that this outspoken directness contrasts as completely with the manners of the settled Syrians and Lebanese of today as it doubtless did with those of the Byzantine Greeks. The cultured Syrian is one of the most charmingly courteous of men and will put any European to shame when he bows him to a seat, with solicitous enquiries regarding his excellency's health. It is fascinating to think that, after twelve centuries, the Syrians still exhibit the courtesy of the Byzantines, the bedouins the rough democracy of the Arab conquerors.

When Muawiya visited Medina for the first time after his accession, he was coldly received by the Companions, the Helpers and the Emigrants, the aged survivors of the days of enthusiasm. He is alleged to have expostulated with a group of these with whom he was seated, saying, "All the people have come to me to give allegiance except you, O Helpers." One of the latter replied curtly, "We have no riding camels." To which Muawiya answered (for of course he had lived in Medina as the secretary of the Apostle), "What has become of all those camels you used to employ to fetch water?" "We lamed them chasing after you and your father after the Battle of Bedr," was the bitter retort. It would be difficult to imagine a more provocative remark, but Muawiya made no reply. The Helper, determined to continue to press his point, then remarked gloomily, "Truly the Apostle of God said to us, 'You will see after me a state of calamity.'" "What did he then command you to do?" enquired the new khalif. "He commanded us to be resigned," replied the Helper with a sigh. "Then be resigned," retorted Muawiya, again one imagines with a humorous twinkle.

The elders of Medina, helpless in face of the military strength of the khalif (and even in face of his wit) comforted themselves with the thought of his eternal damnation, an idea which finds expression in these lines by a poet of that town:

> "The Prince of the Faithful, Muawiya, we greet him,
> In this message from us of the Prophet's own city.
> We will be resigned till the Day when we meet him,
> The last Day of Judgement, the Day without pity."

Finally, a tradition attributes to a contemporary chieftain the saying that he had associated with Muawiya and had never seen a man of greater forbearance, or slower to folly, or more extreme in gravity, than he.

Yet perhaps the most striking tribute to Muawiya's democracy was given by a Greek contemporary, the historian Theophanes, who described him as being the first councillor, not the king or emperor of the Arabs. We, in our times, have seen more than enough of dictators. Yet how few, if any, have we seen who were able to circulate freely among their people, to sit and indulge in open and equal conversation not only with the public but with their political enemies, and to reply to their sarcastic, and even insolent remarks, with quiet good humour. Yet, or perhaps for this very reason, it is recorded that Muawiya was the only khalif against whom there was never any rebellion after his accession.

It has already been mentioned that Muawiya, while Ali was still alive, had appointed Amr ibn al Aasi governor of Egypt, the land which, on his initiative alone, had been conquered by the Arabs. He did not live long to enjoy the peaceful fruits of his many labours. He died in 663, two years after the accession of Muawiya. The character of Amr ibn al Aasi is difficult to assess. Of his courage and initiative, his successful invasion of Egypt at the head of only 3,500 bedouins, is sufficient proof. His subsequent administration of the conquered province seems to have been more enlightened than that of his chief, Umar ibn al Khattab. He devoted a regular proportion of the annual revenue of the country to the repair and development of the irrigation works and he endeavoured to protect the Copts from extortionate taxation. He also re-dug Trajan's canal which the Byzantines had allowed to silt up, thereby making it possible for ships from the Red Sea to sail up to Fustat and thence into the Nile and down to the Mediterranean.[5] As a politician and diplomat he enjoyed a high reputation, from the time of his mission on behalf of Quraish to the Negus of Abyssinia,[6] to his final manœuvres in support of Muawiya against Ali. Yet his conduct of the arbitration at Udroh was deceitful and he may well have been financially corrupt. That he was a poet we know, if only from the few lines of prose which he wrote to Umar ibn al Khattab, describing the life of Egypt. His many recorded witticisms prove the readiness of his sense of humour. But perhaps the most unexpected tribute to his character is that paid by a man who had been intimate with all the great personalities of those stirring days and whose characterization of Amr ibn al Aasi was contained in few words, "I have never seen a gentler companion than he."

It will be recollected that, during the siege of Othman's house prior to his murder, the mutineers had clamoured for the surrender of the unpopular Merwan, who was sheltering with the khalif's household. When Othman was murdered, Merwan escaped with a wound, accompanied Zubair and Talha to Basra and fought against Ali in the Battle of Aisha's camel. When Ali was victorious, Merwan took refuge with Muawiya in Damascus. The new khalif, when the death of Ali had removed all opposition, appointed the hated Merwan to be governor of Medina, an apparent act of retribution for the murder of Othman. But the power had passed from Medina for ever. The remnants of the Companions and their descendants lived there far from the madding crowd. Some passed their days in religious meditation, others in the dissipation of the wealth acquired in the great conquests, on the pleasures of luxury and the charms of the fair sex. The heroic days of Bedr, Uhud and the Arab Apostasy were slowly forgotten.

Over the licentious and turbulent soldiery of Kufa, Muawiya first appointed Mughira ibn Shuba, the adulterer of Basra. A stout, coarse-grained adventurer, with matted hair and a powerful frame, who had lost an eye at the Battle of the Yarmouk, Mughira had been a successful fighter in Persia. He had ruled Kufa before at the end of the time of Umar the second khalif, but had been removed by Othman to make room for an Amaiyid. He had the reputation of a man not easily put to shame, unabashed, brutal and full of courage, cunning and resourcefulness. He was now responsible for Kufa, that is, for Central Iraq, and for Northern Persia. It was no light task. In Iraq the Khariji heretics still conspired for their ideal of the theocratic republic, while the disappointed supporters of Ali and his family regarded the dynasty of Damascus with hatred and resentment. In Northern Persia, the tide of conquest resumed its flow, with Kufa as its base.

But the most remarkable of Muawiya's governors was to be Zayyad "the son of his father", whom we have already more than once had occasion to notice. He was governing South Persia for Ali when the sword of ibn Muljam put an end to his master's career. Nevertheless, so firmly was he established in his capital at Persepolis that he maintained his independent rule over his province for more than a year after Muawiya's accession. It will be remembered that Mughira ibn Shuba had been saved from an ignominious death

[5] Map XXVII. page 239.

[6] Page 49.

by stoning for the Basra adultery by the fact that Zayyad "the son of his father" had withheld his evidence. He had not forgotten the kindness and now acted as mediator to secure the pardon of Zayyad. With the approval of Muawiya, he proceeded to where Zayyad ruled in state in Persepolis (once the city of Cyrus and Darius) and returned bringing Zayyad with him under safe-conduct to Damascus. The new khalif was not the man to alienate a provincial governor of such proved ability. He received him with every mark of honour and confirmed him in his post.

Soon afterwards, a remarkable incident took place. It will be recollected that Zayyad was the son of Sumaiya, a vagrant slave girl of Taif and Mecca, and was of unknown paternity. Suddenly, to the scandal of the devout, Muawiya declared that his own father, old Abu Sofian, was the father of Zayyad by the notoriously promiscuous Sumaiya, and consequently that Zayyad was his own brother. The illegitimate relationship between Abu Sofian and Sumaiya had, of course, occurred before the conversion of the old man to Islam. It was a recognized tenet of the early Muslims that a man converted to Islam could not be blamed for sins committed in the Ignorance. Apart from religion, however, some of the proud Beni Umaiya were by no means flattered by the inclusion in the family tree of a relative of such doubtful parentage. To admit his father's liaison with a woman of notorious immorality was, to say the least of it, an original way of winning over a political opponent. But Muawiya's political sense was not at fault. Zayyad the son of his father now became Zayyad ibn abi Sofian and his interest was thereby firmly attached to the throne. Zayyad was made the governor of Basra, with his jurisdiction extending right across Southern Persia to the River Indus in modern Pakistan. Mughira remained governor of Kufa until his death. He was succeeded by Zayyad, who became simultaneously governor of Kufa and Basra and who thus was Muawiya's *alter ego* in his rule over the whole eastern half of the empire. He maintained an almost regal state, and was preceded and followed wherever he went by troops and heralds.

The provinces of Kufa and Basra were still rent by internal schisms. The dissenters, three hundred of whom had been put to death in Kufa by Mughira, continued to plot, but the principal source of internal strife was the bitterness between the supporters of Muawiya and those of the martyred Ali. Although Zayyad had previously been a servant of the latter, he now employed all his efforts to support the Umaiyids. He is alleged to have said himself that the art of government consisted in the use of lenity without weakness and of severity without brutality. As he is reported to have caused a supporter of Ali to be buried alive, it is difficult to know how he would have defined the brutality which he deprecated.

Persons suspected of disloyalty were arrested and asked their opinions of Ali and Othman. Those who replied that Ali had been a good man and that injustices had been perpetrated during the reign of Othman, paid for their temerity with their lives. In order to enjoy the patronage of Muawiya it was necessary to curse Ali and to praise the martyred Othman. Zayyad was pitiless in his imprisonment and execution of the dissidents, the kharijis and the party of Ali alike, though suspects who secured the remand of their cases to Muawiya himself were often pardoned.

Ruthless as were the methods employed by Zayyad the son of his father, the fickle and turbulent behaviour of the Kufans towards the mild and benevolent Ali when he was their ruler suggests that they deserved a good deal of the severity of which they complained under Mughira and Zayyad. During the régime of Ali the whole of lower Iraq and much of Persia had been in turmoil, the roads unsafe and the frontiers invaded by the unbelievers. No sooner was Zayyad firmly in the saddle than sedition subsided, internal security was perfectly re-established and the Faithful once more surged onwards beneath their victorious banners into India and Turkestan. Such ruthless efficiency on the part of both Muawiya and Zayyad seemed to suggest that perhaps they really were brothers and that old Abu Sofian had actually begotten not one but two statesmen of genius.

## *NOTABLE DATES*

| | |
|---|---|
| Ali defeats the levellers at Nahrawan | March 658 |
| Seizure of Egypt by Amr ibn al Aasi | July 658 |
| Assassination of Ali | 20th January 661 |
| Abdication of Hasan | July 661 |

## *PERSONALITIES*

Muawiya, khalif in Damascus.
Ali, khalif in Kufa.
Amr ibn al Aasi, the conqueror of Egypt } The Arbitrators.
Abu Musa al Ashari, the conquerer of Fars }
Abdul Rahman ibn Muljam, the murderer of Ali.
Hasan, eldest son of Ali, and grandson of the Prophet.
Mughira ibn Shuba, once again governor of Kufa under Muawiya.
Zayyad, the son of his father, governer of Basra and later of Kufa also, as Zayyad ibn abi Sofian.

# XX

# *The Conquests Resumed*

The Caliphate might conceivably be allotted to the worthiest of the Faithful; it might conceivably be hereditary in the family of the Apostle; but Mahomet could never have imagined that it would become hereditary in the family of his bitterest enemy. FREEMAN, *History of the Saracens*

The situation on the accession of Muawiya presented many difficulties. The theocratic bond which had held together the early Caliphate had been destroyed by the murder of Othman. . . . Muawiya's problem was to find a new basis for the Empire. His answer was the transformation from Islamic theocracy to an Arab secular state. . . . Muawiya rarely commanded but was skilful in operating . . . through persuasion and through his personal ability and prestige. PROFESSOR BERNARD LEWIS, *The Arabs in History*

# XX

## THE CONQUESTS RESUMED

AS soon as the civil wars were over and Muawiya was firmly in the saddle, the expansion of the Arab Empire was resumed. While he was engaged in the civil war against Ali, the new khalif had concluded an armistice with Byzantium, even agreeing to pay tribute to Caesar, from whom, however, he obtained hostages for the observance of the truce. Later the hostages were released and hostilities resumed.

At the eastern foot of the Taurus passes lay the open plain of Adana, which was to be the scene of unending frontier warfare for centuries to come, an Arab North-west Frontier similar to the North-West Frontier of India during the period of British rule. From this area, the frontier ran approximately north-east to Marash and Malatia and thence up into Armenia, Georgia and the Caucasus. The narrow pass known in antiquity as the Cilician Gates debouched on to the plain of Tarsus, but was perhaps too easily defended to be used by the Arabs for raiding Byzantium. We are informed therefore that Muawiya made use of Malatia as an advanced base for in-roads into Byzantine territory. He also rebuilt and fortified Marash.

Perhaps because his religious sincerity was impugned by the supporters of Ali and by the Companions in Medina, Muawiya, during the twenty years of his khalifate, 661–680, was untiring in his hostilities against the Byzantines. Perhaps also he sought to obliterate the memory of the tribute which he had paid to them during the years when he was fighting his fellow Muslims. The Arabs did not relish the intense cold of the plateau of Asia Minor in winter, with the result that they normally raided every summer, withdrawing in the autumn, before the cold weather set in. Muawiya, moreover, made the first recorded efforts to organize regular military units. From the time of the Prophet, it will be remembered the Arabs had always fought by tribes, each tribal contingent led by its natural chief. At first, the Arab armies had been paid only from the plunder seized on a campaign, after the deduction of one-fifth and its despatch to the khalif's central treasury in Medina. Umar ibn al Khattab had instituted a pay-roll, but his list of those entitled to pensions was based on the tribal structure.

The existence of a more or less fixed frontier with Byzantium, however, made more regular methods essential. The garrisoning of the fortresses was a dangerous and exhausting service and those engaged on it required especially high rates of pay. Moreover, the soldiers were no longer always Arabs, and frequent mention is made henceforward of contingents from Khurasan or of the transportation of Khurasanis with their families to the north-western passes. Perhaps they were more familiar than the Arabs with cold winters and mountainous country.

Operations were not, however, limited merely to "routine" summer raiding. The khalif determined to launch an attack on the capital of the empire, Constantinople itself. It will be remembered that, ever since he became governor of Syria in 639, Muawiya had appreciated the immense advantages of sea power. The cautious Umar ibn al Khattab had refused to sanction the formation of an Arab fleet, but Othman had eventually allowed himself to be persuaded. The result had been Muawiya's capture of Cyprus and two great sea battles in which the Byzantine fleet had been defeated and scattered. Sea power in the eastern Mediterranean had passed to the Arabs. In 668 (others say 670, so vague are the records of even so important an event) a great Arab fleet sailed unopposed through the Dardanelles. The Arabs landed seven miles from the city of Constantinople, and moved forward to the attack of the imperial capital.

The Muslims, by this time, had acquired a certain skill in siege warfare and were provided with mangonels and equipment for battering the walls and gates and for bombarding the city. They had learned the drill for forming a testudo, joining their shields above their heads to protect themselves from missiles from the walls, and the other time-honoured devices for attacking fortifications. But though they had acquired these skills to some extent, it was not the kind of warfare in which they excelled. We have already seen that the walls of Byzantium had withstood, for many consecutive years, both the wild and undisciplined valour of the Avars and the more regular and technical operations of the armies of Chosroes. The ramparts and towers were of immense height and solidity, while the Byzantines were no longer engaged in operations in distant and half-hostile provinces, but were defending the last refuge of their country, their religion, their wives and their children. Day after day the lines of assaulting Arabs beat in vain against the towering walls, like the furious ocean against the rocky cliffs of some mountainous land. But perhaps the principal instrument which supported the defence and alarmed the attackers was the famous Greek fire. The systems of espionage in use must have been less highly developed than those employed today, when the Byzantines were able for centuries to preserve the secret of this alarming weapon, a form of flame-thrower of which new versions have once again appeared in the field in our own times.

Unable to storm the walls of the great city, the Arabs were nevertheless able to plunder and lay waste the surrounding country on both the European and Asiatic shores. With the autumn, they abandoned their efforts to assault the walls and withdrew to the island of Cyzicus in the Sea of Marmora, eighty miles from Constantinople. For a period of seven years, the Arabs besieged Constantinople in vain, until at length their losses in men, ships and material compelled them to abandon the attempt. It seems almost miraculous in retrospect to remember that Byzantium, so often apparently at its last gasp in the seventh century, was to survive for seven centuries more and—already old—was yet to outlive that energetic, new Arab Empire which was now hammering at its gates.

Europe, since the Renaissance, has lavished its admiration upon the Roman Republic, but the memory of the later Graeco-Roman Empire has rarely met

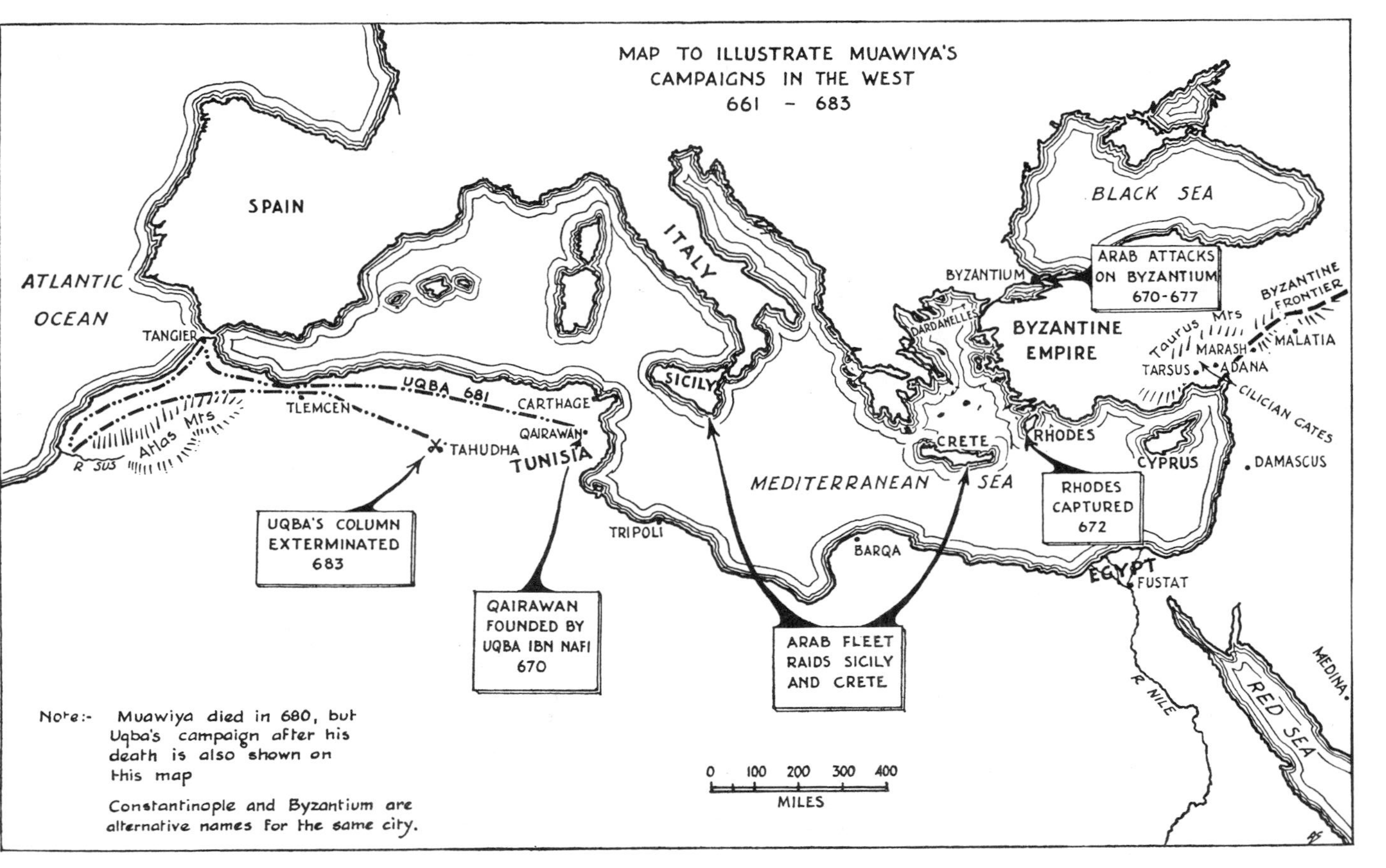
MAP TO ILLUSTRATE MUAWIYA'S
CAMPAIGNS IN THE WEST
661 - 683
SPAIN
ATLANTIC
OCEAN
TANGIER
Atlas Mts
R SUS
TLEMCEN
UQBA 681
CARTHAGE
QAIRAWAN
TAHUDHA
TUNISIA
UQBA'S COLUMN
EXTERMINATED
683
QAIRAWAN
FOUNDED BY
UQBA IBN NAFI
670
TRIPOLI
ITALY
SICILY
MEDITERRANEAN SEA
BARQA
CRETE
ARAB FLEET
RAIDS SICILY
AND CRETE
RHODES
RHODES
CAPTURED
672
CYPRUS
EGYPT
FUSTAT
R NILE
RED SEA
MEDINA
DAMASCUS
BLACK SEA
BYZANTIUM
DARDANELLES
ARAB ATTACKS
ON BYZANTIUM
670-677
BYZANTINE
EMPIRE
Taurus Mts
TARSUS
ADANA
MARASH
MALATIA
BYZANTINE
FRONTIER
CILICIAN GATES
0 100 200 300 400
MILES
Note:- Muawiya died in 680, but
Uqba's campaign after his
death is also shown on
this map
Constantinople and Byzantium are
alternative names for the same city.

Map XXXIV

with honourable mention. Yet by its dogged, last-ditch resistance in the seventh century, it decided the course of European history up to our own times. For if Byzantium had fallen in the 670's, the Arabs might well have swept on through Greece to Italy and France, where no equivalent Power would have stood in their path. Constantinople was not ultimately to fall to the Muslims until 1453, when it was captured by the Ottoman Turks. By that time, Europe had emerged from the Dark Ages and was able to offer an ultimately successful resistance, though the Muslims reached Vienna on more than one occasion. Christendom does not seem to have adequately recognized its debt to the Byzantines.

The failure of Muawiya's great attack on Constantinople did something to revive the weakened prestige of the Byzantine Empire and to reduce the terror hitherto inspired by the Arab name. With the death of Muawiya, which occurred soon afterwards, civil war between the rival branches of Quraish was to break out again and the tremendous fighting power of the Arabs was to be diverted once more from foreign conquests to fratricidal strife.

* * * * *

In describing first the Arab operations against Constantinople under Muawiya, we have departed from strict chronological order. His khalifate began in 661, the siege of Constantinople lasted from 668 or 670 to 677 or thereabouts, and he died in 680. Let us return to the beginning of his reign to consider the many other active campaigns which he promoted during his twenty-year khalifate.

At the beginning of his reign Muawiya had been faced with the problem which, more than once in the last fifty years, has confronted British strategists. It is the struggle between the advocates of the main front and those who support the side-shows, the conflict between the direct and the indirect line of approach. Both in strategy and in tactics, the soldier is often tempted to risk all in an attack on the enemy's key position, which, if captured, will end the struggle at one blow. But the very fact that its loss will mean complete disaster suggests that the enemy's resistance will there be the most desperate. Moreover, if the attacker risks everything in the assault on the key position and fails, he may never have the strength to attack again. The impetus of his offensive will have been lost and the chance of victory gone for ever, at a cost of immense casualties. If, however, he follows the other course, he will merely mask the key position and will divert his efforts to the flanks or to many subsidiary enterprises, which, in the long run, may wear down the enemy's opposition. In any case, the repulse of any of these subsidiary operations will not bring the offensive to a standstill. Those probing attacks which are successful can be energetically exploited and the advantage can be pressed home where actual experiment has shown the enemy to be weakest.

Thus if the effort and the armament expended in vain attacks on the walls of Constantinople had been used elsewhere, they might well have sufficed to conquer Italy, Spain and perhaps France. It is true that Spain was indeed to be conquered some forty years later, but by that time the pristine enthusiasm of the Arabs had yet further waned and their reputation no longer terrorized the world. But in 661 their fame was still terrible and they had never been defeated. If then they had occupied Italy, Spain and France, Constantinople itself could not long have survived.

* * * * *

It will be remembered that when Amr ibn al Aasi had first conquered Egypt, he had sent his nephew, Uqba ibn Nafi, to raid southwards into the Sudan, where indeed he had met with scant success. When Amr ibn al Aasi was re-appointed governor of Egypt by Muawiya in July 658, he again took Uqba with him. The latter was an extremely dashing and enterprising cavalry soldier, ever straining at the leash in search of some new adventure more daring than the last. Amr ibn al Aasi died in Egypt in 663, but Uqba doubtless continued to importune the authorities to send him on an expedition which would enable him—in modern parlance—to see some more active service. Muawiya at last appears to have agreed and Uqba was given command of an army in North Africa. The Byzantines still held Carthage, while the limit of actual Arab authority was only at Barqa. Uqba advanced as far as Tunisia, 1,500 miles from the main Arab base at Fustat. Arab armies had reached the same area before, but lack of a nearer base than Egypt had compelled them each time to abandon their conquests.[1] Uqba rightly appreciated that consolidation could not be effected unless an adequate base were established in the area. From such a base, columns could operate to pacify the surrounding country and a provincial government could be firmly established.

In 670, accordingly, Uqba chose a desert area south of Carthage, marked out a mosque and a house for the governor and established the army base around this nucleus. The new cantonment was Qairawan, which was later to become a great and famous city. Sited some miles inland, it was more congenial to the Arab mind than was Carthage, on the Mediterranean shores, ever exposed to the menace of naval attack. Qairawan, like Kufa, Basra and Fustat, was an Arab military cantonment and base, from which the surrounding country could be dominated.

Uqba was straightforward, outspoken, beloved by his men, perhaps honest, but he was no diplomatist. The Berbers, rather than the few isolated Byzantine garrisons here and there on the coast, were the real defenders of Africa. On several occasions, when the Arabs seemed to be strong, these people expressed themselves ready to accept Islam. But when for some reason or other the Arabs withdrew or passed on, the Berbers recanted from their profession of the faith. The Prophet had usually been mild in his treatment of unbelievers, but apostates were regarded as worthy of death. To the simple mind of Uqba, the Berbers came under this heading and he was ready to punish apostasy among them with death.

For what reason tradition does not relate, shortly after the founding of Qairawan, Uqba was dismissed and Africa, which for a short time under

[1] The ebb and flow which preceded the establishment of Arab rule in North Africa reminds us of the difficulties of communications in North Africa, which we ourselves experienced in the Second World War. The British army, like Uqba based on Egypt, advanced to Barqa, but, weakened by its long communications, was counter-attacked and driven back. Rommel advanced to Alamain with his base at Tripoli, but was himself defeated for the same reason.

his governorship had been made an independent province, was again placed under Egypt. It can only be assumed that unsatisfactory reports had reached Muawiya on the subject of Uqba's administration. The new governor of Egypt was Maslama ibn Mukhalled, who sent a certain Dinar abu al Muhajir, a freed slave of his own, to take over from Uqba. Perhaps the irascible Uqba refused to surrender his command. Perhaps Muawiya himself had sent orders. At any rate, Dinar on his arrival put Uqba in chains. These sudden vicissitudes, from commander-in-chief to prisoner in irons, suggest the communist purges of our own time.

As already stated, the contest in North Africa was three-cornered, the Byzantines, the Berbers and the Arabs constituting three separate groups. The Berbers had apparently been alienated by the perhaps arbitrary methods of Uqba and had allied themselves with the Byzantines against him. It was the policy of Dinar to win over the Berbers and with them to fight the Byzantines.[2] In this he achieved considerable success, especially in the case of Kusaila, the principal Berber leader. Assisted by these new allies, Dinar was able to occupy most of the hinterland of Carthage, though he was unable to capture the city which was firmly held by Byzantium. Moreover, assured by the friendship of the Berbers of the safety of his communications, Dinar was able to advance as far as Tlemcen, near the present frontier between Algeria and Morocco.

The general pattern of the operations in North Africa at this period emerges fairly clearly. The Byzantines held a few points on the seashore, in which they could be supported by sea from Constantinople. They could not, however, offer battle to the Arabs in the open country, unless they enjoyed the support of the Berbers. The Arabs were normally able, whenever they sent an army, to defeat Berbers and Byzantines alike in battle. The Arab problem, however, was not to win battles but to pacify the country and in this Uqba had singularly failed. The distances in Africa were so great that when the Arab armies passed on, the Berbers rose again in their rear and cut their communications. Uqba seems to have endeavoured to deal with this situation by punitive raids, Dinar by conciliation. The Berbers are a stubborn race. Even today, thirteen hundred years after Uqba and Dinar, they still preserve their distinct race and language.

Meanwhile Uqba had returned to Damascus. Muawiya died in 680, and was succeeded by his frivolous son, Yezeed. The new khalif was persuaded to reappoint Uqba, who appeared in Africa once again in 681. Revenge for an injury is sweet to the Arab mentality, and Uqba tasted its sweetness by placing Dinar in chains and dragging him about in this condition wherever he went. Kusaila, who had been co-operating with Dinar, thereupon vanished into the desert, while Uqba, as full of warlike energy as ever, set off on an expedition to the west. Crossing the whole of modern Algeria, he entered the present day territory of Morocco, then still known by its Roman name of Mauritania Tigitana. He captured Tangier, and still unsatisfied, continued down the Atlantic shore as far as the Sus, which flows into the Atlantic at the modern port of Aqadir.

[2] Cambridge Mediaeval History.

However tactless and arrogant Uqba may have been, his qualities as a fighter commanded respect. He apparently marched the 1,500 miles from Qairawan to Aqadir without any venturing to oppose him in arms. Without communications, without supplies and without a base, such an operation was perhaps rather a bedouin super-raid than a territorial conquest. Nevertheless to penetrate one thousand five hundred miles into unknown, hostile territory was no mean feat of courage and endurance. Tradition depicts Uqba as dramatically riding his horse into the Atlantic Ocean and declaiming, sword in hand, "*Allahu akbar*! If my course were not stopped by this sea, I would still ride on to the unknown kingdoms of the west, preaching the unity of God, and putting to the sword the rebellious nations who worship any other god but Him."

The very success of this gallant enterprise had perhaps made this dashing commander over confident. Returning towards the east and apparently under the impression that all opposition was now at an end, he divided his force into several columns. These scoured the country, presumably with the object of effecting a general pacification, a task which he should have accomplished before advancing so far. Perhaps his lack of sympathy with the Berbers made it difficult for him to obtain intelligence, perhaps from over confidence he did not seek it.

Suffice it to say that a small column which he himself was accompanying was ambushed at Tahudha, near the modern town of Biskra, by a force of Berbers led by their chief Kusaila. Uqba and his men fought on until all were killed, including the unfortunate Dinar, who died in his chains. This reverse occurred in the year 683.

As soon as the news of the disaster became known, a general rising of Berbers ensued, all Uqba's conquests were evacuated, including Qairawan, and Barqa became once more the limit of Arab rule in Africa. Yet Uqba had made an Arab conquest of North Africa inevitable, for history has proved again and again that a rising and energetic imperial power is rarely deterred by such a check. On the contrary, the resolve to recover the prestige thus lost renders a reconquest inevitable.

* * * * *

Sicily, as has already been mentioned, was raided more than once by the Arab fleet during the reign of Muawiya. A curious tradition relates that on one occasion the raiders carried off "idols" of gold and silver, studded with pearls. It is perhaps significant of the change of Arab mentality that the khalif, instead of utterly destroying such abominations, sent them on to India where he thought that their sale would fetch a higher price.

In the year 672, an Arab fleet captured Rhodes and the khalif ordered the establishment of a Muslim colony on the island, which was used as an advanced base for the attack on Constantinople and from which Arab vessels were able to attack Byzantine seaborne trade. The island was held for eight years. After the death of Muawiya, it was abandoned. A raid was also directed against Crete, again doubtless in connection with the operations against Byzantium.

Wide and far-reaching as were Muawiya's operations in the west, they led to little permanent advance, most of the gains being lost again when he died. This was primarily due to too wide dispersion, and particularly to the abortive attack on Constantinople. If the strength dissipated at Constantinople had been carefully employed elsewhere, North Africa could easily have been consolidated and possibly also, as already suggested, Italy and Spain. Yet, only twenty years before, the primitive Arabs under Umar ibn al Khattab had simultaneously overthrown the Persian and Byzantine Empires. Thus to advance at the same time on all fronts had become part of their tradition. Under Muawiya the Arabs were an empire, no longer merely hordes of wild tribes. But the burning enthusiasm of the early years no longer drove them onwards to victory or Paradise.

A second cause, however, produced the impression of the futility of Muawiya's operations in the west. His many raids on land and sea were doubtless softening up resistance. No matter what reverses were sustained in Africa, fresh forces would have been sent and the lost ground regained. If Muawiya had lived, Rhodes would have been retained and Sicily probably acquired. But after his death, the Arabs were to be divided against one another once more by twelve years of civil war, during which all expansion to the west came to a standstill. Thus the fruit of Muawiya's operations was lost, before expansion was resumed in the 690's.

* * * * *

If Muawiya's extensive operations in the west seemed to end with little tangible result, the same was not true in the east. In Iraq, he was served by two outstanding commanders. The coarse-grained Mughira ibn Shuba, the adulterer of Basra, was a man of energy and of powerful personality. As governor of Kufa under Muawiya, he not only kept strict order in that turbulent community, but he also urged onwards the armies of Northern Persia. In Basra Zayyad the son of his father, now recognized as the son of Abu Sofian, was a man of even more brilliant talent than Mughira. He was in command of the operations in South Persia. The two worked in cordial co-operation. In 670, half-way through the khalifate of Muawiya, Mughira died. Soon afterwards Zayyad, moving his headquarters to Kufa, was made responsible for all operations in Persia.

The Arabs had reached the Hindu Kush under the khalifate of Othman, but their rule had not been consolidated. Now, under Muawiya, they pressed forward again, advancing to Kabul, which they besieged. A breach was made in the city walls by the Arab mangonels and an assault was launched but failed to break through into the town. At dawn the next morning, the defenders, exhilarated by their repulse of the storming party, threw open one of the gates and sallied out to counter-attack, preceded by an elephant, which was wounded by an Arab warrior. The sally was repulsed and the defenders of the city withdrew. The wounded elephant, however, fell in the gateway, with the result that the gate could not be shut and the Arabs broke into the city over the elephant's body. Twice again, in Muawiya's reign, Kabul rose in revolt, but each time the rebellion was suppressed and the Arabs consolidated

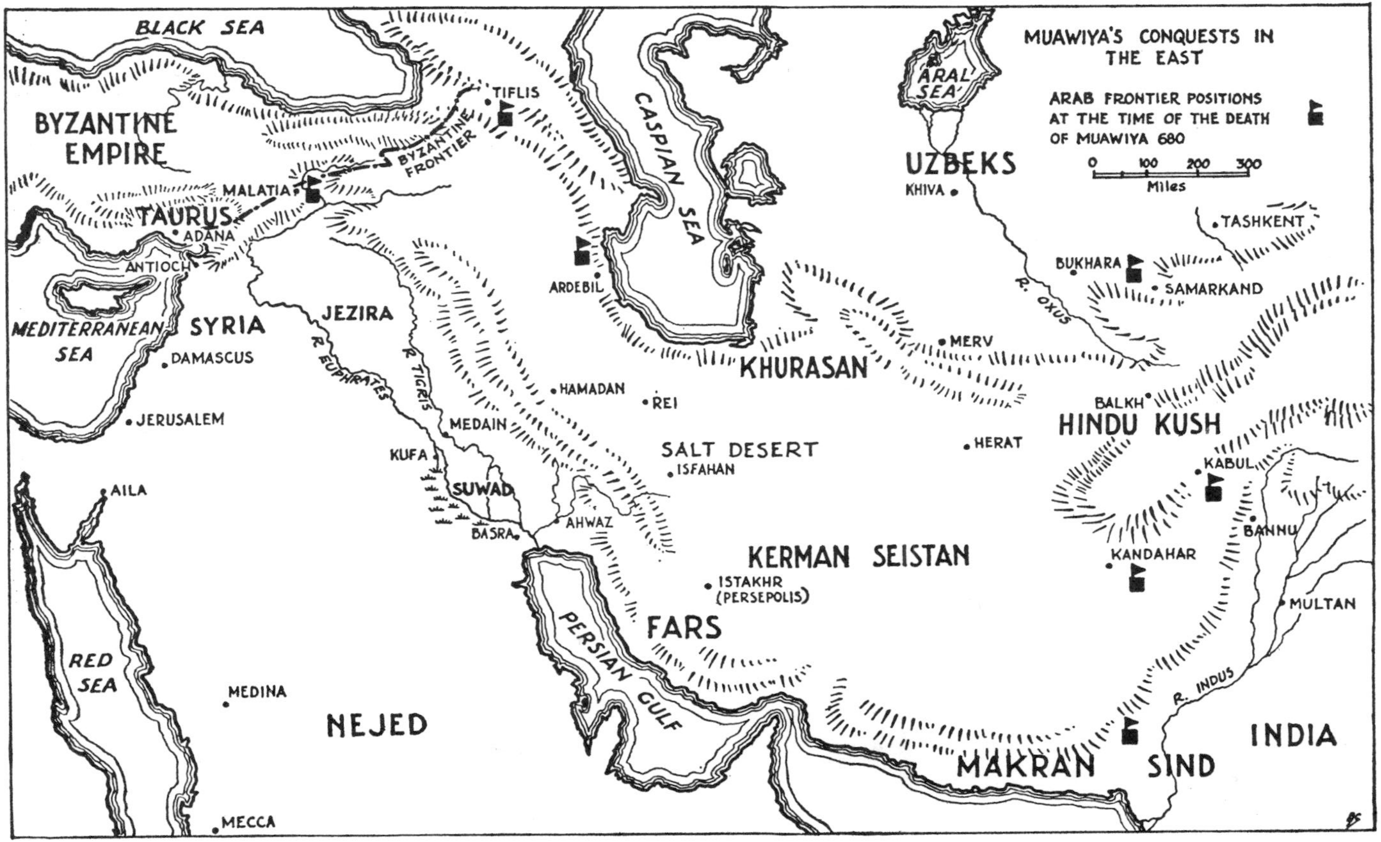

MUAWIYA'S CONQUESTS IN THE EAST
ARAB FRONTIER POSITIONS AT THE TIME OF THE DEATH OF MUAWIYA 680
0 100 200 300
Miles
BLACK SEA
BYZANTINE EMPIRE
TIFLIS
BYZANTINE FRONTIER
MALATIA
TAURUS
ADANA
ANTIOCH
MEDITERRANEAN SEA
SYRIA
DAMASCUS
JERUSALEM
JEZIRA
R. EUPHRATES
R. TIGRIS
MEDAIN
KUFA
SUWAD
BASRA
AILA
RED SEA
MEDINA
MECCA
NEJED
CASPIAN SEA
ARDEBIL
HAMADAN
REI
SALT DESERT
ISFAHAN
AHWAZ
PERSIAN GULF
FARS
ISTAKHR (PERSEPOLIS)
KERMAN
SEISTAN
KHURASAN
MERV
HERAT
ARAL SEA
UZBEKS
KHIVA
R. OXUS
BUKHARA
SAMARKAND
TASHKENT
BALKH
HINDU KUSH
KABUL
BANNU
KANDAHAR
MULTAN
R. INDUS
MAKRAN
SIND
INDIA

Map xxxv

their hold. Colonies of Arabs were settled in some places in Khurasan and Seistan, while, as already mentioned, troops were enlisted in Khurasan to hold the frontier passes of the Taurus mountains against the Byzantines.

Zayyad the son of his father died in 673. His twenty-five-year-old son Ubaidullah ibn Zayyad was appointed governor of Khurasan. In 674, at the head of a force of 24,000 Arabs, he crossed the Oxus and besieged Bukhara, which had apparently been seized by the wife of the Great Khan of the Turks. The city came to terms and was placed under tribute. In 676, Ubaidullah was made governor of Basra, while Saeed, the son of the murdered Khalif Othman, replaced him in Khurasan. Bukhara rebelled but Saeed crossed the Oxus with an army, retook the city and from thence moved on to Samarkand. After desperate fighting, in which Saeed himself lost an eye, the city came to terms and paid tribute.

As in the west, the Arab hold on the country beyond the Oxus was relaxed during the renewed civil wars after the death of Muawiya, but was later resumed and extended. Thus was Islam spread far into Turkestan and Uzbekistan, territories now in the Soviet Union. As a result of these campaigns, there are now more than twenty million Muslims in Soviet Russia.

Further south, an Arab raid reached the area round Bannu, half-way between Kabul and Multan. At about the same time, Kandahar was also occupied. As early as the khalifate of Othman, a reconnaissance had been sent through Makran, with orders to reach the frontiers of India and return to report. The commander of the force formed an unfavourable opinion of the country. "The water supply is scanty," he told the khalif, presumably referring to the deserts of Makran. "A small army would be lost there, and a large army would starve." As a result, Othman forbade any further advance through Makran. The decision was reversed by Muawiya. Under Zayyad the son of his father, Arab arms reached Sind, the delta area of the River Indus. The conquest of Sind was, however, incomplete when Muawiya died and the Arab civil wars were to put an end to further expansion for several years.

In brief, the twenty years of Muawiya's khalifate was a time of intensive military activity. It was also a period of transition. During the khalifates of Abu Bekr and Umar ibn al Khattab, there had been little military planning from headquarters in Medina. It is true that each forward move was sanctioned by the khalif, but it was not designed by him. In each area, it was the local tribes and armies themselves which were clamouring to go forward. As often as not, the khalif refused to sanction the further advance for which the local commanders were pressing. Moreover, the first two khalifs were not under any compulsion to supply money or arms for the wars, indeed rather the reverse. Each campaign furnished sufficient plunder to pay for the next and to remit a handsome balance to Medina.

But when Muawiya came to power, the Prophet had already been dead nearly thirty years. Few of his Companions were left and these were already old. The passionate and wild enthusiasm of the early years was already on the wane. The murder of Othman and the civil war against Ali had resulted in disillusionment. More than anything else, perhaps, the accumulation of wealth, slaves and women had caused a relaxation of morals and a loss of energy. The lean, hardy cavaliers of Arabia had grown fat. Ali when middle-aged had a large stomach. Muawiya, in later life, had become so obese that he was obliged to sit down in the pulpit when preaching.

The momentum of the great conquests had been so tremendous that they swept irresistibly forward without organization, without pay, without plans and without orders. They constitute a perpetual warning to technically advanced nations who rely for their defence on scientific progress rather than the human spirit. But once a great empire had been acquired, organization became inevitable. There were not enough pure-bred Arabs from Central Arabia to conquer the world. Non-Arabs had to be recruited in Khurasan to fight in the West. Christians from Syria and Copts from Egypt had to be employed as officials. Indians with their water-buffaloes from Sind were transported to the marshes of the lower Euphrates and Tigris. Persians from Fars were moved to Antioch. A cosmopolitan empire, with subjects professing different religions, could not constitute a devoted and homogeneous people of high morale, such as the Central Arabians had been twenty-five years earlier.

Muawiya accordingly set himself to organize. During his reign we read for the first time of police forces in Kufa and Basra, normally a sign of an advanced administration. Judges, treasurers and commandants of police are thenceforward appointed in all provinces, as well as governors. Muawiya inaugurated the first postal service and endeavoured to regularize the finances, though this task was rendered more difficult by the fact that the treasury officials in Egypt kept the accounts in Coptic, those in Syria in Greek and those in the former domains of Chosroes in Persian. The language question indeed was becoming a pressing problem. One of the reasons for the brilliant career of Zayyad the son of his father was that he had taken the trouble to learn Persian well. If the Arabs wished to remain in sole control of their great empire, they must become educated. The bedouins, however, regarded education as effeminate. Prowess with lance and sword and open-handed generosity to the guest or the poor were their ideals of manhood, and it was by such means, they justly claimed, that the empire had been conquered.

But while the khalif was faced with these innumerable problems, the rank and file of Arabs were not prepared to admit that the wild enthusiasm of the great conquests could no longer be sustained. Thus we find Uqba ibn Nafi sweeping forward fifteen hundred miles across North Africa until he rode his horse into the Atlantic Ocean. Oblivious of diplomacy or organization, administration or finance, he conceived it to be the Arab vocation to proclaim the Unity of God to a faithless world and to proclaim it by sword and lance, on camel and on horseback. Over the Oxus into the steppes of Central Asia and through the passes of the Hindu Kush into India, the outer wave still pressed on with cries of *Allahu akbar*, unaware that times were changing and that the conquests already achieved could only be retained by organization, justice, administration and finance. For lack of such administrative backing, the conquests they achieved were often lost once more and had to be re-won time and again until an efficient imperial machine could be built up.

In another direction also, the khalifate of Muawiya was a period of transition. It will be remembered that the ideal pursued by Umar ibn al Khattab was that of an Arab super-race, devoted only to government and war, and living in each conquered country in some great military base cantonment, a race apart, not mixing with the native peoples. The rôle of the conquered nations in this Arab Empire was to work and thereby to supply the revenue to support the government and the Arab armies. To ensure the preservation of the system, the Arabs were forbidden to acquire land.

When Muawiya became khalif in 660, Umar's system gradually ceased to be enforced. Arabs were already acquiring landed estates in the Basra area, while others did so also in Persia. The fact that Amr ibn al Aasi had acquired a farm in Beersheba has been mentioned. Probably fewer Arabs settled in Egypt than anywhere else, because the dampness of the climate of the delta was uncongenial to them. An increasing number of Copts, however, became converted to Islam as time went on, thereby becoming the equals of the Arabs and endeavouring, out of social ambition, to become known as Arabs, until finally the name Copt[3] became synonymous with Christian. In a word, all over the empire, the idea of the Arabs as a conquering race apart gradually weakened in the cosmopolitan empire of the sultan-khalifs.

* * * * *

The great failure of Muawiya's reign, in so far as his services to the Arabs were concerned, was his inability to select an acceptable successor. This had indeed been one of the most difficult problems facing Islam from the beginning. The only principle which at first seemed to be partially recognized had been that the khalif was chosen by acclamation by the people of Medina. Meanwhile, however, the capital of the empire had been moved to Damascus and Medina had become no more than a provincial town. Thus the only method for which any precedent existed was no longer applicable.

If any Arab system can be said to have been recognized, it would have been the selection of the most capable member of the ruling family. This was the method ordinarily followed in choosing a tribal chief, but even then it often led to quarrels and armed clashes. Moreover, the feud between Beni Hashim and Beni Umaiya was still so acute that any attempt to choose a successor from Quraish as a whole would probably have given rise to civil war. The modern technique of a nation-wide election was obviously impossible in a largely illiterate society scattered over so immense an area. In any case, even today, elections are rarely advisable among Arabs, who are too personally individualistic to bow willingly to a majority verdict. (Western democracy is not an acceptable form of government for men who insist on complete personal freedom, but for those who are ready to sacrifice a measure of freedom in the interests of order.)

In addition to these complications, Muawiya was doubtless influenced by the fear that if a member of Beni Hashim were nominated to succeed him, he would probably inaugurate his reign by exterminating any likely candidates from Beni Umaiya. For this reason, from Muawiya's point of view, the choice was limited to a member of Beni Umaiya, but it would appear as

[3] Copt is of course originally the same word as Egypt pronounced with a hard g.

though he ought to have chosen the most suitable candidate from that clan. Instead, he nominated his somewhat frivolous and irreligious son, Yezeed.

From the Arab point of view, this selection had many disadvantages. Firstly it promised them an incapable ruler, for the character of Yezeed was well known. Secondly it threatened to establish the principle of hereditary kingship, which was anathema alike to the old Arab spirit and to Muslim religious sentiment. Geographical jealousies were also involved. Medina resented the transfer of the capital to Damascus, and had its own candidates who might establish their court once more in the City of the Prophet. During the brief khalifate of Ali, he had declared Kufa to be his capital, and that fickle and turbulent town still cherished hopes of becoming the centre of the empire. Finally true and conscientious Muslims still regarded the khalif as the sacred successor of the Apostle of God, who should above all be pre-eminent in his religion. The selection of a dissipated young man, brought up in the luxurious and worldly city of Damascus, seemed to them almost blasphemy.

Muawiya was perfectly aware of the obstacles in the way of his son's succession, and determined to overcome them to the best of his ability. He secretly consulted his provincial governors, and endeavoured, by what we should call propaganda methods, to improve his son's reputation among the general public. For the same purpose, Yezeed was sent off to the army besieging Constantinople, that he might win the credit of having served in the holy war. In some cases, cash bribes were handed out to placate the hostility of prominent men. Eventually in 676, provincial governors were instructed to arrange for deputations from the various districts to present themselves in Damascus, ostensibly to request the khalif to nominate his son. When the delegations arrived in the capital, Muawiya consented to grant their petition and Yezeed was duly declared heir apparent in Damascus.

It was soon obvious that Medina was the most hostile city in the empire to the newly nominated heir to the khalifate. Muawiya accordingly determined to proceed to the Holy City in person and to ascertain whether his prestige or his diplomacy could achieve success. Arriving at Medina with an escort of a thousand cavalry, he found the leaders of the opposition to be all themselves aspirants to the succession. The first was Husain, the second son of Ali, for Hasan, the eldest, was already dead. With him was Abdulla, the son of Ali's rival Zubair, who had been killed at the Battle of the Camel. Next came Abdul Rahman, eldest surviving son of Abu Bekr, and finally Abdulla the son of Umar ibn al Khattab. As soon as Muawiya reached Medina, the dissidents left for Mecca. The remainder of the people of the City of the Prophet took the oath to Yezeed.

Under the pretext of performing the lesser pilgrimage, the khalif went on to Mecca, where he endeavoured to persuade the people to agree to the nomination of his son. But when he approached Abdulla the son of Umar ibn al Khattab, the latter replied that there were khalifs before Muawiya who had sons, who were as good as Muawiya's sons, but that their fathers had not nominated them to succeed them. Abdul Rahman the son of Abu Bekr was even more uncompromising, and replied openly that he would oppose

Yezeed's succession, because the selection of a khalif was a matter for decision by the general consent of the Muslims. Abdulla the son of Zubair proved more violent still in his rejection of the candidacy of the son of Muawiya. At length the khalif was obliged to return to Damascus without securing an oath of allegiance from Yezeed's rivals.

Muawiya died in April 680. He had preserved for nearly fifty years some pieces of the hair and parings of the nails of the Apostle of God. When he felt the approach of death, he directed that these be put in his mouth and on his eyes as soon as his life was ended and that he be wrapped for burial in a garment once given him by the Prophet. In this manner, at the age of seventy-seven, he passed peacefully away in his palace in Damascus. Twelve years of fratricidal civil war were to follow his decease.

* * * * *

Thus ended the age of the Great Arab Conquests. In less than fifty years, the bedouins of Arabia had established the greatest empire in the world of their day, and one of the greatest in history. No empire of comparable size has ever been conquered in so short a time, except that of Alexander the Great, which, however, fell to pieces on his death. The Arab Empire was to endure complete for two and a half centuries and gradually shrinking in extent for seven hundred years.

It is of interest to compare it in other respects to that of Alexander which covered to some extent the same territory. In one way the two form a complete contrast, for Alexander's empire owed its existence to the almost superhuman figure of one man. It has been well said, on the other hand, that the Arabs built their empire in spite of and not owing to their leaders.

The Arab conquests were unique in another respect. Before they began, the people of Arabia were looked upon with contempt by the Great Powers of the then world. The Yemen had been an Abyssinian and then a Persian colony. The only two Arab rulers worthy of the name had been subordinate princes of the Byzantine and the Persian Empires. As soldiers, the Arabs of the times of Ignorance had been a negligible quantity. The Greeks, on the other hand, were the most famous soldiers of their day, long before Alexander embarked on his career of conquest. The Roman Empire took centuries to build. France had been the leading power of Europe long before the birth of Napoleon. The Arabs were unique in the torrential speed of their flood of conquests which started from nothing.

The fifty years from 630 to 680 utterly transformed the world. Nothing has ever been the same again. In classical times, the Mediterranean was a Roman lake. It was the heart and centre of their empire, the medium in which they travelled from province to province. The north coast of Africa was part of the same world as France, Spain and Italy. The "East" began at the frontier between Rome and Persia, now approximately the border between Syria and Iraq. The Arab conquests divided the Mediterranean into northern and southern halves. Although the countries of the Arab Empire were by no means homogeneous, and North Africa even today differs profoundly from Arabia, yet superficially the conquests imposed a similar manner of life from Persia—

even from India—to Morocco, that way of life which today we call Eastern. It is difficult for us to realize that Algeria and Morocco were once homogeneous with Spain and Italy.

There are many shades of meaning to the word great. Yet in general we associate that adjective with something more than mere size. We seek for some quality of soul or spirit before we are willing to describe a man or an action as great. The Muslims were later on, after the civil wars, to resume their conquests. North Africa was to be consolidated, Spain was to be conquered, France and Italy were to be invaded, Malta and Sicily occupied. But these operations were no longer purely Arab. The empire had become multiracial. Nor perhaps were they great, for they were no longer inspired by the white-hot and passionate dedication of the first fifty years of the Great Arab Conquests.

## *NOTABLE DATES*

| | |
|---|---|
| Muawiya sole khalif | July, 661 |
| Death of Amr ibn al Aasi | 663 |
| Death of Mughira ibn Shuba | 670 |
| Foundation of Qairawan by Uqba ibn Nafi | 670 |
| Arab attack on Byzantium | 670 |
| Capture of Rhodes | 672 |
| Death of Zayyad the son of his father | 673 |
| Campaign against Bukhara by Ubaidullah ibn Zayyad | 674 |
| Ubaidullah made governor of Basra | 676 |
| Yezeed declared heir-apparent | 676 |
| Siege of Byzantium abandoned | 677 |
| Death of Muawiya | 680 |

## *PERSONALITIES*

Muawiya ibn abi Sofian, the khalif.
Uqba ibn Nafi, invader of North Africa as far as the Atlantic.
Mughira ibn Shuba, governor of Kufa and North Persia.
Zayyad the son of his father, governor of Basra and South Persia and finally of all Iraq and Persia.
Ubaidullah ibn Zayyad, governor of Khurasan and then of Basra.
Saeed the son of the Khalif Othman, governor of Khurasan.
Yezeed, son and heir of Muawiya.

| | |
|---|---|
| Husain ibn Ali ibn abi Talib<br>Abdulla ibn Zubair<br>Abdul Rahman ibn abi Bekr<br>Abdulla ibn Umar ibn al Khattab | Rivals of Yezeed and future aspirants to the Khalifate. |

# *Epilogue*

# EPILOGUE

FEW will deny that the events described in this book have changed the history of the world. They have also profoundly affected our lives and are still affecting them day by day. Our neglect of the history of these events has prevented us from understanding, and thence from handling wisely, our relations with the Arabs and with Muslims in general. It is therefore worth our while briefly to summarize a few of the lessons which we can deduce from our narrative.

The Muslim way of life draws its origin from two principal sources—firstly, the message left by Muhammad himself, and secondly, the customs of the people of Arabia in the seventh century. The easiest method for us to follow in this enquiry will be to discuss different subjects, examining how each has been affected by these two sources.

*Social Relations*

Broadly speaking, the Prophet appears to have been a kindly man. His sympathy for the poor and the weak, his lack of interest in money, his love of children and his feeling for personal cleanliness have all passed into the Muslim way of life. There is a tenderness and a pity in the Arab community which Europeans often miss.

The Arab way of life in the seventh century, on the other hand, was hard and often cruel. The absence of any form of central government led to the punishment of criminals by the injured party or his relatives. The most conspicuous example of this state of affairs was the blood feud. There were no police, no laws and no judges to punish the murderer. As a result, the relatives of the victim attempted to kill the murderer or, if that were impossible, one of his relatives. The same law applied to lesser injuries, such as wounds, blows or thefts. This system of reprisals led, as we have seen, to many cruel and savage actions.

Since the seventh century, many Muslim states have, at various times, established efficient legal systems and police forces, rendering private retaliation unnecessary, but the idea of revenge dies hard. In a wider sense, the right, and even the duty, of revenge has survived all modern reforms, for as a result of these early origins, it has become an accepted moral principle. This, it seems to me, is one of the directions in which Christianity differs most from Islam. Christians are never entitled to return evil for evil. In Islam, retaliation is a right, in some cases being even regarded as a moral duty.

Muhammad, as we have seen, was more influenced in his lifetime by Judaism than by Christianity. Moreover, the seventh century Arabs were doubtless in much the same state of social development as the Old Testament Hebrews. Abraham and Moses were their revered Prophets as much as, or more than, Christ. The Old Testament is often inspired by the same ideas, both of an eye for an eye and a tooth for a tooth, and also of the duty of massacring unbelievers. To love their neighbour and to hate their enemy was an accepted moral attitude to the ancient Hebrews and the seventh-century Arabs alike.

The Arab community of the seventh century has also bequeathed to Muslims a strong feeling of family obligation, a viewpoint which has both its good and bad aspects, but which is quite strange to the modern West. In Muslim society, the family will always care for its old people, its orphans, its idiots, its ne'er-do-wells and even its delinquents. In this it offers a marked contrast to the modern West where relatives are all too often looked upon as disagreeable acquaintances, and where the misfits are frequently left to their fate or thrust into public institutions. If Islam is not a welfare state, it at least produces whole welfare families where everyone is cared for, whether they deserve it or not. Yet family devotion has the drawback that a state servant may be tempted to rob the government or accept bribes, in order, for example, to give his children a good education or to pay for medical treatment for an old mother.

The Prophet was fond of women and Islam sanctions a maximum of four wives and also permits concubinage. In actual fact, the numbers of the sexes are approximately equal, so it is of course impossible for the great majority of men to have more than one wife. As against this permissible indulgence, Muhammad was extremely severe in his dealing with extra-conjugal relations. Adultery was normally punished by death. Any form of dalliance or flirtation was severely repressed. The present laxity of sexual relations in the Christian world fills good Muslims with horror. Thus adherents of both religions are inclined to regard those of the other faith as sexually immoral.

*Government*

As already indicated, the fact that Muhammad combined civil and religious authority has introduced a basic difference between Christian and Muslim states. All through history, until the last forty years, Muslim rulers have normally combined civil and religious control. This system avoided conflicts between the civil and religious authorities, but it also enabled the ruler to use, against his political opponents, those punishments which the Prophet pronounced against apostates. Perhaps the most difficult problem for the non-Muslim is presented by the fact that Muhammad made use of assassination against his enemies. As everything which the Apostle did must be right, some politicians here find justification for the removal of their opponents by the same method.

Muhammad, as we have seen, was not only the Prophet but the ruler of his people. The greater part of his career was spent in a bitter moral, political and military struggle for sheer survival. In these precarious circumstances, his followers obeyed his every word, for they believed him to receive his instructions directly from God. His first successors, as we have seen, endeavoured in all things exactly to imitate his conduct, in his method of government as much as in his private life. As a result of this early precedent, Muslim rule has always been autocratic, as was that of the Prophet and his successors. But although Abu Bekr and Umar were autocrats, they were not haughty despots, living in isolation from their subjects. They were extremely accessible, democratic and patriarchal. The traditional Muslim ruler is therefore autocratic, but is restrained from tyranny by a powerful tradition of benevolence and patriarchy.

Reference has already been made to the difficulties experienced in choosing the Prophet's successors. Heredity was never admitted by the Arabs as a sufficient basis for succession. In the selection of ordinary chiefs, the most suitable candidate of the ruling family was normally chosen. In the selection of a khalif, the most natural choice, and that which in theory was made in the cases of the first four, was that of the most suitable Muslim leader. In practice the difficulty of selecting the best candidate and the resulting danger of civil war, often resulted in the use of primogeniture in later Muslim dynasties. The Arabs, however, have never accepted the principle of the automatic succession of the eldest son.

Particularly is it noticeable that the idea of government by groups of men—cabinets, parliaments or committees—has no precedent at all in Arab history. Their idea of government is always one man. In theory he is chosen by the people. He must be humble, accessible, benevolent, pious and hospitable. Arrogant despots cannot be tolerated but nevertheless executive power must be vested in one man alone. All these traditions can be traced from the seventh century.

At various times since 1918, the Western Powers have painstakingly built up democratic, elective institutions in the countries of the Middle East. In every case, within a few years, these constitutions have collapsed and military dictators have assumed power. Perhaps this is not to be wondered at, for the military dictator is nearer to time-honoured Arab tradition than is Western democracy.

*War*

The Arabians in the seventh century were extremely war-like, but their methods of fighting were primitive. They relied on their military spirit and on individual personal courage rather than on the science of war. The tradition has survived to this day and has often cost the Muslims dear, in contests with more business-like killers, who fight to win. Every Muslim child is brought up on the accounts of the Prophet's life and the Arab conquests and thus the tradition of personal bravery, to the neglect of skill, has been perpetuated until now, even in distant Muslim countries, although it was originally applicable to Central Arabia alone.

The Byzantine and the Persian armies, it must be realized, were the leading military forces of their time. Many works on military history and the art of war were studied by their officers. The two armies had military traditions centuries old. They were equipped with the latest technical weapons, and regarded such backward races as the Arabs with no little contempt. The great Arab conquests, therefore, contain not a few lessons for ourselves, the principal of which is that it is an error to rely solely on technical superiority to win wars. The Persians and the Byzantines were war-weary, sophisticated, perhaps cynical. Many of their subjects were disloyal. They disliked wars and a what's-the-good-of-it-all-anyway attitude had undermined their morale. The Arabs were, on the contrary, simple, enthusiastic and willing to die. We tend to forget that these, not science or education, are the basic qualities of a soldier.

Much confusion exists today regarding the military value of Arabs. The first Arab conquerors made little or no attempt to convert the conquered populations to Islam. They insisted only that the subject peoples pay extra taxes with humility. Socially the defeated were reduced to the level of second-class citizens, to use a modern phrase, but they were not urged to be Muslims. If, however, any members of the conquered races were voluntarily converted to Islam, they automatically became the equals of their conquerors, and were able to mix and to intermarry with them. Before long they came to be regarded as "Arabs", even if (as was the case with many of them) they had not a drop of Arabian blood in their veins. Thus inevitably the terms Muslim and Arab became synonymous.

Yet there is undoubtedly a superficial similarity in the Arabic-speaking races from the borders of Persia to Morocco. This resemblance must be principally attributed, not to racial origins, but to the influence of culture and religion. Admission to social equality with the Arabs involved not only conversion to Islam but also the adoption of the Arabic language, which led to a common literature and education.

The relation between the Arabic-speaking races today is not unlike that shared by the nations of Europe. To us in Britain and to one another, Greeks and Norwegians may be foreigners, but to Asians all the peoples of Europe and North America appear similar, for they share the common heritage of Christendom. Yet in the crises of life, Norwegians and Greeks behave differently. Their common cultural and religious heritage is not strong enough to eliminate their respective racial characteristics. Thus the term Arabs, if applied to all the peoples from Persia to Morocco is comparable to the designation Europeans—a group sharing much the same cultural and religious heritage, though possessing widely different racial characteristics.

Discussion of the meaning of the word Arab is not purely academic, but may have an important political aspect. If one Arab country invades or attacks another, it may claim that all Arabs are one single nation and therefore that their action must be considered as a domestic, internal affair, in which neither the United Nations nor any other non-Arab organization can have any concern. If, on the other hand, we consider the relation between one Arab country and another to be comparable to that between the nations of Western Europe, then the invasion of one Arab country by another becomes international aggression, which it is presumably incumbent upon the United Nations to prevent. This is yet another example of the relevance of history to our present day affairs.

The story of the first fifty years of Arab conquests reveals many characteristic qualities which are still true to life in so far as the Central Arabians are concerned, for these people are unchanged since the days of the Prophet. Hardy, independent and full of military virtues, they nevertheless still rely on courage rather than on science. Yet, given anything like the same standards of training and equipment, they might well be the equals of any soldiers on earth. Islam is essentially a soldier's religion because it originated from this hardy and warlike race. The remaining Arabic-speaking peoples of today, however, vary immensely in their military qualities, with the result that it is quite impossible to generalize concerning them, as many people try to do.

Another remarkable peculiarity of the Central Arabian is his frankness and straightforward outlook. His speech is simple and direct without titles or elaborate forms of politeness. To him an enemy is an enemy and his tendency is to deal with him by physical violence. In these respects, the Syrians, the Lebanese and the Greeks offer a striking contrast, for they are essentially intellectual, courteous and subtle. Their instinct is to dispose of their enemies by more circuitous methods than hitting them on the head with an axe. Living in an intellectual world, they are reluctant to accept a rough and ready compromise instead of the theoretically correct solution of a problem. These few examples may suffice to illustrate the widely different, sometimes diametrically opposed, racial characteristics which distinguish the different peoples who share in common the Arabic language and the Muslim religion.

* * * * *

The relations between Christianity and Islam today justify a brief comment. As Muhammad himself declared, Judaism, Christianity and Islam are three related religions. If we consider them alone, their differences may appear profound, but when we compare them to Hinduism, Buddhism or communist atheism, they appear, by contrast, closely connected with one another. Yet many people regard Christianity and Islam as the great rival religions. This illusion takes its origin, I believe, from political rather than religious causes.

As our narrative has shown, the first Arab conquerors regarded Byzantium as their principal enemy. In the subsequent Arab conquests of North Africa and Spain, in the Crusades, in the invasion of the Balkans by the Turks, and in their long hostilities with Czarist Russia, nearly all Muslim wars have been directed against Christians. Conflicts between Muslims and Hindus in India have been on an altogether smaller scale and Muslims have scarcely ever been involved in hostilities against Jews except in the last forty years in Palestine.

This long-standing rivalry between Christians and Muslims has been due to political and geographical accident rather than to basic religious differences. Now that materialist atheism is challenging all spiritual values, the two religions might well make common cause against those who deny the existence of God altogether. There is, I believe, an immense field in which the two could co-operate.

* * * * *

The Arabic-speaking world, after four centuries of obscurity, is once again playing its part in history. It is both our duty and our interest to study more thoroughly the history and mentality of this group of races, which have to their credit so long and illustrious an historical record.

# GENERAL CHRONOLOGY

| | YEAR A.D. |
|---|---|
| Birth of Muhammad | 570 |
| Abyssinian advance on Mecca (year of the Elephant) | 570 |
| Persian occupation of the Yemen | 574 |
| Abolition of Beni Ghassan Dynasty by Byzantines | 581 |
| Marriage of Muhammad to Khadija | 595 |
| Invasion of Byzantine Empire by Chosroes | 602 |
| Abolition of Lakhmide Dynasty by Persia | 602 |
| Heraclius proclaimed Emperor | 610 |
| Muhammad's vision of the Archangel Gabriel | 610 |
| Muhammad migrates to Medina | 622 |
| Heraclius sails from Byzantium to outflank Persians | 622 |
| Battle of Bedr | 624 |
| Battle of Uhud | 625 |
| Siege of Medina by Quraish | 627 |
| Assassination of Chosroes. Perso-Byzantine peace | 628 |
| Pilgrimage of Hudeibiya | 628 |
| Battle of Mota | 629 |
| Muslim capture of Mecca | 630 |
| Death of Muhammad | 632 |
| Campaigns of the Apostasy | 632–633 |
| Accession of King Yezdegird | 632 |
| Capture of Hira | 633 |
| Invasion of Palestine and Jordan | 633–634 |
| Khalid's march across the desert | 634 |
| Battle of Babylon in Iraq | 634 |
| Battle of Ajnadain in Palestine | 634 |
| Death of Abu Bekr | 634 |
| First battle of the Yarmouk | 634 |
| Battle of the Bridge in Iraq | 634 |
| Capture of Damascus | 635 |
| Battle of Buwaib in Iraq | 635 |
| Second battle of the Yarmouk | 636 |
| Battle of Qadasiya | 637 |
| Occupation of Medain | 638 |
| Foundation of Kufa | 639 |
| Invasion of Egypt | 640 |
| Death of Heraclius | 641 |
| Surrender of Babylon | 641 |
| Arab occupation of Alexandria | 642 |
| Battle of Nehawand | 642 |
| Assassination of Umar ibn al Khattab | 644 |

| | |
|---|---|
| Conquest of Cyprus | 649 |
| Death of Yezdegird | 652 |
| Assassination of Othman | 656 |
| Battle of the Camel | 656 |
| Battle of Siffeen | 657 |
| Assassination of Ali | 661 |
| Foundation of Qairawan | 670 |
| Arab siege of Byzantium | 670–677 |
| Death of Muawiya | 680 |

# *Index*

# INDEX

Most Arabic names consist of the personal name of the individual followed by the personal name of his father. For example, John son of Thomas, Muhammad son of Abdulla.

It is the custom in England to index such names under the second name, that is under the name of the father. Thus John the son of Thomas is indexed as "Thomas, John the son of". This practice has in general been followed in the present index. In the case of important people, the name has been entered twice—for example under John and under Thomas, with a cross-reference. In the case of lesser characters, the name will usually be found under that of the father. Thus Jareer son of Abdulla is shown not under Jareer but under "Abdulla, Jareer ibn".

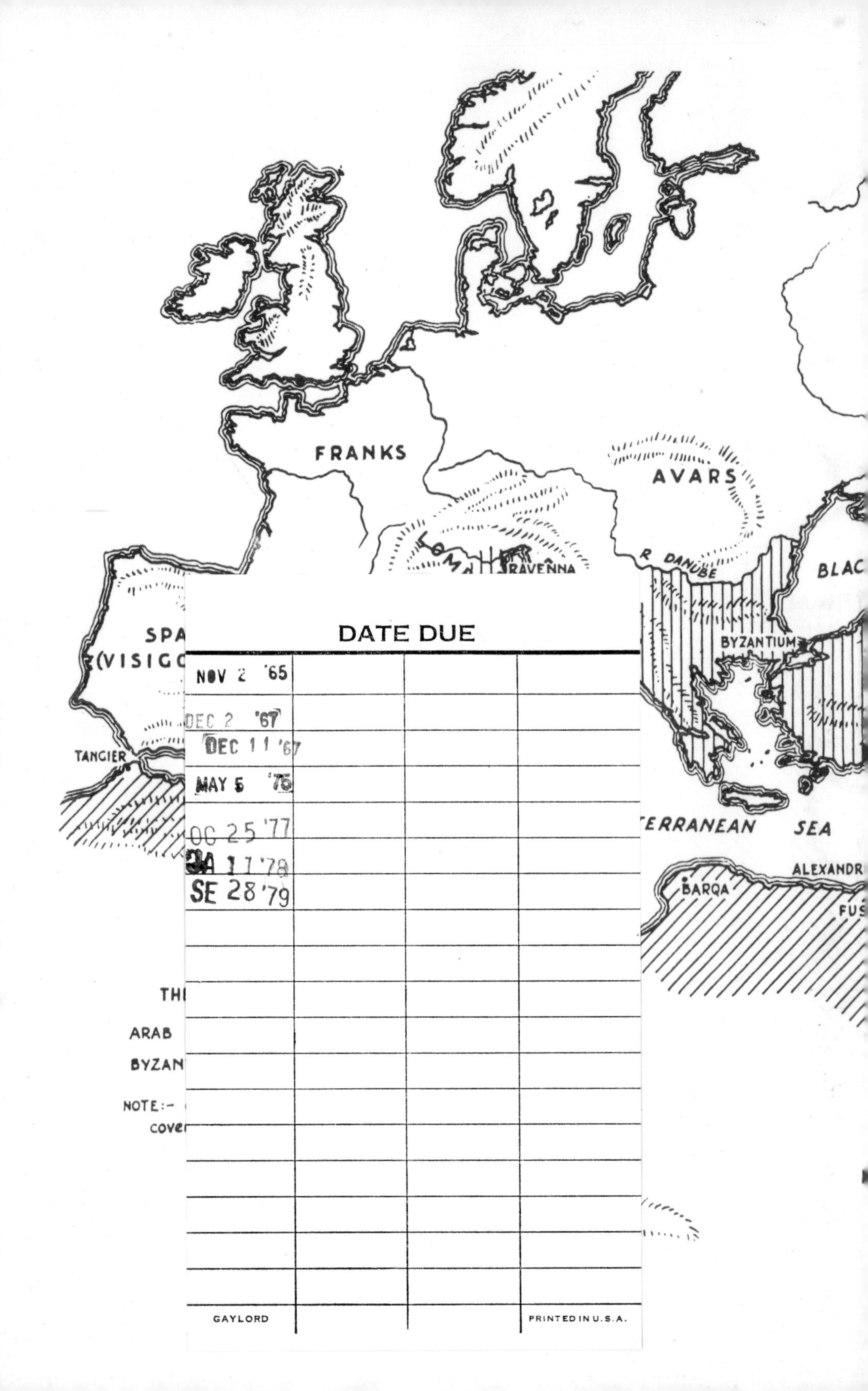
FRANKS
AVARS
R DANUBE
RAVENNA
BYZANTIUM
TANGIER
SEA
BARQA
ARAB
NOTE:-
DATE DUE
NOV 2 '65
DEC 2 '67
DEC 11 '67
MAY 5 '75
OC 25 '77
SE 28 '79
GAYLORD
PRINTED IN U.S.A.